Frommer's® 98

Las Vegas

by Mary Herczog and Rick Garman

Macmillan • USA

ABOUT THE AUTHORS

Mary Herczog lives in Los Angeles and works in the film industry. As a freelance writer, her work has appeared in several major publications (the *Los Angeles Times* and *Rolling Stone,* among others) and essay collections, as well as *Frommer's Los Angeles.* She still isn't sure when to hold and when to hit in blackjack.

When not found slouched in front of a slot machine with a glazed look in his eye mumbling incoherently to himself, **Rick Garman** is an award-winning playwright whose plays *17 Days* and *Mountains* have been produced in Los Angeles and around the country.

MACMILLAN TRAVEL

A Simon & Schuster Macmillan Company
1633 Broadway
New York, NY 10019

Find us online at **www.frommers.com** or
on America Online at Keyword: **Frommers**.

ISBN 0-02-861639-1
ISSN 0899-3262

Editor: Douglas Stallings
Production Editor: Phil Kitchel
Design by Michele Laseau
Digital Cartography by Ortelius Design & John Decamillis

SPECIAL SALES

Bulk purchases (10+ copies) of Frommer's and selected Macmillan travel guides are available to corporations, organizations, mail-order catalogs, institutions, and charities at special discounts, and can be customized to suit individual needs. For more information write to: Special Sales, Macmillan General Reference, 1633 Broadway, New York, NY 10019.

Manufactured in the United States of America

Contents

6　Dining in Las Vegas　104

7　What to See & Do in Las Vegas　155

List of Maps

ACKNOWLEDGMENTS

Thanks to Doug Stallings, Becka Hemingway, Cheryl Ladd-Campbell, Jan Laverty, James Randi, Paula Tevis, Mr. Wayne Newton, Cary Hern, "Uncle" Lou, Kelly Benway, Bob Bell, Barbara Ciarlantini, Tom Hawley, Brittany and Kitty, Chuck Taggert, Jesse Garon, and *Scope* magazine.

AN INVITATION TO THE READER

In researching this book, we discovered many wonderful places—hotels, restaurants, shops, and more. We're sure you'll find others. Please tell us about them, so we can share the information with your fellow travelers in upcoming editions. If you were disappointed with a recommendation, we'd love to know that, too. Please write to:

Frommer's Las Vegas '98
Macmillan Travel
1633 Broadway
New York, NY 10019

AN ADDITIONAL NOTE

Please be advised that travel information is subject to change at any time—this is especially true of prices. We therefore suggest that you write or call ahead for confirmation when making your travel plans. The authors, editors, and publisher cannot be held responsible for the experiences of readers while traveling. Your safety is important to us, however, so we encourage you to stay alert and be aware of your surroundings. Keep a close eye on cameras, purses, and wallets, all favorite targets of thieves and pickpockets.

WHAT THE SYMBOL MEANS

✪ Frommer's Favorites

Hotels, restaurants, attractions, and entertainment you should not miss.

The following abbreviations are used for credit cards:

AE	American Express	ER	enRoute
CB	Carte Blanche	JCB	Japan Credit Bank
DC	Diners Club	MC	MasterCard
DISC	Discover	V	Visa

FIND FROMMER'S ONLINE

Arthur Frommer's Outspoken Encyclopedia of Travel (www.frommers.com) offers more than 6,000 pages of up-to-the-minute travel information—including the latest bargains and candid, personal articles updated daily by Arthur Frommer himself. No other Web site offers such comprehensive and timely coverage of the world of travel.

Introducing Las Vegas

"The point about [Las Vegas], which both its critics and its admirers overlook, is that it's wonderful and awful *simultaneously.* So one loves it and detests it at the same time."
— David Spanier, *Welcome to the Pleasure Dome: Inside Las Vegas*

As often as you might have seen it on TV or in a movie, there is nothing that prepares you for that first sight of Las Vegas. The skyline is hyperreality, a mélange of the Statue of Liberty, a giant lion, a pyramid and a Sphinx, and preternaturally glittering buildings. At night, it's so bright, you can actually get disoriented—and also get a sensory overload that can reduce you to hapless tears or fits of giggles. And that's without setting foot inside a casino, where the shouts from the craps tables, the crash of coins from the slots, and general roar combine into either the greatest adrenaline rush of your life or the eleventh pit of hell.

Las Vegas is a true original; there is nothing like it in America or arguably the world. In other cities, hotels are built near the major attractions. Here, the hotels *are* the major attractions. For that matter, what other city has a skyline made up almost entirely of buildings from other cities' skylines? Instead of historical codes to follow, builders in Vegas have to worry about the height of the roller coaster in their hotel.

The result of all this is that once you go to Vegas, you will want to come back again, if only to make sure you didn't dream it all. It's not just the casinos with their nonstop action and sound, it's not the almost blinding lights, it's not the buildings that seek to replicate some other reality (Rome, New York, ancient Egypt), it's not the mountains of shrimp at the buffets, the wedding chapels that will gladly unite two total strangers in holy wedlock, it's not the promise of free money. It's the whole package. It's the Megabucks slots. It's Frank and Dino and Sammy. It's Elvis—the Fat Years. It's volcanoes and white tigers and cocktail waitresses dressed in Roman togas. It's cheesy and sleazy and artificial and wholly, completely unique. It's wonderful. It's awful. It's wonderfully awful and awfully wonderful. Love it, loathe it, or both, no one has ambivalent feelings about Vegas.

Las Vegas can be whatever the visitor wants, and for a few days, the visitor can be whatever he or she wants. Just be prepared to leave all touchstones with reality behind. Just for this time, you will rise at noon and gorge on endless amounts of rich food at 3am. You will watch your money grow or (more probably) shrink. You will watch a volcano explode and pirates fight the British. And after awhile, it will all seem pretty normal. This is not a cultural vacation, okay? Save the thoughts of museums and historical sights for the real New York, Egypt and Rome. Vegas is about fun. Go have some. Go have too much. It won't be hard.

The Vegas of the Rat Pack years, classic old Las Vegas, does not exist any more. Even as ancient civilizations are replicated, "old" in Vegas terms is anything over a decade. Indeed, by the end of 1998, thanks to tear downs and renovations, there will be nothing original left on the Strip. In a way that is both admirable and ghastly, and also part of what makes Vegas so *Vegas*. What other city can completely shed its skin in such a short amount of time?

But as much as one might mourn the loss of such landmarks as the Sands and regret the upcoming change in the facade of Caesars Palace, one has to admit that time marches on, and Vegas has to keep pace. Nostalgia for the vanished does not mean you can't enjoy what turns up in its place. Even as you might sneer at the sheer gaudy tastelessness of it all, if you stop to think about it, what's out there in plain view is undeniably remarkable.

And when it's all lit up at night—well, even those who have lived here for years agree there is nothing like the sight of the Strip in all its evening glory. "It still takes my breath away, even after all this time," says one long-time resident. Everything is in lights in Vegas; hotels, casinos, 7-Elevens, the airport parking garage. Stand still long enough, and they'll probably cover you in neon.

Oh, the gambling? Yes, there is plenty of that. Which is much like saying there is plenty of sand at the beach. Let's not kid ourselves; that's the main attraction of Vegas. The rest—the buffets, the shows, the cartoonish buildings—is so much window dressing to lure you and your money to the city. But even a nongambler can have a perfectly fine time in Vegas, though the lure of countless slot machines has tempted even the most puritan of souls in their day.

Unfortunately, the days of an inexpensive Las Vegas vacation are gone. Once, the hotels used to undercharge for everything, figuring this made the guest feel more inclined to drop bigger bucks at the tables, and feel better about it. The modern hotels don't seem to care how they get your money, and besides, they have big construction costs to recoup. The cheap buffets and meal deals still exist, as do some cut-rate rooms, but both are likely to prove the old adage about getting what you pay for. If all you are looking for is fuel and a place to catch a quick nap, they'll do just fine. Be prepared to pay if you are looking for glamour and fine dining.

But free drinks are still handed to anyone lurking near a slot, and if show tickets aren't in the budget, you won't lack for entertainment. Free lounge shows abound, and the people-watching opportunities alone never pall. From the Armani-clad high rollers in the Baccarat rooms to the polyester-sporting couples at the nickel slots, Vegas contains a cross section of America.

Yes, it's noisy and chaotic. Yes, it's gotten more and more like Disneyland for adults. Yes, it's a shrine to greed and the love of filthy lucre. Yes, there is little ambience and even less "culture." Yes, someone lacking self discipline can come to great grief.

But in its own way, Vegas is every bit as amazing as the nearby Grand Canyon, and every bit as much a must-see. It's one of the Seven Wonders of the Artificial World. And everyone should experience it at least once—and might find themselves coming back for more.

1 Frommer's Favorite Las Vegas Experiences

- **A Stroll on the Strip After Dark.** You haven't really seen Las Vegas until you've seen it at night. This neon wonderland is the world's greatest sound and light show. Begin at Luxor and work your way down past the incredible new New York New York. If your strength holds out, you will end at Circus Circus, where live acrobat acts take place over head while you gamble. Make plenty of stops en route to take in the ship battle at Treasure Island, see the Mirage volcano erupt, and enjoy the light, sound, and water show at Bally's.
- **Casino-Hopping on the Strip.** The interior of each lavish new hotel-casino is more outrageous and giggle-inducing than the last. Just when you think they can't possibly top themselves, they do. From Rome to ancient Egypt, from a rain forest to a pirate's lair, from King Arthur's castle to New York City, it is still all, totally, completely, and uniquely Las Vegas.
- **The Penny Slots at the Gold Spike.** Where even the most budget-conscious traveler can gamble for hours.
- **A Creative Adventures Tour.** Char Cruze provides personalized tours that unlock the mysteries of the desert canyons and make regional history come vibrantly alive.
- **A Dinner Show at Ceasars Magical Empire.** A solid dinner plus hours of entertainment, including your own personal magic show, make this one of the best values in Vegas, and a heck of a good time.
- **Buffets.** They may no longer be the very best of bargains, as the cheaper ones do not provide as good food as the more pricey ones, but there is something about the endless mounds of food that just screams "Vegas" to us.
- **Cirque du Soleil.** You haven't really seen Cirque du Soleil until you've seen it at Treasure Island, with a showroom equipped with state-of-the-art sound and lighting systems, and a seemingly infinite budget for sets, costumes, and high-tech special effects. It's an enchantment.
- **An Evening in Glitter Gulch.** Set aside an evening to tour downtown hotels and take in the overhead light show of the Fremont Street Experience. Unlike the lengthy and exhausting Strip, you can hit 17 casinos in about 5 minutes.
- **The Liberace Museum.** It's not the Smithsonian, but then again, the Smithsonian doesn't have rhinestones like these. Nowhere else but here.
- **Your Favorite Headliners.** As soon as you arrive in town, pick up a show guide and see who's playing during your stay.
- **Finding the Worst Lounge Shows.** Some feel this is the ultimate Vegas experience and dedicate many an evening to it. Be sure to watch out for Cook E. Jarr and the Crumbs.
- **The Shopping Forum at Caesars Palace.** This is an only-in-Vegas shopping experience—an arcade replicating an ancient Roman streetscape, with classical piazzas and opulent fountains. Don't miss the scary audio-animatronic statues as they come to glorious, cheesy life.

Impressions

There are no innocent bystanders in Las Vegas. Nobody comes to Las Vegas to be innocent.

—Michael Ventura, *The Death of Frank Sinatra*

• **A Hike or Picnic at Valley of Fire State Park.** More thrilling natural wonders majestic to explore: sandstone canyons, cliffs, rock formations, and Native American petroglyphs.

2 The City Today & Tomorrow

Las Vegas is on a roll. A major resort, New York New York, went up in 1997, and Bellagio, the latest creation from Steve Wynn, owner of the Mirage and Treasure Island, will open in 1998. At this writing, another 11,500 rooms in five new megaresorts and additions to existing properties are under construction; that figure will more than double by the turn of the century (see chapter 5 for more details on upcoming hotels). No matter how many rooms the town builds, tourists just keep arriving to fill them up. Las Vegas's room inventory is already the largest of any city in the nation. And at 90%, its room occupancy rate is also one of the highest.

But Las Vegas isn't resting on its laurels. Hoteliers are very aware that if occupancy rates are to keep pace with burgeoning room counts, tourists must be lured to the town. Gone are the days when a hotel could simply offer a casino, a show, and some formula restaurants. Today, each new property has to do something spectacular to garner attention (from rooftop roller coasters to celebrity-chef restaurants), while existing hotels frantically renovate in hopes of competing successfully with sensationalist newcomers.

The phenomenal growth in tourism (the city had about 30 million visitors last year) is paralleled by a population explosion. Las Vegas has had a 26% increase in its population over the last 5 years, and between 4,000 and 6,000 people are relocating into the area monthly. This is the only city in America where the phone book is published twice a year, in order to keep up with all the changes and newcomers. While this has been terrific for the local economy, it has caused many problems, such as congested highways and insufficient schools and services. For tourists, the town's all-too-rapid growth is most evident along the Strip, which is totally inadequate to accommodate us in such huge numbers. While monorails and other traffic solutions are under consideration, Strip traffic remains frustratingly bumper-to-bumper at almost all times.

Snarled traffic notwithstanding, the excitement generated by new hotels, restaurants, and sightseeing options easily outweighs the inconveniences. Every year, the Strip undergoes a major change, gaining an erupting volcano here, a towering Eiffel Tower or Empire State Building there. Downtown Las Vegas is also spiffing up, proud of its new look centered on the Fremont Street Experience. Each time, you think, "They can't possibly top this." And yet, they do. And one thing's for sure—somehow, they always will.

3 A Look at the Past

Dateline

■ A.D. 1150 Anasazi leave the area. Nomadic Paiutes become the dominant group.

■ 1831–48 Artesian spring waters of Las Vegas serve as a watering place on the Old Spanish Trail.

continues

For many centuries the land that would become Nevada was inhabited only by several Native American tribes: the Paiute, Shoshone, and Washoe. It wasn't until 1826 that Europeans set foot in the future state, and not until 1829 that Rafael Rivera, a scout for Mexican traders, entered a verdant valley nurtured by desert springs and called it Las Vegas ("the meadows"). From 1831 to 1848 these springs served as a watering place on the Old Spanish Trail for trading caravans plying the route between Santa Fe and the California coast. Explorer, soldier, and pathfinder Col. John C. Frémont (for whom the main thoroughfare downtown is named) rested near the headwaters of Las Vegas Springs on an overland expedition in 1844. A decade later Congress established a monthly mail route through Las Vegas Springs. And in 1855 Mormon leader Brigham Young sent 30 missionaries to Las Vegas to help expand Mormonism between Salt Lake City and southern California. Just north of what is today downtown (what would these missionaries think if they could see it now?) the Mormon colony built an adobe fort and dwellings. They raised crops, baptized Paiutes, and mined lead in the nearby mountains. However, none of these ventures proved successful, and the ill-fated settlement was abandoned after just 3 years.

The next influx into the area came as a result of mining fever in the early 1860s, but this soon subsided. However, gold prospector Octavius Decatur Gass stayed behind and, in 1865, built the 640-acre Las Vegas Ranch using structures left by the Mormons as his base. Since Gass controlled the valley's water, he finally found "gold" offering services to travelers passing through. Gass planted crops and fruit orchards, started vineyards, raised cattle, established cordial relations with the Paiutes (he even learned their language), and served as a legislator. This became the first significant settlement in the area. By 1900 the Las Vegas valley had a population of 30.

A TENT CITY IN THE WILDERNESS The city of Las Vegas was officially born in 1905 when the Union Pacific Railroad connecting Los Angeles and Salt Lake City decided to route its trains through this rugged frontier outpost, selected for its ready supply of water and the availability of timber in the surrounding mountains. On a sweltering day in May, 1,200 townsite lots were auctioned off to eager pioneers and real estate speculators who had come from all over the country. The railroad depot was located at the head of Fremont Street (site of today's Amtrak station). Championing the spot was Montana senator William Clark, who had paid the astronomical sum (for that time) of $55,000 for the nearby Las Vegas Ranch and springs. The coming of a railroad more or less ensured the growth of the town. As construction began, tent settlements, saloons, ramshackle restaurants, boardinghouses, and shops gradually emerged. The early tent hotels

- **1855** Mormon colony of 30 missionaries establishes settlement just north of today's downtown. Unsuccessful in its aims, the colony disbands in 1858.
- **1864** President Lincoln proclaims Nevada 36th state of the Union. Las Vegas, however, is still part of the Territory of Arizona.
- **1865** Gold prospector Octavius D. Gass builds Las Vegas Ranch, the first permanent settlement in Las Vegas, on site of the old Mormon fort.
- **1880s** Due to mining fever, the population of Nevada soars to more than 60,000 in 1880. The Paiutes are forced onto reservations.
- **1895** San Franciscan inventor Charles Fey creates a three-reel gambling device—the first slot machine.
- **1907** Fremont Street, the future "Glitter Gulch," gets electric lights.
- **1909** Gambling is made illegal in Nevada, but Las Vegas pays little heed.
- **1911** William Howard Taft, first American president to pass through Las Vegas, waves at residents from his train.
- **1928** Congress authorizes construction of Hoover Dam 30 miles away, bringing thousands of workers to the area. Later, Las Vegas will capitalize on hundreds of thousands who come to see the engineering marvel.
- **1931** Gambling is legalized once again.
- **1932** The 100-room Apache Hotel opens Downtown.
- **1933** Prohibition is repealed. Las Vegas's numerous speakeasies become legit.
- **1934** The city's first neon sign lights up the Boulder Club downtown.

continues

- **1941** The luxurious El Rancho Las Vegas becomes the first hotel on the Strip. Downtown, the El Cortez opens.
- **1946** Benjamin "Bugsy" Siegel's Flamingo extends the boundaries of the Strip. Sammy Davis Jr. debuts at the Last Frontier. Downtown (dubbed "Glitter Gulch") gets two new hotels: the Golden Nugget and the Eldorado.
- **1947** United Airlines inaugurates service to Las Vegas.
- **1948** The Thunderbird becomes the fourth hotel on the Strip.
- **1950** The Desert Inn adds country club panache to the Strip.
- **1951** The first of many atom bombs is tested in the desert just 65 miles from Las Vegas. An explosion of another sort takes place when Frank Sinatra debuts at the Desert Inn.
- **1952** The Club Bingo (opened in 1947) becomes the desert-themed Sahara. The Sands's Copa Room enhances the city's image as an entertainment capital.
- **1954** The Showboat pioneers buffet meals and bowling alleys in a new area of Downtown.
- **1955** The Strip gets its first high-rise hotel, the nine-story Riviera, which pays Liberace the unprecedented sum of $50,000 to open its showroom. The Riviera is the ninth hotel on the Strip. A month later, the Dunes becomes the 10th.
- **1956** The Fremont opens downtown, and the Hacienda becomes the southernmost hotel on the Strip.

continues

charged a dollar to share a double bed with a stranger for eight hours!

By present-day standards, the new town was not a pleasant place to live. Prospectors' burros roamed the streets braying loudly, generally creating havoc and attracting swarms of flies. There were no screens, no air conditioners, no modern showers or baths (the town's bathhouse had but one tub) to ameliorate the fierce summer heat. The streets were rutted with dust pockets up to a foot deep that rose in great gusts as stage coaches, supply wagons, and 20-animal mule teams careened over them. It was a true pioneer town, complete with saloon brawls and shoot-outs. Discomforts notwithstanding, gaming establishments, hotels, and nightclubs—some of them seedy dives, others rather luxurious—sprang up and prospered in the Nevada wilderness. A red-light district emerged on Second Street between Ogden and Stewart avenues. And gambling, which was legal until 1909, flourished.

THE EIGHTH WONDER OF THE WORLD
For many years after its creation, Las Vegas was a mere whistle-stop town. That all changed in 1928 when Congress authorized the building of nearby Boulder Dam (later renamed Hoover Dam), bringing thousands of workers to the area. In 1931 gambling once again became legal in Nevada, and Fremont Street's gaming emporiums and speakeasies attracted workers from the dam. Upon the dam's completion, the Las Vegas Chamber of Commerce worked hard to lure the hordes of tourists who came to see the engineering marvel (it was called "the Eighth Wonder of the World") to its casinos. Las Vegas was about to make the transition from a sleepy desert town to "a town that never sleeps." But it wasn't until the early years of World War II that visionary entrepreneurs began to plan for its glittering future.

LAS VEGAS GOES SOUTH   Contrary to a popular conception, Bugsy Siegel didn't actually stake a claim in the middle of nowhere—he just built a few blocks south of already existing properties. Development a few miles south of Downtown on Highway 91 (the future Strip) was already underway in the 1930s, with such establishments as the Pair-O-Dice Club and the Last Frontier. And in 1941 El Rancho Vegas, ultraluxurious for its time, was built on the same remote stretch of highway (across the street from where the Sahara now stands). According to legend, Los Angeles hotelier Thomas E. Hull had been driving by the site when his car broke down.

Noticing the extent of passing traffic, he decided to build there. Hull invited scores of Hollywood stars to his grand opening, and El Rancho Vegas soon became the hotel of choice for visiting film stars. Beginning a trend that still continues today, each new property tried to outdo existing hotels in luxurious amenities and thematic splendor. In 1943 the Last Frontier (the Strip's second hotel) created an authentic western setting by scouring the Southwest in search of authentic pioneer furnishings for its rooms, hiring Zuni craftsmen to create baskets and wall hangings, and picking up guests at the airport in a horse-drawn stagecoach. Las Vegas was on its way to becoming the entertainment capital of the world.

Las Vegas promoted itself in the 1940s as a town that combined Wild West frontier friendliness with glamour and excitement. As chamber of commerce president Maxwell Kelch aptly put it in a 1947 speech, "Las Vegas has the impact of a Wild West show, the friendliness of a country store, and the sophistication of Monte Carlo." Throughout the decade, the city was largely a regional resort—Hollywood's celebrity playground. Clara Bow and Rex Bell (a star of westerns) bought a ranch in Las Vegas where they entertained such luminaries as the Barrymores, Norma Shearer, Clark Gable, and Errol Flynn. The Hollywood connection gave the town glamour in the public's mind. So did the mob connection (something Las Vegas has spent decades trying to live down), which became clear early on when notorious underworld gangster Benjamin "Bugsy" Siegel (with partners Lucky Luciano and Meyer Lansky) built the fabulous Flamingo, a tropical paradise and "a real class joint." In 1947 the Club Bingo opened across the street from El Rancho Vegas, bringing a new game to town.

A steady stream of name entertainers came to Las Vegas. In 1947 Jimmy Durante opened the showroom at the Flamingo. Other headliners of the 1940s included Dean Martin and Jerry Lewis, tap-dancing legend Bill "Bojangles" Robinson, the Mills Brothers (who first recorded "Bye-Bye Blackbird"), skater Sonja Henie, and Frankie Laine. Future Las Vegas legend Sammy Davis Jr. debuted at El Rancho Vegas in 1945.

While the Strip was expanding, downtown kept pace with new hotels such as the El Cortez and the Golden Nugget. By the end of the decade, Fremont Street was known as "Glitter Gulch," its profusion of neon signs proclaiming round-the-clock gaming and entertainment.

- **1957** The Dunes introduces bare-breasted showgirls in its *Minsky Goes to Paris* revue. The most luxurious hotel to date, the Tropicana, opens on the Strip.
- **1958** The 1,065-room Stardust opens as the world's largest resort complex with a spectacular show from France, the *Lido de Paris.*
- **1959** The Las Vegas Convention Center goes up, presaging the city's future as a major convention city. Another French production, the still-extant *Folies Bergére,* opens at the Tropicana.
- **1960** The Rat Pack, led by Chairman of the Board Frank Sinatra, holds a 3-week "Summit Meeting" at the Sands. A championship boxing match, the first of many, takes place at the Convention Center. El Rancho Las Vegas, the Strip's first property, burns to the ground.
- **1963** McCarran International Airport opens. Casinos and showrooms are darkened for a day as Las Vegas mourns the death of Pres. John F. Kennedy.
- **1965** The 26-story Mint alters the Fremont Street skyline. Muhammad Ali defeats Floyd Patterson at the Las Vegas Convention Center.
- **1966** The Aladdin, the first new hotel on the Strip in 9 years, is soon eclipsed by the unparalleled grandeur of Caesars Palace. The Four Queens opens Downtown. Howard Hughes takes up residence at the Desert Inn. He buys up big chunks of Las Vegas and helps erase the city's gangland stigma.
- **1967** Elvis Presley marries Priscilla Beaulieu at the

continues

Aladdin, the city's all-time most celebrated union.

- **1968** Circus Circus gives kids a reason to come to Las Vegas.
- **1969** The Landmark and the International (today the Hilton) open within a day of each other on Paradise Road. Elvis Presley makes a triumphant return headlining at the latter.
- **1973** The ultraglamorous 2,100-room MGM Grand assumes the mantle of "world's largest resort." Superstars of magic, Siegfried and Roy, debut at the Tropicana.
- **1976** Fittingly, pioneer aviator Howard Hughes dies aboard a plane en route to a Houston hospital. Martin and Lewis make up after a 20-year feud.
- **1978** Leon Spinks dethrones "the Greatest" (Muhammad Ali) at the Las Vegas Hilton. Crime solver Dan Tanna (Robert Urich) makes the streets of *Vega$* safer, and better known.
- **1979** A new international arrivals building opens at McCarran International Airport.
- **1980** McCarran International Airport embarks on a 20-year, $785 million expansion program. Las Vegas celebrates its 75th birthday. A devastating fire destroys the MGM Grand, leaving 84 dead and 700 injured. Bally's takes over the property.
- **1981** Siegfried and Roy begin a record-breaking run in their own show, *Beyond Belief,* at the Frontier.
- **1982** A Las Vegas street is named Wayne Newton Boulevard.

continues

THE 1950S: BUILDING BOOMS AND A-BOMBS

Las Vegas entered the new decade as a city (no longer a frontier town) with a population of about 50,000. Photographs indicate that Las Vegas was more glamorous in the 1950s than it is today. Men donned suits and ties, women floor-length gowns, to attend shows and even for casino gambling. Hotel growth was phenomenal. The Desert Inn, which opened in 1950 with headliners Edgar Bergen and Charlie McCarthy, brought country club elegance (including an 18-hole golf course and tennis courts) to the Strip. In 1951 the Eldorado Club downtown became Benny Binion's Horseshoe Club, which would gain fame as the home of the annual World Series of Poker. In 1954 the Showboat sailed into a new area east of Downtown. Although people said it could never last in such a remote location, they were wrong. The Showboat not only innovated buffet meals and a bowling alley (106 lanes to date) but offered round-the-clock bingo. In 1955 the Côte d'Azur–themed Riviera became the ninth big hotel to open on the Strip. Breaking the ranch-style mode, it was, at nine stories, the Strip's first high-rise. Liberace, one of the hottest names in show business, was paid the unprecedented sum of $50,000 a week to dazzle audiences in the Riviera's posh Clover Room. The 15-story Fremont Hotel Downtown became the highest building in Las Vegas; and the Hacienda extended the boundaries of the Strip by opening 2 miles south of the nearest resort. Elvis appeared at the New Frontier in 1956 but wasn't a huge success; his fans were too young to fit the Las Vegas tourist mold. In 1957 the Tropicana joined the Hacienda at the far end of Las Vegas Boulevard. In 1958 the $10 million, 1,065-room Stardust upped the spectacular stakes by importing the famed *Lido de Paris* from the French capital. It became one of the longest running shows ever to play Las Vegas.

Throughout the 1950s, most of the above-mentioned hotels competed for performers whose followers spent freely in the casinos. The advent of big-name Strip entertainment tolled a death knell for glamorous nightclubs in America; owners simply could not compete with the astronomical salaries paid to Las Vegas headliners. Major '50s stars of the Strip included Rosemary Clooney, Nat King Cole, Peggy Lee, Milton Berle, Judy Garland, Red Skelton, Ernie Kovacs, Abbott and Costello, Fred Astaire and Ginger Rogers, the Andrews Sisters, and Marlene Dietrich. Two performers whose names have ever since been linked to Las Vegas—Frank

Sinatra and Wayne Newton—made their debuts there. Mae West not only performed in Las Vegas, but cleverly bought up a half mile of desolate Strip frontage between the Dunes and the Tropicana.

Competition for the tourist dollar also brought nationally televised sporting events such as the PGA's Tournament of Champions to the Desert Inn golf course (the winner got a wheelbarrow filled with silver dollars). In the 1950s the wedding industry helped make Las Vegas one of the nation's most popular venues for "goin' to the chapel." Nevada requires no blood test or waiting period. Celebrity weddings of the 1950s that sparked the trend included singer Dick Haymes and Rita Hayworth, Joan Crawford and Pepsi chairman Alfred Steele, Carol Channing and TV exec Charles Lowe, and Paul Newman and Joanne Woodward.

On a grimmer note, the '50s also heralded the atomic age in Nevada, with nuclear testing taking place just 65 miles northwest of Las Vegas. A chilling 1951 photograph shows a mushroom-shaped cloud from an atomic bomb test visible over the Fremont Street horizon. Throughout the decade, about one bomb a month was detonated in the nearby desert.

- **1989** Steve Wynn makes headlines with his spectacular Mirage, fronted by an erupting volcano. He signs Siegfried and Roy to a 5-year $57 million showroom contract (since extended)!
- **The 1990s** The medieval Arthurian realm of Excalibur opens as the new "world's-largest-resort" title holder with 4,032 rooms, a claim it relinquishes when the MGM Grand's new 5,005-room megaresort/theme park opened in 1994. Other properties to come aboard in the 1990s include the Debbie Reynolds Hotel, Luxor Las Vegas, Treasure Island, The Hard Rock, the Monte Carlo, and the Stratosphere.

THE 1960S: THE RAT PACK AND A PACK RAT   The very first month of the new decade made entertainment history when the Sands hosted a 3-week "Summit Meeting" in the Copa Room presided over by "Chairman of the Board" Frank Sinatra with Rat Pack cronies Dean Martin, Sammy Davis Jr., Peter Lawford, and Joey Bishop (all of whom happened to be in town filming *Oceans Eleven*).

On November 25, 1963, Las Vegas mourned the death of Pres. John F. Kennedy with the rest of the nation. Between 7am and midnight, all the neon lights went off, casinos stood empty, and showrooms were dark.

The building boom of the '50s took a brief respite. The Strip's first property, the El Rancho Vegas, burned down in 1960. And the first new hotel of the decade, the first to be built in 9 years, was the exotic Aladdin in 1966. A year after it opened the Aladdin hosted the most celebrated Las Vegas wedding of all time when Elvis Presley married Priscilla Beaulieu. In 1966 Las Vegas also hailed Caesar—Caesars Palace, that is—a Lucullan pleasure palace whose grand opening was a million-dollar, 3-day Roman orgy with 1,800 guests.

During the '60s, negative attention focused on mob influence in Las Vegas. Of the 11 major casino hotels that had opened in the previous decade, 10 were believed to have been financed with mob money. Attorney General Robert Kennedy ordered the Department of Justice to begin serious scrutiny of Las Vegas gaming operations. Then, like a knight in shining armor, Howard Hughes rode into town. He was not,

Impressions

We loved Vegas because we know the house rules, which are as follows: As long as you don't bother the other customers, you can do anything. That's the promise of Vegas: Anything.

—Michael Venture, *Las Vegas: The Odds on Anything*

however, on a white horse. Ever eccentric, he arrived (for security rather than health reasons) in an ambulance. The reclusive billionaire moved into a Desert Inn penthouse on Thanksgiving Day 1966 and did not set foot outside the hotel for the next 4 years! It became his headquarters for a $300 million hotel- and property-buying spree, which included the Desert Inn itself (in 1967). Hughes was as "bugsy" as Benjamin Siegel any day, but his pristine reputation helped bring respectability to the desert city and lessen its gangland stigma. For a while, it worked.

Las Vegas became a family destination in 1968 when Circus Circus burst on the scene with the world's largest permanent circus and a "junior casino" comprising dozens of carnival midway games on its mezzanine level. In 1969 the Landmark and the dazzling International (today the Hilton) ventured into a new area of town: Paradise Road near the Convention Center. That same year Elvis made a triumphant return to Las Vegas at the International's showroom and went on to become one of the city's all-time legendary performers. His fans had come of age.

Hoping to establish Las Vegas as "the Broadway of the West," the Thunderbird Hotel presented Rodgers and Hammerstein's *Flower Drum Song*. It was a smash hit. Soon the Riviera picked up *Bye, Bye, Birdie,* and, as the decade progressed, *Mame* and *The Odd Couple* played at Caesars Palace. While Broadway played the Strip, production shows such as the Dunes's *Casino de Paris* became ever more lavish, expensive, and technically innovative. Showroom stars of the 1960s included Barbra Streisand, Phyllis Diller, Carol Burnett, Little Richard (who billed himself as "the bronze Liberace"), Louis Armstrong, Bobby Darin, the Supremes, Johnny Carson, Bob Newhart, the Smothers Brothers, and Aretha Franklin. Liza Minnelli filled her mother's shoes, while Nancy Sinatra's boots were made for walking. And Tom Jones wowed 'em at the Flamingo.

THE 1970S: MERV, MIKE, MGM & MAGIC   In 1971 the 500-room Union Plaza opened at the head of Fremont Street on the site of the old Union Pacific Station. It had what was, at the time, the world's largest casino, and its showroom specialized in Broadway productions. The same year talk show host Merv Griffin began taping at Caesars Palace, taking advantage of a ready supply of local headliner guests. He helped popularize Las Vegas even more by bringing it into America's living rooms every afternoon. Rival Mike Douglas soon followed suit at the Las Vegas Hilton.

The year 1973 was eventful: The Holiday Inn (today Harrah's) built a Mississippi riverboat complete with towering smokestacks and foghorn whistle, which was immediately dubbed "the ship on the Strip." Dean Martin headlined in the celebrity room of the magnificent new MGM Grand, named for the movie *Grand Hotel*. And over at the Tropicana, illusionists extraordinaire Siegfried and Roy began turning women into tigers and themselves into legends in the Folies Bergére.

Two major disasters hit Las Vegas in the 1970s. First, a flash flood devastated the Strip, causing more than $1 million in damage. Hundreds of cars were swept away in the raging waters. Second, gambling was legalized in Atlantic City. Las Vegas's hotel business slumped as fickle tourists decided to check out the new East Coast gambling mecca.

On a happier note, audiences were moved when Frank Sinatra helped to patch up a 20-year feud by introducing Dean Martin as a surprise guest on Jerry Lewis's 1976

Muscular Dystrophy Telethon at the Sahara. Martin and Lewis hugged and made up. Who would cross Sinatra?

As the decade drew to a close, Dan Tanna began investigating crime in glamorous *Vega$*, an international arrivals building opened at McCarran International Airport, and dollar slot machines caused a sensation in the casinos. Hot performers of the '70s included Ann-Margret, Tina Turner, Englebert Humperdinck, Bill Cosby, Sonny and Cher, Tony Bennett, Mel Tormé, Bobby Darin, Gregory Hines (with his brother and dad), Donny and Marie, the Jackson 5, Gladys Knight and the Pips, and that "wild and crazy guy" Steve Martin. Debbie Reynolds introduced her daughter Carrie with a duet performance before a Desert Inn audience. Shirley MacLaine began an incarnation at the Riviera. And country was now cool; the names Johnny Cash, Bobby Gentry, Charlie Pride, and Roy Clark went up in marquee lights.

THE 1980S: THE CITY ERUPTS Las Vegas was booming once again. McCarran Airport began a 20-year, $785 million expansion program. On a tragic note, in 1980 a devastating fire swept through the MGM Grand, leaving 84 dead and 700 injured. Shortly thereafter, Bally acquired the property and reopened the MGM Grand.

Siegfried and Roy were no longer just the star segment of various stage spectaculars. Their own show, *Beyond Belief,* ran for 6 years at the Frontier, playing a record-breaking 3,538 performances to sellout audiences every night. It became the most successful attraction in the city's history.

In 1989 Steve Wynn made Las Vegas sit up and take notice. His gleaming white and gold Mirage was fronted by five-story waterfalls, lagoons, and lush tropical foliage—not to mention a 50-foot volcano that dramatically erupted, spewing great gusts of fire another 50 feet into the air every 15 minutes after dark! Wynn gave world-renowned illusionists Siegfried and Roy carte blanche (and more than $30 million) to create the most spellbinding show Las Vegas had ever seen.

Stars of the '80s included Eddie Murphy, Don Rickles, Roseanne Barr, Dionne Warwick, Paul Anka, the Captain and Tennille, Donna Summer, Rich Little, George Carlin, Barry Manilow, Bernadette Peters, and Diahann Carroll. Country continued to be cool, as evidenced by frequent headliners Willie Nelson, Kenny Rogers, Dolly Parton, Crystal Gale, Merle Haggard, and Barbara Mandrell. Joan Rivers posed her famous question, "Can we talk?" and bug-eyed comic Rodney Dangerfield complained he got "no respect."

THE 1990S: KING ARTHUR MEETS KING TUT The decade began with a blare of trumpets heralding the rise of a turreted medieval castle fronted by a moated drawbridge and staffed by jousting knights and fair damsels. Excalibur's interior had so many stone castle walls that a Strip comedian quipped "it looks like a prison for Snow White." Excalibur also reflects the '90s marketing trend to promote Las Vegas as a family vacation destination.

Several sensational megahotels have opened on the Strip since 1993, and they're all running at close to 100% occupancy, as are older properties benefiting from the visitor excitement they've generated. They include the *new* MGM Grand Hotel,

Favorite Vegas Movies from the Mayor of Las Vegas

Jan Laverty is the mayor of Las Vegas.

- *Oceans 11*
- *Viva Las Vegas*

(10 Other Vegas Movies the Mayor Didn't Pick & Possible Reasons Why)

- *Leaving Las Vegas.* Alcoholics and hookers are not good role models.
- *One from the Heart.* Shot on a sound stage rather than in Las Vegas.
- *Vegas Vacation.* Griswald family *not* typical Vegas tourists.
- *Casino.* Puts the squeeze on heads rather than on wallets.
- *They Came to Rob Las Vegas.* The title says it all.
- *The Electric Horseman.* Robert Redford successfully steals valuable horse from casino.
- *Indecent Proposal.* Robert Redford successfully wins million dollars from casino.
- *Con Air.* In the real Vegas, planes land at the airport, not on the Strip.
- *Showgirls.* Need we say more?
- *Honeymoon in Vegas.* Beats us. Who doesn't love Flying Elvii?

backed by a full theme park (it ended Excalibur's brief reign as the world's largest resort); the Luxor Las Vegas, and Steve Wynn's Treasure Island.

On October 27, 1993, a quarter of a million people crowded onto the Strip to witness the implosion of the 37-year-old Dunes Hotel. Vegas-style, it went out with a bang. Later that year a unique pink-domed, 5-acre indoor amusement park, Grand Slam Canyon, became part of the Circus Circus Hotel. In 1995 the Fremont Street Experience was completed, revitalizing Downtown Las Vegas. Closer to the Strip, rock restaurant magnate Peter Morton opened the Hard Rock Hotel, billed as "the world's first rock 'n' roll hotel and casino." The year 1996 saw the advent of the French Riviera–themed Monte Carlo and the Stratosphere, its 1,149-foot tower the highest building west of the Mississippi. The unbelievable New York New York arrived in 1997. As the millennium approaches, Las Vegas is flourishing as never before, and the ongoing metamorphosis of the Strip continues to thrill visitors who find a dramatic new streetscape every time they visit.

4 Recommended Books

If you believe in "reading more about it," here are a very select few of our favorites you might turn to.

McCracken, Robert D., *Las Vegas: The Great American Playground* (University of Nevada Press, 1997). A comprehensive history of Las Vegas.

Spanier, David, *Welcome to the Pleasure Dome: Inside Las Vegas* (University of Nevada Press, 1992). First-person history and analysis of the Las Vegas phenomenon.

Thompson, Hunter S., *Fear and Loathing in Las Vegas* (Random House, 1971). The gonzo journalist and his Samoan lawyer head to Sin City for the all-time binge. An instant classic, soon (or at last) to be a movie starring Johnny Depp.

Tronnes, Mike, ed., *Literary Las Vegas* (Henry Holt, 1995). A terrific collection of different essays and excerpts from books about Vegas.

Planning a Trip to Las Vegas

Before any trip, you need to do a bit of advance planning. When should I go? Should I take a package deal or make my own hotel and airline reservations? Will there be a major convention in town during my visit? We'll answer these and other questions for you in this chapter, but you might want to read through the sightseeing and excursions in chapters 7 and 11 for some ideas on how to spend your time if you tire of gambling.

1 Visitor Information

For advance information call or write the **Las Vegas Convention and Visitors Authority,** 3150 Paradise Rd., Las Vegas, NV 89109 (☎ **800/332-5333**). They can send you a comprehensive packet of brochures, a map, a show guide, an events calendar, and an attractions list; help you find a hotel that meets your specifications (and even make reservations); and tell you if a major convention is scheduled during the time you would like to visit Las Vegas. Or stop by when you're in town. They're open Monday to Friday 8am to 6pm and Saturday and Sunday 8am to 5pm.

Another excellent information source is the **Las Vegas Chamber of Commerce,** 711 E. Desert Inn Rd., Las Vegas, NV 89109 (☎ **702/735-1616**). Ask them to send you their *Visitor's Guide,* which contains extensive information about accommodations, attractions, excursions, children's activities, and more. They can answer all your Las Vegas questions, including those about weddings and divorces. They're open Monday to Friday 8am to 5pm.

And for information on all of Nevada, including Las Vegas, contact the **Nevada Commission on Tourism** (☎ **800/638-2328**). They have a comprehensive information packet on Nevada.

If you're surfing the Net, you can get information about Las Vegas from these Web sites:

- **The Las Vegas Index:** http://lvindex.com
- **Las Vegas Online:** http://www.infi.net/vegas/vlv/
- **Vegas.net,** an on-line magazine: http://vegasnet.com
- **Where To In Las Vegas** magazine: http://a1-lasvegas-wt.com
- The **"Official" Las Vegas Leisure Guide and Resource Directory:** http://www.pcap.com

What Things Cost in Las Vegas	U.S. $
Taxi from airport to the Strip	8–12.00
Taxi from airport to downtown	15–18.00
Minibus from the airport to the Strip	3.50
Minibus from the airport to downtown	4.75
Double room at the Desert Inn (very expensive)	175–185.00
Double room at the MGM Grand (expensive)	69–119.00
Double room at Residência Nazareth (budget)	51.00
Double at Circus Circus (inexpensive)	36–65.00
Five-course tasting menu at Gatsby's without tax or tip, with wines (very expensive)	65–85.00
Three-course dinner at Chin's without tax or tip (moderate)	20.00
Three-course dinner at Stage Deli without tax or tip (moderate)	20.00
Three-course dinner at Stage Deli without tax or tip (moderate)	15.00
All-you-can-eat buffet dinner at Circus Circus	4.99
All-you-can-eat- buffet dinner at Caesars Palace	13.95
Bottle of beer	2.50
Coca-Cola	1.50
Cup of coffee	1.50
Roll of ASA 100 color film, 36 exposures	4.70
Show ticket for *Country Fever* (including a drink and a basket of chicken tenders; tax and gratuity extra	25.00
Show ticket for *Enter the Night* (including two drinks; tax and gratuity extra)	35.00
Show ticket for headliners at Caesars (including tax; drinks extra)	45–75.00
Show ticket for *Siegfried and Roy* (including two drinks, tax, souvenir brochure, and gratuity)	89.95

2   When to Go

Since most of a Las Vegas vacation is usually spent indoors, you can have a good time here year-round. The most pleasant seasons, as you'll see from the chart below, are spring and fall, especially if you want to experience the great outdoors. Weekdays are slightly less crowded than weekends. Holidays are always a mob scene and come accompanied by high hotel prices. Hotel prices also skyrocket when big conventions and special events are taking place. The slowest times of year are June and July, the week before Christmas, and the week after New Year's. If a major convention is to be held during your trip, you might want to change your date.

THE CLIMATE

One thing you'll hear again and again is that even though Las Vegas gets very hot, the dry desert heat is not unbearable. This is true. The humidity averages a low 22%, and even on very hot days there's apt to be a breeze. Also, except on the hottest summer days, there's relief at night when temperatures often drop as much as 20°. But

Las Vegas Advisor

Professional gambler and longtime Las Vegas resident Anthony Curtis, author of *Bargain City: Booking, Betting, and Beating the New Las Vegas,* knows all the angles for stretching your hotel, restaurant, and, most important, gaming dollar. His 12-page monthly newsletter, the *Las Vegas Advisor,* is chock-full of insider tips on how to maximize your odds on every game, which slot tournaments to enter, casino promotions that represent money-making opportunities for the bettor, where to obtain the best fun books, which hotel offers a 12-ounce margarita for 99¢ or a steak dinner for $3, what are the best buffet and show values in town, and much, much more. Subscribers get more than $400 worth of coupons for discounts on rooms, meals, show tickets, and car rentals, along with free slot plays, two-for-one bets, and other perks. A subscription is $45 a year, a single issue $5. To subscribe call ☎ **800/244-2224** or send a check to Las Vegas Advisor, 3687 S. Procyon St., Las Vegas, NV 89103.

it also gets really cold, especially in the winter, when at night it can drop to 30° and lower. The breeze can also become a cold, biting wind. If you aren't traveling in the height of summer, bring a wrap. Also, remember your sunscreen and hat—even if it's not all that hot, you can burn very easily and fast. (You should see all the lobster-red people in the casinos at night.)

Las Vegas's Average Temperatures (°F)

	Jan	Feb	Mar	Apr	May	June	July	Aug	Sept	Oct	Nov	Dec
Average	44	50	57	66	74	84	91	88	81	67	54	47
Avg. High	55	62	69	79	88	99	105	103	96	82	67	58
Avg. Low	33	39	44	53	60	68	76	74	65	53	41	36

LAS VEGAS CALENDAR OF EVENTS

You may be surprised that Las Vegas does not offer as many annual events as most tourist cities. The reason is Las Vegas's very raison d'être: the gaming industry. This town wants its visitors spending their money in the casinos, not off at Renaissance fairs and parades. When in town, check the local paper and call the **Las Vegas Convention and Visitors Authority** (☎ **702/892-0711**), **Las Vegas Events** (☎ **702/731-2115**), or the **Chamber of Commerce** (☎ **702/735-1616**) to find out about other events scheduled during your visit.

January
- **The PBA Classic.** The Showboat Hotel, 2800 Fremont St. (☎ **702/385-9150**), hosts this major bowling tournament every January.

March
- **The PBA Invitational.** Another major annual bowling tournament, also at the Showboat Hotel.

April
- **The World Series of Poker.** This famed 21-day event takes place at Binion's Horseshoe Casino, 128 Fremont St. (☎ **702/382-1600**), in late April and early May, with high-stakes gamblers and show-biz personalities competing for six-figure purses. There are daily events with entry stakes ranging from $125 to

Major Convention Dates for 1998–99

Listed below are Las Vegas's major annual conventions with projected attendance figures for 1998, and, where available, for 1999.

Consumer Electronics Show
1998: Jan 8–11   100,000
1999: Jan 7–10   100,000

Souvenir Super Show
1998: Jan 18–21 50,000

Shooting, Hunting, Outdoor Trade Show
1998: Jan 27–30   35,000

Western Shoe Associates
1998: Feb 8–11   25,000

Men's Apparel Guild in California (Magic)
1998: Feb 18–21   70,000

Associated Surplus Dealers
1998: Feb 22–26 50,000

Ski Industries of America
1998: Mar 2–6   28,000

Networld/Interop
1998: May 4–8   60,000

International Council of Shopping Centers
1997: May 18–20   35,000

Associated Surplus Dealers
1998: Aug 16–20   32,000

Specialty Equipment Market Association
1998: Nov 3–6   60,000

Softbank Comdex
1998: Nov 16–19   190,000

$5,000. To enter the World Championship Event (purse $1 million), players must put up $10,000. It costs nothing to go watch the action.

- **TruGreen-ChemLawn Las Vegas Senior Classic.** This 4-day event in mid- to late April or early May takes place at the Tournament Players Club (TPC), The Canyons, 9851 Canyon Run Dr., in nearby Summerlin. For details and driving information, call ☎ 702/382-6616.

June

- **Helldorado.** This Elks-sponsored Western heritage celebration takes place over a several day period in mid-June. It includes a bull riders, a trail ride, a barbecue, and four major Professional Rodeo Cowboys Association (PRCA) rodeos at the Thomas and Mack Center at UNLV. For information call the Elks Lodge (☎ **702/870-1221**) or check the local papers. The ticket office number is ☎ 702/895-3900.

September

- **Oktoberfest.** This boisterous autumn holiday is celebrated from mid-September through the end of October at the Mount Charleston Resort (☎ **800/955-1314** or 702/872-5408) with music, folk dancers, sing-alongs around a roaring fire, special decorations, and Bavarian cookouts.

October

- **PGA Tour Las Vegas Invitational.** This 5-day championship event, played on three local courses, is televised by ESPN. For details call ☎ 702/382-6616.

December

- **National Finals Rodeo.** This is the Super Bowl of rodeos, attended by close to 170,000 people each year. The top 15 male rodeo stars compete in six different events: calf roping, steer wrestling, bull riding, team roping, saddle bronc riding, and bareback riding. And the top 15 women compete in barrel racing. An all-around "Cowboy of the Year" is chosen. In connection with this event, hotels book

Fun Fact

In 1995, Don Harrington entered a satellite event at the World Series of Poker for just $220, won his way into the $10,000 buy for the Championship Event, and went on to win the $1 million prize.

country stars in their showrooms, and there's a cowboy shopping spree—the NFR Cowboy Christmas Gift Show, a trade show for western gear—at Cashman Field.

Where: At the 17,000-seat Thomas and Mack Center of UNLV. When: For 10 days during the first 2 weeks of the month. How: Order tickets as far in advance as possible (☎ **702/895-3900**).

- **Las Vegas Bowl Week.** A championship football event in mid-December pits the winners of the Mid-American Conference against the winners of the Big West Conference. The action takes place at the 32,000-seat Sam Boyd Stadium. Call ☎ 702/895-3900 for ticket information.

- **Western Athletic Conference (WAC) Football Championship.** This collegiate championship event takes place the first week in December. Call ☎ 792/731-5595 for ticket information. Tickets prices range from $15 to $100.

- **New Year's Eve.** This is a biggie (reserve your hotel room early). Downtown, Fremont Street is closed to traffic between Third and Main streets, and there's a big block party with two dramatic countdowns to midnight (the first is at 9pm, midnight on the East Coast). Of course, there are fireworks.

  There's also a big New Year's Eve gala at the Mount Charleston Resort (☎ **800/955-1314** or 702/872-5408). Make dinner reservations early and book a cabin for the night. See chapter 11 for details.

3 Tips for Travelers with Special Needs

FOR PEOPLE WITH DISABILITIES   Write or call **The Independent Living Program,** Nevada Association for the Handicapped, 6200 W. Oakey Blvd., Las Vegas, NV 89102 (☎ **702/870-7050**). They can recommend hotels and restaurants that meet your needs, help you find a personal attendant, advise about transportation, and answer all questions.

In addition, the **Nevada Commission on Tourism** (☎ **800/638-2328**), offers a free accommodations guide to Las Vegas hotels that includes access information.

Two helpful travel organizations—**Accessible Journeys** (☎ **800/TINGLES** or 610/521-0339) and **Flying Wheels Travel** (☎ **800/535-6790** or 507/451-5005)—offer tours, cruises, and custom vacations worldwide for people with physical disabilities; Accessible Journeys can also provide nurses/companions to travelers. **The Guided Tour Inc.** (☎ **800/783-5841** or 215/782-1370) has tours for people with physical or mental disabilities, the visually impaired, and the elderly.

Mobility International USA, P.O. Box 10767, Eugene, OR 97440 (☎ **503/343-1284**), offers accessibility and resource information to its members. Membership ($25 a year) includes a quarterly newsletter called *Over the Rainbow.*

There's no charge for help via telephone (accessibility information and more) from the **Travel Information Service,** Moss Rehab Hospital (☎ 215/456-9600). Another organization, the **Society for the Advancement of Travel for the Handicapped** (SATH), 347 Fifth Ave., Suite 610, New York, NY 10016 (☎ **212/447-7284**), charges $5 for sending requested information.

Recommended books: Twin Peaks Press, Box 129, Vancouver, WA 98666 (☎ **360/694-2462**), specializes in books for people with disabilities. Write for their *Disability Bookshop Catalog,* enclosing $5.

Greyhound (☎ **800/752-4841**) allows a disabled person to travel with a companion for a single fare. Call at least 48 hours in advance to discuss this and other special needs.

Airlines don't offer special fares to the disabled. When making your flight reservations, ask where your wheelchair will be stowed on the plane and if your guide dog may accompany you.

FOR SENIORS   Always carry some form of photo ID that includes your birth date so you can take advantage of discounts wherever they're offered. And it never hurts to ask.

If you haven't already done so, consider joining the **American Association of Retired Persons** (☎ **800/424-3410** or 202/434-2277). Annual membership costs $8 per person or couple. You must be at least 50 to join. Membership entitles you to many discounts. Write to Purchase Privilege Program, AARP Fulfillment, 601 E St. NW, Washington, DC 20049, to receive their *Purchase Privilege* brochure, a free list of hotels, motels, and car-rental firms nationwide that offer discounts to AARP members.

New Year's Eve in Las Vegas

Over the last couple of years, more and more people have been choosing Las Vegas as their party destination for New Year's Eve. In fact, some estimates indicate that by the time you read this, there will be more people ringing in the new year in Nevada than in New York City's Time Square.

From experience, we can tell you that there are a lot of people who come here on December 31. We mean a lot of people. It seemed that it may very well have been the entire population of the western United States, but we didn't stop to count. (Neither did anyone else, but here's what we know from last year; almost *all* the 94,000 hotel rooms were sold out by 201,000 visitors. Nearly 400,000 total jammed the Strip to watch the Hacienda implode. Another 25,000 paid $10 apiece to experience New Year's Eve from the Fremont St. Experience.) Traffic is a nightmare, parking (at least legally) is next to impossible, and there is not one square inch of the place that isn't occupied by a human being. Las Vegas doesn't really need a reason to throw a party, but when an event like this comes along they do it up right. A major portion of the strip is closed down, sending the masses and their mass quantities of alcohol into the street. Each year's celebration is a little different but usually includes a street-side performance by a major celebrity, confetti, the obligatory countdown, fireworks, and an occasional building implosion (The Hacienda on New Year's '97).

Of course there will always be the die-hard gamblers. New Year's '96 at the Stardust Casino was something like this: From outside you heard the countdown ("Three! Two! One!") and everyone in the casino looked up from their slot machines, their glazed eyes clearing slightly as some portion of their brain registered the fact that something important was happening. A few mumbled "Happynewyear," and then the coins started dropping again.

We would say that all then returned to normal, but it's hard to apply that phrase to Las Vegas with a straight face.

Elderhostel is a national organization that offers low-priced educational programs for people over 55 (your spouse can be any age; a companion must be at least 50). Programs are generally a week long, and prices average about $355 per person, including room, board, and classes. For information on programs in Nevada call or write Elderhostel headquarters, 75 Federal St., Boston, MA 02110 (☎ **617/ 426-7788**), and ask for a free catalog.

Greyhound also offers discounted fares for senior citizens. Call your local Greyhound office for details.

FOR FAMILIES   Las Vegas in the '90s is discussed in the "Especially for Kids" suggestions in chapter 7 and chapter 5. See the "Family-Friendly" boxes for suggestions for hotels, restaurants, and shows. Here are also a few general suggestions to make traveling with kids easier.

If they're old enough, let the kids write to various tourist offices for information and color brochures. If you're driving, give them a map on which they can outline the route. Let them help decide your sightseeing itinerary.

Although your home may be toddler-proof, hotel accommodations are not. Bring blank plugs to cover outlets and whatever else is necessary.

Carry a few simple games to relieve the tedium of traveling. Packing snacks will also help and save money. If you're using public transportation (airlines, bus), always inquire about discounted fares for children.

Children under 12, and in many cases even older, stay free in their parents' rooms in most hotels. Look for establishments that have pools and other recreational facilities (see "Family-Friendly Hotels" in chapter 5).

FOR GAYS & LESBIANS   The *Las Vegas Bugle,* a monthly magazine serving the gay community, provides information about bars, workshops, local politics, support groups, shops, events, and more. A subscription costs $20 for 12 issues. For details call ☎ **702/369-6260.** See also listings for gay bars in chapter 10.

4 Getting There

BY AIR
THE MAJOR AIRLINES
The following airlines have regularly scheduled flights into Las Vegas (some of these are regional carriers, so they may not all fly from your point of origin): **Air Canada** (☎ 800/776-3000), **Alaska Airlines** (☎ 800/426-0333), **America West** (☎ 800/ 235-9292), **American/American Eagle** (☎ 800/433-7300), **American Trans Air** (☎ 800/543-3708), **Canadian International** (☎ 800/426-7000), **Condor** (☎ 800/ 524-6975), **Continental** (☎ 800/525-0280), **Delta/Skywest** (☎ 800/221-1212), **Frontier** (☎ 800/432-1359), **Hawaiian** (☎ 800/367-5320), **Kiwi** (☎ 800/ 538-5494), **Midway** (☎ 888/226-4392), **Midwest Express** (☎ 800/452-2022), **Northwest** (☎ 800/225-2525), **Reno Air** (☎ 800/736-6247), **Southwest** (☎ 800/ 435-9792), **Sun Country** (☎ 800/359-6786), **TWA** (☎ 800/221-2000), **United** (☎ 800/241-6522), **USAir** (☎ 800/428-4322), and **Western Pacific** (☎ 800/ 930-3030).

We've always enjoyed Southwest's relaxed attitude and their service leaves few complaints. However, they mostly feature first come, first served seating, so if you want to avoid that, you can't go wrong with United.

FINDING THE BEST AIRFARE
Generally, the least expensive fares (except for special packages and special-promotion discount fares you see announced in newspaper travel sections) are

advance-purchase fares that involve certain restrictions. For example, in addition to paying for your ticket 3 to 21 days in advance, you may have to leave or return on certain days, stay a maximum or minimum number of days, and so on. Also, advance-purchase fares are often nonrefundable. Nonetheless, the restrictions are usually within the framework of one's vacation plans, and savings of $500 and more are not unusual. It's also possible to get a really good airfare combined with your hotel room and perhaps even a car rental by purchasing a **package.**

THE LAS VEGAS AIRPORT

Las Vegas is served by **McCarran International Airport,** 5757 Wayne Newton Blvd. (☎ **702/261-5743** or TDD **702/261-3111**), just a few minutes' drive from the southern end of the Strip. It's a big, modern airport, and rather unique in that it includes a casino area with more than 1,000 slot machines. Although these are reputed to offer lower paybacks than hotel casinos (the airport has a captive audience and doesn't need to lure repeat customers), it's hard to resist throwing in a few quarters while waiting for luggage to arrive. We actually know someone who hit a $250 jackpot there on his way out of town, thereby recouping most of his gambling losses at the last possible moment. He was surprised, too.

AIRPORT TRANSPORTATION Getting to your hotel from the airport is a cinch. **Bell Trans** (☎ **702/739-7990** or fax 702/384-2283) runs 20-passenger mini-buses daily between the airport and all major Las Vegas hotels and motels almost around the clock (4:30am to 2am). There are several other companies that run similar ventures—just stand outside on the curb and one will be flagged down for you. Buses from the airport leave about every 10 minutes. For departure from your hotel, call at least 2 hours in advance (though often you can just flag one down outside any major hotel). The cost is $3.50 per person each way to Strip and Convention Center area hotels, $4.75 to Downtown properties (any place north of the Sahara Hotel and west of I-15).

Even less expensive are **Citizen's Area Transit (CAT)** buses (☎ **702/ CAT-RIDE**). The no. 108 bus departs from the airport and will take you to the Stratosphere where you can transfer to the 301, which stops close to most Strip and Convention Center area hotels. The no. 109 bus goes from the airport to the Downtown Transportation Center at Casino Center Blvd. and Stewart Ave. The fare for is $1.50, 50¢ for seniors and children. *Note:* If you have heavy luggage, you should know that you might have a long walk from the bus stop to your door (even if it's right in front of your hotel).

RENTING A CAR All of the major car-rental companies are represented in Las Vegas. We like **Allstate** (☎ **800/634-6186** or 702/736-6148), the least expensive of the airport-based car-rental agencies. Besides the usual mix, their fleet of more than 1,500 vehicles includes an inventory of 15 passenger vans, four-wheel drives, Jeeps, minivans, sports cars, and convertibles. We've found this local, family owned company (the largest independent operator in Las Vegas) friendly and competent, with an invariably charming staff at the airport. They're open 24 hours. And they've agreed to offer our readers a **20% discount off regular rental rates** at any Allstate location (just show the agent your copy of this book). In addition to McCarran Airport, there are Allstate car desks at the Aladdin, Riviera, Stardust, and Jackie Gaughan's Plaza hotels, and the company offers free pickup anywhere in Las Vegas.

National companies with outlets in Las Vegas include **Alamo** (☎ 800/327-9633), **Avis** (☎ 800/367-2847), **Budget** (☎ 800/922-2899), **Dollar** (800/842-2054), **Enterprise** (☎ 800/325-8007), **Hertz** (☎ 800/654-3131), **National** (☎ 800/ 227-7368), and **Thrifty** (☎ 800/367-2277)

Driving Distances to Las Vegas (in miles)			
Chicago	1,766	New York City	2,564
Dallas	1,230	Phoenix	286
Denver	759	Salt Lake City	421
Los Angeles	269	San Francisco	586

BY CAR

The main highway connecting Las Vegas with the rest of the country is I-15; it links Montana, Idaho, and Utah with southern California. From the East Coast, take I-70 or I-80 west to Kingman, Arizona, and then U.S. 93 north to Downtown Las Vegas (Fremont Street). From the south, take I-10 west to Phoenix and then U.S. 93 north to Las Vegas. From San Francisco, take I-80 east to Reno and then U.S. 95 south to Las Vegas. If you're driving to Las Vegas be sure to read the driving precautions under "By Car" in chapter 4's "Getting Around" section.

PACKAGE DEALS

When you make reservations on any airline, also inquire about money-saving packages that include hotel accommodations, car rentals, tours, and so forth with your airfare.

For instance, at press time, a **Delta Dream Vacation** package leaving from New York could cost as little as $342.50 per person based on double occupancy, including round-trip coach air transportation, two nights at your choice of several major casino hotels, a rental car for 24 hours, airport transfers, and bonus discounts and admissions. At press time Southwest Airlines was offering round-trip airfare from Los Angeles with two nights at several different hotels complete with ground transportation; per person based on double occupancy, for the Mirage it was $174, and for the Golden Nugget $119. (Of course, this was midweek.) Similar packages are available from such companies as **American Airlines Fly Away Vacations, America West Vacations,** and **USAir Vacations.**

Prices vary according to the season, seat availability, hotel choice, whether you travel midweek or on the weekend, and other factors. Since even an advance-purchase round-trip fare between New York and Las Vegas can easily be $100 or $200 more than the above-quoted figure, it seems almost insane not to book a less expensive package that includes so many extras.

CHARTER FLIGHTS

Similar to airline packages, charter flights are booked by tour operators who buy up all (or most of) the seats on an airplane and put together packages that include airfare and other features—perhaps accommodations, shows, meals, car rentals, airport transfers, and/or attractions tickets. The operators then sell these charters through travel agents. It can be worth your while to compare charter offerings to major airline packages. Most travel agents know which tour operators specialize in Las Vegas charters. If yours does not, ask them to investigate packages offered by **Funjet Vacations** (☎ 800/558-3050), **Hamilton, Miller, Hudson and Fang** (☎ 800/669-4466), **MLT Vacations** (☎ 800/328-0025), and **Adventure Tours** (☎ 800/638-9040).

For Foreign Visitors 3

This chapter will provide some specifics about getting to the United States as economically and effortlessly as possible, plus some helpful information about how things are done in Las Vegas, from receiving mail to making a local or long-distance telephone call.

1 Preparing for Your Trip

ENTRY REQUIREMENTS

DOCUMENT REGULATIONS   Canadian citizens may enter the United States without visas; they need only proof of residence.

Citizens of the United Kingdom, New Zealand, Japan, and most other western European countries traveling on valid passports may not need a visa for fewer than 90 days of holiday or business travel to the United States, providing that they hold a round-trip or return ticket and enter the United States on an airline or cruise line that participates in the visa waiver program.

(Note that citizens of these visa-exempt countries who first enter the United States may then visit Mexico, Canada, Bermuda, and/or the Caribbean islands and then reenter the States, by any mode of transportation, without needing a visa. Further information is available from any U.S. embassy or consulate.)

Citizens of countries other than those stipulated above, including citizens of Australia, must have two documents: a valid **passport,** with an expiration date at least 6 months later than the scheduled end of the visit to the United States; and a **tourist visa,** available without charge from the nearest U.S. consulate. To obtain a visa, the traveler must submit a completed application form (either in person or by mail) with a 1 1/2-inch square photo and demonstrate binding ties to a residence abroad.

Usually you can obtain a visa at once or within 24 hours, but it may take longer during the summer rush from June to August. If you cannot go in person, contact the nearest U.S. embassy or consulate for directions on applying by mail. Your travel agent or airline office may also be able to provide you with visa applications and instructions. The U.S. consulate or embassy that issues your visa will determine whether you will be issued a multiple- or single-entry visa and if any restrictions regarding the length of your stay will apply.

MEDICAL REQUIREMENTS No inoculations are needed to enter the United States unless you are coming from, or have stopped over in, areas known to be suffering from epidemics, particularly cholera or yellow fever.

If you have a disease requiring treatment with medications containing narcotics or drugs requiring a syringe, carry a valid, signed generic prescription from your physician to allay any suspicions that you are smuggling drugs. The prescription brands you are accustomed to buying in your country may not be available in the United States.

CUSTOMS REQUIREMENTS Every adult visitor may bring in, free of duty: 1 liter of wine or hard liquor; 200 cigarettes or 100 cigars (but no cigars from Cuba) or 3 pounds of smoking tobacco; and $100 worth of gifts. These exemptions are offered to travelers who spend at least 72 hours in the United States and who have not claimed them within the preceding 6 months. It is altogether forbidden to bring foodstuff (particularly cheese, fruit, cooked meats, and canned goods) and plants (vegetables, seeds, tropical plants, and so on) into the country. Foreign tourists may bring in or take out up to $10,000 in U.S. or foreign currency with no formalities; larger sums must be declared to customs on entering or leaving.

INSURANCE

Unlike most other countries, the United States does not have a national health system. Because the cost of medical care is extremely high, we strongly advise all travelers to secure health coverage before setting out on their trip. You may want to take out a comprehensive travel policy that covers (for a relatively low premium) sickness or injury costs (medical, surgical, and hospital); loss or theft of your baggage; trip-cancellation costs; guarantee of bail in case you are arrested; and costs of accident, repatriation, or death. Such packages (for example, "Europe Assistance" in Europe) are sold by automobile clubs at attractive rates, as well as by insurance companies and travel agencies.

MONEY

The U.S. monetary system has a decimal base: One American dollar ($1) = 100 cents (100¢). Dollar bills commonly come in $1 (a "buck"), $5, $10, $20, $50, and $100 denominations (the last two are not welcome when paying for small purchases and are usually not accepted in taxis or at subway ticket booths). There are six coin denominations: 1¢ (one cent or "penny"); 5¢ (five cents or "nickel"); 10¢ (ten cents or "dime"); 25¢ (twenty-five cents or "quarter"); 50¢ (fifty cents or "half dollar"); and the rare $1 piece.

Traveler's checks in U.S. dollars are accepted at most hotels, motels, restaurants, and large stores. Sometimes picture identification is required. American Express, Thomas Cook, and Barclay's Bank traveler's checks are readily accepted in the United States. Do not bring traveler's checks denominated in other currencies.

Credit cards are the method of payment most widely used: Visa (BarclayCard in Britain), MasterCard (EuroCard in Europe, Access in Britain, Chargex in Canada), American Express, Discover, Diners Club, JCB, and Carte Blanche, in descending order of acceptance. You can save yourself trouble by using "plastic" rather than cash or traveler's checks in almost all hotels, motels, restaurants, and retail stores. You must have a credit or charge card to rent a car. It can also be used as proof of identity or as a "cash card" enabling you to draw money from automatic-teller machines (ATMs).

If you plan to travel for several weeks or more in the United States, you may want to deposit enough money into your credit-card account to cover anticipated expenses

We are going to do something they can't top. In this town, you've got to move ahead in quantum jumps.

—Lee Fisher, PR representative for the Dunes, in 1963
upon bringing the Casino de Paris revue to the hotel.

and avoid finance charges in your absence. This also reduces the likelihood of your receiving an unwelcome big bill on your return.

You can telegraph money, or have it telegraphed to you very quickly using the **Western Union** system (☎ **800/325-6000**).

SAFETY

While tourist areas are generally safe, crime is on the increase everywhere, and U.S. urban areas tend to be less safe than those in Europe or Japan. Visitors should always stay alert. This is particularly true of large U.S. cities, including Las Vegas.

Remember also that hotels are open to the public, and in a large hotel, security may not be able to screen everyone entering. Always lock your room door—don't assume that once inside your hotel you are automatically safe and no longer need to be aware of your surroundings. In Las Vegas, many hotels check room keys at the elevators at night, providing some extra security. Many Las Vegas hotels also have in-room safes; if yours doesn't and you're traveling with valuables, put them in a safety-deposit box at the front desk.

DRIVING

Safety while driving is particularly important. Question your rental agency about personal safety, or ask for a brochure of traveler safety tips when you pick up your car. Obtain written directions, or a map with the route marked in red, from the agency showing how to get to your destination. And, if possible, arrive and depart during daylight hours.

Recently more and more crime has involved cars and drivers. If you drive off a highway into a doubtful neighborhood, leave the area as quickly as possible. If you have an accident, even on the highway, stay in your car with the doors locked until you assess the situation or until the police arrive. If you are bumped from behind on the street or are involved in a minor accident with no injuries and the situation appears to be suspicious, motion to the other driver to follow you to either a police station, gas station, or some other well populated area. Never get out of your car in such situations.

If you see someone on the road who indicates a need for help, do not stop. Take note of the location, drive on to a well-lighted area, and telephone the police by dialing ☎ 911. Park in well-lighted, well-traveled areas if possible.

Always keep your car doors locked, whether attended or unattended. Never leave any packages or valuables in sight. If someone attempts to rob you or steal your car, do not try to resist the thief/carjacker—report the incident to the police department immediately.

2 Getting to the United States

For an extensive listing of airlines that fly into Las Vegas, see "Getting There" in chapter 2. Travelers from overseas can take advantage of the advance-purchase fares offered by all the major U.S. and European carriers.

A number of U.S. airlines offer service from Europe to the United States. If they do not have direct flights from Europe to Las Vegas, they can book you straight through on a connecting flight. You can make reservations by calling the following numbers in London: **American** (☎ 0181/572-5555), **Continental** (☎ 4412/9377-6464), **Delta** (☎ 0800/414-767), and **United** (☎ 0181/990-9900).

And of course many international carriers serve LAX and/or San Francisco International Airport. Helpful numbers to know include **Virgin Atlantic** (☎ 0293/747-747 in London), **British Airways** (☎ 0345/222-111 in London), and **Aer Lingus** (☎ 01/844-4747 in Dublin, or 061/415-556 in Shannon). **Quantas** (☎ 008/177-767 in Australia) has flights from Sydney to Los Angeles and San Francisco; you can also take United from Australia to the West Coast. **Air New Zealand** (☎ 0800/737-000 in Auckland, or 643/379-5200 in Christchurch) also offers service to LAX. Canadian readers might book flights on **Air Canada** (☎ in Canada 800/268-7240, or 800/361-8620), which offers direct service from Toronto, Montreal, Calgary, and Vancouver to San Francisco and Los Angeles.

The visitor arriving by air, no matter what the port of entry, should cultivate patience and resignation before setting foot on U.S. soil. Getting through immigration control may take as long as 2 hours on some days, especially summer weekends, so have your guidebook or something else to read handy. Add the time it takes to clear customs and you will see you should make a very generous allowance for delay in planning connections between international and domestic flights—figure on 2 to 3 hours at least.

In contrast, for the traveler arriving by car or by rail from Canada, the border-crossing formalities have been streamlined to the vanishing point. And for the traveler by air from Canada, Bermuda, and some places in the Caribbean, you can sometimes go through customs and immigration at the point of departure, which is much quicker.

3 Getting Around the United States

On their transatlantic or transpacific flights, some large U.S. airlines (for example, TWA, American, Northwest, United, and Delta) offer travelers special discount tickets under the name **Visit USA,** allowing travel between U.S. destinations at minimum rates. They are not on sale in the United States and must be purchased before you leave your point of departure. This system is the best, easiest, and fastest way to see the United States at low cost. You should obtain information well in advance from your travel agent or the office of the airline concerned, since the conditions attached to these discount tickets can be changed without advance notice.

Bus travel in the United States can be both slow and uncomfortable; however, it can also be quite inexpensive. **Greyhound,** the sole nationwide bus line, offers an **Ameripass** for unlimited travel throughout the United States. Greyhound's phone number is ☎ 800/231-2222. At press time, prices were $179 for 7 days, $289 for 15 days, $399 for 30 days, and $559 for 60 days. Though bus stations are often located in undesirable neighborhoods, the one in Las Vegas is conveniently located in a safe part of downtown.

There is currently no **rail** service to Las Vegas.

FAST FACTS: For the Foreign Traveler

Automobile Organizations   Auto clubs will supply maps, suggested routes, guidebooks, accident and bail-bond insurance, and emergency road service. The major auto club in the United States, with hundreds of offices nationwide, is the **American Automobile Association (AAA).** Members of some foreign auto clubs have reciprocal arrangements with the AAA and enjoy its services at no charge. If you belong to an auto club, inquire about AAA reciprocity before you leave. The AAA can provide you with an **International Driving Permit** validating your foreign license, although drivers with valid licenses from most home countries don't really need this permit. You may be able to join the AAA even if you are not a member of a reciprocal club. To inquire, call the nearest office, which is in Carson City (☎ 702/883-2470). In addition, some automobile rental agencies now provide these services, so you should inquire about their availability when you rent your car.

Automobile Rentals   To rent a car you need a major credit or charge card. A valid driver's license is required, and you usually need to be at least 25 years old. Some companies do rent to younger people but add a daily surcharge. Be sure to return your car with the same amount of gas you started out with; rental companies charge excessive prices for gasoline. For car-rental companies in Las Vegas, see "Renting a Car" in chapter 2.

Business Hours   Offices are usually open weekdays from 9am to 5pm. Banks are open weekdays from 9am to 3pm or later, although there's 24-hour access to the automatic-teller machines (ATMs) at most banks and other outlets. In Las Vegas, money is also available around the clock at casino cages—and every casino has at least one ATM machine. Shops, especially those in shopping complexes, tend to stay open late: until about 9pm weekdays and until 6pm weekends.

Climate   See "When to Go" in chapter 2.

Currency   See "Preparing for Your Trip" earlier in this chapter.

Currency Exchange   The "foreign-exchange bureaus" so common in Europe are rare in the United States. They're at major international airports, and there are a few in most major cities, but they're nonexistent in medium-size cities and small towns. Try to avoid having to change foreign money, or traveler's checks denominated other than in U.S. dollars, at small-town banks, or even at branches in a big city; in fact leave any currency other than U.S. dollars at home (except the cash you need for the taxi or bus ride home when you return to your own country); otherwise, your own currency may prove more nuisance to you than it's worth.

Las Vegas casinos can exchange foreign currency, usually at a good rate.

Drinking Laws   The legal age to drink alcohol is 21.

Electric Current   The United States uses 110–120 volts AC (60 cycles), compared to 220–240 volts AC (50 cycles), as in most of Europe. Besides a 100-volt converter, small appliances of non-American manufacture, such as hair dryers or shavers, will require a plug adapter with two flat, parallel pins. The easiest solution to the power struggle is to purchase dual-voltage appliances that operate on both 110 and 220 volts and then all that is required is a U.S. adapter plug.

Embassies and Consulates   All embassies are located in the nation's capital, Washington, D.C. In addition, several of the major English-speaking countries also have consulates in San Francisco or in Los Angeles.

The embassy of **Australia** is at 1601 Massachusetts Ave. NW, Washington, DC 20036 (☎ **202/797-3000**); a consulate-general is at 1 Bush St., Suite 700, San Francisco, CA 94104 (☎ **415/362-6160**). The embassy of **Canada** is at 501 Pennsylvania Ave. NW, Washington, DC 20001 (☎ **202/682-1740**); the nearest consulate is at 300 South Grand Ave., 10th Floor, California Plaza, Los Angeles, CA

90071 (☎ **213/346-2700**). The embassy of the **Republic of Ireland** is at 2234 Massachusetts Ave. NW, Washington, DC 20008 (☎ **202/462-3939**); a consulate is at 44 Montgomery St., Suite 3830, San Francisco, CA 94104 (☎ **415/ 392-4214**). The embassy of **New Zealand** is at 37 Observatory Circle NW, Washington, DC 20008 (☎ **202/328-4848**); the nearest consulate is at 12400 Wilshire Blvd., Suite 1150, Los Angeles, CA 90025 (☎ **310/207-1605**). The embassy of the **United Kingdom** is at 3100 Massachusetts Ave. NW, Washington, DC 20008 (☎ **202/462-1340**); the nearest consulate is at 1 Sansome St., Ste. 850, San Francisco, CA 94104 (☎ **415/981-3030**).

If you are from another country, you can get the telephone number of your embassy by calling "Information" (directory assistance) in Washington, D.C. (☎ **202/ 555-1212**).

Emergencies   Call ☎ **911** for fire, police, and ambulance. If you encounter such traveler's problems as sickness, accident, or lost or stolen baggage, call Traveler's Aid, an organization that specializes in helping distressed travelers. In Las Vegas, there is an office in McCarran International Airport (☎ 702/798-1742), which is open daily from 8am to 5pm. Similar services are provided by Help of Southern Nevada, 953-35B E. Sahara Ave., Suite 208, at Maryland Parkway in the Commercial Center on the northeast corner (☎ 702/369-4357). Hours are Monday to Friday, from 8am to 4pm.

Holidays   On the following national legal holidays, banks, government offices, post offices, and many stores, restaurants, and museums are closed: January 1 (New Year's Day), third Monday in January (Martin Luther King Jr. Day), third Monday in February (Presidents' Day), last Monday in May (Memorial Day), July 4 (Independence Day), first Monday in September (Labor Day), second Monday in October (Columbus Day), November 11 (Veterans Day/Armistice Day), fourth Thursday in November (Thanksgiving Day), and December 25 (Christmas Day). The Tuesday following the first Monday in November is Election Day.

Legal Aid   If you are stopped for a minor infraction (for example, of the highway code, such as speeding), never attempt to pay the fine directly to a police officer; you may be arrested on the much more serious charge of attempted bribery. Pay fines by mail, or directly into the hands of the clerk of the court. If accused of a more serious offense, it is best to say and do nothing before consulting a lawyer. Under U.S. law, an arrested person is allowed one telephone call to a party of his or her choice. Call your embassy or consulate.

Mail   You may receive mail c/o General Delivery at the main post office of the city or region where you expect to be. The addressee must pick it up in person, and must produce proof of identity (driver's license, credit card, passport).

Mailboxes are blue with a red-and-white logo, and carry the inscription U.S. MAIL. Within the United States, it costs 20¢ to mail a standard-size postcard. Letters that weigh up to 1 ounce cost 32¢, plus 23¢ for each additional ounce. A postcard to Mexico costs 30¢, a $^{1}/_{2}$-ounce letter 35¢; a postcard to Canada costs 30¢, a 1-ounce letter 40¢. A postcard to Europe, Australia, New Zealand, the Far East, South America, and elsewhere costs 40¢, while a letter is 50¢ for each $^{1}/_{2}$ ounce. In Las Vegas, the closest post office to the Strip is behind the Stardust Hotel at 3100 S. Industrial Rd., between Sahara Avenue and Spring Mountain Road (☎ 800/ 297-5543). The main post office is at 1001 E. Sunset Rd., same phone number. It's open Monday to Friday from 8:30am to 5pm. You can also mail letters and packages at your hotel, and there's a full-service U.S. Post Office in the Forum Shops in Caesars Palace.

Medical Emergencies   See "Emergencies" above.

Taxes   In the United States there is no VAT (value-added tax) or other indirect tax at a national level. There is a $10 customs tax, payable on entry to the United States, and a $6 departure tax. Sales tax of 7% is levied on goods and services by state and local governments, however, and is not included in the price tags you'll see on merchandise. There is also a hotel tax of 8%. These taxes are not refundable.

Telephone and Fax   Pay phones can be found on street corners, as well as in bars, restaurants, public buildings, stores and at service stations. Some accept 20¢, most are 25¢. If the telephone accepts 20¢, you may also use a quarter (25¢) but you will not receive change.

In the past few years, many American companies have installed "voice-mail" systems, so be prepared to deal with a machine instead of a receptionist if calling a business number. Listen carefully to the instructions (you'll probably be asked to dial 1, 2, or 3 or wait for an operator to pick up); if you can't understand, sometimes dialing 0 will put you in touch with an operator within the company. It's frustrating even for locals!

For long-distance or international calls, it's most economical to charge the call to a telephone charge card or a credit card; or you can use a lot of change. The pay phone will instruct you how much to deposit and when to deposit it into the slot on the top of the telephone box.

For long-distance calls in the United States, dial 1 followed by the area code and number you want. For direct overseas calls, first dial 011, followed by the country code (Australia, 61; Republic of Ireland, 353; New Zealand, 64; United Kingdom, 44; and so on), and then by the city code (for example, 71 or 81 for London, 21 for Birmingham, 1 for Dublin) and the number of the person you wish to call.

Before calling from a hotel room, always ask the hotel phone operator if there are any telephone surcharges. There almost always are, and they often are as much as 75¢ or $1, even for a local call. These charges are best avoided by using a public phone, calling collect, or using a telephone charge card.

For reversed-charge or collect calls and for person-to-person calls, dial 0 (zero, not the letter "O") followed by the area code and number you want; an operator will then come on the line, and you should specify that you are calling collect, or person-to-person, or both. If your operator-assisted call is international, immediately ask to speak with an overseas operator.

Telephone Directory   The local phone company provides two kinds of telephone directories. The general directory, called the "white pages," lists businesses and personal residences separately, in alphabetical order. The first few pages are devoted to community-service numbers, including a guide to long-distance and international calling, complete with country codes and area codes.

The second directory, the "yellow pages," lists all local services, businesses, and industries by type, with an index at the back. The listings cover not only such obvious items as automobile repairs by make of car, or drugstores (pharmacies), often by geographical location, but also restaurants by type of cuisine and geographical location, bookstores by special subject and/or language, places of worship by religious denomination, and other information that a visitor might otherwise not readily find. The yellow pages also include city plans or detailed area maps, often showing postal ZIP codes and public transportation.

For local directory assistance ("Information"), dial **411;** for long-distance information dial 1, then the appropriate area code and **555-1212.**

Most hotels have fax machines available for their customers, and there is usually a charge to send or receive a facsimile. You will also see signs for public faxes in the windows of small shops.

Time   Nevada is on Pacific time, which is 3 hours earlier than on the U.S. East Coast. For instance, when it is noon in Las Vegas, it is 3pm in New York and Miami; 2pm in Chicago, in the central part of the country; and 1pm in Denver, Colorado, in the midwestern part of the country. Nevada, like most of the rest of the United States, observes daylight saving time during the summer; in late spring, clocks are moved ahead 1 hour and then are turned back again in the fall. This results in lovely long summer evenings, when the sun sets as late as 8:30 or 9pm.

Tipping   Some rules of thumb: bartenders, 10% to 15%; bellhops, at least 50¢ per bag, or $2 to $3 for a lot of luggage; cab drivers, 10% of the fare; chambermaids, $1 per day; checkroom attendants, $1 per garment; hairdressers and barbers, 15% to 20%; waiters and waitresses, 15% to 20% of the check; valet parking attendants, $1; showroom maitre d's, see chapter 10 for details; casino dealers, a few dollars if you've had a big win.

Getting to Know Las Vegas 4

Located in the southernmost precincts of a wide, pancake-flat valley, Las Vegas is the biggest city in the state of Nevada. Treeless mountains form a scenic backdrop to hotels awash in neon glitter. For tourism purposes, the city is quite compact.

1 Orientation

VISITOR INFORMATION

All major Las Vegas hotels provide comprehensive tourist information at their reception and/or sightseeing and show desks. Other good information sources are: the **Las Vegas Convention and Visitors Authority,** 3150 Paradise Rd., Las Vegas, NV 89109 (☎ **702/ 892-0711**, Monday to Friday 8am to 6pm, Saturday and Sunday 8am to 5pm); the **Las Vegas Chamber of Commerce, 711 E. Desert Inn Rd., Las Vegas, NV 89109** (☎ **702/735-1616**, Monday to Friday 8am to 5pm), and, for information on all of Nevada, including Las Vegas, the **Nevada Commission on Tourism** (☎ **800/638-2328**).

FOR TROUBLED TRAVELERS

The **Traveler's Aid Society** is a social-service organization geared to helping travelers in difficult straits. Their services might include reuniting families separated while traveling, feeding people stranded without cash, or even emotional counseling. If you're in trouble, seek them out. In Las Vegas there is a Traveler's Aid office at McCarran International Airport (☎ **702/798-1742**). It's open daily from 8am to 5pm. Similar services are provided by **Help of Southern Nevada,** 953-35B E. Sahara Ave. (suite 208), at Maryland Parkway in the Commercial Center (☎ **702/369-4357**). Hours are Monday to Friday 8am to 4pm.

CITY LAYOUT

There are two main areas of Las Vegas, the Strip and downtown. For many people, that's all there is to Las Vegas. But there is actually more to the town than that; maybe not as glitzy and glamorous—okay, definitely not—but you will find still more casino action on Paradise Road and in east Las Vegas, mainstream and alternative culture shopping on Maryland Parkway, and different restaurant choices all over the city. Confining yourself to the Strip and downtown is fine for the first-time visitor, but repeat customers (and you will be) should get out there and explore. Las Vegas Boulevard South (the Strip) is Ground Zero for addresses; anything crossing it will start with 1 East and 1 West (and go up from there) at that point.

THE STRIP

The Strip is probably the most famous $3^1/_2$-mile stretch of highway in the nation. Officially Las Vegas Boulevard South, it contains most of the top hotels in town and offers almost all of the major showroom entertainment. We divide the Strip into three sections: **South Strip** can be roughly defined as the portion of the Strip south of Harmon Avenue, including the MGM Grand, the Monte Carlo, the New York New York, and the Luxor hotels. **Mid-Strip** is a long stretch of the street between Harmon Avenue and Spring Mountain Road, including Caesars, the Mirage and Treasure Island, Bally's, the Flamingo Hilton, and Harrah's. **North Strip** stretches north from Stardust Road all the way to the Stratosphere Tower and includes the Stardust, Sahara, Riviera, Desert Inn, and Circus Circus. It's on the Strip where a first time visitor will, and probably should, spend the bulk of their time. If mobility is a problem, then it's probably the South and Midstrip locations that are the best bets.

CONVENTION CENTER

This area east of the Strip has grown up around the Las Vegas Convention Center. Las Vegas is one of the nation's top convention cities, attracting more than 2.9 million conventioneers each year. The major hotel in this section is the Las Vegas Hilton, but in recent years Marriott has built Residence Inn and Courtyard properties here, and the Hard Rock Hotel has opened. You'll find many excellent smaller hotels and motels southward along Paradise Road. All of these offer close proximity to the Strip.

DOWNTOWN

Also known as "Glitter Gulch" (narrower streets make the neon seem brighter), downtown Las Vegas, which is centered on Fremont Street between Main and 9th streets, was the first section of the city to develop hotels and casinos. With the exception of the Golden Nugget, which looks like it belongs in Monte Carlo, this area has traditionally been more casual than the Strip. But with the advent of the Fremont Street Experience (see chapter 7 for details), downtown is experiencing a revitalization. The area is clean, the crowds low key and friendly, and the light show over head as silly as anything on the Strip. Don't overlook it. Las Vegas Boulevard runs all the way into Fremont Street downtown (about a 5-minute drive from Stratosphere if traffic is good).

BETWEEN THE STRIP & DOWNTOWN

The area between the Strip and downtown is a seedy stretch dotted with tacky wedding chapels, bail-bond operations, pawnshops, and cheap motels.

However, the area known as the **Gateway District** (roughly north and south of Charleston to the west of Las Vegas Boulevard South) is slowly but surely gaining a name for itself as an actual artists colony. Studios, small cafes, and other signs of life are springing up, and it is hoped this movement will last.

2 Getting Around

It shouldn't be too hard to navigate your way around. For the most part, you won't have to.

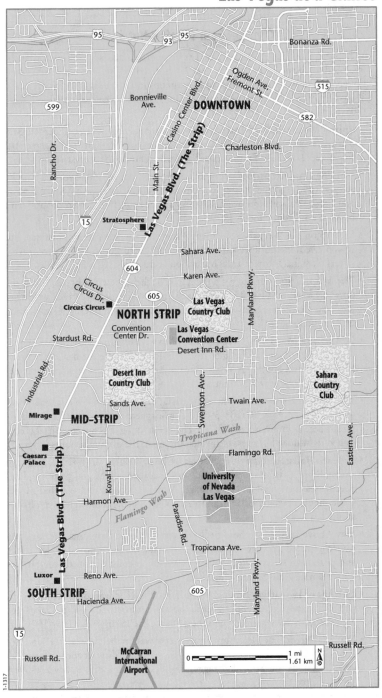

DOWNTOWN

Bonanza Rd.

Ogden Ave.
Fremont St.

Bonnieville
Ave.

Charleston Blvd.

Rancho Dr.

Main St.

Casino Center Blvd.

Stratosphere

Las Vegas Blvd. (The Strip)

Sahara Ave.

Karen Ave.

Maryland Pkwy.

Circus
Circus Dr.

Circus Circus

NORTH STRIP

Las Vegas
Country Club

Convention
Center Dr.

Las Vegas
Convention Center

Stardust Rd.

Desert Inn Rd.

Industrial Rd.

Desert Inn
Country Club

Sahara
Country
Club

Sands Ave.

Swenson Ave.

Twain Ave.

Mirage

MID-STRIP

Eastern Ave.

Tropicana Wash

Caesars
Palace

Flamingo Rd.

Koval Ln.

University
of Nevada
Las Vegas

Harmon Ave.

Flamingo Wash

Paradise Rd.

Tropicana Ave.

Luxor

Reno Ave.

Las Vegas Blvd. (The Strip)

SOUTH STRIP

Hacienda Ave.

Maryland Pkwy.

Russell Rd.

Russell Rd.

McCarran
International
Airport

0   1 mi
                 1.61 km

N

1-1317

Chopper Tom's Traffic Hot Spots

"Chopper" Tom Hawley has watched Las Vegas grow since he was a little kid catching lizards in the desert back in the '60s. A self-described "traffic geek," Tom's traffic reports can be seen mornings and afternoons in Las Vegas on Channel 3. He also co-anchors "The Morning Report" from 7am to 9am on radio station KVBC (105.1 FM).

- **Spring Mountain/I-15 Interchange:** This interchange will be undergoing reconstruction through early 1999. Your best bet is the Desert Inn Superarterial to get over I-15. Use Tropicana or Sahara to get onto the Interstate.

- **Flamingo and the Strip:** Pedestrian underpasses here should have been built by August 1998, but the project fell apart in a squabble between Mirage Resorts and Caesars Palace. Now overhead walkways are being built, and probably won't be done until sometime in 1999.

- **U.S. 95 on the West side of Town:** A huge freeway expansion is planned, but it won't be done until well after the year 2000. During rush hour, try surface streets like Charleston or Lake Mead Boulevard.

- **The Strip:** If you want to get a good look at the spectacular hotels, this is the only way to go, and you'll probably even enjoy taking plenty of time waiting at the lights. But if you just want to get to your destination fast, use Okavol Lane or Paradise Road.

- **I-215/Lake Mead Dr./Green Valley Pkwy.:** This three-way interchange is under construction to give motorists a quick new route for driving between Henderson and South Las Vegas. But until the work wraps up around the beginning of 1999, it will be a mess.

- **The Spaghetti Bowl:** If you want pasta, try Battista's Hole in the Wall, 4041 Audrie St. (☎ 702/733-3950). The Spaghetti Bowl is what locals call the mess where I-95 intersects U.S. 95. The whole thing is being completely redesigned right now, but most of the detours are in the overnight hours.

- **Ride the Rails:** At this writing, battles are being fought over which rails will go where. Right now, monorails already exist between MGM and Bally's and between Treasure Island and the Mirage. A system between Bellagio and Monte Carlo should open in fall 1998, and another one is being planned between Bally's an the Las Vegas Hilton.

- **Stay Above It All:** Overhead pedestrian walkways at Tropicana and the Strip were completed a couple of years ago, and dramatically improved vehicle traffic and pedestrian safety. Other walkways are under construction on the Strip at both Flamingo and Spring Mountain.

- **The Age of Industrial:** An upgrade of Industrial Road was completed last year, with extra lanes and smooth travel all the way from Russell Road to Oakey. It's a great alternative when I-15 and the Strip are backed up.

- **Do D.I. Direct:** The Desert Inn Superarterial was finished in March 1995, with 2 miles of nonstop travel between Paradise and Valley View. It goes up over I-15 and down under the Strip. The biggest thrill ride this side of the New York New York roller coaster!

BY CAR

We highly recommend a rental car for Vegas tourists. The Strip is too spread out for walking, downtown is too far away for a cheap cab ride, and public transportation is ineffective at best. Plus, further visits call for further exploration in still more parts of the city, and a car brings freedom. You should note that places with addresses some 60 blocks east or west from the Strip are actually less than a 10-minute drive—provided there is no traffic. However, if you plan to confine yourself to one part of the Strip (or one cruise down to it) or to Downtown, your feet will suffice.

Note: If you can, avoid driving during peak rush hours, especially if you have to make a show curtain. Parking is usually a pleasure, since all casino hotels offer valet service. That means that for a mere $1 tip you can park right at the door. (Though the valet usually fills up on busy nights.) Furthermore, though bus tours are available to nearby attractions, a car lets you explore at your own pace rather than according to a tour schedule. See "Renting a Car" in chapter 2 for information and toll-free numbers of companies with offices in Las Vegas.

Since driving on the outskirts of Las Vegas—for example, coming from California—involves desert driving, you must take certain precautions. It's a good idea to check your tires, water, and oil before leaving. Take at least five gallons of water in a clean container that can be used for either drinking or the radiator. Pay attention to road signs that suggest when to turn off your car's air conditioner. And don't push your luck with gas—it may be 35 miles, or more, between stations. If your car overheats, do not remove the radiator cap until the engine has cooled, and then remove it only very slowly. Add water to within an inch of the top of the radiator.

BY TAXI

Since cabs line up in front of all major hotels, an easy way to get around town is by taxi. Cabs charge $2.20 at the meter drop and 30¢ for each additional one-fifth of a mile. A taxi from the airport to the Strip will run you $8 to $12, from the airport to downtown $15 to $18, and between the Strip and downtown about $7 to $10. You can often save money by sharing a cab with someone going to the same destination (up to five people can ride for the same fare).

If you want to call a taxi, any of the following companies can provide one: **Desert Cab Company** (☎ 702/376-2688), **Whittlesea Blue Cab** (☎ 702/384-6111), and **Yellow/Checker Cab/Star Company** (☎ 702/873-2000).

BY PUBLIC TRANSPORTATION

The no. 301 bus operated by **Citizens Area Transit** (☎ 702/CAT-RIDE) plies a route between the Downtown Transportation Center (at Casino Center Boulevard and Stewart Avenue) and a few miles beyond the southern end of the Strip. The fare is $1.50 for adults, 50¢ for seniors (62 and older) and children 5 to 17, and free for those under 5. CAT buses run 24 hours a day and are wheelchair-accessible. Exact change is required, but dollar bills are accepted.

Or you can hop aboard a classic streetcar replica run by **Las Vegas Strip Trolley** (☎ 702/382-1404). These old-fashioned dark-green vehicles have interior oak paneling and are comfortably air-conditioned. Like the buses, they run northward from Hacienda Avenue, stopping at all major hotels en route to the Sahara, and then looping back via the Las Vegas Hilton. They do not, however, go to the Stratosphere Tower or Downtown. Trolleys run about every 15 minutes daily between 9:30am and 2am. The fare is $1.30 (under 5 free), and exact change is required.

❓ Did You Know?

- Las Vegas (Sin City) has more churches per capita than any other city in America.
- Illusionists Siegfried and Roy have sawed a woman in half more times than anyone else.
- Visitors on a trail ride once brought a horse into the crowded casino of the Thunderbird Hotel. They put a pair of dice between his lips at the craps table, and he threw a natural seven.
- In January, a Las Vegas visitor can ski the snowy slopes of Mount Charleston and water-ski on Lake Mead in the same day.
- Former Pres. Ronald Reagan performed at the Last Frontier in 1954. Those who saw him said he was a pretty good song and dance man.
- Bandleader Xavier Cugat and Spanish bombshell singer Charo were the first couple to exchange vows at Caesars Palace, 2 days after its 1966 opening.

FAST FACTS: Las Vegas

Ambulances   See "Emergencies," below.

Area Code   702

Baby-Sitters   Contact Around the Clock Child Care (☎ 800/798-6768 or 702/365-1040). In business since 1985, this reputable company clears its sitters with the health department, the sheriff, and the FBI, and carefully screens references. Charges are $38 for 4 hours for one or two children, $7.50 for each additional hour, with surcharges for additional children and on holidays. Sitters are on call 7 days a week, 24 hours a day, and they will come to your hotel. Call at least 2 hours in advance.

Banks   Banks are generally open 9 or 10am to 3pm, and most have Saturday hours. See also "Cash and Credit," below.

Car Rentals   See "Getting Around," above.

Cash and Credit   It's extremely easy, too easy, to obtain cash in Las Vegas. Most casino cashiers will cash personal checks and can exchange foreign currency, and just about every casino has a machine that will provide cash on a wide variety of credit cards.

Climate   See "When to Go" in chapter 2.

Convention Facilities   Las Vegas is one of America's top convention destinations. Much of the action takes place at the Las Vegas Convention Center, 3150 Paradise Rd., Las Vegas, NV 89109 (☎ 702/892-0711). The largest single-level convention center in the world, its 1.3 million square feet includes 89 meeting rooms. And this immense facility is augmented by the Cashman Field Center, 850 Las Vegas Blvd. N., Las Vegas, NV 89101 (☎ 702/386-7100). Under the same auspices, Cashman provides another 98,100 square feet of convention space.

Currency Exchange   Most Las Vegas hotels can exchange foreign currency. There's also a currency exchange desk run by Travelex in the ticketing area on the first level of McCarran International Airport.

Dentists and Doctors   Hotels usually have lists of dentists and doctors should you need one. In addition, they are listed in the Centel Yellow Pages.

For dentist referrals you can also call the Clark County Dental Society (☎ 702/255-7873), weekdays 9am to noon and 1 to 5pm; when the office is closed, a recording will tell you whom to call for emergency service.

For physician referrals, call Desert Springs Hospital (☎ 800/842-5439 or 702/733-6875). Hours are Monday to Friday 8am to 5pm.

Drugstores   Sav-on is a large 24-hour drugstore and pharmacy close to the Strip at 1360 E. Flamingo Rd., at Maryland Parkway (☎ 702/731-5373 for the pharmacy, 702/737-0595 for general merchandise). White Cross Drugs, 1700 Las Vegas Boulevard South (☎ 702/382-1733), open daily 7am to 1am, will make pharmacy deliveries to your hotel during the day.

Dry Cleaners   Things spill, and silk stains. When in need, come to Steiner Cleaners, 1131 E. Tropicana (corner of Maryland Parkway, in the Vons Shopping Center) (☎ 702/736-7474), open Monday to Friday from 7am to 6:30pm, Saturday 8am to 6pm, closed Sunday. Not only did they clean all the costumes for the movie *Casino,* but they were Liberace's personal dry cleaners for years.

Emergencies   Dial 911 to contact the police or fire departments or to call an ambulance.

Emergency services are available 24 hours a day at University Medical Center, 1800 W. Charleston Blvd., at Shadow Lane (☎ 702/383-2661); the emergency room entrance is on the corner of Hastings and Rose streets. Sunrise Hospital and Medical Center, 3186 Maryland Pkwy., between Desert Inn Road and Sahara Avenue (☎ 702/731-8080), also has a 24-hour emergency room. For more minor problems, if you are on the Strip, the Imperial Palace has a 24-hour urgent care facility, the Resorts Medical Center, an independently run facility on the 8th floor, with doctors and X-ray machines; it's located at 3535 Las Vegas Boulevard South, between Sands and Flamingo (☎ 702/731-3311).

Highway Conditions   For recorded information, call ☎ 702/486-3116.

Hot Lines   The Rape Crisis Center (☎ 702/366-1640), Suicide Prevention (☎ 702/731-2990), Poison Emergencies (☎ 800/446-6179).

Information   See "Visitor Information," earlier in this chapter.

Libraries   The largest in town is the Clark County Library branch at 1401 Flamingo Rd., at Escondido Street, on the southeast corner (☎ 702/733-7810). Hours are Monday to Thursday 9am to 9pm, Friday and Saturday 9am to 5pm, Sunday 1 to 5pm.

Liquor and Gambling Laws   You must be 21 to drink or gamble. There are no closing hours in Las Vegas for the sale or consumption of alcohol, even on Sunday.

Newspapers and Periodicals   There are two Las Vegas dailies: the *Las Vegas Review Journal* and the *Las Vegas Sun.* The *Review Journal*'s Friday edition has a helpful "Weekend" section with a comprehensive guide to shows and buffets. And at every hotel desk, you'll find dozens of free local magazines, such as *Vegas Visitor, What's On in Las Vegas, Showbiz Weekly,* and *Where to in Las Vegas,* that are chock-full of helpful information. The International Newsstand carries a vast selection of virtually ever major U.S. city newspaper and many international ones; they probably don't have everything, but we tried and couldn't find one they had missed; 3900 Maryland Pkwy., in Citibank Plaza; ☎ 702/796-9901. Open Monday to Sunday from 8:30am to 9pm.

Parking   Valet parking is one of the great pleasures of Las Vegas and well worth the dollar tip (given when the car is returned) to save walking a city block from the far reaches of a hotel parking lot, particularly when the temperature is over 100°. Another summer plus: The valet will turn on your air-conditioning, so you don't have to get in an "oven on wheels."

Police   For nonemergencies call ☎ 702/795-3111. For emergencies call ☎ 911.

Post Office   The most convenient post office is immediately behind the Stardust Hotel at 3100 Industrial Rd., between Sahara Avenue and Spring Mountain Road (☎ 800/297-5543). It's open Monday to Friday 8:30am to 5pm. You can also mail letters and packages at your hotel, and there's a full-service U.S. Post Office in the Forum Shops in Caesars Palace.

Safety   In Las Vegas, vast amounts of money are always on display, and criminals find many easy marks. Don't be one of them. At gaming tables and slot machines, men should keep wallets well concealed and out of the reach of pickpockets, and women should keep handbags in plain sight (on laps). Outside casinos, popular spots for pickpockets and thieves are restaurants and outdoor shows, such as the volcano at Mirage or at the Treasure Island pirate battle. Stay alert. Unless your hotel room has an in-room safe, check your valuables in a safety-deposit box at the front desk.

Show Tickets   See chapter 10 for details on obtaining show tickets.

Taxes   Clark County hotel room tax is 8%; the sales tax is 7%.

Taxis   See "Getting Around, By Taxi" earlier in this chapter.

Time Zone   Las Vegas is in the Pacific time zone, 3 hours earlier than the East Coast, 2 hours earlier than the Midwest.

Veterinarian   If Fido or Fluffy gets sick while traveling, go to the West Flamingo Animal Hospital. It's open 24 hours and they take DISC, MC, V, and have an ATM machine; 5445 Flamingo near Decater (☎ 702/876-2111).

Weather and Time   Call ☎ 702/248-4800.

Weddings   Las Vegas is one of the easiest places in the world to tie the knot. There's no blood test or waiting period, the ceremony and license are inexpensive, chapels are open around the clock, and your honeymoon destination is right at hand. More than 101,000 marriages are performed here each year. Get a license Downtown at the Clark County Marriage License Bureau, 200 S. 3rd St., at Bridger Avenue (☎ 702/455-3156). Open 8am to midnight Monday to Thursday and from 8am Friday through midnight Sunday. On legal holidays they're open 24 hours. The cost of a marriage license is $35, the cost of the ceremony, another $35.

Accommodations in Las Vegas

If there's one thing Vegas has, it's hotels. Big hotels. Here you'll find 19 of the 20 largest hotels in the world. And rooms: 105,000 rooms, to be exact—or at least exact at this writing. Every 5 minutes, or so it seems, someone is putting up a new giant hotel, or adding another 1000 rooms to an already existing one. So finding a place to stay in Vegas should be the least of your worries.

Or is it?

When a convention, a fight, or some other big event is happening— and these things are always happening—darn near all of those 105,000 rooms are going to be sold out. (Over the course of last year, the occupancy rate for hotel rooms in Las Vegas ran at about 90%.) A last-minute Vegas vacation can turn into a housing nightmare. If possible, plan in advance so you can have your choice: Ancient Egypt or Ancient Rome? New York or New Orleans? Strip or downtown? Luxury or economy? Vegas has all that and way too much more.

The bottom line is that with a few sometimes subtle differences, a hotel room is a hotel room is a hotel room. After you factor in location, price, and whether you have a pirate-loving kid, there isn't that much difference between rooms, except for perhaps size and the quality of their surprisingly similar furnishings. Price isn't even always a guideline; prices in Vegas are anything but fixed, so you will notice wild ranges (the same room can routinely go for anywhere from $60 to $250, depending on demand), and even that range is negotiable if it's a slow time. (Though such times are less and less common thanks to the influx of conventions.)

Yes, if you pay more you will probably (but not certainly) get a "nicer" establishment and clientele to match (perhaps not so many loud drunks in the elevators). On the other hand, if a convention is in town the drunks will be there; they will just be wearing business suits and/or funny hats. And frankly, the big hotels, no matter how fine, are mass-producing rooms; at 3,000 or more a pop, they are the equivalent of Sixties tract housing. Consequently, even in the nicest hotels you can (and probably will) encounter plumbing noises, overhear conversations from other rooms, or get woken by the maids as they knock on the doors next to yours that don't have the "do not disturb" sign up.

1 Best Bets

- **Best for Conventioneers/Business Travelers:** The **Las Vegas Hilton,** 3000 Paradise Rd., adjacent to the Las Vegas Convention Center and the setting for many on-premises conventions, offers extensive facilities along with helpful services such as a full business center.

- **Best Elegant Hotel:** Country club elegance is the keynote of the **Desert Inn Country Club Resort and Casino,** 3145 Las Vegas Blvd. S. In its European-style casino, gaming tables are comfortably spaced; the glitzy glow of neon is replaced by the glitter of crystal chandeliers; and the scarcity of slot and video poker machines eliminates the usual noisy jangle of coins. Extensive facilities are complemented by attentive personal service. This is the most prestigious hotel address in town.

- **Best Archetypically Las Vegas Hotel:** By the end of 1998, there aren't going to be any. Las Vegas hotels are one and all doing such massive face lifts that the archetype is going to be but a memory. Still, despite some major face lifts, **Caesars Palace,** 3570 Las Vegas Blvd. S., will probably continue to embody the excess and, well, downright silliness that used to characterize Vegas—and to a certain extent still does.

- **Best Swimming Pool:** The **Mirage,** 3400 Las Vegas Blvd. South, and the **Flamingo Hilton,** 3555 Las Vegas Blvd. S., probably tie for most stunning; both feature lushly landscaped areas, with trees galore, amorphously shaped pools with water slides and waterfalls, plus kiddie pools, Jacuzzis, and, in the case of the Flamingo, swan- and duck-filled ponds and islands of flamingos and African penguins. Far more Vegas, however, is the **Tropicana,** 3801 Las Vegas Blvd. S., where you'll also find a swim-up bar/blackjack table.

- **Best Health Club:** Like sumptuous swimming pools, deluxe state-of-the-art health clubs are the rule in Las Vegas hotels. Most exclusive (the fee is $18 per visit) and extensively equipped is the club at the **Mirage,** offering a full complement of machines—some with individual TVs (headphones are supplied), free weights, private whirlpool rooms as well as a large whirlpool and saunas, a thoroughly equipped locker room, and comfortable lounges in which to rest up after your workout. An adjoining salon offers every imaginable spa service. Steve Wynn works out here almost daily, as do many celebrity guests.

- **Best Hotel Dining/Entertainment:** Food aficionados will be thrilled with the nationally renowned celebrity chefs at the **MGM Grand,** 3799 Las Vegas Blvd. S. You'll find restaurants by Mark Miller, Emeril Lagasse, and Wolfgang Puck, as well as one of the best restaurants in Vegas: the Grand's gourmet room Gatsby's. There's also a re-creation of Hollywood's famed Brown Derby here.

- **Best for Twentysomethings Through Baby Boomers:** The **Hard Rock Hotel,** 4455 Paradise Rd., which bills itself as the world's "first rock 'n' roll hotel and casino" and "Vegas for a new generation." Aficionados of Hard Rock clubs won't mind the noise level, but we aren't sure about everyone else.

- **Best Interior:** For totally different reasons, it's a tie between **New York New York,** 3790 Las Vegas Blvd. S., and the **Mirage.** The latter's tropical rain forest and massive coral-reef aquarium behind the registration desk may not provide as much relaxation as a Club Med vacation, but they're a welcome change from the general hubbub that is usual for Vegas. Speaking of hubbub, New York New York has cornered the market on it, but its jaw-dropping interior, with its extraordinary attention to detail (virtually every significant characteristic of New York City is recreated somewhere here) makes this a tough act to beat. Ever.

- **Best for Families:** It's a classic. **Circus Circus,** 2880 Las Vegas Blvd. S., has almost unlimited activities for kids—ongoing circus acts, a vast video-game arcade, a carnival midway, and a full amusement park.
- **Best Rooms:** On the strip, they're at the **Mirage;** downtown, they're at the **Golden Nugget,** 129 E. Fremont St. The rooms actually look almost identical, though the former are done in more earth tones, while golds are the hallmark of the latter. In both hotels, each room has a marble entryway, a half-canopy bed, a dressing table with lighted lamp, comfortable overstuffed chairs in the single-bed rooms, and a lush (if average sized) marbled bathroom. You feel special in them.
- **Best Noncasino Hotel:** The very upscale **Alexis Park Resort,** 375 E. Harmon Ave., is the choice of many visiting celebrities and headliners. Many of its rooms have working fireplaces and/or Jacuzzis, and guests are cosseted with can-do concierge service.
- **Best Casinos:** Our favorite places to gamble are anywhere we might win. But we also like the **Mirage** (lively, beautiful, and not overwhelming), **Caesers Palace** (because the cocktail waitresses are dressed in togas), **New York New York** (because of the aforementioned attention to detail; it almost makes losing fun!), and **Main Street Station,** 200 N. Main St., (because it's about the most smoke-free casino in town, and because it's pretty).
- **Best Downtown Hotel:** It's a tie. The upscale **Golden Nugget** is exceptionally appealing in every aspect. The **Main Street Station,** which has done a terrific job of renovating an older space, now evokes turn-of-the century San Francisco, with great Victorian details everywhere, solidly good restaurants, and surprisingly nice rooms for an inexpensive price.
- **Best Views:** From high-floor rooms at the **Stratosphere,** 2000 Las Vegas Blvd. S., you can see the entire city.

2 Coming Attractions

The recent hotel building boom has meant that several legendary old timers—the Dunes, Sands, and Hacienda hotels, all Strip residents of 4 decades or more—have bitten the dust recently. Locals vainly decry the loss of historic properties in this current climate (even Bugsy Siegel's vast suite at the Flamingo, complete with trap door escape routes and tunnels, has been demolished), but the process is unstoppable. Actually, by the end of 1998, nothing on the Strip will be original, since Caesers, Aladdin, and the Sahara will all have changed their facades, as the Flamingo and others did long ago, and the last of the old hotels will be but memories.

The new era of hotels was ushered in by the Mirage, and everyone since then has been trying to up the ante. Last year, 1997, saw the opening of the Orleans just before the New Year (contributing over 800 new rooms with plans already afoot to double that). New York New York, which set yet another level of stupendous excess, which will surely remain unmatched. At least until the rumored Venice hotel, complete with canals and gondolas, makes the scene in a few years. And then something else will come along and top that. It's one of the things you can count on in Vegas. By the year 2000, you can expect another 20,000 hotel rooms to be added.

Here's what's on tap for the next couple years:

- **Project Paradise** was supposed to open in 1998, but as of this writing that appears to have been optimistic. The Circus Circus venture will be located south of Luxor and will be connected to that property and sister Excalibur by air-conditioned walkways. In addition to the resort, there will be a new **Four Seasons** ultraluxury hotel. Total room count for both hotels is over 4,000.

Our Top Five Ideas for New Hotels

Perhaps one of the most fascinating things about this city is the fact that its identity is stolen from other locations. Within city limits you have (or will have) New York, Paris, Venice, New Orleans (many times over), Rio de Janeiro, ancient Rome, Algiers, medieval Europe, Egypt, Monte Carlo, the French Riviera, and the old West. Note, please, that you will not see a Las Vegas–themed anything in any of these places. Or anywhere else for that matter. No, Vegas seems determined to recreate skylines as opposed to building one of its own. With that in mind, we offer a few suggestions for the latest and greatest amusement park, er, hotel/casino. (And lest you think we went overboard, remember, there is an Ellis Island Casino already.)

Butte, Montana, Hotel and Casino Imagine the wonder of Montana's Big Sky country with a whole lot of neon added. An animatronic buffalo stampede happens out front every hour for free, and the explosive roller coaster, the Unabombadier, offers unparalleled thrills. Just be careful crossing the driveways and in the parking garages—there are no speed limits.

Hotel Seattle Bill Gates's first foray into the casino and hotel business.

Dakota The centerpiece here is the life-size recreation of Mount Rushmore that comes to animatronic life every 15 minutes to pass out 2-for-1 coupons at the Dakota Buffet.

St. Louis Theme Park Located behind the St. Louis Hotel and Casino, don't miss the Arch Coaster (which only makes one loop, but it's a doozie), the Arch Sling-Shot, Arch Water Ride, and Pirates of the Arch.

Hoover Dam Hotel & Casino Why drive thirty miles? See a ¼-scale replica right here on the Las Vegas Strip!

- The ITT Corporation (owner of Caesars and the Desert Inn, as well as Planet Hollywood International) recently announced plans for **Planet Hollywood** casino resort here adjacent to the Desert Inn. Budgeted at $830 million, this 3,200-room hotel was originally scheduled for completion in 1999, though the project has been put on a slow-down recently. Expect this place to win the theme-restaurant-run-amok contest.
- In 1999 you'll be able to go from New York to France in just a few minutes as Bally's opens its 3,000-room **Paris Casino Hotel** next door to its existing property. It plans on being a faithful recreation of "The City of Lights" at the turn of the century, complete with a 540-foot replica of the Eiffel Tower.
- The mother of all new projects is tentatively called **Venice** and will be the largest hotel in the world with over 6,000 rooms. It may also be the most expensive to build, as its canals-and-gondolier theme is supposed to rack up a price tag near $2 billion. It will be located on the former site of the Sands directly across the street from the Mirage.

3 Three Questions to Ask Before You Book a Room

WHERE SHOULD I STAY?

Your two main choices for location are the Strip and downtown. The Strip is undeniably the winner, especially for the first-timers, if only by sheer overwhelming force. On the other hand, it is also crowded, overly confining, and strangely claustrophobic. The hotels only look close together; in reality, those are mostly large properties, and it's a long (and often very hot or very cold) walk from one place to the next.

Contrast that with downtown, which is nowhere near as striking, but five minutes can put you in about seventeen different casinos. The Fremont Street upgrade has turned a rapidly declining area into a very pleasant place to be, and the crowds reflect that: They just seem nicer and more relaxed, with the result that a better time can be had there. Since it's only a 5-minute ride by car between downtown and Strip hotels (the Convention Center is more or less in between), there's no such thing as a bad location if you have access to a car. If money is no object, a $10 cab ride separates the Strip from downtown.

For those of you depending on public transportation: While the bus ride between Downtown and the Strip is short in distance, it can be long in time stuck in traffic. You should also be aware that the buses become quite crowded once they reach the Strip and may pass by a bus stop if no one signals to get out and the driver does not wish to take on more passengers. Without a car, your ease of movement between areas of town is, therefore, limited.

But for first timers, frankly, there probably isn't any point to staying anywhere but the Strip; you are going to spend most (if not all) of your time there anyway. For future visits, however, strongly consider Downtown.

But even Strip location isn't the end of the debate. Staying at on the **South Strip** end means an easy walk (sometimes in air-conditioned comfort) to the MGM Grand, New York New York, Tropicana, Luxur, and Excalibar—all virtually on one corner. **Mid-Strip** has Caesars, the Mirage, Treasure Island, Bally's, the Flamingo Hilton, Harrah's, and so forth. The **North Strip** gets you the Riveria, Desert Inn, Sahara, Stardust, and Circus Circus, though with a bit more of a walk between them. For this reason, if mobility is a problem and you want to see more than just your own hotel casino, probably the South and Midstrip locations are the best bets.

The Laughlin Alternative

Okay, worst case scenario: There is not a hotel room to be had for love or money in all of Las Vegas. Well, maybe for money but you just can't count that high. Consider this seemingly radical alternative: the little town of Laughlin. Less than an hour away by car, Laughlin is also a gambling town. What it offers you are name-brand hotels like the Flamingo Hilton, Harrah's, and Golden Nugget, among many others. On a recent Super Bowl weekend, when most rooms in Vegas were sold out, outrageously priced, or both, Laughlin had plenty of rooms available in the $25 to $45 range. Even taking in account the cost of rental car and gas, this still allows you to have full day's and evening's worth of gambling in Vegas and a budget-conscious place to stay. The only thing you miss out on is being able to walk outside and immediately be on the Strip, but there's enough neon here too that you can pretend. One caveat is the narrow, two-lane road that you have to take to get there can be intimidating if you aren't used to such roads, but plans are in the works to upgrade it to a four-lane divided highway.

For more information call **Reservations Plus** (☎ 800/805-9528).

Reservations Services

If you get harried when you have to haggle, use a free service offered by **Reservations Plus**, 2275 A Renaissance Dr., Las Vegas, NV 89119 (☎ **800/805-9528;** fax 702/795-8767). They'll find you a hotel room in your price range that meets your specific requirements. Because they book rooms in volume, they are able to get discounted rates. Not only can they book rooms, but they can arrange packages (including meals, transportation, tours, show tickets, car rentals, and other features) and group rates.

The **Las Vegas Convention and Visitors Authority** also runs a room reservations hot line (☎ **800/332-5334**), which can be helpful. They can apprise you of room availability, quote rates, contact a hotel for you, and tell you when major conventions will be in town.

WHAT AM I LOOKING FOR IN A HOTEL?

Consider also what you want from a hotel. If gambling is not your priority, what are you doing in Vegas? Just kidding. But if you want something quieter, consider a hotel without a casino. Make certain it has a pool, however, especially if you need some recreation; there is nothing so boring as a noncasino, nonpool Vegas hotel. Particularly if you have kids.

Casino hotels, by the way, are not always a nice place for children. It used to be that the casino was a separate section in the hotel and children were not allowed inside (we have fond memories of standing just outside the casino line, watching our dads put quarters in a slot machine "for us"). But in almost all the new hotels, you have to walk through the casino to get anywhere—the lobby, the restaurants, the outside world. This makes sense from the hotel's point of view; it gives you many opportunities to stop and drop a quarter or 10 in a slot.

But this often major, crowded trek gets wearying for adults; it's far worse for kids. The rule is that kids can walk through the casinos, but they can't stop, even to gawk for a second at someone hitting a jackpot nearby. The casino officials who will immediately hustle said child away are just doing their job, but, boy, it's annoying.

So take this (and what a hotel offers that kids might like) into consideration when booking a room. Note also that those gorgeous hotel pools are often cold and not very deep; they look like places you would want to linger, but often (from a kid's point of view) they are not. Plus, the pools close early. (Hotels want you inside gambling, not outside swimming.)

Ultimately, though, if the town is busy, nab any room you can, especially if you get a price you like. How much time are you going to spend in the room anyway?

WHAT WILL I HAVE TO PAY?

As far as prices go, keep in mind that our price categories are rough guidelines at best. If you see a hotel that appeals to you, even if it seems out of your price range, give a call anyway. They might be having a special, a slow week, some kind of promotion, or they may just like the sound of your voice (we have no other explanation for it). You could end up with a hotel in the "expensive" category offering you a room for $35 a night. Since it's a toll-free call, it's a worth a try.

You can also call the **Las Vegas Convention and Visitors Authority** (☎ **800/ 332-5333**) to find out if an important convention is scheduled at the time of your planned visit; if so, you might want to change your date. Some of the most popular conventions are listed under "When to Go" in chapter 2. Remember also that the best deals are offered midweek by the hotels, when prices can drop dramatically. If possible, go then.

We've classified all our hotel recommendations based on the average rack rate you can expect to be quoted for a double room on an average night (*not* when the Consumer Electronics Show is in town, *not* on New Year's Eve). Your *actual* rate may be a little less than this if you stay only Sunday through Thursday and a little more than this if you stay Friday and Saturday. Expect to pay more than $100 for a **Very Expensive** room; expect to pay between $75 and $100 for an **Expensive** room; expect to pay between $50 and $75 for a **Moderate** room; and expect to pay less than $50 for an **Inexpensive** room.

Of course, you can expect significant savings if you book a money-saving package deal, like those described in chapter 2. And on any given night when business is slow, you might be able to stay at a "very expensive" hotel for a "moderate" price.

4 South Strip

VERY EXPENSIVE

Carriage House

105 E. Harmon Ave., between Las Vegas Blvd. S. and Koval Lane, Las Vegas, NV 89109. ☎ **800/ 221-2301** or 702/798-1020. Fax 702/798-1020, ext. 112. 154 suites. A/C TV TEL. $135 studio for 1 or 2; $165 1-bedroom condo for up to 4; $275 2-bedroom condo for up to 6. Inquire about lower-priced packages. AE, CB, DC, DISC, MC, V. Free parking (self).

Housed in a nine-story stucco building fronted by palm trees, this friendly, low-key resort hotel has a loyal repeat clientele. It's entered via a large, comfortably furnished lobby where guests enjoy a complimentary Monday afternoon manager's reception with hors d'oeuvres and wine. And the hotel caters to kids with welcome bags of cookies at check-in and gratis VCRs and movies on request; the front desk maintains a nice-sized movie library.

Attractive suites, with brass-trimmed lacquer or bleached-oak furnishings, have small sitting areas and fully equipped kitchenettes (most with dishwashers). One-bedroom units have full living rooms and dining areas, with phones, radios, and TVs in both rooms. Two-bedroom/two-bath condominiums have a king-size bed in each bedroom and a queen sleeper sofa in the living room. Both the rooms and the public areas are immaculate. Free local phone calls are a plus.

Dining/Entertainment: Kiefers, perched on the ninth floor, offers a romantic, candlelit setting and superb skyline views via a wall of windows. Tuesday through Saturday a pianist entertains in an adjoining lounge with a small dance floor. The menu highlights steak, seafood, and pasta dishes. Breakfast and dinner only.

Services: Complimentary transportation 7am to 10:30pm to/from airport. Pay-per-view.

Facilities: Tour and show desks, coin-op washers/dryers, Har-Tru tennis court lit for night play (no charge for play, balls, or racquets), swimming pool/sundeck, whirlpool.

EXPENSIVE

✪ MGM Grand Hotel/Casino

3799 Las Vegas Blvd. S., at Tropicana Ave., Las Vegas, NV 89109. ☎ **800/929-1111** or 702/ 891-7777. Fax 702/891-1112. 4,254 rms, 751 suites. A/C TV TEL. $69–$119 standard double; $79–$129 concierge floor double with breakfast; $99–$2,500 suite. Extra person $10. Children under 12 stay free in parents' room. AE, DC, DISC, MC, V. Free parking (self and valet).

The MGM Grand has recently completed one of the most amusing renovations in Vegas. When it first opened, the billion-dollar property, spread over 112 acres, had a *Wizard of Oz* theme. The outside was a shocking shade of emerald green, some door handles had "Oz" on them, rainbows were everywhere, and right in the center was a giant animatronic reenactment of MGM's most famous movie. Outside was a theme park, which initially charged an exorbitant entry fee.

That has changed. The outside is still green, but now the MGM Grand is The City of Entertainment, which means the theme is *all* MGM movies, not just one specific film beloved by children. Gone is the Oz attraction (though it may reappear at a later date in a different, less prominent part of the hotel), to be replaced by a Rain Forest Cafe—something more appealing to adults. Relegated to a basement location is the large arcade. Gone is the cartoonish lion at the entrance, to be replaced by a classier, "liquid gold" Leo. He'll be surrounded by 80-foot video screens so that, as your plane comes in for a landing, you can watch Tom Jones performing. Really. Gone, too, is much of the theme park, to be replaced by a convention center. Why? Well, probably because the great "Vegas Is for Families" experiment failed. But if you ask anyone in town on the record, they will deny ever catering to families. Given the original look of the MGM and what is coming in its place, that seems especially disingenuous.

But practical. The MGM did seem a bit cheesy (particularly if you contrast it to the even older, original MGM Grand, the elegant place that was destroyed in one of the worst hotel fires in history). As one of the world's largest hotels, it was also overwhelming and hard to navigate. The eighty 42-inch TV monitors (apprising registering guests of hotel happenings) in the otherwise lovely and vast, white marble lobby only added to the chaotic confusion a guest might feel.

But the renovations are seeking to fix all that. The TV monitors remain, but the lobby is now immediately accessible from outside. The redesign will attempt to create some more intimate corners, and has already made navigating the still immense place somewhat easier. (It's actually kind of amusing how they are now backing away from bragging about their size and moving more toward trying to hide that fact.) And the staff, confirms a recent guest, couldn't be more helpful and friendly. Throughout, the theme of The City of Entertainment will be repeated, as old movies are evoked in the decor (though considerable green and the odd rainbow still remain). In certain areas (like the restaurant row), the look is meant to suggest a behind-the-scenes view of a film studio back lot.

The rooms will give no cause for complaint. They are decorated in four distinct motifs. Most glamorous are the Hollywood rooms furnished in two-tone wood pieces (bird's-eye maple on cherry), with gold-flecked walls (hung with prints of Humphrey Bogart, Marilyn Monroe, and Vivien Leigh as Scarlett), gilded moldings, and beds backed by mirrors. Oz-themed rooms still have emerald-green rugs and upholstery, silver and gold star-motif wallpaper, bright poppy-print bedspreads, and tasseled green drapes; walls are hung with paintings of Dorothy and friends. In the Casablanca rooms—decorated in earth tones with shimmery fabrics and pecan/walnut furnishings and moldings—artworks depict Moroccan scenes such as an Arab marketplace. And the cheerful Old South rooms feature 18th-century–style furnishings and faux-silk beige damask walls hung with paintings of southern belles and scenes from *Gone With the Wind.* All rooms offer gorgeous marble baths.

Dining/Entertainment: MGM houses the most prestigious assemblage of dining rooms of any hotel in town. Four cutting-edge stars in the Las Vegas culinary galaxy—the **Wolfgang Puck Café,** Emeril Lagasse's **New Orleans Fish House, Gatsby's,** and Mark Miller's **Coyote Café**—along with buffet offerings, are described

South Strip Accommodations

Carriage House **4**	Holiday Inn Casino Boardwalk **1**	New York New York **3**
Excalibur **6**	Luxor Las Vegas **8**	Orleans **9**
MGM Grand Hotel/Casino **5**	Monte Carlo Resort & Casino **2**	Tropicana Resort & Casino **7**

in chapter 6. Indeed, Emeril's and Gatsby's vie for the honor of best restaurant in Vegas. The **Oz Buffet** is described in chapter 6. In addition, the following dining facilities comprise a restaurant row between the casino and the theme park.

Heralding the restaurant area's new Hollywood theme is the plush and luxurious **Brown Derby,** modeled after the legendary Los Angeles celebrity haunt where Louella Parsons and Hedda Hopper held court in the 1940s. It's not in a giant hat, though. Like the original, its walls are lined with caricatures of celebrities (a caricaturist on the premises draws customers for a fee), and signature dishes on its largely steak/chops/seafood menu include Cobb salad and grapefruit cake. A handsome mahogany-paneled bar adjoins. Lunch and dinner are served.

Another new facility here consists of two distinct dining areas, **La Scala** and **Tre Visi.** Both serve regional Italian fare. The very elegant La Scala (named for the Milan opera house), has walls hung with opera posters and antique musical instruments. It's open for dinner only. Fronted by an imposing Doric colonnade suggestive of a Roman ruin, with columned archways inside framing scenes of ancient Rome, the more casual Tre Visi serves lunch and dinner.

Dragon Court is an elegant restaurant with textured gold wall coverings and purple and gold fleur-de-lis pattern carpeting. Eclectic Chinese fare is featured. Only dinner is served.

A food court, done in a Farmer's Market, outdoor theme, features **McDonald's, Hamada's Orient Express, Mamma Ilardo's Pizzeria, Nathan's** (hot dogs and fries), and a **Häagen-Dazs** ice cream outlet that also features espresso and cappuccino. The

Stage Deli Express, a cafeteria-style offshoot of the New York original, serves up traditional deli sandwiches; seating overlooks race and sports book action.

Benninger's, off the casino, provides gourmet coffees and scrumptious fresh-baked pastries (great bear claws here). In addition, there are many restaurants and fast-food places in the theme park.

The Center Stage and Betty Boop lounges offer entertainment nightly. The circular Flying Monkey Bar and the Santa Fe Lounge offer live music. A talking robotic horse and jockey spout sports data at the Turf Club Lounge in the race and sports book area.

Services: 24-hour room service, foreign-currency exchange, guest-relations desk, shoe shine (in men's rooms).

Facilities: Casino; MGM Grand Adventures Theme Park; full-service health spa and health club; full-service unisex hair/beauty salon; four night-lit tennis courts with pro shop (lessons available); huge, beach-entry swimming pool with waterfall; a vast sundeck area with a Jacuzzi, pool bar, and cabanas equipped with cushioned chairs and towels that rent for $20 per day; a 30,000-square-foot video arcade (including virtual-reality games); carnival midway with 33 games of skill; business center; florist; shopping arcade; two wedding chapels (in the theme park); show/sports event ticket desks; car-rental desk; sightseeing/tour desks; America West airline desk.

The **MGM Grand Youth Center,** a first-rate facility for children ages 3 to 16, has separate areas for different age groups. The center has a playhouse and tumbling mats for toddlers, a game room, extensive arts and crafts equipment, video games, a dining area, and a large-screen TV/VCR for children's movies. Accompanied by professional counselors, youngsters can visit the theme park or the swimming pool, take excursions to nearby attractions, have meals, and participate in all sorts of entertainment and activities (☎ **702/891-3200** for details and prices).

Monte Carlo Resort & Casino

3770 Las Vegas Blvd. S., between Flamingo Rd. and Tropicana Ave., Las Vegas, NV 89109. ☎ **800/311-8999** or 702/730-7777. Fax 702/730-7250. 2,759 rms, 255 suites. A/C TV TEL. Sun–Thurs $69–$199 double, Fri–Sat $99–$269; suites $139–$339. Extra person $15. Children under 12 stay free in parents' room. AE, CB, DC, DISC, MC, V. Free parking (self and valet).

The newest resort on the Strip, the massive Monte Carlo is the world's seventh-largest hotel. It's fronted by Corinthian colonnades, triumphal arches, splashing fountains, and allegorical (and slightly naughty) statuary, with an entranceway opening on a bustling casino. A separate entrance in the rear of the hotel leads to a splendid marble-floored, crystal-chandeliered lobby evocative of a European grand hotel. Palladian windows behind the registration desk overlook a salient feature: the hotel's 20,000-acre pool area, a lushly landscaped miniature water park with a 4,800-foot wave pool, a surf pond, waterfalls, and a "river" for tubing. Also notable is the Monte Carlo's spa, offering extensive workout facilities, hot and cool whirlpools, steam and sauna, and numerous services (massage, facials, sea-salt scrubs, seaweed wraps, and more). Workout clothing and toiletries are provided.

Spacious rooms with big marble baths exude a warmly traditional European feel. Striped tan wallpapers with fleur-de-lis friezes create a neutral backdrop for rich cherrywood furnishings and vivid floral-print fabrics and carpeting. Cable TVs are equipped with hotel-information channels, keno, and pay-movie options. A concierge level for VIPs is on the 32nd floor.

Dining/Entertainment: The Monte Carlo's **Pub and Brewery, Dragon Noodle Company,** and buffet room are described in chapter 6.

A wall of stained-glass windows, beveled mirrors, rich mahogany paneling, plush leather booths, and elegantly appointed tables lit by shaded candle lamps set an

For the grand debut of Monte Carlo as a resort in 1879 the architect Charles Garnier designed an opera house for the Place du Casino and Sarah Bernhardt read a symbolic poem. For the debut of Las Vegas as a resort in 1946 Bugsy Siegel hired Abbott and Costello, and there, in a way, you have it all.
—Tom Wolfe, *Las Vegas (What?) . . . (Can't hear you! Too noisy) Las Vegas!!!!*

opulent tone at **Blackstone's Steak House.** Dinner only; entrees such as mesquite-grilled steaks, seafood, prime rib, and roast duck Grand Marnier.

At the **Market City Caffe,** a tempting antipasto bar (with dozens of items ranging from roasted potato salad to mussels marinara), a display kitchen housing an oak-burning pizza oven, and wooden bins overflowing with fruits and vegetables create a warmly colorful interior. Lunch and dinner daily.

The plant-filled, sky-ceilinged 24-hour cafe has a whimsical magic/fantasy theme; delightful murals depict clowns, court jesters, and harlequins. Additional venues include a food court (with branches of **Nathan's, McDonald's, Sbarro, Häagen-Dazs,** and a first-rate bagel bakery), a pool-area snack bar, and several lounges, most notably the plush Houdini's, it's magic theme honoring illusionist Lance Burton, who headlines at the hotel's showroom.

Services: 24-hour room service, foreign currency exchange, shoe shine, limo rental.

Facilities: Casino, car-rental desk, four tennis courts, sightseeing/tour/show desk, barber/beauty salon, vast swimming pool, kiddie pool, whirlpool, water attractions (see above), wedding chapel, full business center, large video-game arcade, large shopping arcade.

✪ New York New York

3790 Las Vegas Blvd. S., at Tropicana Ave., Las Vegas, NV 89109. ☎ **800/693-6763** or 702/740-6969. Fax 702/740-6920. 2034 rms. A/C TV TEL. Sun–Thurs from $89 double, Fri–Sat from $129 double. Extra person $20. AE, CB, DC, DISC, MC, V. Free parking (self and valet).

Just when you think Las Vegas has it all and has done it all, they go and do something like this. New York New York is just plain spectacular. Even the jaded and horrified have to admit it. You can't miss the hotel, it's that little (Hah!) building on the corner of the Strip and Tropicana that looks like the New York City skyline: the Empire State Building, the Chrysler Building, the Public Library, down to the 150-foot Statue of Liberty and Ellis Island, all built to approximately one-third scale. And as if that isn't enough, they threw in a roller coaster running around the outside and into the hotel and casino itself.

And inside, it all gets better. There are details everywhere—so many, in fact, that the typical expression on the face of casino-goers is slack-jawed wonder. If you enter the casino via the Brooklyn Bridge (the walkway from the Strip), you find yourself in a replica of Greenwich Village, down to the cobblestones, the manhole covers, the tenement buildings, and the graffiti. (Yes, they even re-created that. You should see the subway station.) The main casino area is done as Central Park, complete with trees, babbling brooks, streetlamps, and footbridges. The change carts are little Yellow Cabs. The reception area and lobby are done in belle epoque, art deco, golden age of Manhattan style; you feel like breaking out into a 1930s musical number while standing there. It really is impossible to adequately describe the sheer mind-blowing enormity of the thing. So we are just going to leave it at: *Wow.* The word *subtle* was obviously not in the lexicon of the designers. It's hard to see how Vegas can ever top this, but then again that's been said before.

Upstairs—oh, yes, there's much more—is the arcade, which is Coney Island themed (naturally), and just as crowded as the real thing, as kids play boardwalk games in the hopes of winning tickets redeemable for cheap prizes. (This helps them learn about gambling at an early age.) The line for the roller coaster (lengthy at this writing) is here. There are many restaurants, all housed in buildings that fit the theme of whatever New York neighborhood is represented in that particular part of the hotel.

Rooms are housed in different towers, each with some New York–inspired name. (Disappointingly, they are not inside the buildings of the skyline—it would have been quite fun to stay in the Empire State Building.) Truthfully, the place is so massive that finding your way to your room can take awhile. There are 64 different styles of rooms, and they are all smashing. Each essentially is done up in a hard-core art deco style: various shades of inlaid wood, rounded tops to the armoires and headboards, usually shades of brown and wood colors. However, some of the rooms are down-right tiny (just like New York again!), and in those all this massively detailed decoration could be overwhelming, if not suffocating. The bathrooms are also small, but with black, marble-topped sinks, which again lend a glamorous '20s image. The amenities come in bottles shaped like the NYC skyline—these are the sort you want to stash in your suitcase to take home!

The march to the pool will in some cases trot you right down that Central Park bridge—wave to all the restaurant patrons as you parade in your swimsuit. The pool is the only disappointment; though fairly large with a waterfall, it's shallow and ringed on one side by the parking garage. The roller coaster regularly screams by overhead.

Cranks would have us note that coming here is not like going to the real New York. On the other hand, given how crowded it is (being the newest and hottest game in town, everyone wants to come check it out, and stays to play) and how noisy, it kind of is just like being in New York. Especially with the all too realistic traffic and parking nightmares. In short, New York New York is not only overcrowded, but perhaps not as efficient as it should be. Though staying here seems irresistible, it may be worth waiting until some of the newness has worn off (that should be by early 1998) or certainly until another new, fabulous place opens up. But this hasn't stopped many from staying here; a mere 6 months after opening, hotel representatives announced they were doing so well they were planning to add another 1,000 rooms.

Dining/Entertainment: As mentioned above, presently New York New York is still so new that everyone is coming there, which means the restaurants and snack bars are almost always crowded, particularly within 2 hours (in either direction) of a meal time. This translates to long lines and waits, and occasionally less than terrific service. Too bad; the food looks tasty, and they have several brand-name restaurants here that provide a welcome relief from some of the dreck found in Vegas hotels. Plan to either bring a book, eat at really off hours, or skip it all together until (again) the newness has worn off a touch.

The **Motown Cafe** is described in chapter 6.

Il Fornaio is a reliable chain, featuring nouvelle Italian cuisine (meaning lighter sauces based on olive oil rather than tomatoes). They also make their own delicious bread, and some terrific pastries.

Chin-Chin is another chain, somewhat less reliable (it gets mixed reviews from diners), featuring Szechuan and Cantonese, with some Polynesian and Pacific Rim tossed in.

Gallagher's Steak House is an upscale steak house, most notable for the huge cuts of raw meat that are in the windows, attracting many bemused looks.

America is the 24-hour coffee shop. Scattered throughout the property are also a pizza place (featuring slices and long lines), a deli, barbecue, Mexican, and **Nathan's** hot dogs, which no New York–themed hotel should be without (though the dogs cost quite a bit more than the buck they will set you back in NYC). **Schraft's Ice Cream** has also been resurrected here; at $2.50 for a scoop, it's pricey, but so good it's worth it.

There are several festive and beautifully decorated bars throughout the property. At the Bar at Times Square, a lighted ball drops every night at midnight, to recreate the famous New Year's Eve event in the real location. New Year's Eve every night: A terrific promotion, or hell on earth?

A production called MADhattan will be opening by 1998.

Services: Concierge, courtesy limo, currency exchange, dry cleaning, express checkout, laundry, newspaper delivery, room service, safety deposit boxes, video rentals, valet and self-parking.

Facilities: Beauty salon, car rental, arcade, pool, tour desk. The spa is smaller than average and merely adequate, but at $15 a day it is slightly cheaper than other major hotels.

Tropicana Resort & Casino

3801 Las Vegas Blvd. S., at Tropicana Ave., Las Vegas, NV 89109. ☎ **800/634-4000** or 702/739-2222. Fax 702/739-2469. 1,884 rms, 130 suites (for high rollers only). A/C TV TEL. Sun–Thurs from $75 double, Fri–Sat from $129. Extra person $15. Children under 18 stay free in parents' room. AE, CB, DC, DISC, MC, V. Free parking (self and valet).

This long-time denizen of the Strip is looking great since a major renovation in 1995. The entranceway is now a colorful Caribbean-village facade; there are nightly laser light shows on the Outer Island corner facing the Strip; pedestrian skywalks across the Strip link the Trop with the MGM Grand, the Excalibur, and the Luxor; and the resort's resident bird and wildlife population has dramatically increased. The Trop today comprises a lush landscape of manicured lawns, towering palms, oleanders, weeping willows, and crepe myrtles. There are dozens of waterfalls, thousands of exotic flowers, lagoons, and koi ponds. And flamingos, finches, black swans, mandarin ducks, African crown cranes, cockatoos, macaws, toucans, and Brazilian parrots live on the grounds. There's even a wildlife walk (home to pygmy marmosets, boa constrictors, and others) inside the resort itself.

Rooms in the Paradise Tower are traditional, with French provincial furnishings and turn-of-the-century wallpapers. Island Tower rooms, more befitting a tropical resort, are decorated in pastel colors like pale pink and sea-foam green, with splashy print bedspreads and bamboo furnishings; some have beds with mirrored walls and ceilings. Motel rooms out back can be tiny and oddly shaped. All Trop rooms have sofas and safes; TVs offer Spectravision movies, account review, video checkout, and channels for in-house information.

Dining/Entertainment: Mizuno's, a beautiful teppanyaki dining room, is detailed in chapter 6, as are the Trop's buffet offerings.

El Gaucho is an elegantly rustic Argentine steak house, with rough-hewn log beams overhead and pecky-pine walls hung with cowhides, antlers, serapes, branding irons, and gaucho gear. Steaks, chops, prime rib, and seafood come with traditional accompaniments. Dinner only.

Papagayo's is a colorful Mexican eatery behind a wrought-iron gate, where cream stucco walls are adorned with Mexican rugs and Diego Rivera prints. Lunch and dinner.

Coming by 1998 is **Peitro's,** a gourmet room.

Calypso's, the Trop's 24-hour coffee shop, is the most cheerful in town. Decorated in bright island colors, it has a wall of windows overlooking waterfalls, weeping willows, and palm-fringed ponds filled with ducks and flamingos. Traditional (and very tasty) coffee-shop fare is augmented by interesting items ranging from Caribbean shrimp sate to bacon-stuffed cheese quesadillas. An extensive Chinese menu is available nightly from 6pm to midnight.

The **Players Deli,** sandwiched between the casino and the pool, is a unique cafeteria-cum-gaming room where slot and video poker machines are equipped with handy pullout dining ledges. Gamblers can also snack here at poker tables or in a small keno lounge or sports book. Hot and cold sandwiches, salads, and snack fare (nachos, chicken wings) are featured. Open daily from 10am to 10pm.

Down a level from the casino, in the Atrium Shopping area, is a **Baskin-Robbins** ice-cream parlor. The Atrium Lounge in the casino offers a variety of live music nightly after 5pm. The Coconut Grove Bar serves the pool area, and the Tropics Bar is between the two towers on the wildlife walk.

Services: 24-hour room service, shoe shine.

Facilities: Casino, health club (a range of machines, treadmills, exercise bikes, steam, sauna, Jacuzzi, massage, and tanning room), video-game arcade, tour and show desks, wedding chapel, car-rental desk, beauty salon and barbershop, business center, travel agent, shops (jewelry, chocolates, women's footwear, logo items, women's fashions, sports clothing, gifts, newsstand).

Three swimming pools (one Olympic size) and three whirlpool spas are located in a 5-acre garden with 30 splashing waterfalls, lagoons, and lush tropical plantings. One pool has a swim-up bar/blackjack table.

MODERATE

Excalibur

3850 Las Vegas Blvd. S., at Tropicana Ave., Las Vegas, NV 89109. ☎ **800/937-7777** or 702/597-7777. Fax 702/597-7040. 4,032 rms. A/C TV TEL. $49–$119 for up to 4 people. Children under 17 stay free in parents' room, children over 17 pay $12. Rates are higher during holidays and convention periods. AE, CB, DC, DISC, MC, V. Free parking (self and valet).

Now this is kitsch. One of the largest resort hotels in the world, Excalibur (aka "the Realm") is a gleaming white, turreted castle complete with moat, drawbridge, battlements, and lofty towers. And it's huger than huge. Apparently, the creators thought there were a lot of Arthur and Guenevere wannabes out there. And probably they are right; but do we really need a medieval, forest-themed, knights-running-amok hotel in which to act out our fantasies?

Needless to say, this is not historically accurate. But it is hilarious. What it is not, is comfortable, which is actually historically accurate since big castles were not traditionally warm, cozy, inviting places. Excalibur is just too darn big, a chaotic frenzy at all times. Even the must-see factor fades quickly.

But do check it out. And while you are at it, have fun by having the hotel page you and your friends: "Lady Doe to the white courtesy phone" or "Sir Jones to the house phone." Really, they do this. The second floor holds the recently refurbished Medieval Village site of Excalibur's restaurants and quaint shops along winding streets and alleyways, a sort of permanent Renaissance Faire. Which could be reason enough to stay away. On the Village's Jester's Stage, jugglers, puppeteers, and magicians amuse guests with free 20-minute performances throughout the day. Up here you can access the new enclosed, air-conditioned moving sidewalk that connects with the Luxor.

Below the casino level is the Fantasy Faire, housing a very dark and large video-game arcade, dozens of medieval-themed carnival games, and two "magic motion machine" theaters featuring high-tech visual thrills; the thrills include simulated roller coaster and runaway train adventures and an outer space demolition derby directed by George Lucas, enhanced by hydraulically activated seats that synchronize with the on-screen action.

The rooms maintain the Arthurian motif with walls papered to look like stone castle interiors. Oak furnishings are heraldically embellished; mirrors are flanked by torchier sconces; bedspreads have a fleur-de-lis theme; and prints of jousting knights adorn the walls. Guests who have stayed in Tower 2 have complained about the noise from the roller coaster across the street at New York New York. It shuts down at 11pm, so early birds should probably stay in a different part of the hotel.

Note: If you should accidentally drop your wallet exiting a cab outside the Excalibur, don't expect to ever see it again. But that is probably true for any Vegas hotel.

Dining/Entertainment: Camelot, Excalibur's fine dining room, offers continental fare in a rustic castle setting, with murals of Camelot's pristine lakes and verdant forests forming an idyllic backdrop. Dinner only.

Sir Galahad's, a prime rib restaurant, occupies a candlelit "castle" chamber with massive oak beams and wrought-iron candelabra chandeliers overhead. The specialty is prime rib, carved tableside and served with soup or salad, mashed potatoes, creamed spinach, and Yorkshire pudding. Dinner only is served.

Wild Bill's, a Western-themed restaurant and dance hall, has beveled-glass doors punctured by "bullet holes," walls adorned with rodeo murals, and booths separated by large wagon wheels. A rustic bar nestles in one corner. Country music is played during the day; at night there's live music for dancing. No, we don't know what it has to do with King Arthur either. Entrees include steak, ribs, catfish, and burgers. Dinner only.

Lance-a-Lotta Pasta replicates a flamboyant Italian village, complete with strolling guitarists. The menu lists pizzas and pastas, subs and hero sandwiches. They serve huge portions, and many locals say this is their favorite place in town for pasta; dinner only.

Café Expresso, a window operation off Lance-a-Lotta Pasta, serves espresso, cappuccino, and pastries. It has several tables in the Medieval Village.

The **Sherwood Forest Cafe,** its entrance guarded by a sentry of lavender dragons (kids love to climb on them), is Excalibur's 24-hour facility. A low-priced children's menu is a plus.

Another heraldic dining room, the **Round Table Buffet,** is described in chapter 6. Other facilities include three snack bars. The Village Pub is an Alpine-themed bar in the Medieval Village; the Minstrel's Theatre Lounge offers live entertainment nightly (during the day, movies and sporting events are shown on a large-screen TV); there are several bars in the casino (most interesting of these is King George's, featuring international beers and microbrews); and a snack and cocktail bar serves the North pool.

Services: 24-hour room service, free gaming lessons, shoe shine, foreign-currency exchange.

Facilities: Casino, tour and show desks, state-of-the-art video-game arcade, wedding chapel (you can marry in medieval attire), unisex hairdresser, car-rental desk, a parking lot that can accommodate RVs, shops (see chapter 9). There are two large, beautifully landscaped swimming pools complete with waterfalls and water slides and an adjoining 16-seat whirlpool spa.

Holiday Inn Casino Boardwalk

3750 Las Vegas Blvd. S., between Harmon and Tropicana aves., Las Vegas , NV 89109. ☎ **800/HOLIDAY,** 800/635-4581, or 702/735-2400. Fax 702/730-3166. Web site www. hiboardwalk.com. 641 rms, 12 suites, 2 executive suites. A/C TV TEL. $39–$109 double; $250–$495 one-bedroom suite, $495–$895 two-bedroom suite. Extra person $15. Rates may be higher during special events. Children 19 and under stay free in parents' room. AE, DC, DISC, JCB, MC, V. Free parking (self and valet).

This is just like a Holiday Inn, only in Vegas you *gotta* have a theme, and the hotel just finished an extensive renovation to give it a more attractive Coney Island and Boardwalk flavor, inside and especially out. The facade is kind of fun, with clowns and games and mannequins dressed in turn-of-the-century clothes. Of course, this is completely eclipsed by New York New York just a few doors (in Strip terms) down. After all, the roller coaster on the outside of this hotel is just a facade.

Still, being a Holiday Inn means you know what you are getting in terms of quality, and the Strip location is a good one. Also, you don't have to walk through the casino to get to the lobby, which is a plus. On the other hand, it's a bit pricey, at the high end for what are standard Holiday Inn hotel rooms. The ones in the new 16-story tower, decorated in vibrant colors with cherrywood furnishings and prints of Coney Island adorning the walls, are perhaps a bit nicer than the older units, which are pleasantly done up in soft pastels with blond wood furnishings. All offer cable TVs with pay-movie options. Irons and ironing boards are in the rooms.

Dining/Entertainment: A big draw is the **Cyclone Coffee Shop,** a 24-hour facility decorated with murals of the Coney Island boardwalk and adorable roller-coaster-motif lighting fixtures. Well worth a visit even if you're staying elsewhere, it has some of the best bargain meals in town (see chapter 6 for details).

Coney's, totally replicating the feel of a beach restaurant, serves boardwalk fare: fresh roasted corn on the cob, fresh-cut fries, pizza, and cheesesteak sandwiches. Other facilities include a 24-hour deli in the casino, an ice cream/yogurt parlor, and two casino bars; a buffet room is under construction.

Services: 24-hour room service, shoe shine.

Facilities: Casino, two small swimming pools, shops, coin-op washers/dryers, video-game arcade and shooting gallery, sightseeing/show/tour desk, car-rental desk. Guests can use health club facilities nearby.

✪ Luxor Las Vegas

3900 Las Vegas Blvd. S., between Reno and Hacienda aves., Las Vegas, NV 81119. ☎ **800/288-1000** or 702/262-4000. Fax 702/262-4452. 4,500 rms, 488 suites. A/C, TV, TEL. Sun–Thurs $49–$259 double, Fri–Sat $99–$299 double; $179–$279 concierge level; $99–$329 Jacuzzi suite, $500–$800 for other suites. Extra person $10. Children under 12 stay free in parents' room. AE, CB, DC, DISC, MC, V. Free parking (self and valet).

By the time this book comes out, Luxor will have completed a $300 million renovation and expansion. Cheese fans will be disappointed to learn that the Egyptian fantasma that set the pace for all others isn't all that tacky anymore. Oh sure, the main hotel is still a 30-story bronze pyramid, complete with a really tall, 315,000-watt light beam at the top. (The Luxor says that's because the Egyptians believed their souls would travel up from heaven in a beam of light; we think it's really because it gives them something to brag about: "The most powerful beam on earth!") Sure, replicas of Cleopatra's Needle and the Sphinx still grace the outside, but the interior redesign has been made much more inviting, classier, and functional.

Guests now enter on the casino level (as opposed to one level up in the past) and are adjunct to the lobby, which used to be a hike away. The lobby has been redone in marble and cherry wood—vaguely art deco, which was influenced by Egyptian Revival anyway. It's one of the nicest lobbies in town. There is also a separate lobby in the two new towers, which is exclusively for tour groups. Even the Egyptian touches that remain have taken on a grand air rather than that of a theme park. (The tacky and overpriced Cleopatra's Barge ride down the "Nile" is gone for good.) It's kind of impressive, unless of course you've actually been to Egypt and seen the real statues of Ramses. Don't fear; the talking animatronic camels are back.

The rooms have had a freshening up in the pyramid. High-speed "inclinator" elevators run on a 39° angle, making the ride up to your room a bit of a thrill. Sloped window walls remind you you're in a pyramid. *Note:* In the pyramid, most baths have showers only, no tubs. The rooms are probably better in the new tower. Featuring fine art deco and Egyptian furnishings, they were full of nice touches. Huge armoires house not only the TV but closet space. The marble bathrooms have phones, vanity mirrors, and hair dryers. Even the floor lamps are interesting. This is one of the few rooms in Las Vegas that stands out. You know you are in the Luxor when you are in these rooms, as opposed to the cookie-cutter decor usually found in town. Especially desirable are a group of suites with glamorous art deco elements, private sitting rooms, refrigerators, and, notably, Jacuzzis by the window (enabling you to soak under the stars at night). And we would love to meet whomever is going to rent the new 4,000-square-foot luxury suite at the top of the tower.

Alternative culture denizens might be made aware that at least one multiply tattooed and pierced soul was asked to leave the Luxor gift shop, despite an armload of packages, because they "don't allow gang activity in the casino." This may be what happens when you upgrade your image.

Dining/Entertainment: The Luxor's **Pharaoh's Pheast** buffet is discussed in chapter 6.

To enter **Isis,** a gourmet room, you'll pass through a colonnade of caryatid statues. Within, replicas of artifacts from King Tutankhamen's tomb are on display in glass cases, and a golden statue of Osiris forms a visual centerpiece. A harpist plays during dinner. The classic continental menu features items such as braised breast of pheasant filled with foie gras and pistachio. Dinner only.

The **Sacred Sea Room** has gold walls adorned with murals and hieroglyphics depicting fishing on the Nile. Turquoise mosaic tiles on the ceiling suggest ocean waves, and the dining-at-sea ambience is further enhanced by a central ship's hull and mast. Fresh- and saltwater seafood arrives daily from both coasts. Dinner only.

The 24-hour **Pyramid Café**—its booths flanked by palm trees and foliage—replicates the interior of a pyramid. Like the decor, the menu has an Egyptian theme with a small nod to Middle Eastern cuisine. Most menu items, however, are of the predictable Las Vegas hotel coffee-shop genre. A $2.99 late-night breakfast of sirloin steak, eggs, hash browns, and toast is served daily except Wednesday from 11pm to 6am.

Other venues are a deli off the casino and a **Swensen's Ice Cream** shop on the attraction level.

The plush Nefertiti's Lounge features live bands for dancing nightly; off-hours sporting events are aired on a large-screen TV. The Obelisk Bar and Anteroom Lounge serve the casino. Tut's Hut specializes in Polynesian drinks and Otemanu Hot Rock samplers (seafood, tenderloin, chicken, pork, or vegetables grilled at your table and served with plum, peanut, mustard, and teriyaki dipping sauces). The Sportsbook Lounge, adjoining the race and sports book, airs sports action on TV monitors overhead. And the Oasis Terrace and Bar provides poolside food and drinks.

Services: 24-hour room service, foreign-currency exchange, shoe shine.

Facilities: Casino; full-service unisex hair salon; complete spa and health club (with a full range of machines, free weights, steam, sauna, and Jacuzzi; massage, facials, herbal wraps, and other beauty treatments available); VirtuaLand, an 18,000-square-foot video arcade that showcases Sega's latest game technologies; car-rental desk; tour/show/sightseeing desks.

The hotel has five pools, with the main one an immense palm-fringed swimming pool (palms even grow right in the pool) with outdoor whirlpool, kiddie pool, pool-accessories shop, and luxurious cabanas (cooled by misting systems and equipped with rafts, cable TVs, phones, ceiling fans, tables and chairs, chaise longues, and refrigerators stocked with juices and bottled water) that rent for $75 a day.

INEXPENSIVE

✪ Orleans

4500 W. Tropicana Ave., west of Strip and I-15, Las Vegas, NV 89103. ☎ **800/ORLEANS** or 702/365-7111. Fax 702/365-7505. AOL Keyword: Coast Casinos. 840 rooms, 30 suites. $39–$79 standard double; $89–$125 one-bedroom suite. A/C TV TEL. AE, DC, DISC, MC, V. Free parking (self and valet).

Just opened in December 1997, the Orleans is owned by the same company that owns the Barbary and Gold Coast casinos. It's a little out of the way, but as construction is completed on an upcoming 12-screen movie complex, complete with food court and day care center, this becomes an increasingly attractive option to staying on the hectic Strip. Its facade is aggressively fake New Orleans, more reminiscent of Disneyland than the Big Easy. Inside it's much the same. But a bright casino (complete with Cajun and zydeco music over the loud speakers) and a policy of handing out Mardi Gras beads at all the restaurants and bars (ask if you haven't gotten yours) make for a pleasantly festive atmosphere. However, we could do without those scary mannequins simulating Mardi Gras fun leaning over French Quarter–style railings above the casino.

If the prices hold true (as always, quotes vary), this hotel is one of the best bargains in town, despite the location. The rooms are particularly nice—the largest in town, so the hotel claims, next to Rio's. They all have a definite New Orleans French feel. They are L-shaped with a seating alcove by the windows, and come complete with slightly turn-of-the-century style overstuffed chair and sofa. The beds have brass headboards, the lamps (including some funky iron floor lamps) look antique, lace curtains flutter at the windows. The one drawback is that all these furnishings, and the busy floral decorating theme, makes the room, particularly down by the seating area in front of the bathrooms, seem crowded. Still, it's meant to evoke a cozy, warm Victorian parlor, which traditionally is very overcrowded, so maybe it's successful after all. The medium-sized bathrooms are also nice, but there is no closet, only a rod for hanging clothes. Suites are, depending on your taste, even more grand and spectacular, but they have a different look, so they could also be disappointing. They have a grand looking wood bar, richly upholstered chairs; the bathrooms are very fancy with dark wood and marble and a big oval tub. They also have four TVs!

Two medium-sized pools with grass and cabanas opened in the summer 1997.

Dining/Entertainment: At this writing, the hotel was still finishing off much of its property, so still to come are a number of restaurants, including a 500-seat food court buffet, a New Orleans–themed restaurant/nightclub/lounge with live entertainment, an oyster bar, a gumbo house, sushi and margarita bars, plus a cafe serving specialty coffees and beignets.

You would think something called Orleans would open up their Louisiana restaurants first, but that is not the case. First came **Vito's** Italian, a fancy Italian place complete with piano bar from 1 to 3am.

🤸 Family-Friendly Hotels

As repeatedly mentioned in their individual listings, most of the hotels are backing away from being perceived as a place for families. Still, anything with a serious theme and/or outlets for kids, as the following all have, is probably better than a regular hotel.

Circus Circus (see p. 81)   Centrally located on the Strip, this is our first choice if you're traveling with the kids. The hotel's mezzanine level offers ongoing circus acts daily from 11am to midnight, dozens of carnival games, and an arcade with more than 300 video and pinball games. And behind the hotel is a full amusement park.

Excalibur (see p. 52)   Also owned by Circus Circus, Excalibur features a whole floor of midway games, a large video-game arcade, crafts demonstrations, free shows for kids (puppets, jugglers, magicians), and thrill cinemas. It has child-oriented eateries and shows (details in chapter 10).

Luxor Las Vegas (see p. 54)   Another Circus Circus property. Kids will enjoy VirtuaLand, an 18,000-square-foot video-game arcade that showcases Sega's latest game technologies. Another big attraction here is the "Secrets of the Luxor Pyramid," a high-tech adventure/thrill ride using motion simulators and IMAX film.

The MGM Grand Hotel, Casino, and Theme Park (see p. 45)   This resort is backed by a 33-acre theme park and houses a state-of-the-art video-game arcade and carnival midway. A unique offering here is a youth center for hotel guests ages 3 to 16, with separate sections for different age groups. Its facilities range from a playhouse and tumbling mats for toddlers to extensive arts and crafts equipment for the older kids.

Canal St. Grill is a modern steak and seafood place.

Don Miguel's, a basic but satisfying Mexican restaurant, makes its own tortillas, and you can watch.

Courtyard Cafe is the 24-hour coffee shop. **Terrible Mike's** offers fast food. **Kate's Korner** has ice cream. Five bars are throughout the property, plus the Bourbon St. Lounge, which features live bands at night.

The Branson Theater is their 827-seat theater featuring live entertainment.

Services: Room service, safety deposit boxes, courtesy bus to/from airport and the Strip.

Facilities: Beauty salon, business center, game room/arcade, 70-lane bowling alley, wedding chapel, 40,000 square feet of meeting space (with more on the way), two swimming pools.

5 Mid-Strip

VERY EXPENSIVE

Bally's Las Vegas

3645 Las Vegas Blvd. S., at Flamingo Rd., Las Vegas 89109. ☎ **800/634-3434** or 702/739-4111. Fax 702/794-2413. 2,549 rms, 265 suites. A/C TV TEL. $95–$135 double; $35 more for concierge floor (incl. breakfast); $300–$2,500 suite. Extra person $15. Children 18 and under stay free in parents' room. AE, CB, DC, JCB, MC, V. Free parking (self and valet).

Bally's recently completed a $72 million renovation, which included the construction of a monorail that whisks passengers from its downstairs shopping level (a bit of a hike from the casino) to the MGM Grand. More noticeable is its elaborate new facade, a plaza containing four 200-foot people movers that transport visitors to and from the Strip via a neon-lit arch surrounded by cascading waters and lush landscaping. Light, sound, and water shows take place here every 20 minutes after dark.

The minute you step from its glittering entranceway into its light and airy casino, you'll notice that Bally's is one of the most cheerful hotels on the Strip. A whimsical mural of Las Vegas scenes backs the registration desk. A virtual "city within a city," Bally's offers a vast array of casino games, superb restaurants, entertainment options, shops, and services. During your Las Vegas stay, you need never step outside.

Large rooms are decorated in teal, mauve, and earth tones. All have sofas. TVs offer video checkout, not to mention cash-advance capability for your credit card. The 22nd floor is a concierge level.

Dining/Entertainment: Seasons, its interior modeled after a grand salon at Versailles, is an ornate setting of crystal chandeliers, gilded plasterwork and trellises, and elegantly draped private alcoves backed by gilt-framed mirrors. Cuisine is continental. Dinner only.

Bally's Steakhouse exudes an aura of substantial comfort. Gleaming brass chandeliers are suspended from a gorgeous oak-and-mahogany ceiling, and diners are ensconced in leopard-skin booths and black leather armchairs. A traditional steak and seafood menu is complemented by an extensive wine list; dinner only.

Al Dente has an expanse of marble flooring and art-deco maple and black lacquer columns where planters of greenery create intimate dining areas. Its menu offers delicious pastas, thin-crust pizzas with California-style toppings, and other Italian entrees; dinner only.

Las Olas is a charming candlelit Mexican eatery fronted by a lounge with a tiered fountain. The dining area, its walls hung with rugs and embroideries, displays Mexican statuary and pottery in wall niches. Breakfast, lunch, and dinner are served.

There's also a bright and cheerful 24-hour coffee shop, and food outlets in the shopping mall include a branch of New York's **Stage Deli.**

The mermaid-themed Bubbles Bar serves the casino. In addition, On the Rocks, a poolside bar with a lovely terrace cooled by ceiling fans, specializes in tropical drinks and wines by the glass. And the Terrace Café, a seasonal poolside eatery, offers light fare during the day. See also "Buffets and Sunday Brunches" in chapter 6.

Services: 24-hour room service, guest-services desk, shoe shine, foreign-currency exchange.

Facilities: Casino, tour and show desks, car-rental desk, small video-game arcade, shopping arcade (see chapter 9), wedding chapel, men's and women's hair salons, state-of-the-art health spa and fitness center, eight night-lit tennis courts and pro shop (lessons available), two basketball courts.

A gorgeous palm-fringed sundeck surrounds an Olympic-size swimming pool, one of the most beautiful in Las Vegas. There's a whirlpool, and guests can rent private cabanas with stocked refrigerators, TVs, ceiling fans, rafts, and private phones for $60 to $85 a day.

Bellagio

Corner of Las Vegas Blvd. S. and Flamingo Rd.

Steve Wynn's latest amazing upscale resort is due to open in late 1998, on the site of the legendary Dunes Hotel. The Bellagio is inspired by the eponymous Italian village that overlooks Lake Como. The front of the property will feature a 12-acre lake,

Mid-Strip Accommodations

Bally's Las Vegas **12**
Barbary Coast Hotel & Casino **8**
Bellagio **11**
Bourbon Street **9**
Caesars Palace **7**
Center Strip Inn **13**
Flamingo Hilton **6**

Harrah's Las Vegas **3**
Imperial Palace **5**
Maxim **10**
Mirage **4**
Rio Hotel & Casino **14**
Treasure Island at the Mirage **1**
Vagabond Inn **2**

the setting for water-ballet extravaganzas (more free shows!) and a replica of an Italian Village. The grounds will be some of the most lushly landscaped, with classical gardens, fountains and pools. The hotel will have 3,000 rooms and 270 suites. All this comes with a hefty price tag: $1.3 billion. For that price, it better be good. Knowing Wynn, it will be.

✪ Caesars Palace

3570 Las Vegas Blvd. S., just north of Flamingo Rd., Las Vegas, NV 89109. ☎ **800/634-6661** or 702/731-7110. Fax 702/731-6636. 3,200 rms. A/C TV TEL. From $99 standard double, $109–$500 "run of house deluxe" double; $549–$1,000 suite. Extra person $20. Children under 12 stay free in parents' room. AE, CD, DC, DISC, MC, V. Free parking (self and valet).

Since 1966, Caesers has stood as simultaneously the ultimate in Vegas luxury and the nadir (or pinnacle, depending on your values) of Las Vegas cheese. It's the most Vegas-style hotel you'll find. Or at least it was. By the end of 1997, most of that will have changed. Caesers is undergoing a massive $300 million renovation, inside and out. Don't worry, the Roman theme will remain. But as with everything else in Vegas, it has been upgraded to, let's say, a nicer neighborhood in Rome.

When Caesers was originally built to reflect Roman decadence, its designers probably had no idea how guffaw-inducing this would be some years later. It's the level of kitsch all should aspire to: Roman colonnades, Roman pillars, gigantic faux marble Roman statues, staff attired in gladiator outfits—it's splendidly ridiculous. It's what Vegas ought to be.

But all things change, and Caesers has been outshined over the years by more modern glamour. And frankly, that facade was looking dated 2 decades ago. So, like all of Vegas, they upgrade. The dark and smoky Romanesque design is being replaced by a brighter, more upscale theme; tacky '70s neon and mirrors have been replaced by beiges, earth tones, and hand-painted murals (specially commissioned). It's all generally lighter, brighter, and perhaps closer to the elegance Caesers originally sought to evoke. But never fear, the Roman statues still remain, as do the toga'd cocktail waitresses, and so should Caeser's giggle factor. Unfortunately, the fate of the entrance fountains (which landed permanently in Vegas legend when Evel Knievel attempted to jump over them) remains in question.

Past or future, Caesers remains spectacular. From the Roman temples, heroic arches, golden charioteers, and 50-foot Italian cypresses of its entrance, to the overwhelming interiors, it's the spectacle a good Vegas hotel should be. A moving sidewalk carries you into the Forum shops and the casino. The shops are in the grandest mall you can imagine (think the *La Dolce Vita* walk on the Via Veneto), covered by a sky that is supposed to change during the day to reflect the passing of time. (How Vegas is that, by the way, that you can't see the real sky, but we will simulate it for you?) These high-rent boutiques (Armani, Versace) lead to a group of animatronic Roman statues that come to life every hour to mumble something about bacchanals and the good life. That is probably supposed to subliminally make you want to gamble more and otherwise live it up, provided of course Caesars benefits. It's somewhat creepy, but the crowd eats it up.

Caesers is also known for its luxurious rooms and service. (Long lines at the reservation desk are sometimes relieved by gratis champagne.) The lobbies that lead to the rooms are stunning, all marble, dark greens and mahogany trim. Accommodations occupy (ultimately) four towers, and there are too many decorator schemes to describe here. You'll likely enjoy a lavish bath with marble floor, European fixtures, and oversized marble tubs (about half are Jacuzzis). (*Note:* Some of the rooms have lavish tubs in the middle of the room, which can be uncomfortable if you want to shower and don't want this to turn into a spectator sport.) Art in the rooms keeps to the Greco-Roman theme (some have classical sculptures in niches), furnishings tend to neoclassic styles; Roman columns, pilasters, and pediments are common. Many rooms have four-poster beds with mirrored ceilings, and all are equipped with three phones (bedside, bath, and desk), cable TVs with HBO, a gaming instruction channel (with cameo appearances by hotel headliners like Natalie Cole and Johnny Mathis), and in-house information stations. All rooms have private safes, hair dryers, irons and ironing boards, and lighted closets.

Still more things to take advantage of, in addition to the fine restaurants and the aforementioned Forum Shops (which are quite pleasant to stroll through), is the OMNIMAX Theatre (described in chapter 7) and Caesers Magical Empire (described in chapter 7).

Dining/Entertainment: Caesars has a well-deserved reputation for superior in-house restaurants. There are nine in the hotel, plus dining facilities in The Forum shopping area. All are highly recommended.

The hotel's premier restaurant, the exquisite **Palace Court,** and **Bacchanal,** which re-creates a multicourse Roman feast, are both described in chapter 6 along with the hotel's food court and buffets.

Neros, specializing in prime aged steaks and fresh seafood at dinner, has an extensive wine list. Its lunch menu features international contemporary fare. The restaurant's newly refurbished octagonal design is a contemporary interpretation of the

Spanish Madejar style, with an eight-pointed star radiating from the ceiling. Padded, sound absorbing walls make for a more intimate dining experience.

Just off the casino is the elegant Japanese restaurant **Ah'So,** which will be remodeled this year. No word yet on how it will look.

Primavera, the Italian restaurant, is not just being totally remodeled, but moved, along with the **Empress Court** Cantonese restaurant. Both will overlook the pool, with Primavera on the pool level and Empress Court above it. Both are supposed to have al fresco dining.

Cafe Roma, Caesars' comfortable, 24-hour casual-dining venue, offers international buffets and a menu that runs the gamut from filet mignon to chicken quesadillas, as well as burgers, salads, and sandwiches. A Chinese menu is available from 5pm to 1:15am.

Restaurants in The Forum Shops arcade include **Spago** (Wolfgang Puck's famed establishment), **The Palm, Planet Hollywood,** and the **Stage Deli**—all discussed in chapter 6. Some new additions will be added by late 1997.

There are several casino lounges, among them the Olympic Lounge and La Piazza Lounge offering nightly live entertainment in the Olympic Casino. The **Palace Court Terrace** (an ultraelegant, romantic piano bar) is one of my favorite Las Vegas nightspots. See also **Cleopatra's Barge** (a nightclub).

Services: 24-hour room service, shoe shine, complimentary gaming lessons, valet and dry cleaning services.

Facilities: Three casinos, two extensive shopping arcades (see chapter 9), state-of-the-art video arcade, American Express office, full-service unisex salon, show desks, car-rental desk.

Caesars' swimming pool area, which was already magnificent, is being completely remodeled at this time in an elaborate classical Roman theme, with pediments, columns, and templelike structures. A new health spa will be open by 1998, and should feature extensive workout equipment as well as a steam room, sauna, whirlpool, tanning beds, massage, aromatherapy, facials, and a sundeck.

Also under construction are 113,000 square feet of meeting space and 250,000 square feet of additional retail space for The Forum Shops. These should be finished by the time you read this.

EXPENSIVE

Flamingo Hilton

3555 Las Vegas Blvd. S., between Sands Ave. and Flamingo Rd., Las Vegas, NV 89109. ☎ **800/ 732-2111** or 702/733-3111. Fax 702/733-3353. 3,642 rms, 176 suites, 201 time-share units. A/C TV TEL. $69–$205 double; $250–$580 suite. Extra person $16. Children 18 and under stay free in parents' room. Inquire about packages and time-share suites. AE, CB, DC, DISC, JCB, MC, V. Free parking (self and valet).

The Flamingo has changed a great deal since Bugsy Siegel opened his 105-room oasis "in the middle of nowhere" in 1946. It was so luxurious for its time that even the janitors wore tuxedos. Jimmy Durante was the opening headliner, and the wealthy and famous flocked to the tropical paradise of swaying palms, lagoons, and waterfalls. While the Flamingo is a senior citizen on the Strip with a colorful history, a fresh, new look, enhanced by a recent $130 million renovation and expansion, has made Siegel's "real class joint" better than ever. Still, reaching the outside world (the Strip and Flamingo competitors) can be difficult; there is a lot of casino between you and the lobby, and then again between you and the street.

For those planning some leisure time outside the casino, the Flamingo's exceptional pool area, spa, and tennis courts are a big draw. One of the two best in Vegas, the pool is smashing, with countless trees and foliage, live birds, two water slides, waterfalls, and so on. Although the water can be a little chilly, kids should be able to spend hours in there.

Rooms occupy six towers and are variously decorated. Some are done up in soft blues and peach for a resort look enhanced by pretty fabrics, light painted-wood furnishings, and lovely watercolors of tropical scenes. Others use soft earth tones, forest green, or coral. All accommodations offer in-room safes; TVs have in-house information and gaming-instruction stations, a keno channel, video checkout, message retrieval, and account review.

Dining/Entertainment: The Old West **Beef Baron,** heralded by golden steer heads and a mural of a cattle roundup, bills itself as "a steakhouse forged in the spirit of our first great cattle ranchers." They usually offer steak and seafood specials for a decent price; dinner only.

Fronted by a tiered terra-cotta fountain, **Alta Villa** is designed to suggest an Italian village, with a vaulted ceiling, a trellised grape arbor under a painted sky, and grapevine-motif carpeting. A pretty ceramic-tiled exhibition kitchen is a focal point. A traditional Italian menu is featured; dinner only.

Peking Market's interior simulates an open marketplace in a bustling Chinese city. A central wood-burning brick oven casts a warm glow; dinner only.

The candlelit **Flamingo Room** is adorned with murals of flamingos, flamingo sculptures, and glass etched with flamingos; it offers piano-bar music at dinner. One of the draws here is an extensive salad bar supplemented by smoked whitefish and salmon, and crab and shrimp salads. The menu highlights steak and seafood dishes; full American breakfasts are also served here; dinner only.

Hamada of Japan is a softly lit, teak-beamed restaurant centered by a small rock garden. Some of the seating is at teppanyaki grill tables, and there's also a sushi bar. Come by for a Japanese breakfast of fish, raw egg, sticky beans, rice, soup, pickles, vegetables, and seaweed. It's open for all meals.

Lindy's Deli, a pleasant and spacious 24-hour coffee shop, offers appetizing smoked fish platters (salmon, whitefish, sturgeon) with bagels and cream cheese, corned beef and pastrami sandwiches, matzo ball soup, and other traditional Jewish deli items in addition to typical Las Vegas coffee-shop fare.

Bugsy's Deli, offering sandwiches on fresh-baked breads, is a casual self-service eatery just off the casino. The Pool Grille serves up light fare, and a snack bar serves the race and sports book area. Bugsy's Bar, festooned with orange and pink neon flamingo feathers, occupies a central position in the casino. And the Rainbow Bar, off the casino, has a wall of windows overlooking palm trees and waterfalls.

The Flamingo's Paradise Garden Buffet is described in chapter 6.

Services: 24-hour room service, guest services desk, translation services (interpreters are available for more than 35 languages; gaming guides are available in six languages).

Facilities: Casino, car-rental desk, tour and show desks, full-service beauty salon/ barber shop, wedding chapel, four night-lit championship tennis courts with pro shop and practice alley (tennis clinics and lessons are available), shopping arcade (see chapter 9 for details).

Five gorgeous swimming pools, two Jacuzzis, water slides, and a kiddie pool, are located in a 15-acre Caribbean landscape amid lagoons, meandering streams, fountains, waterfalls, a rose garden, and islands of live flamingos and African penguins. Ponds are filled with ducks, swans, and koi, and a grove of 2,000 palms graces an expanse of lawn.

A health club offers a variety of universal weight machines, treadmills, stair machines, free weights, sauna, steam, a TV lounge, and hot and cold whirlpools.

Shifting Sands: Tribute to a Las Vegas Legend

The Sands Hotel, closed last year, had been a Las Vegas landmark since 1952. It was the seventh resort to open on the Strip. New York show producer and Copacabana nightclub owner Jack Entratter was one of its original backers, and he used his showbiz contacts to bring superstar entertainment and gorgeous showgirls to the Copa Room stage. Danny Thomas was the room's opening headliner; Jimmy Durante, Red Skelton, Debbie Reynolds, and Jerry Lewis were among those who made regular appearances; and Louis Armstrong and Metropolitan Opera star Robert Merrill performed together for a memorable two weeks in 1954. Entrater's efforts not only put the Sands on the map, but helped establish Las Vegas as America's entertainment capital.

However, the Sands was probably most famous as the home of the notorious Rat Pack (Frank Sinatra, Sammy Davis Jr., Dean Martin, Peter Lawford, and Joey Bishop) and the site of their 3-week "Summit Meeting" in January 1960. No other Las Vegas show tickets have ever been more coveted or difficult to obtain. One night Sinatra picked up Sammy Davis Jr. bodily and said, "Ladies and gentlemen, I want to thank you for giving me this valuable NAACP trophy." He then dropped Davis into the lap of a man in a ringside seat who happened to be Sen. John F. Kennedy. Davis looked up and quipped, "It's perfectly all right with me, Senator, as long as I'm not being donated to George Wallace or James Eastland." The Rat Pack returned to the Copa stage in 1961 for an onstage birthday party for Dean Martin with a 5-foot-high cake in the shape of a whiskey bottle. Martin threw the first slice, and a food fight ensued. The riotous clan kept Las Vegas amused during most of the decade. By the way, Frank Sinatra and Mia Farrow were married at the Sands several eons ago.

Exercise tapes are available, and spa services include massage, soap rub, salt glow, tanning beds, and oxygen pep-up.

✪ Harrah's Las Vegas

3475 Las Vegas Blvd. S., between Flamingo and Spring Mountain rds., Las Vegas, NV 89109. ☎ **800/HARRAHS** or 702/369-5000. Fax 702/369-5008. 2,600 rms, 45 suites, 55 executive suites. A/C TV TEL. $75–$289 standard double, $99–$329 deluxe double; $195–$1,000 suite. Extra person $15. Children 12 and under stay free in parents' room. AE, CB, DC, DISC, MC, V. Free parking (self and valet).

A recent radical facelift has completely transformed Harrah's. It used to look like a Mississippi River showboat, but now looks nothing like that. It's more elegant, with a European carnival theme. Everywhere there are large murals celebrating different international festivals accented by lots of marble, bright colors, mirrors, and gold trim. A neat trick involving the confetti-strewn pattern carpeting and the fiber-optic fireworks on the ceiling combine to make a festive effect. They have removed Jackson Square, an outdoor shopping area, and replaced it with Carnival Court, which should be a festive, palm-fringed shopping/entertainment plaza where strolling entertainers will perform. It will also have a bandshell.

Overall, Harrah's has done a terrific job with its remodeling, creating a comfortable and fun environment while somehow eschewing both kitsch and the haughtiness that follows in the wake of other hotel conversions' more upscale images.

The rooms are also light and festive, with marble fixtures and light wood accents. All the rooms are larger than average; the points that emerge from both the old and the new tower wings translate inside into an extra triangle of space for a couch and table. Spacious minisuites in this section, offering large sofas and comfortable armchairs, are especially desirable. In all rooms, TVs offer hotel-information and keno channels, pay movies, Nintendo, and video account review and checkout.

Dining/Entertainment: The plush **Claudine's** is a romantic turn-of-the-century setting for steak and seafood meals. After you dine, relax over drinks in the adjoining piano bar lounge; dinner only.

Most of the new restaurants were still being completed as we went to press. The **Range Steakhouse** will be one of the few hotel restaurants that overlooks the Strip. **Asia** will feature a mixture of Chinese and other Asian cuisines. The **Garden Cafe** will be the 24-hour coffee shop. **Club Cappocino** will serve specialty coffees and home baked pastries. **Andreotti's** will serve Italian foods in an outdoor Tuscan-inspired atmosphere. **Winning Streaks,** the sports book restaurant and pub, will feature solid hamburgers.

Several new bars are also in the works. Of special mention, La Playa is an open-air lounge with a beach-gone-crazy theme. It will be the only bar on the Strip with outdoor seating, right on the Strip and will feature live Caribbean reggae bands.

In the lobby are a **TCBY** and an espresso/pastry cart for quick breakfasts.

See also the buffet listings in chapter 6.

Services: 24-hour room service (including a special pizza and pasta menu), complimentary gaming lessons.

Facilities: Casino, car-rental desk, tour and show desks, nice sized video-game arcade, coin-op laundry, shops (see chapter 9 for details), unisex hair salon.

Harrah's has a beautiful, Olympic-size swimming pool and sundeck area with waterwall and trellised garden areas, a whirlpool, kids' wading pool, cocktail and snack bar, and poolside shop selling T-shirts and sundries.

The hotel's health club will be remodeled, doubling in size, by 1998; previously it was one of the better facilities on the Strip, offering Lifecycles, treadmills, stair machines, rowing machines, lots of Universal equipment, free weights, whirlpool, steam, sauna, and massage; there are two TVs and a VCR for which aerobic exercise tapes are available.

✪ Mirage

3400 Las Vegas Blvd. S., between Flamingo Rd. and Sands Ave., Las Vegas, NV 89109. ☎ **800/ 627-6667** or 702/791-7111. Fax 702/791-7446. 3,044 rms, 279 suites. A/C TV TEL. Sun–Thurs, $79–$399 double, Fri–Sat and holidays $159–$399; $250–$3,000 suite. Extra person $30. AE, CB, DC, DISC, MC, V. Free parking (self and valet).

We really like this place. Actually, ask around; most visitors and locals agree. Even if they haven't stayed here, the majority consider it the most beautiful hotel in Vegas. From the moment you walk in and breathe the faintly tropically perfumed air (we think it's vanilla) and enter the lush rain forest, you just know that you are on vacation. It's a totally different experience from most Vegas hotels, where you step inside the door and are immediately the victim of a sensory assault.

The Mirage was Steve Wynn's first from-the-ground-up project; it seems funny now, but back in 1989, this was considered a complete gamble that was sure to be a failure. That was before the hotel opened, mind you. On opening day the crowds

Impressions

Supercalafragilisticexpialadocious!
— Governor Bob Miller's reaction upon first visiting the Mirage

nearly tore the place down getting inside, and the Mirage soon made its money back. Now it is the model all recent hotels follow.

Occupying 102 acres, the Mirage is fronted by more than a city block of cascading waterfalls and tropical foliage centering on a very active "volcano," which, after dark, erupts every 15 minutes, spewing fire 100 feet above the lagoons below. To be honest, it's not very volcano-like; if you've seen the movie, you are going to be disappointed. Instead of lava flow, expect a really neat light show, and you won't mind a bit. (In passing, that volcano cost $30 million, which is equal to the entire original construction cost for Caesers next door.) The lobby is dominated by 53-foot, 20,000-gallon simulated coral reef aquarium stocked with more than 1,000 colorful tropical fish, including six sharks. This gives you something to look at while waiting (never for long) for check in. Be sure to say hi to Sidney, the really big fish. (You'll know which one he is.) Sidney is a grouper, which means he can change his gender according to need. Seven inches when he first went into the tank at the Mirage's opening, he now weighs, well, a whole lot. We find his leisurely progress through the tank Zen-like.

Next it's through the rain forest, which occupies a 90-foot domed atrium—a path meanders through palms, banana trees, waterfalls, and serene pools. If we must find a complaint with the Mirage, it's with the next bit, as you have to negotiate 8 miles (or so it seems) of casino mayhem to get to your room, the pool, food, or the outside world. (On the other hand, the sundries shop is located right next to the guest room elevators, so if you forgot toothpaste, you don't have to travel miles to get more.) The formerly tropical-themed rooms have been redone in varying neutrals, with liberal use of muted gold. A marble entryway, mirrors, vanity table, and canopy over the bed's headboard give even the standards a luxurious appearance. The bathrooms are marble and slightly on the small size, depending on the room. Oak armoires house 25-inch TVs, and phones are equipped with fax and computer jacks. Further up the price scale are superdeluxe rooms with whirlpool tubs. By the way, when you ring anywhere in the hotel (front desk, restaurant reservations, the spa) whomever answers the phone greets you by name ("How can I help you Ms. Jones?"), thanks, apparently, to a sophisticated caller-ID system. It takes you aback at first, but one has to admit it is a nice, personal touch in a large facility. The staff continues the helpful touches; any problems that may arise are quickly smoothed out.

Off the casino is a habitat for Siegfried and Roy's white tigers, a plaster enclosure that allows for photo taking and "aaaahhhs." Out back is the pool, one of nicest in Vegas (it has a quarter-mile shoreline), a tropical paradise of waterfalls, trees, water slides, and so forth. It looks inviting, but truth be told is sometimes on the chilly side and isn't very deep. But it's so pretty you hardly care. Behind the pool is the Dolphin habitat and the new Siegfried and Roy's Secret Garden, which has a separate admission.

Dining/Entertainment: The **Noodle Kitchen,** a very authentic Asian restaurant, and the **Mirage Buffet** are detailed in chapter 6.

Kokomo's, situated in the tropical rain forest atrium, offers seating under bamboo-thatched roofing and trellised bougainvillea vines. Some tables overlook lagoons and waterfalls. The menu highlights steaks, chops, prime rib, and seafood. All meals are served. This is a beautiful place to eat, certainly, but somewhat pricy for the privilege. All meals are served.

Mikado, under a starlit sky, offers diners a candlelit setting with a sunken tropical rock garden, lotus pond, and sheltering pines. Teppanyaki cooking is featured along with à la carte Japanese specialties and a sushi bar; dinner only.

At **Moongate,** also under the stars, seating is in an open courtyard defined by classical Chinese architectural facades and tiled rooflines. White doves perch on cherry tree branches, and intricately hand-carved walls frame a moongate tableau. The menu offers Cantonese and Szechuan specialties; dinner only.

A cobblestone passage evoking a European village street leads to **Restaurant Riva,** a very pretty dining room. Candlelit at night, its walls are hung with gilt-framed still-life paintings and its windows with swagged draperies. Sophisticated northern Italian fare is served; dinner only.

Off the same quaint street is the **Bistro,** a charming belle epoque setting with rich mahogany paneling, Toulouse-Lautrec–style murals, and pink-cloth-covered tables lit by shaded brass oil lamps. Fare is French/continental; dinner only.

A branch of **California Pizza Kitchen,** under a thatch-roofed dome, is in the center of the casino overlooking the race and sports book. A bank of video monitors lets you follow the action while dining on oak-fired pizzas with toppings ranging from duck sausage to goat cheese. Calzones, salads, and pasta dishes here, too. All entrees are under $11.

The Caribe Café, a festive 24-hour coffee shop, adheres to the tropical theme. It's designed to suggest an open-air Caribbean village. Additional food and beverage facilities include an ice-cream parlor; the Paradise Café, an alfresco terrace with umbrella tables overlooking the pool (drinks and light fare are served); the Lagoon Saloon in the rain forest, specializing in tropical drinks and offering live music for dancing until 1am Sunday to Wednesday; the Baccarat Bar, where a pianist entertains nightly (jackets required for men); the poolside Dolphin Bar, and the Sports Bar in the casino.

Services: 24-hour room service, overnight shoe shine on request, morning newspaper delivery.

Facilities: Casino, car-rental desk, shops (Siegfried and Roy and Cirque du Soleil merchandise and others), unisex hairdresser and salon offering all beauty services, video arcade, business-services center. A free tram travels between the Mirage and Treasure Island almost around the clock.

The Mirage Day Spa teems with friendly staff anxious to pamper the customers, bringing you iced towels to cool you during your workout and refreshing juices afterward. After a workout in the gym, soak in the soothingly darkened Jacuzzi, take a steam, a sauna, a shower, and you'll be prepared for an evening of wild abandon. All the regular spa services are available, but a flat $20 charge for use of the above facilities is sufficient to make you relaxed and happy. Aveda and other fancy, name-brand products in the dressing room along with hair dryers, an endless supply of towels, cold drinks, and encouragement, make this a blessed retreat in a wild town.

Free swimming lessons and water aerobics classes take place daily at the pool. Private poolside cabanas (equipped with phones, TVs, free snacks and soft drinks, refrigerators, misting systems, rafts, and radios) can be rented for $85 a day.

Rio Hotel & Casino

3700 W. Flamingo Rd., at I-15, Las Vegas, NV 89103. ☎ **800/752-9746** or 702/252-7777. Fax 702/252-0080. 2,582 suites. A/C TV TEL. $95 Sun–Thurs, $149 Fri–Sat. Extra person $15. Inquire about golf packages. AE, CB, DC, MC, V. Free parking (self and valet).

The Rio Hotel confounded expectations by not only succeeding in a somewhat removed area away from the Strip, but it also thrived there. It recently completed an immediately popular $200 million addition: a new 41-story tower and the Masquerade Village. Diverging from the rest of the tropically themed hotel, this latter simulates a European village, complete with shops, restaurants, and a bizarre live action show in the sky. The addition is actually quite nice—not only is the architecture, in its faux way, aesthetically pleasing, but this part of the casino is much more airy, thanks to the very tall ceilings.

Rio pushes itself as a "carnival" atmosphere hotel, which in this case means the same hectic, crowded, noisy conditions you can expect to find in Brazil during carnival time. The older section's low ceilings only seem to accentuate how crowded the area is in both the number of people and the amount of stuff (slot machines, gaming tables). Out back is a pool with a sandy beach, and two new pools in imaginative fish and shell shapes that seem inviting until you get up close and see how small they are. It could be especially disappointing after you have braved the long, cluttered walk (particularly from the new tower rooms) to get there.

The rooms are touted because of their size; every one is a "suite," which does not mean two separate rooms, but rather one large one with a sectional, corner sofa and coffee table at one end. The dressing areas are certainly larger than average and feature a number of extra amenities, such as refrigerators (unusual for a Vegas hotel room), coffeemakers, and small snacks. Windows, running the whole length of the room, are floor to ceiling, with a pretty impressive view. The furniture does not feel like hotel room standard, but otherwise, the decor (shades of green) is fairly bland and nothing to get excited about. Expect, by the way, a long wait on the phone for reservations, and a not very helpful staff.

Attempting to compete with Treasure Island's free pirate show, and to keep shoving that party, carnival theme down your throat, there is a new, live-action show called "The Masquerade Show in the Sky." Three differently themed shows alternate, from noon to 10pm Sunday through Tuesday, from 1pm to 11pm Thursday through Saturday (it's dark Wednesday). Sets modeled after Mardi Gras floats (sort of) move on grids set in the ceiling, filled with costumed performers who lip sync to songs designed to rev up the crowd, but not continue the theme (Motown hits, for example). These floats are best viewed from the second floor of the Village. Down below, dancers do their thing on a stage, while even stranger costumes (ostriches, dragons) prance next to them. Guests can also don costumes and ride a float, but you have to pay for the privilege. All this party atmosphere, by the way, is strictly for adults; they actively discourage guests from bringing children.

Dining/Entertainment: Fiore (the Rio's premier restaurant), the **All American Bar and Grille,** and the hotel's first-rate buffet are all described in chapter 6.

In the elegant **Antonio's,** an Italian restaurant, the centerpiece of the room is a marble-columned rotunda in which a crystal chandelier is suspended from a recessed Mediterranean-sky ceiling. Other focal points are an exhibition kitchen and a magnificent marble display table brimming with tempting antipasto selections; dinner only.

Napa is a new addition, featuring country French gourmet cuisine. They have more than 600 selections of wine, and you can watch food preparation in the kitchen. Dinner only is served, Wednesday to Sunday.

Mask is an Asian restaurant set in a simulated rain forest; dinner only.

Mama Marie's Cuccini is a moderately priced Italian restaurant catering to "family style dining." It features extremely ordinary Italian food. Lunch and dinner are served.

Bamboleo is a combination Brazilian/Argentinean/Mexican place, open for lunch and dinner.

The **Voodoo Cafe,** set atop the 41st floor of the new Tower, promises to offer New Orleans–style food, live jazz and dancing, along with a view.

Buzio's Seafood Restaurant overlooks a palm-fringed pool. Massive alabaster chandeliers and flowering plants are suspended from a lofty canvas-tent ceiling, and a marble counter faces an exhibition kitchen. Lunch and dinner are available daily.

The **Beach Café,** also overlooking the pool and sandy beach, is the Rio's tropically festive 24-hour facility. Besides regular coffee-shop fare, it features Mexican, Italian, and Polynesian/Chinese specialties. Delicious fresh-baked desserts are a plus.

Toscano's Deli, off the casino, not only looks like a New York delicatessen but serves up a creditable pastrami or corned beef on rye. It also features pizza, pastas, and a wide array of first-rate fresh-baked breads, cakes, and pastries.

Check out the **Nawlins** store, which features beignets (french donuts liberally covered in powdered sugar; make sure they give you lots and eat all of them) made from genuine Café Du Monde mix. They cost a bit more than at the real McCoy, but you aren't at the real McCoy, anyway.

You might consider checking out the **Wine Cellar Tasting Room,** which bills itself as "the world's largest and most extensive collection of fine wines." Maybe, maybe not. Tasting here costs about $15 for three wines; open daily.

The Ipanema Piano Bar features live music Sunday through Friday. Mambo's Entertainment Lounge in the casino has dancing from 9pm to 3am (except Sunday). Another casino bar is under a fantasy coral reef with fish swimming overhead. Drinks, tropical and otherwise, are available poolside from the open-air Coco-Bana or a service window off Buzio's.

Services: 24-hour room service, guest-services desk, foreign-currency exchange, shoe shine, complimentary shuttle bus to/from the MGM and the Forum Mall.

Facilities: Casino, tour and show desks, unisex hair salon (all beauty services, including massage and facials), small video-game arcade, fitness room (stair machine, rowing machine, Lifecycle, four-station exercise machine), shops (gifts, clothing for the entire family, logo merchandise). Three whirlpool spas nestle amid rocks and foliage, there are two sand volleyball courts, and blue-and-white-striped cabanas (equipped with rafts and misting coolers) can be rented for $8 per hour or $25 per day.

✪ Treasure Island at the Mirage

3300 Las Vegas Blvd. S., at Spring Mountain Rd., Las Vegas, NV 89177-0711. ☎ **800/ 944-7444** or 702/894-7111. Fax 702/894-7446. Web site www.treasureislandlasvegas.com. 2,679 rms, 212 suites. A/C TV TEL. From $69 double; from $109 suite. Extra person $30. Inquire about packages. AE, DC, DISC, JCB, MC, V. Free parking (self and valet).

They will deny it now if you ask them, but Treasure Island was originally conceived (more or less) as the family alternative to the more grown-up Mirage. Why else would you build a hotel that is essentially a blown up version of Disneyland's Pirates of the Caribbean? But that's all behind them. Sure, the pirate theme remains with a vengeance, complete with plenty of skulls, crossbones, treasure chests, pirate ships' figureheads, animatronic skeletons, and pirate nautical paraphernalia. But a $25 million face-lift has added more marble and gilded the bones, so to speak (actually, literally in some cases). It's still Pirates of the Caribbean, but with lots and lots of money thrown at it. Despite this, it still remains a top family choice and many kids are often running about, which some vacationers may not find desirable.

This is modern Vegas kitsch; not nearly as out there as, say, Excalibur, but loads of fun to gawk at anyway. The outside is an entire 18th-century pirate village, with the front consisting of a wooden dock from which spectators can view the free live-action, pirate stunt show that plays every 90 minutes. The rooms continue the Caribbean theme; in other words, expect a lot of sand. And parchment. It's not quite as opulent as the Mirage, but comfortable. They do have a modern phone system with icons on the buttons so you can easily get connected to the spa or make dinner reservations without fumbling for the right extension. Turndown service is available if you request it. For those of us who get disoriented in these giant hotels, the hallways have different wallpaper patterns, so you know instantly which of the several choices is yours. Best of all, Strip-side rooms have a view of the pirate battle—views are best from the sixth floor on up. The pool is nothing special—medium to large but with none of the massive foliage and other details that makes the one at the Mirage stand out.

Dining/Entertainment: The hotel's premier restaurant, the **Buccaneer Bay Club,** is described in chapter 6, as are its buffet offerings.

Madame Ching's, luxurious, romantically lit (red silk globe lights are suspended from lotus medallions), and adorned with Chinese paintings, ceramics, sculpture, and lacquer screens, is a good choice for intimate dining. The regional Chinese fare is excellent, and Western pastries are a dessert option; dinner only. Madame Ching, by the way, was a notorious 19th-century female pirate.

The Plank, designed on the unlikely theme of a pirate's library, comprises a warren of cozy rooms where books and curios are displayed in leaded-glass cases. Its ambience is a mix of gleaming brass, polished burl, and musty leather-bound volumes. The menu features seafood and mesquite-grilled steaks and prime rib; dinner only.

The **Black Spot Grille,** its name notwithstanding, is an Italian "sidewalk cafe" set off from the shopping arcade by lacy iron grillwork. Its Italian village ambience is reflected in a Venetian *putti* (cherub) fountain, festival lanterns strung overhead, and faux bougainvillea draped from terra-cotta eaves. Lunch and dinner; almost all menu items are under $10. It's a good place for a tasty, late-night snack.

The very comfortable **Lookout Café,** Treasure Island's 24-hour coffee shop, has an arched beamed ceiling suggestive of a ship's underdeck. Walls are hung with muskets, daggers, and pirate booty from the seven seas, and amber broken-bottle sconces provide soft lighting. From 4pm to midnight, a full prime rib dinner is $9.95.

Just across from Mutiny Bay (the video-game arcade) is Sweet Revenge, an ice-cream/frozen yogurt parlor. The Quarterdeck Deli, a cafeteria off the casino, serves items ranging from pastrami to potato pancakes. And the Island Snack Bar offers light fare and nonalcoholic specialty drinks by the pool.

Captain Morgan's Lounge is a piano bar that overlooks the casino. The Battle Bar, in the casino near the race and sports book, airs athletic events on TV monitors overhead and offers live music nightly except Monday. More importantly, it provides patio seating overlooking Buccaneer Bay; for the best possible view of the ship battle, arrive at least 45 minutes before the show and snag a table by the railing. The ornate, crystal-chandeliered Swashbuckler's specializes in ice cream drinks and a 24-ounce rum concoction served in a skull mug; you can play progressive video poker while imbibing. And in the pool area is the simpatico Island Bar offering frozen specialty drinks; it's cooled by a misting system in summer.

Services: 24-hour room service, limo rental, foreign currency exchange, shoe shine (in men's room in the lobby and casino).

Facilities: Casino, tour and sightseeing desks, car-rental desk, travel agency, Mutiny Bay (an 18,000-square-foot, state-of-the-art video game arcade and carnival midway; one highlight is a full-size Mazda Miata motion-simulator ride), two wedding chapels, full-service unisex salon (days of beauty are an option), and a shopping arcade (for details, see chapter 9). A full-service spa and health club with a complement of machines, sauna, steam, whirlpool and massage, on-site trainers, TVs and stereos with headsets, and anything else you might need (including a full line of Sebastian grooming products in the women's locker rooms). A free tram travels between Treasure Island and the Mirage almost around the clock. For a good photo op, sit in the front of the first car; as you leave the loading dock, note how the Mirage, palm trees and a bit of the New York New York skyline are framed in an attractive, and nearly surreal, manner.

A large, free-form swimming pool with a 230-foot loop slide has a beautifully land-scaped sundeck area amid palms and flower beds. There's a kiddie pool and whirl-pool, and cabanas (equipped with overhead fans, small refrigerators, phones, cable TVs, rafts, tables, and chairs) can be rented for $75 a day.

MODERATE

Barbary Coast Hotel & Casino

3595 Las Vegas Blvd. S., at Flamingo Rd., Las Vegas, NV 89109. ☎ **800/634-6755** or 702/737-7111. Fax 702/737-6304. 200 rms. A/C TV TEL. Sun–Thurs, $39–$75 double; Fri–Sat and holidays $100. Extra person $10. Children under 12 stay free in parents' room. AE, CB, DC, DISC, JCB, MC, V. Free parking (self and valet).

Evoking the romantic image of turn-of-the-century San Francisco but not quite as nicely as Main St. Station downtown, the Barbary Coast enjoys a terrific Strip loca-tion. The casino is adorned with $2 million worth of magnificent stained-glass skylights, and the extremely charming, Victorian-style rooms make for an opulent setting. The latter, decorated in shades of rose and gray, have half-canopied brass beds, gaslight-style lamps, lace-curtained windows, and pretty floral carpets. All ac-commodations include little sitting parlors with entrances framed by floral chintz curtains.

Dining/Entertainment: Michael's, the Barbary Coast's premier restaurant, is flamboyantly Victorian—an intimate dining room with white marble floors, red satin damask wall coverings, plush red velvet booths, and a gorgeous stained-glass dome overhead. The menu highlights steaks and seafood; dinner only.

The **Victorian Room,** open 24 hours, is another attractive, turn-of-the-century venue. Its extensive menu runs the gamut from burgers to broiled Alaskan crab legs; in addition, Chinese entrees are offered at lunch and dinner.

Two bars serve the casino.

Services: 24-hour room service, shoe shine.

Facilities: Casino, Western Union office, tour and show desks, gift shop.

Bourbon Street

120 E. Flamingo, between the Strip and Koval Lane, Las Vegas, NV, 89109. ☎ **800/634-6956** or 702/737-7200. Fax 702/794-3490. 149 standard rooms, 9 minisuites, 8 executive suites. A/C TV TEL. $39–$99 standard double; $59–$109 minisuite; $69–$209 executive suite. AE, CB, DC, DISC, MC, V. Free parking (self and valet).

Note: At press time, this hotel was without a casino. Plans are afoot to restore the gaming license, so it should be back in operation by 1998.

A small hotel located just steps from one of the busiest corners of the strip (Caesars, Bally's, Flamingo Hilton) Bourbon Street is a cheap alternative to its fancier neigh-bors. It has a common New Orleans theme (don't you wonder how many hotels in New Orleans have a Vegas theme?) that is a bit worn in places but not shabby. Pres-ently the empty casino area is disconcerting and is probably what is giving the hotel a ghost town air. That's nothing that a few dozen slot machines and a couple of loud craps tables won't cure.

The rooms are basic, functional, and not particularly memorable. However, they are clean, well decorated, and the windows open (which is always nice); there are coffeemakers, modem hook-ups, in-room movies, and, perhaps most importantly, they can be really cheap. What more do you want?

Dining/Entertainment: A very inexpensive 24-hour restaurant that specializes in Italian fare and has one bar.

Services: Baby-sitting, laundry/dry cleaning, and room service.

Facilities: Tour desk, meeting space, nonsmoking floors.

Impressions

There was a magic in this place. It was like stepping back into the frontier. Casino owners were king. They owned the town. They were glamorous. They had beautiful women and lots of money.

—Steve Wynn, on Las Vegas when he visited as a boy

Imperial Palace

3535 Las Vegas Blvd. S., between Sands Ave. and Flamingo Rd., Las Vegas, NV 89109. ☎ **800/634-6441** or 702/731-3311. Fax 702/735-8328. Web site www.imperial-palace.com. 2,400 rms, 300 suites, 15 executive suites. A/C TV TEL. $29–$99 double; $59–$129 "luv tub" suite, $89–$199 other suites. Extra person $15. Inquire about packages. AE, CB, DC, DISC, MC, V. Free parking (self and valet).

Though appearing even older than its 17 years, the Imperial Palace has much more going for it than first impression might give. The Strip location, right in the middle of the action, can't be beat. The standard rooms are just that, but they all have balconies, which is exceedingly rare in Vegas. The "luv tub" rooms are a great deal; for the price, you get a larger bedroom (with a mirror over the bed!) while the larger than usual bathroom features a 300-gallon sunken "luv tub" (with still more mirrors). A perfect Vegas hoot. Given the slightly larger size of the "luv tub" rooms, that $59 low-end fee plus the location make them one of the best bargains on the Strip. The room amenities are all environmentally aware; biodegradable paper containers featuring cruelty- and animal-free products. They are in an "ongoing" process of upgrading the furniture. TVs offer in-house information channels, video message review and checkout, and pay-per-view movies. The hotel spa, while perhaps nothing hugely special, is more than adequate for exercise needs and is relatively inexpensive—$10 for all day. And the hotel also has a well-appointed 24-hour urgent care clinic, open to the public, which given the location—in the middle of the aforementioned action—is well worth knowing about. The pool is fairly large, with a waterfall and a Jacuzzi. From April to October, they hold "luaus" at night out here, a Polynesian revue and buffet. Expect tiki torches.

A unique feature here is the Imperial Palace Auto Collection of more than 800 antique, classic, and special-interest vehicles spanning a century of automotive history (details in chapter 7). Don't forget the Breathalyzers on the way to the parking garage.

Dining/Entertainment: Embers, the Imperial Palace's plush gourmet room, has burgundy silk-covered walls, spacious candlelit booths, and a smoked-mirror ceiling with recessed pink neon. The menu features steak and seafood entrees, along with pasta dishes; flambé desserts are a specialty; dinner only.

The Ming Terrace, fronted by a bamboo ricksha, achieves additional Eastern ambience from Chinese screens and painted fans. The menu features Mandarin, Cantonese, and Szechuan specialties; dinner only.

The **Rib House** is a rustic setting with exposed-brick walls and heavy oak dividers defining seating areas. A warm, cozy glow emanates from frosted-glass sconces, candlelit tables, and a working fireplace. Barbecued ribs and chicken are specialties; dinner only.

The Seahouse, a casual nautically themed restaurant softly lit by ship's lanterns, features fresh seafood; if you're not a fish fancier you might order filet mignon béarnaise or charbroiled chicken breast with sautéed mushrooms; dinner only.

The 24-hour pagoda-like **Teahouse** offers (in addition to the usual burgers, salads, sandwiches, and full entrees) buffet brunches weekdays ($5.95) and champagne

Sunday brunches ($6.50) from 8am to 3pm. A prime rib and champagne dinner is featured nightly from 5 to 10pm for $7.95.

Pizza Palace is an ordinary (but friendly) Italian eatery with red-and-white checkered tablecloths and big tufted-leather booths. It serves regular and deep-dish pizzas, Italian sandwiches, and pasta dishes. An antipasto salad bar is a plus. Lunch and dinner are offered.

The **Emperor's Buffet,** on the third floor, has a South Seas decor composed of thatched roofing, bamboo and rattan paneling, and Polynesian carvings. All meals are served.

Betty's Diner, in the shopping arcade, serves sandwiches, pizza, nachos, hot dogs, malts, and ice-cream sundaes. Burger Palace is attractively decorated with sports-themed murals. Adjoining it is the Sports Bar where you can follow the races over cocktails. There are a total of 10 cocktail bars/lounges in the hotel, including the Mai Tai Lounge on the main floor and the Poolside Bar (both specializing in exotic Polynesian drinks), and the Ginza, Geisha, Sake, and Kanpai bars serving the casino.

Services: 24-hour room service, free gaming lessons, shoe shine in casino.

Facilities: Casino, health club (machines, free weights, sauna, steam, massage, tanning, TV lounge), show and tour desks, car-rental desk, travel agency, unisex hairdresser, wedding chapel, shopping arcade. An Olympic-size swimming pool is backed by a rock garden and waterfalls, and its palm-fringed sundeck area also has a Jacuzzi.

Maxim

160 E. Flamingo Rd., between the Strip and Koval Lane, Las Vegas, NV 89109. ☎ **800/ 634-6987** or 702/731-4300. Fax 702/735-3252. 757 rms, 38 suites. A/C TV TEL. $25–$209 double. Extra person $10. Children under 4 stay free in parents' room. AE, DISC, DC, MC, V. Free parking (self and valet).

Another older hotel, the Maxim has a dark interior and seems stuck in the seventies (check out the glitzy lights in the casino). Most of Maxim's business is senior citizens. The recently redone rooms are small and standard hotel, though the colors are more modern. All offer TVs with pay-movie options and in-house information channels. If you prefer, you can rent a "players suite" with a whirlpool tub in the bedroom and a separate living room with wet bar.

The pool is very small, and the deck area often looks shabby (the sun's reflection off the hotel ages the surfacing fast). Still, Maxim's is only a block off the Strip, so the location is a definite advantage. And as far as ambience, consider Maxim's the neighborhood bar of casinos. Frankly, sometimes a smaller hotel is also boon; after all, when you tell your friends, "Meet me by the elevator," they don't ask which one.

Dining/Entertainment: The Treehouse is the Maxim's 24-hour coffee shop, a dimly lit facility (it's a bit claustrophobic actually) with many tables overlooking the casino. The portions are large, and the waitresses tell you to finish all your food, and bring you chicken soup if you have a cold. In addition to the requisite coffee-shop fare, it features daily specials such as a New York steak or prime rib dinner for $4.95.

More cheerful is **Jack's Colossal Deli,** a plant-filled self-service "sidewalk cafe" with a window wall and red-and-green-striped booths under an awning. There's also an interior room. Light fare (fresh-baked breakfast pastries, tacos, chili, salads, sandwiches, homemade soups) is served daily. All meals are served.

The **Grand Buffet,** served on the mezzanine level, is rather elegant, especially at dinner when tables are candlelit and a pianist entertains on a baby grand. Dinner ($6.95) is served nightly, plus a weekday brunch buffet and Saturday and Sunday champagne brunch ($7.95).

There are two casino cocktail lounges, the **Waterfall** and Cloud Nine.

Services: Room service, shoe shine.

Facilities: Casino, car-rental desk, tour and show desks, small video-game arcade, gift shop (it also carries resort wear, liquor, luggage, jewelry, and logo items), beauty salon/barbershop, pool and sundeck with seasonal poolside bar.

INEXPENSIVE

Center Strip Inn

3688 Las Vegas Blvd. S., at Harmon Ave., Las Vegas, NV 89109. ☎ **800/777-7737** or 702/ 739-6066. Fax 702/736-2521. 105 rms, 51 suites. A/C TV TEL. Sun–Thurs, $39.95–$49.95 double, Fri–Sat & holidays, from $79.95 double; suites (for up to 4): $79.95 Sun–Thurs, higher Fri–Sat, and special events. Rates include continental breakfast. Mention you read about the Center Strip in Frommer's for a $5 discount Sun–Thurs. AE, DC, DISC, MC, V. Free parking at your room door.

This centrally located little motel is owned and operated by Robert Cohen, who is usually on the premises making sure guests are happy. He's a bit of an eccentric, and his hotel doesn't fit into any expected budget-property pattern. For example, the rooms have video-cassette players, and a selection of about 1,000 movies can be rented for just $2 each. Local calls and use of a fax machine are free. Breakfast consists of bagels, Danish, juice, and coffee, and free coffee is available in the lobby all day. A free pasta dinner is offered daily (subject to availability). Also available at the front desk: irons, hair dryers, and gratis bath amenities.

The rooms, situated in two-story white stucco buildings, are standard motel units equipped with small refrigerators and safes. Suites offer kitchenettes, tubs with whirlpool jets, and steam rooms.

There's no on-premises restaurant, but numerous hotel restaurants (including ultimately Bellagio) are within easy walking distance, and you can have pizza delivered to your room. You'll also get a coupon for an all-you-can-eat $5.95 buffet for two at the Aladdin across the street. Facilities include a swimming pool and sundeck and a car-rental desk; the front desk can arrange tours.

Cohen also operates two Downtown properties: **The Crest Budget Inn** (207 N. 6th St., Las Vegas, NV 89101; ☎ **800/777-1817** or 702/382-5642) and **The Downtowner** (129 N. 8th St., Las Vegas, NV 89101; ☎ **800/777-2566** or 702/ 384-1441). If you mention this book, you'll pay just $24.95 a night Sunday to Friday, $39.95 Saturday. However, you get what you pay for.

Vagabond Inn

3265 Las Vegas Blvd. S., just south of Sands Ave., Las Vegas, NV 89109. ☎ **800/828-8032,** 800/522-1555, or 702/735-5102. Fax 702/735-0168. 126 rms. A/C TV TEL. Sun–Thurs, $42–$95 standard double, $65–$125 king room; Fri–Sat, $52–$110, $72–$150. Rates include continental breakfast. AE, CB, DC, DISC, MC, V. Free self parking.

A central location just across the street from Treasure Island (a cool place from which to watch the pirate battle—drag out a lawn chair), plus clean, nicely decorated basic motel rooms, make this a viable choice. One-third of the rooms have patios or balconies, and all offer cable TVs with pay-movie options. King rooms have wet bars and refrigerators. A wide selection of complimentary bath amenities is available at the front desk, and free coffee is served in the lobby around the clock, as is a daily continental breakfast of juice, fruit, and pastries. Facilities include coin-op washers and dryers. There's a swimming pool but no restaurant. A gratis airport shuttle and free local calls are pluses.

6 North Strip

VERY EXPENSIVE

✪ Desert Inn Country Club Resort & Casino

3145 Las Vegas Blvd. S., between Desert Inn Rd. and Sands Ave., Las Vegas, NV 89109. ☎ **800/ 634-6906** or 702/733-4444. Fax 702/733-4744. 566 rms, 136 suites/minisuites. A/C TV TEL. $175–$185 double; $215–$225 minisuite; $350–$555 suite. Extra person $35. Children under 12 stay free in parents' room. AE, CB, DC, DISC, JCB, MC, V. Free parking (self and valet).

The Desert Inn has long been the most glamorous and gracious of Vegas hotels; coming here means leaving the hectic Strip action behind. The Desert Inn considers itself more a resort than a hotel, and the property and prices reflect this. The property has just undergone a serious renovation. The look now reflects a turn-of-the-century Palm Beach resort, with elegant, clean, and spare lines. (Frankly, the time period of the decor is not turn-of-the-century in many parts, but let's not be picky.) As with most Vegas renovations, the look of everything is lighter, brighter and cleaner— apparently, in the '90s, sand tone, rather than dark, means glamour. The clientele this attracts is middle to upper class, with a large convention crowd, thanks to their close proximity to the Sands Convention Center.

The Desert Inn's history dates from its opening in 1950, with Edgar and Charlie McCarthy premiering in the showroom. Howard Hughes (and later his estate) owned the hotel from 1967 to 1988, and he lived here in the late 1960s. (Actually, legend has it that from the day he checked in to the day he left, via a back door, he was never seen by a single hotel employee. It was during this time he may or may not have been picked up on the highway outside of town by Melvin Drummar and may or may not have rewarded Melvin by making him his heir.) Since this is more resort than hotel, expect first-rate service all the way (indeed, when a mix-up happened with a spa reservation, the matter was dealt with much more efficiently and sweetly than at other hotels in Vegas). Travelers, too, like the on-site golf course, which is quite a good one. And there are five tournament-class tennis courts, all lit for night play; expert instruction and practice ball machines are available.

The newly redone rooms (in light golds and greens) feel spacious, with comfortable armchairs and matching hassocks. The fluffy bed coverings appear lusher than usual, and the mattresses are very firm. Rooms have views of either the Strip or the golf course (the latter helps really give the feel of a getaway), and some even have small balconies, though they are more for air currents than actual standing. Each room has a very big closet with an iron and ironing board. Business travelers will be pleased that the phone lines have modem connections. Cable TVs feature pay-movie options as well as gaming instruction and hotel-information channels. The bathrooms are perhaps the best in Vegas: beautiful and large, done in black and gray granite with double sinks, a separate enclosure for the toilet, and a glass shower separate from the tub. Amenities include a big basket of Neutrogena products, a phone, and hair dryer.

Dining/Entertainment: See chapter 6 for details on the opulent **Monte Carlo Room.**

Portofino, previously a Northern Italian restaurant, is now an upscale Mediterranean cuisine. It overlooks the casino (which isn't very noisy).

At **Ho Wan,** an upscale Cantonese/Szechuan restaurant, a traditional Chinese interior is currently undergoing total renovation to a more contemporary Asian decor, and a new menu is also in the works.

Terrace Pointe, a delightful plant-filled 24-hour coffee shop with a windowed wall overlooking the pool, offers an American/continental à la carte menu along with

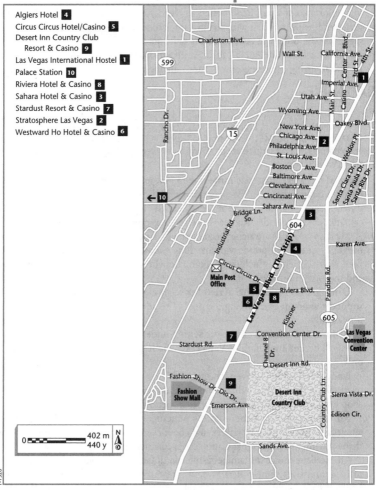

Algiers Hotel **4**
Circus Circus Hotel/Casino **5**
Desert Inn Country Club
    Resort & Casino **9**
Las Vegas International Hostel **1**
Palace Station **10**
Riviera Hotel & Casino **8**
Sahara Hotel & Casino **3**
Stardust Resort & Casino **7**
Stratosphere Las Vegas **2**
Westward Ho Hotel & Casino **6**

Asian specialties and buffet breakfasts and lunches. An omelet station is featured every morning, and, at lunch, there's a carving station.

A posh new steakhouse is also in the works. The newly remodeled Starlight Theatre, a plush casino lounge, features name entertainment at night; it's a romantic setting for cocktails and dancing, one of two casino bars. And even the furthest booth has a fine view of the stage.

Services: 24-hour room service, concierge, shoe shine.

Facilities: Golf course, five tennis courts, swimming pool (some suites have private swimming pools).

The Desert Inn Spa is very beige, large, and pristine. The well-equipped gym has the benefit of actual windows and natural light, something you rarely see in Las Vegas unless you're outside. The placement of the soaking pools in another area with bright, natural light makes the sauna experience feel a little less private than at other spas, but since the other naked women don't resemble showgirls, it's not in the least uncomfortable. If a staff person offers to blend you a complimentary smoothie, don't turn her down. As you sit wrapped in a thick robe, waiting to be called for your massage, that smoothie will taste especially delicious.

Other facilities include a casino, tour and show desks, car-rental desk, beauty salon/barbershop, business center, shops, including golf and tennis pro shops.

EXPENSIVE

Riviera Hotel & Casino

2901 Las Vegas Blvd. S., at Riviera Blvd., Las Vegas, NV 89109. ☎ **800/634-6753** or 702/ 734-5110. Fax 702/794-9451. 1,978 rms, 158 suites. A/C TV TEL. $59–$95 double; $125–$500 suite. Extra person $20. Inquire about "Gambler's Spree" packages. AE, CB, DC, MC, V. Free parking (self and valet).

Opened in 1955 (Liberace cut the ribbon and Joan Crawford was official hostess of opening ceremonies), the Riviera is styled after the luxurious casino resorts of the Côte d'Azur. Its original nine stories made it the first "high-rise" on the Strip. Several towers later, the present-day Riviera is as elegant as ever.

Accommodations are richly decorated with handsome mahogany furnishings and burgundy or teal bedspreads with matching gold-tasseled drapes. Half the rooms offer pool views. Amenities include in-room safes and cable TVs with pay-movie options and in-house information stations.

Dining/Entertainment: Kristofer's, an elegant tropically themed steak and seafood restaurant overlooking the pool. The adjoining lounge serves poolside fare; dinner only.

Ristorante Italiano, a romantic setting under a simulated starlit sky, has a window wall backed by murals of Venice. Classic Italian specialties are featured; dinner only.

Kady's is the Riviera's very cheerful 24-hour restaurant, with a wall of windows overlooking the pool as well as outdoor patio seating. Along with the usual coffee-shop fare, Kady's menu offers Jewish deli specialties.

Rik' Shaw (don't ask me what the punctuation means) features Chinese fare in an elegant candlelit room with crystal chandeliers and mirrored columns. The fan-shaped menu lists traditional Cantonese specialties; dinner only.

An excellent choice for families is the Mardi Gras Food Court, which, unlike most of its genre, is extremely attractive. White canvas umbrella tables and Toulouse-Lautrec–style murals create a comfortable French cafe ambience. Food choices are wide-ranging, including burgers, pizza, gyros, falafel, and Chinese fare. The food court is adjacent to the video-game arcade, so you can relax over espresso while the kids run off and play. Open daily until midnight.

There are two casino bars, the Splash Bar and Le Bistro Lounge; the latter offers nightly live entertainment.

Services: 24-hour room service, shoe shine.

Facilities: Casino (one of the world's largest), large arcade with carnival and video games, well-equipped health club (full complement of cardio and weight machines, free weights, steam, sauna, tanning, facials, salt/soap rubs, massage), Olympic-size swimming pool and sundeck, wedding chapel, beauty salon/barbershop,

---

Fun Fact

In Martin Scorsese's movie Casino, starring Robert De Niro, Joe Pesci, and Sharon Stone, the Riviera stood in for the fictional Tangiers.

comprehensive business-services center, America West airlines desk, tour and show desks, car-rental desk, shops (see chapter 9 for details), two Har-Tru tennis courts lit for night play. A unique feature here: a wine-tasting booth operated by Nevada's only winery.

MODERATE

Palace Station

2411 W. Ave, Las Vegas, NV 89102. ☎ **800/634-3101** or 702/367-2411. Fax 702/221-6510. 943 rooms, 86 suites. AC TV TEL. $59–$169 double; $95–$1,000 suite. AE, CB, DC, DISC, MC, V. Free parking (valet and self).

Another in the series of early California, vaguely Victorian-influenced hotels, the Palace Station is situated by itself, which makes it ideal for those looking to keep away from the bustle of the Strip and downtown. A train theme runs through, complete with old train artifacts. In the lobby are several antique slot machines, which are always fun to look at (nope, you can't play them, but the odds probably stink anyway). The Palace Station comes off as slightly more stylish than some hotels Downtown. The larger-than-it-appears casino (it's actually quite big) attracts many locals, which makes for a more relaxed atmosphere.

The hotel is split into two parts, consisting of the original buildings plus the newer (1991) tower. The older section is out back, a motel-style building by the pool. The rooms in this section have a mix of newer and slightly chipped dark wood furniture. With views only of the parking lot, they are small, dark, and only have showers. For the price, they aren't worth it. Better are the Tower rooms, which are larger, brighter, and newer in feel (possibly thanks to the lighter color schemes—the decor is along the same lines). Floors 6 and above have mountain and Strip views. The corner rooms have extra large bathrooms (though all are spacious enough and have bathtubs), with a separate changing room that has two sinks. The suites, mostly along the Victorian line, are quite nice indeed, prettily decorated, spacious and quite luxurious. This is a place best to stay in if you can get the low-end price or you want to stay away from the crush of the Strip or downtown.

Dining/entertainment: Guadalajara Bay is their Mexican restaurant, featuring 15 different kinds of salsas. It was recently voted best Mexican restaurant by the *Las Vegas Review Journal.* Lunch and dinner are served.

Pasta Palace features Italian food; dinner only.

The **Iron Cafe** is their 24-hour coffee shop, that also serves Chinese food until 11pm. Scattered throughout the property is a Burger King, Pizza Place, and TCBY yogurt. There are two bars, which make large margaritas for 99¢.

Services: Room service, laundry and dry cleaning, Express check-out.

Facilities: Pool, beauty salon, car rental, game room/arcade, tour desk.

Sahara Hotel & Casino

2535 Las Vegas Blvd. S., at E. Sahara Ave., Las Vegas, NV 89109. ☎ **800/634-6666** or 702/737-2111. Fax 702/737-2027. 1,945 rms, 90 suites, A/C TV TEL. $35–$55 standard double, $55–$85 deluxe double; $200–$600 suite. Extra person $10. Children under 14 stay free in parents' room. AE, CB, D, DC, MC, V. Free parking (self and valet).

One of the few venerable hotel casinos remaining in Vegas (it's come a long way since it opened in 1952 on the site of the old Club Bingo), the Sahara is in the process of undergoing a major face lift. The two-part process should be completed by 1998; certainly by then more than half the rooms will have been redecorated, and the hotel's front will be completely different—think onion domes and other Eastern-type detailing. Unfortunately, this includes the loss of the landmark sign, once the tallest in Vegas. (The new one, featuring a camel, is frankly going to look just as dated even more quickly.) The point is not only to keep up with the Joneses—as the newer, glitzy hotels make the old ones seem not just quaint but shabby—but also to attempt to unify the theme. This means trying to make things more like Morocco, though the reality seems to include all of North Africa (hence towers called Tangiers, Egyptian artwork, and so on).

The room decor suffers from overkill, with stars and stripes assaulting the eyes and not looking terribly Moroccan (but then again, neither does Morocco). The boldly striped bedspreads on the otherwise comfortable beds are a particular mistake. The windows open, which is unusual for Vegas.

There is a handsome Olympic-sized pool, done in Moroccan mosaic tiles, possibly with a bathing platform in the middle. It should be noted that the Sahara feels they are not as well equipped as other hotels for children and discourage you from bringing yours.

Dining/Entertainment: *Note:* With the remodeling, some of these places might be either gone or moved, and there may be some newer places as well.

The House of Lords is a plush continental restaurant with a suit of armor in its entrance foyer and a stunning mahogany ceiling within. You'll dine on fancy fare with sorbet served between courses and complimentary petit fours as a finale; dinner only.

La Terrazza, an Italian restaurant, is an intimate bilevel grotto with a wall of windows overlooking the pool and tables lit by silk-shaded candle lamps; dinner only.

The Mexican Village is housed in a room that was originally the exotic setting for a Polynesian dinner show. It still has a few private dining gazebos that used to comprise VIP seating. Ask for them when you reserve if you have at least three in your party. Fare is Mexican; dinner only. The adjoining Acapulco Cantina, backed by a tropical aquarium, serves margaritas, Mexican beers, and light fare.

The **Caravan Coffee Shop,** a 24-hour facility off the casino with windows overlooking the pool, serves all the requisite coffee-shop fare. A steak and lobster dinner with salad, potato, and vegetable is just $7.77. A steak and eggs breakfast served from 11pm to 6am is $2.95.

The **Turf Club Deli,** next to the Race and Sports Center, features Jewish deli fare: homemade matzo ball soup, lox and bagels, pickled herring, and pastrami on rye. Open 10am to 8pm; everything on the menu is under $6.

Bar/lounges include two 24-hour casino bars (the Safari Bar and the Sports Book Bar), plus the Casbah Lounge offering top-notch live entertainment daily from 2pm to 6pm and 7pm to 4am. The Oasis Buffet is detailed in chapter 6.

Services: 24-hour room service.

Facilities: Casino, beauty salon/barbershop, car-rental desk, tour and show desks, shops (see chapter 9), video-game arcade. The Sahara has a large swimming pool and sundeck with a pool shop and poolside bar in nearby thatched-roof structures. A smaller pool shares the same courtyard setting.

Stardust Resort & Casino

3000 Las Vegas Blvd. S., at Convention Center Dr., Las Vegas, NV 89109. ☎ **800/634-6757** or 702/732-6111. Fax 702/732-6257. Web site www.vegas.com./hotel/star. 2,335 rms, 160 suites. A/C TV TEL. Tower rooms and suites, $60–$1,000; Motor Inn rooms, $36–$200 (2-person max). Extra person $10. Children 12 and under stay free in parents' room. AE, CB, D, DC, JCB, MC, V. Free parking (self and valet).

Opened in 1958, the Stardust is a longtime resident of the Strip, its 188-foot starry sign one of America's most recognized landmarks. Today, fronted by a fountain-splashed exterior plaza, the Stardust has kept pace with a growing city. In 1991, it added a 1,500-room tower and a 35,000-square-foot state-of-the-art meeting and conference center, part of a comprehensive $300 million expansion and renovation project. It's a likable hotel, but has no personality, despite being the only star of *Showgirls.* (It was probably chosen for it's oh-so-Vegas lightbulb-intensive facade.)

Rooms in the Towers are perfectly adequate, nice even, but frankly, completely forgettable. If you must know more, the 32-story West Tower rooms are decorated in rich, earth tones with black accents and bedspreads and drapes in bold abstract prints. East Tower rooms are light, airy, and spacious, with peach carpeting and attractive green floral-print bedspreads, upholstered headboards, and draperies. You can rent an adjoining parlor room with a sofa bed, Jacuzzi tub, refrigerator, and wet bar— a good choice for families. Also quite nice are Villa rooms in two-story buildings surrounding a large swimming pool. Decorated in soft Southwestern pastels, they have private shaded patios overlooking the pool. The least expensive rooms are in the Stardust's Motor Inn—four two-story white buildings with shuttered windows set far back on the property. In the past, they were rundown motel rooms, but have been redecorated in more cheerful colors. A suite can be better, but it is a long walk to your hotel. Motor Inn guests can park at their doors. All Stardust accommodations offer in-room safes, and TVs have Spectravision movie options and in-house information channels.

Dining/Entertainment: William B's is an elegant steak-and-seafood restaurant fronted by a handsome bar/lounge. Flambé desserts are a house specialty; dinner only.

Tres Lobos is an attractive restaurant designed to resemble the open courtyard of a hacienda. A plush adjoining lounge specializes in many-flavored margaritas. *Las Vegas Review Journal* readers recently voted this the city's best Mexican restaurant; dinner only.

Toucan Harry's Coffee Shop, the Stardust's 24-hour facility, is a lushly tropical setting under a tented fabric ceiling. In addition to a vast array of sandwiches, salads, and full entrees (including many low-fat, low-cholesterol items), Harry's features a full Chinese menu with more than 50 dishes.

Ralph's Diner reflects America's current nostalgia craze. Fifties rock 'n' roll tunes emanate from an old-fashioned jukebox, and waitresses garbed in classic white diner uniforms sometimes dance to the music. It's not a quiet place. All-American fare is served, an old-fashioned soda fountain turns out desserts, and low-priced blue-plate specials are offered daily. All meals served; everything is under $10 (most are under $7).

Tony Roma's, which you may know from other locations, has a home at the Stardust; more about it, and the Stardust's **Warehouse Buffet,** in chapter 6.

The Short Stop is a snack bar in the race and sports book area of the casino. There are eight bars and cocktail lounges in the hotel, including the Terrace Bar in the casino with an alfresco seating area overlooking the pool and the Starlight Lounge, featuring live music nightly.

Services: 24-hour room service, shoe shine, free ice on every floor.

Facilities: Casino, beauty salon/barbershop, video-game arcade, car-rental desk, show desk, shops (gifts, candy, clothing, jewelry, logo items, liquor). There are two large swimming pools, one in the Villa section, the other between the East and West Towers. Both have attractively landscaped sundecks and poolside bars; the Towers pool area has three whirlpool spas. Guests can use the Las Vegas Sporting House directly behind the hotel, a state-of-the-art, 24-hour health club; its extensive facilities are detailed in chapter 7.

Stratosphere Las Vegas

2000 Las Vegas Blvd. S., between St. Louis St. and Baltimore Ave., Las Vegas, NV 89104. ☎ **800/99-TOWER** or 702/380-7777. Fax 702/383-5334. 1,278 rms, 222 suites. A/C TV TEL. Sun–Thurs, $39–$93 double; Fri–Sat $59–$129; $69–$400 suites. Extra person $15. Children

18 and under stay free in parents' room. Rates may be higher during special events. AE, CB, DC, DISC, JCB, MC, V. Free parking (self and valet).

A really neat idea, in that Vegas way, in a really bad location. At 1,149 feet, it's the tallest building west of the Mississippi. In theory, this should have provided yet another attraction for visitors; climb (okay, elevator) to the top and gaze at the stunning view. But despite being on the Strip, it's a healthy walk from anywhere—the nearest casino is the Sahara, which is five very long blocks away. This and possibly the hefty price charged for the privilege of going up in said Tower may have conspired to keep the crowds away. Stay away they did; the hotel is in severe financial trouble, and construction on additions and upgrades has halted.

But in an effort to lure crowds back, prices have dropped, and some changes have been made. The casino has been toned down (previously it was a World's Fair theme; now it's more temperate and adult looking). The shopping arcade, again with a "major cities" theme, has been expanded slightly. You can still ride the incredible thrill rides (provided the wind isn't blowing too hard that day) on top of the tower: the world's highest roller-coaster (it careens around the outer rim of the tower 909 feet, 108 stories, aboveground) and the Big Shot, a fabulous free-fall ride that thrusts passengers up and down the tower at speeds of up to 45 miles per hour. (One thrill ride aficionado called the Big Shot the scariest thing he had ever ridden.) Indoor and outdoor observation decks do offer stunning city views you will ever see, especially at night.

The rooms are furnished in handsome, Biedermeier-style cherrywood pieces with black lacquer accents. Enhanced by bright abstract paintings, they offer TVs with in-house information channels and pay-movie options, safes, phones with modem ports, and hair dryers and cosmetic mirrors in the bath. Ask for a high floor when you reserve to optimize your view.

Dining/Entertainment: Two notable restaurants here are the revolving **Top of the World,** featuring panoramic vistas of Las Vegas from 800 feet; **Big Sky,** offering all-you-can-eat barbecue dinners. They're described in chapter 6, where you'll also find details about the hotel's buffet room.

At the delightful **Ferraro's,** sky-painted ceilings, trompe l'oeil effects, and stunning murals create the illusion that you're dining in an Italian courtyard.

The 24-hour **Sister's Cafe and Grille,** its corrugated tin roofing and bayou murals designed to suggest a rustic Louisiana fishing camp, adds Cajun/Creole specialties to the more traditional Las Vegas coffee shop fare.

A Nathan's, McDonald's, and Rainforest Cafe are in the Tower Shops area, along with a pizzeria, Jitters (a gourmet coffee shop), and a Häagen-Dazs outlet. Roxy's Diner is a '50s-themed eatery.

Bars and lounges include the Images Cabaret; the L'Isles Bar featuring live Caribbean/reggae music and tropical drinks; a cocktail lounge on the 107th floor; and the Big Sky Lounge adjacent to the restaurant, which features country music nightly after 8pm.

Services: 24-hour room service, foreign currency exchange.

Facilities: Casino, guest services desk, tour and show desk, video-game arcade, shopping arcade, three wedding chapels (offering incredible views from the 103rd floor), car-rental desk. An exercise facility, child care center, and vast resort-style pool and sundeck are in the works.

INEXPENSIVE

Algiers Hotel

2845 Las Vegas Blvd. S., between Riviera Blvd. and Sahara Ave., Las Vegas, NV 89109. ☎ **800/732-3361** or 702/735-3311. Fax 702/792-2112. 105 rms, 1 suite. A/C TV TEL. Sun–Thurs, from

$40 double, Fri–Sat & holidays from $55 double. Extra person $10. Children under 12 stay free in parents' room. AE, CB, DC, DISC, MC, V. Free self parking at your room door.

A venerable denizen of the Strip, the Algiers opened in 1953. However, a recent multimillion dollar renovation—including landscaping (note the lovely flower beds out back) and a new facade with a 60-foot sign—brought rooms and public areas up to date. There's no casino here, though you can play video poker in the bar. Neat two-story, aqua-trimmed peach stucco buildings house nice-sized rooms (with dressing areas) that are clean and spiffy looking. Free local calls are a plus. Facilities include a medium-sized pool and palm-fringed sundeck.

The cozy Algiers Restaurant and Lounge is a local hangout frequented by state and city politicians and journalists. It has a copper-hooded fireplace and walls hung with historic Las Vegas photographs of pretower Strip hotels (Dunes, Sands, Flamingo), Liberace cutting the ribbon at the opening of the Riviera, Clara Bow and Joey Adams with the owner of the now-defunct Thunderbird, and many more. A glassed-in cafe overlooks the pool. The restaurant serves all meals, including many steak and seafood specialties, barbecued baby back ribs, and low-calorie dishes. There are souvenir shops, a jeweler, and a car-rental office out front. Also on the premises is the famed Candlelight Chapel, where many celebrities have tied the knot over the last three decades.

The Algiers is a good choice for families, right across the street from Circus Circus with its many child-oriented facilities and a half block from Wet 'n' Wild. It's also within walking distance of the Las Vegas Convention Center and the Stratosphere Tower.

✪ Circus Circus Hotel/Casino

2880 Las Vegas Blvd. S., between Circus Circus Dr. and Convention Center Dr., Las Vegas, NV 89109. ☎ **800/444-CIRC,** 800/634-3450, or 702/734-0410. Fax 702/734-2268. 3,744 rms. A/C TV TEL. Sun–Thurs, $39–$79 double, Fri–Sat, $59–$99. AE, CB, DC, DISC, MC, V. Free parking (self and valet).

Perhaps the strongest evidence that things are changing in Las Vegas is the massive remodeling and renovation of this classic hotel and casino. The circus theme remains, but Jumbo the Clown has been replaced by commedia dell'arte harlequins. In other words, like everyone else, even the venerable Circus Circus, once the epitome of kitsch, is trying to be taken more seriously. Gone are the bright primary colors and garish trims (murals, carpeting) and instead are subtle, muted tones and more high-rent touches that appeal less to big-top buffs and more to the Cirque de Soleil crowd.

Don't come expecting an adult atmosphere; the circus theme remains and the kid appeal along with it. The midway level features dozens of carnival games, a large arcade (more than 300 video and pinball games), trick mirrors, and ongoing circus acts under the big top from 11am to midnight daily. The world's largest permanent circus according to the *Guinness Book of World Records,* it features renowned trapeze artists, stunt cyclists, jugglers, magicians, acrobats, and high-wire daredevils. Spectators can view the action from much of the midway or get up close and comfy on benches in the performance arena. There's a "be-a-clown" booth where kids can be made up with washable clown makeup and red foam rubber noses. They can grab a bite to eat in **McDonald's** (also on this level), and since the mezzanine overlooks the casino action, they can also look down and wave to Mom and Dad—or more to the point, Mom and Dad can look up and wave to the kids without having to stray too far away from the blackjack table. Circus clowns wander the midway creating balloon animals and cutting up in various ways.

There is also the upgraded Grand Slam Canyon indoor theme park out back and an all new shopping arcade decorated with replicas of turn-of-the-century circus posters.

The Circus Circus is what the whole hep world would be doing on Saturday night if the Nazis had won the war.
—Hunter S. Thompson, *Fear and Loathing in Las Vegas.*

The thousands of rooms here occupy sufficient acreage to warrant a free Disney World–style aerial shuttle (another kid pleaser) and minibuses connecting its many components. Tower rooms have just slightly better than average, brand-new hotel room furnishings and offer safes, and TVs are equipped with in-house information and gaming-instruction stations. The Manor section comprises five white, three-story buildings out back, fronted by rows of cypresses. Manor guests can park at their doors, and a gate to the complex that can be opened only with a room key assures security. These rooms are usually among the least expensive in town, but we've said before and we'll say again: You get what you pay for.

All sections of this vast property have their own swimming pools; additional casinos serve the main tower and Skyrise buildings; and both towers provide covered parking garages.

Dining/Entertainment: Highly esteemed by locals, **The Steak House** is elegant and candlelit, its cherry-paneled walls hung with gilt-framed oil landscapes. Shelves of books and green glass chandeliers create a clubby look. A plush lounge adjoins. Open for dinner and Sunday brunch.

The very reasonably priced **Pink Pony** is Circus Circus's cheerful bubble-gum pink and bright red 24-hour eatery, with big paintings of clowns on the walls and pink pony carpeting. It offers a wide array of coffee-shop fare, including a number of specially marked "heart-smart" (low-fat, low-cholesterol) items.

Stivali's is its new fancy Italian dining room, located in the new shopping arcade. Lunch and dinner are served.

The brass-railed Pizzeria is in the main casino. Latte Express, featuring gourmet coffees, adjoins. Two 24-hour eateries, the **Westside Deli** (in the Main Tower's casino) and the Skyrise Snack Bar (near the race and sports book), round out food options here. The Promenade Cafe is the new coffee shop in the shopping arcade.

In addition there are seven casino bars throughout the Circus Circus complex, notably the carousel-themed Horse-A-Round Bar on the midway level.

The Circus Buffet is discussed in chapter 6.

Services: 24-hour room service (continental breakfast and drinks only), shoe shine.

Facilities: Three casinos, wedding chapel, tour and show desks, car-rental desk, unisex hairdresser, two swimming pools, two video-game arcades, shops (see chapter 9), Grand Slam Canyon Theme Park (see chapter 7).

Adjacent to the hotel is **Circusland RV Park,** with 384 full-utility spaces and up to 50-amp hookups. It has its own 24-hour convenience store, swimming pools, saunas, Jacuzzis, kiddie playground, fenced pet runs, video-game arcade, and community room. The rate is $12 Sunday to Thursday, $16 Friday and Saturday, $18 holidays.

Westward Ho Hotel & Casino

2900 Las Vegas Blvd. S., between Circus Circus Dr. and Convention Center Dr., Las Vegas, NV 89109. ☎ **800/634-6803** or 702/731-2900. 656 rms, 121 suites. A/C TV TEL. $36.90–$56 double; $76 suite. Extra person $10. MC, V. Free parking at your room door.

Located next door to Circus Circus, the Westward Ho is fronted by a vast casino, with rooms in two-story buildings that extend out back for several city blocks. In fact, the property is so large that a free bus shuttles regularly between the rooms and the casino 24 hours a day. There are three swimming pools and three whirlpool spas to serve all areas.

The rooms are clean and adequately furnished motel units. A good buy here: two-bedroom suites with 1¹/₂ baths, living rooms with sofa beds, and refrigerators; they sleep up to six people.

There's a 24-hour restaurant in the casino under a stained-glass skylight dome. It serves a buffet breakfast, brunch and dinner, as well as an à la carte menu featuring traditional coffee-shop fare. Other facilities include a tour desk, free airport shuttle, a gift shop, a casino lounge where a three-piece country band entertains Monday to Saturday from 7pm to 1am, and a deli in the casino serving sandwiches, ribs, and half-pound extra-long hot dogs.

7 Convention Center & Paradise Road

VERY EXPENSIVE

Alexis Park Resort

375 E. Harmon Ave., between Koval Lane and Paradise Rd., Las Vegas, NV 89109. ☎ **800/ 582-2228** or 702/796-3300. Fax 702/796-4334. 500 suites. A/C MINIBAR TV TEL. $99–$139 1-bedroom suite, $175–$250 1-bedroom loft suite, $350–$1,500 larger suite. Extra person $15. Children 18 and under stay free in parents' room. AE, CB, DC, DISC, JCB, MC, V. Free parking (self and valet).

A low-key atmosphere, luxurious digs, and superb service combine to make Alexis Park the hotel choice of many showroom headliners and visiting celebrities. Alan Alda, Alec Baldwin, Whitney Houston, Robert de Niro, Dolly Parton, and Garth Brooks are just a few of the superstars who've chosen this resort's discreet elegance over the glitzier Strip hotels. It's the kind of place where you can get a phone at your restaurant table or your suit pressed at 3am.

You'll sense the difference the moment you approach the palm-fringed entrance-way, fronted by lovingly tended flower beds and a rock waterfall. The elegant lobby has comfortable sofas amid immense terra-cotta pots of ferns, cacti, and calla lilies, and there's notably fine artwork throughout the public areas.

Spacious suites are decorated in light resort colors with taupe lacquer furnishings. Loft suites have cathedral ceilings. All are equipped with refrigerators, wet bars, two-line phones (one in each room of your suite) with computer jacks, and TVs (also one in each room) with HBO and pay-movie options. More than a third of the suites have working fireplaces and/or Jacuzzi tubs.

Dining/Entertainment: Pegasus, an exquisite award-winning gourmet dining room, is described in chapter 6.

The **Pisces Bistro,** under a 30-foot domed ceiling with planters of greenery cascading from tiers overhead, provides live entertainment Tuesday through Saturday nights (see chapter 10) and serves drinks, pizzas, salads, sandwiches, a few full entrees (steak, seafood, pasta), and desserts, both inside and on a patio overlooking the pool.

Services: 24-hour room service, concierge.

Facilities: Gift shop, unisex hair salon, health club (including a good complement of workout equipment, whirlpool, massage, steam, and sauna).

Behind the hotel are beautifully landscaped grounds with palm trees and pines, streams and ponds spanned by quaint bridges, gazebos, rock gardens, flower beds, and oleanders. Here you'll find a large fountain-centered swimming pool, two smaller pools, cabana bars, three whirlpool spas, umbrella tables, table tennis, and a nine-hole putting green.

Courtyard Marriott

3275 Paradise Rd., between Convention Center Dr. and Desert Inn Rd., Las Vegas, NV 89109. ☎ **800/321-2211** or 702/791-3600. Fax 702/796-7981. 137 rms, 12 suites. A/C TV TEL. Sun–Thurs, $109 double; Fri–Sat, $119; $119–$129 suite. Convention rates can be higher. AE, CB, DC, DISC, MC, V. Free parking at your room door.

Housed in three-story terra-cotta–roofed stucco buildings, in an attractively landscaped setting of trees, shrubbery, and flower beds, the Courtyard is a welcome link in the Marriott chain. The concept for these limited-service, lower-priced lodgings (though not especially low-priced for Las Vegas) was developed in the 1980s, and this particular property opened in 1989. Although the services are limited, don't picture a no-frills establishment. This is a beautiful hotel, with a pleasant, plant-filled lobby and very nice rooms indeed.

Like its public areas, the rooms, most with king-size beds, still look spanking new. Decorated in shades of gray-blue, mauve, and burgundy, with sofas and handsome mahogany furnishings (including large desks), they offer TVs with multiple On-Command movie options. All rooms have balconies or patios.

Dining/Entertainment: Off the lobby is a light and airy plant-filled restaurant with glossy oak paneling and tables. It serves buffet breakfasts, as well as à la carte lunches (mostly salads and sandwiches); light fare is available from 5 to 10pm. Adjoining is a comfortable lobby lounge with plush furnishings, a large-screen TV, and a working fireplace. Drinks are served here from 4 to 10pm. You can also enjoy breakfast in this lounge and catch a morning TV news show.

Services: Room service 4 to 10pm, complimentary airport shuttle.

Facilities: Small exercise room, medium-size swimming pool with adjoining whirlpool, picnic tables and barbecue grills, coin-op washers/dryers.

✪ The Hard Rock Hotel & Casino

4455 Paradise Rd., at Harmon Ave., Las Vegas, NV 89109. ☎ **800/473-ROCK** or 702/693-5000. Fax 702/693-5010. 311 rms, 24 suites, 4 executive suites. A/C TV TEL. Sun–Thurs, $75–$250 double, Fri–Sat, $145–$300; from $250 suite. Extra person $25. Children 12 and under stay free in parents' room. AE, CB, DC, DISC, MC, V. Free parking (self and valet).

Owner Peter Morton, who bills his Hard Rock Hotel and Casino as "Vegas for a New Generation," sent out invitations to the property's March 1995 opening inscribed on casino chips bearing the image of Jimi Hendrix. Dozens of celebrities flew in for the festivities, which included concerts by the Eagles and Sheryl Crow. Everything here is rock-themed, from the Stevie Ray Vaughan quote over the entrance ("When this house is a rocking, don't bother knocking, come on in") to the vast collection of music memorabilia displayed in public areas. The house is always "a rocking" (the pulsating beat emanates from hundreds of speakers throughout the property), and the cheerful casino features piano-shaped roulette tables and guitar-neck-handle slot machines. Even the walls of the bell desk are lined with gold records.

Large, attractive rooms, decorated in earth tones with photographs of rock stars adorning the walls, have beds with leather headboards and French windows that actually open to fresh air (a rarity in Las Vegas). Uncharacteristically large 27-inch TVs (most hotel sets are smaller since they want you in the casino, not staring at the tube) offer pay movie options and special music channels.

Dining/Entertainment: The Hard Rock's premier restaurant, **Mortoni's,** is a beauty. Parchment-yellow walls are hung with vintage photographs such as a tuxedoed James Dean at a Hollywood party; Humphrey Bogart, Frank Sinatra, and Grace Kelly at Chasen's in the 1940s; and stills from Las Vegas movies. Furnishings are butter-soft plush red leather. Large windows overlook the pool area, where,

Accommodations East of the Strip

Alexis Park Resort **10**
Best Western Mardi Gras Inn **5**
Courtyard Marriott **4**
Debbie Reynolds Hotel/Hollywood Movie Museum **3**
Emerald Springs Holiday Inn **8**
Fairfield Inn by Marriott **6**
The Hard Rock Hotel & Casino **11**
La Quinta Inn **7**
Las Vegas Hilton **1**
Motel 6 **12**
Residence Inn by Marriott **2**
Sam's Town **13**
Super 8 Motel **9**

Rock 'n' Roll Minimuseum

Fronted by a 90-foot Fender Stratocaster guitar, the Hard Rock is a rock 'n' roll museum displaying a collection of rock-legend memorabilia. Not to be a killjoy, but much of it comes off as rock star discards (and tax write-offs.) There is a large tribute to the late Kurt Cobain, including "I Hope I Die Before I Get Old," a poem written by Pearl Jam's Eddie Vedder after Cobain's death. Though well intentioned, the display can strike one as inappropriate, especially given how Cobain's mixed feelings toward fame contributed in part to his suicide. Still, there are certainly some exhibits that buffs, and others, will find worth viewing:

- Elvis' gold lamé jacket.
- Guitars from Nirvana, ZZ Top, Bruce Springsteen, Bill Haley (from the movie *Rock Around the Clock*), Eric Clapton, and many others.
- James Brown's shoe shine stand (where he wrote songs when he was a kid) and his "King of Soul" cape and crown.
- The dresses the Supremes wore on the *Ed Sullivan Show.*
- A piece of the plane that carried Otis Redding to his death in the late '60s.
- Pete Townshend's smashed guitar from the *Late Night with David Letterman* show.
- The artist formerly known as Prince's handwritten lyrics for a song from *Purple Rain.*
- "Maestro of Love" Barry White's Lifetime Achievement Award.
- The white suit worn by Mick Jagger when he was released from a U.K. jail in the late '60s.
- Greg Allman's favorite biker jacket.
- A collection of surfboards belonging to the Beach Boys.
- An XXL jacket worn on tour by Meat Loaf.
- Las Vegas hotel menus signed by Elvis and Jimi Hendrix.
- More than 500 merchandising items manufactured with the Beatles' images.
- The piano on which Al Green composed "Take Me to the River."

weather permitting, you can dine outdoors at umbrella tables. The fare is Italian, and portions are vast; dinner only.

Mr. Lucky's 24/7 is the hotel's round-the-clock coffee shop, displaying rock memorabilia and old Las Vegas hotel signs. California-style entrees and pizzas are offered in addition to the usual Las Vegas menu.

The **Hard Rock Cafe** (details in chapter 6) is adjacent to the hotel.

The Center Bar in the casino is under a glowing purple dome, from which a globe inscribed with the words "One Love, One World" is suspended. The Beach Club Bar serves light fare and frozen drinks poolside. And the Viva Las Vegas Lounge, off the casino, has a video wall where four monitors display rapid-paced rock footage.

Services: 24-hour room service, concierge.

Facilities: Small video-game arcade, gift/sundry shop and immense Hard Rock retail store, show desk (for **The Joint** only; tickets to other shows can be arranged by the concierge), health club (offering a full complement of Cybex equipment, stair machines, treadmills, massage, and steamrooms).

The Hard Rock has one of the most gorgeous pool areas in Las Vegas, complete with a palm-fringed sandy beach, grassy expanses of lawn, a vast, free-form sand-bottomed pool with a water slide and 150 speakers providing underwater music, several whirlpools, and raft rentals. Luxurious poolside cabanas (equipped with TVs, phones, misters, and refrigerators) can be rented for $55 to $85 a day.

✪ Las Vegas Hilton

3000 Paradise Rd., at Riviera Blvd., Las Vegas, NV 89109. ☎ **800/376-7917** or 702/732-7111. Fax 702/732-5790. 3,174 rms, 305 suites, A/C TV TEL. $95–$279 double. Extra person $25. Children of any age stay free in parents' room. Inquire about attractively priced golf and other packages. CB, DC, DISC, ER, MC, V. Free parking (self and valet).

This is really quite a classy hotel, which is probably why so many business travelers prefer it. (That, and the location next to the convention center.) The lobby, glittering with massive chandeliers and gleaming marble, is lovely, and the casino is actually separate from it. There are quite a few terrific restaurants, plus the largest hotel convention and meeting facilities in the world. Their nightclub (called The Nightclub) is a great place to hang in the evening, and features regular sets by dance music star Kristine W. Colonel Tom Parker's memorial service was held here in the hotel. And one of Elvis' sequined jumpsuits is enshrined in a glass case in the front (he played here).

A serious renovation is adding a number of new shops, plus Star Trek: The Experience, a themed attraction, which should be open by 1998 (the available details are in chapter 7). They want to start attracting more of a leisure crowd, but you do have to wonder how all these additions might change the otherwise high-rent atmosphere.

The rooms are undergoing a remodeling and will have partly marble floors and slightly larger marble bathtubs. Each has a small dressing area outside the bathroom. The rooms are nothing particularly special in terms of decor, but they are very comfortable. Some have views of the adjacent 18-hole golf course. They do feature automatic check-out on the TV and a hotline number on the phone that sends you directly to housekeeping. All offer TVs (cached in handsome armoires) with HBO, On-Command pay-movie options, an in-house information channel, and video checkout capability.

Dining/Entertainment: Bistro Le Montrachet is reviewed in chapter 6.

Most dramatic of the Hilton's restaurants is **Benihana Village,** a pagoda-roofed Oriental fantasyland with cascading waterfalls and meandering streams, spanned by quaint wooden bridges. You'll enjoy dancing water displays and fiber-optic fireworks while you dine. The Village houses three restaurants and a lounge. On one side of the central waterway is the **Garden of the Dragon,** its entrance presided over by a fiery-eyed dragon atop a pagoda. The menu offers regional Chinese specialties; dinner only.

Across the stream is the **Seafood Grille,** fronted by a colorful Asian marketplace aclutter with barrels of eggs (above which are animated hens in wooden cages) and displays of fish, fruits, and vegetables. Seating is under a pagoda eave, walls are hung with fishing nets, and wooden columns are embellished with Chinese kites; dinner only.

At the far end, occupying two dining levels, is a branch of **Benihana,** with a restrained Japanese shoji-screen decor and teppanyaki-grill tables. It's solid Japanese food, but that show, with the chef slicing, dicing, and whirling away at your table, is still a kitsch thrill; dinner only.

Near the entrance to this exotic restaurant complex is the Kabuki Lounge, an inviting setting for cocktails.

The **Hilton Steakhouse,** which also serves seafood and chops, offers a warmly intimate wood-paneled interior with candlelit tables; dinner only.

Another beef eatery is the **Barronshire Room,** where an English club ambience is created by high-backed burgundy leather booths and armchairs, crystal chandeliers and sconces, and walls hung with gilt-framed oil paintings. The restaurant is patterned after the renowned Barronshire Inn in southern England; dinner only.

At the simpatico **MargaritaGrille,** Mexican music, pots of cacti, and displays of papier-mâché birds and pottery combine to create a south-of-the-border ambience. The Grille's bar is quite popular for cocktails and Mexican appetizers; dinner only.

Andiamo, a charming Italian *ristorante,* seats diners amid planters of ficus trees and terra-cotta columns. Above the brass- and copper-accented exhibition kitchen is a colorful display of Italian food products. All pasta and bread served here is made fresh on the premises; dinner only.

Finally there's **The Coffee Shop,** a Southwestern 24-hour facility where lush faux foliage, including hibiscus draped from driftwood beams overhead, gives the room a cheerful ambience. Traditional Las Vegas coffee-shop fare is supplemented by Mexican specialties.

Additional facilities include a branch of **TCBY** and a cappuccino and pastry cart in the lobby. There are seven bar/lounges at the Hilton. In addition, the Garden Snack Bar serves the pool deck; the Paddock Snack Bar in the race and sports book features pizza, sandwiches, and other light fare items (not oats); and the Nightclub, a first-rate casino lounge, which features live entertainment nightly. See also the buffet listings in chapter 6. *Note:* Children 12 and under dine in any Hilton restaurant for half the listed menu prices.

Services: 24-hour room service, foreign-currency exchange.

Facilities: Casino, car-rental desk, tour desk, travel agency, shops, small video-game arcade, business service center (faxing and express mail), multiservice beauty salon/barbershop, jogging trail, 18-hole golf course.

The third-floor roof comprises a beautifully landscaped 8-acre recreation deck with a large swimming pool, a 24-seat whirlpool spa, six Har-Tru tennis courts lit for night play, Ping-Pong, and a putting green. Also on this level is a luxurious, 17,000-square-foot, state-of-the-art health club offering Nautilus equipment, Lifecycles, treadmills, rowing machines, three whirlpool spas, steam, sauna, massage, and tanning beds. Guests are totally pampered: all toiletries are provided; there are comfortable TV lounges; complimentary bottled waters and juices are served in the canteen; and beauty services include facials, oxygen pep-up, and spa body treatments.

EXPENSIVE

La Quinta Inn

3970 Paradise Rd., between Twain Ave. and Flamingo Rd., Las Vegas, NV 89109. ☎ **800/ 531-5900** or 702/796-9000. Fax 702/796-3537. 176 rms, 5 suites. A/C TV TEL. $85–$95 standard double, $89–$99 executive double; $115–$125 suite. Rates include continental breakfast; inquire about seasonal discounts. AE, CB, DC, DISC, MC, V. Free parking (self).

With its four mission-style buildings forming a U around a large courtyard, this La Quinta offers a tranquil alternative to the razzle-dazzle of Strip hotels. Although you're just a minute (and a gratis shuttle ride) from major casinos, you'll feel like you're staying in a countryside retreat. Lovely grounds, with manicured lawns, lovingly tended flower beds, and a charming stone fountain, offer rustic benches, lawn games (croquet, badminton, volleyball), barbecue grills, and picnic tables.

Accommodations are immaculate and attractive. Executive rooms feature one queen-size bed, a small refrigerator, a wet bar, and a microwave oven. Double queens are larger but have no kitchen facilities. And spacious one- and two-bedroom suites contain large living rooms (some with sofa beds), dining areas, and full kitchens. Most accommodations have patios or balconies, and all feature baths with oversized whirlpool tubs. TVs offer satellite channels and HBO.

Dining/Entertainment: Complimentary continental breakfast (juice, bagels, cereal, muffins, fresh fruit, beverages) is served daily in the Patio Café.

Facilities: Car rentals/tours arranged at the front desk, coin-op washers/dryers, medium-size swimming pool and adjoining whirlpool. A free 24-hour shuttle offers pickup and return to and from the airport and several Strip casino hotels.

✪ Residence Inn by Marriott

3225 Paradise Rd., between Desert Inn Rd. and Convention Center Dr., Las Vegas, NV 89109. ☎ **800/331-3131** or 702/796-9300. 144 studios, 48 penthouses. A/C TV TEL. $89–$169 studio; $109–$219 penthouse. Rates include continental breakfast. AE, CB, DC, DISC, MC, V. Free parking (self).

Staying here is like having your own apartment in Las Vegas. The property occupies seven acres of perfectly manicured lawns, tropical foliage, and neat flower beds. It's a great choice for families and business travelers. Monday through Friday, they offer a free light dinner with beer, wine and soda.

Accommodations, most with working fireplaces, are housed in condolike, two-story wood and stucco buildings, fronted by little gardens. Studios have adjoining sitting rooms with sofas and armchairs, dressing areas, and fully equipped eat-in kitchens complete with dishwashers. Every guest receives a welcome basket of microwave popcorn and coffee. TVs offer visitor-information channels and VCRs (you can rent movies nearby), and all rooms have balconies or patios. Duplex penthouses, some with cathedral ceilings, add an upstairs bedroom (with its own bath, phone, TV, and radio) and a full dining room.

Dining/Entertainment: A big continental buffet breakfast (fresh fruit, yogurt, cereals, muffins, bagels, pastries) is served each morning in the gatehouse, a delightful cathedral-ceilinged lobby lounge with a working fireplace. There's comfortable seating amid planters of greenery. Daily papers are set out here each morning; there's a large-screen TV and a stereo for guest use; and a selection of toys, games, and books is available for children. Weekday evenings from 5:30 to 7pm, complimentary buffets with beverages (beer, wine, coffee, soda), fresh popcorn, and daily varying fare soup/salad/sandwiches, tacos, Chinese, barbecue, spaghetti, and so on) are served in the gatehouse. This cocktail-hour spread affords an opportunity to socialize with other guests, a nice feature if you're traveling alone.

Services: Local restaurants deliver food, and there's also a complimentary food-shopping service. Maids wash your dishes.

Facilities: Car-rental desk, barbecue grills, coin-op washers/dryers, sports court (paddle tennis, volleyball, basketball). There's a good-size swimming pool and whirlpool with a sundeck. Guests can use the health club next door at Courtyard Marriott (details below).

MODERATE

Best Western Mardi Gras Inn

3500 Paradise Rd., between Sands Ave. and Desert Inn Rd., Las Vegas, NV 89109. ☎ **800/634-6501** or 702/731-2020. Fax 702/733-6994. 315 minisuites. A/C TV TEL. $40–$125 double. Extra person $8. Children 18 and under stay free in parents' room. AE, CB, DC, DISC, JCB,

Cheap Hotel Alternatives

If you are determined to come to Vegas during a particularly busy season, and you are finding yourself shut out of the prominent hotels, here is a list of moderate to very inexpensive alternatives. We haven't inspected all the rooms or evaluated the service at these places, but most of these are major chain hotels, which brings with it a certain amount of quality control. All are located in decent neighborhoods, and a drive-by indicates that they seem to be well cared for.

On or Near the Strip

Best Value Inn, 167 E. Tropicana; ☎ **702/795-3311**
Budget Suites of America, 1500 Stardust; ☎ **702/732-1500**
Budget Suites of America, 4205 W. Tropicana; ☎ **702/889-1700**
Comfort Inn, 211 E. Flamingo; ☎ **800/634-6774**
Howard Johnson Hotel, 3111 W. Tropicana; ☎ **800/654-2000**
Quality Inn, 377 E. Flamingo; ☎ **800/221-2222**
Travelodge, 3735 S. Las Vegas Blvd.; ☎ **800/225-3050**

Paradise Road & Vicinity

Budget Suites of America, 3684 Paradise; ☎ **702/699-7000**
Crowne Plaza, 4255 Paradise Rd.; ☎ **800/2-CROWNE**

Airport Vicinity

Best Western McCarren, 4970 Paradise Rd.; ☎ **800/528-1234**
Comfort Inn South, 5075 Koval Lane; ☎ **800/221-2222**
Days Inn Airport, 5100 Paradise Rd.; ☎ **800/634-6439**
Howard Johnson Airport, 5100 Paradise Rd.; ☎ **800/446-4656**

Downtown & Vicinity

Best Western Main Street, 100 N. Main St.; ☎ **800/528-1234**
Best Western Mariana, 1322 E. Fremont; ☎ **800/528-1234**
Budget Inn, 301 S. Main St.; ☎ **702/385-5560**
Econo Lodge, 520 S. Casino Center; ☎ **800/233-7706**
Econo Lodge, 1150 S. Las Vegas Blvd.; ☎ **800/424-4777**
Travelodge, 2028 E. Fremont; ☎ **800/578-7878**

East Las Vegas & Vicinity

Budget Suites of America, 4625 Boulder Highway; ☎ **702/454-4625**
Budget Suites of America, 4855 Boulder Highway; ☎ **702/433-3644**
Motel 6 Boulder Highway, 4125 Boulder Highway; ☎ **800/466-8356**
Super 8 Motel, 5288 Boulder Highway; ☎ **800-825-0880**

West Las Vegas & Vicinity

Motel 6, 5085 Industrial Rd. (South Las Vegas); ☎ **800/466-8356**
EZ-8 Motel, 4201 S. Industrial Rd. (South Las Vegas); ☎ **800/32-MOTEL**

MC, V. Free parking at your room door.

Opened in 1980, this well-run little casino hotel has a lot to offer. A block from the convention center and close to major properties, its three-story building sits on nicely landscaped grounds with manicured lawns, trees, and shrubbery. There's a gazebo out back where guests can enjoy a picnic lunch.

Accommodations are all spacious, queen-bedded minisuites with sofa-bedded living room areas and eat-in kitchens, the latter equipped with wet bars, refrigerators, and coffeemakers. All are attractively decorated and offer TVs with HBO and pay-movie options. Staying here is like having your own little Las Vegas apartment.

Dining/Entertainment: A pleasant restaurant/bar off the lobby, open from 6:30am to 11pm daily, serves typical coffee-shop fare; a 12-ounce prime rib dinner here is just $8.95.

Services: Free transportation to/from airport and major Strip hotels.

Facilities: Small casino (64 slots/video poker machines), small video-game arcade, car-rental desk, tour and show desks, coin-op washers/dryers, unisex hairdresser, gift shop, RV parking. The inn has a large swimming pool with a duplex sundeck and whirlpool.

Debbie Reynolds Hotel/Hollywood Movie Museum

305 Convention Center Dr., between Las Vegas Blvd. S. and Paradise Rd., Las Vegas, NV 89109. ☎ **800/633-1777** or 702/734-0711. Fax 702/734-7548. 153 rms, 39 suites, 39 executive suites. A/C TV TEL. Standard $75–$99; $129–$200 suites. Extra person $10. AE, CB, DC, DISC, MC, V. Free parking (self and valet).

Note: At press time, in addition to having lost its gaming license (so the hotel currently has no casino), the Debbie Reynolds Hotel has filed for bankruptcy. At attempt to sell the hotel has fallen through, but Ms. Reynolds and her organization insist that the hotel will stay open and that Ms. Reynolds will continue to perform there, but obviously under the circumstances the future of the place must remain in some doubt.

In 1993, America's sweetheart, musical-comedy star Debbie Reynolds, took over the 12-story Paddlewheel Hotel, transforming its signature paddlewheel facade into a neon-lit revolving film reel and inserting color photographs of Hollywood icons into the frames. Why did Debbie buy a hotel? Ever the vivacious entertainer, she had long dreamed of creating a performance space to her own specifications as well as a museum to house her massive collection of Hollywood memorabilia (see chapter 7). Her Hollywood-glamour concept is an exciting one. Not only does she perform in the showroom, but she has created an after-hours lounge where Strip entertainers (many of whom are her friends) can unwind and take the stage after their shows.

The lobby here is a minimuseum of Hollywood memorabilia: The Baccarat crystal chandeliers overhead are from the film *The Great Waltz,* the marble-topped console tables were used on the sets of *Camille* and *Marie Antoinette,* and a teak opium bed and side chairs from *The Good Earth* are on display. You can even sit down (an unusual feature for a Las Vegas hotel lobby) on a high-backed burgundy brocade ottoman from the 1932 movie *Grand Hotel.*

Large rooms offer great views of the Strip from picture windows. All have sizable dressing areas, TVs with Spectravision movie options, and phones with call waiting. Some accommodations also offer refrigerators, hair dryers, and coffeemakers. In keeping with the hotel's Hollywood theme, walls are hung with large black-and-white photographs of movie legends (perhaps Gable and Lombard will be watching over you). The top three floors house luxurious time-share units; call for details.

Dining/Entertainment: The 24-hour Celebrity Café serves as both a hotel coffee shop and a lounge where Debbie and her Strip entertainer friends can hang out and perform until the wee hours on weekend nights.

And Bogie's Bar, its back wall lined with Bogart movie stills, serves the casino.

Services: 24-hour room service.

Facilities: Large swimming pool with bilevel sundeck, whirlpool, saunas, gift shop, sightseeing/show/tour desk. A large shopping center, just across the street, has a drugstore/pharmacy, post office, dry cleaner, and coin-op laundry. Guests can enjoy health club privileges nearby.

Emerald Springs Holiday Inn

325 E. Flamingo Rd., between Koval Lane and Paradise Rd., Las Vegas, NV 89109. ☎ **800/ 732-7889** or 702/732-9100. Fax 702/731-9784. 132 rms, 18 suites. A/C TV TEL. $69–$99 studio; $99–$129 Jacuzzi suite, $129–$175 hospitality suite. Extra person $15. Children 18 and under stay free in parents' room. AE, CB, DC, DISC, MC, V. Free parking (self).

Housed in three mauve-trimmed peach stucco buildings, Emerald Springs offers a friendly, low-key alternative to the usual glitz and glitter. It's entered via a charming, marble-floored lobby with a waterfall fountain and lush, faux tropical plantings under a domed skylight. Off the lobby is a comfortably furnished lounge with a large-screen TV and working fireplace. Typical of the inn's hospitality is a bowl of apples for the taking at the front desk. And weeknights from 10:30pm to midnight you can "raid the icebox" at the Veranda Café, which offers complimentary cookies, peanut butter and jelly sandwiches, and coffee, tea, or milk. Although your surroundings here are serene, you're only three blocks from the heart of the Strip.

Public areas and rooms here are notably clean and spiffy. Pristine hallways are hung with nice abstract paintings and have small seating areas on every level, and rooms are beautifully decorated in teal and mauve with bleached-oak furnishings. Even the smallest accommodations (studios) offer small sofas, desks, and armchairs with hassocks. You also get two phones (desk and bedside), an in-room coffeemaker (with gratis coffee), and a wet bar with refrigerator. TVs (concealed in an armoire) have HBO and pay-movie options; VCRs are available on request. There's a separate dressing room and a hair dryer in the bath. Suites add a living-room area with a large-screen TV to the above, an eat-in kitchenette with a microwave oven, a larger dressing room, and a Jacuzzi tub. Hospitality suites feature sitting room areas and dining tables.

Dining/Entertainment: Just off the lobby (you can hear the splashing of the fountain and waterfall), the **Veranda Café** offers both indoor and alfresco dining, the latter on a covered patio overlooking the pool. It serves buffet breakfasts and à la carte lunches (burgers, salads, deli sandwiches) and dinners (light fare plus entrees). A comfortable bar/lounge with video poker games adjoins.

Services: Concierge, complimentary limousine transportation to and from the airport and nearby casinos between 6:30am and 11pm (van service available 11pm to 6:30am), room service, business services, gratis newspapers available at the front desk.

Facilities: Fitness room, nice sized pool/sundeck and whirlpool in an attractively landscaped setting.

Fairfield Inn by Marriott

3850 Paradise Rd., between Twain Ave. and Flamingo Rd., Las Vegas, NV 89109. ☎ **800/ 228-2800** or 702/791-0899. Fax 702/791-0899. Web site: www.marriot.com. 129 rms. A/C TV TEL. $61–$150 for up to 5 people. Rates include continental breakfast. AE, CB, DC, DISC, MC, V. Free parking (self).

This pristine property, opened in 1990, is a pleasant place to stay. It has a comfortable lobby with sofas and armchairs, a simpatico setting in which to plan your day's activities over a cup of coffee, tea, or hot chocolate (provided gratis all day).

Rooms are cheerful. Units with king-size beds have convertible sofas, and all accommodations offer well-lit work areas with desks; TVs have free movie channels as well as pay-movie options. Local calls are free.

Breakfast pastries, fresh fruit, juice, and yogurt are served in the lobby each morning, and many restaurants are within easy walking distance. Facilities include a pool/whirlpool and sundeck with umbrella tables. A free shuttle goes to and from the airport every 30 minutes between 6am and midnight. Car rentals and tours can be arranged. The front desk offers warm hospitality.

INEXPENSIVE

Motel 6
195 E. Tropicana Ave., at Koval Lane, Las Vegas, NV 89109. ☎ **800/4-MOTEL-6** or 702/798-0728. Fax 702/798-5657. 602 rms. A/C TV TEL. Sun–Thurs, $33.99 single, Fri–Sat, $51.99 single. Extra person $6. Children under 17 stay free in parents' room. AE, CB, DC, DISC, MC, V. Free parking at your room door.

Fronted by a big neon sign, Las Vegas's Motel 6 is the largest in the country, and it happens to be a great budget choice. Most Motel 6 properties are a little out of the way, but this one is quite close to major Strip casino hotels (the MGM is nearby). It has a big, pleasant lobby, and the rooms, in two-story cream stucco buildings, are clean and attractively decorated. Some rooms have showers only, others, tub/shower baths. Local calls are free and your TV offers HBO.

Three restaurants (including a pleasant 24-hour family restaurant called **Carrows**) adjoin. On-premises facilities include a large, well-stocked gift shop, vending machines, a tour desk, two nice-size swimming pools in enclosed courtyards, a whirlpool, and coin-op washers/dryers.

Super 8 Motel
4250 Koval Lane, just south of Flamingo Rd., Las Vegas, NV 89109. ☎ **800/800-8000** or 702/794-0888. 290 rms. A/C TV TEL. Sun–Thurs, $41–$43 double, Fri–Sat, $56–$58 double. Extra person $8. Children 12 and under stay free in parents' room. Pets $8 per night (one pet only). AE, CB, DC, DISC, MC, V. Free parking (self).

Billing itself as "the world's largest Super 8 Motel," this friendly property occupies a vaguely Tudor-style stone and stucco building. Coffee is served gratis in a pleasant little lobby furnished with comfortable sofas and wing chairs. Rooms are clean and well maintained. Some have safes, and TVs offer free movie channels.

Dining/Entertainment: The nautically themed **Ellis Island Restaurant,** open 24 hours, offers typical coffee-shop fare at reasonable prices. In the adjoining bar—a library-like setting with shelves of books and green marble tables—sporting events are aired on TV monitors. There's also a bar in the casino with a karaoke machine.

Services: Limited room service via Ellis Island, free airport transfer.

Facilities: Casino (actually located next door at Ellis Island; race book and 50 slot/poker/21 machines), small kidney-shaped pool/sundeck and adjoining whirlpool, car-rental desk, coin-op washers/dryers.

8 East Las Vegas

✪ Sam's Town Hotel & Gambling Hall
5111 Boulder Hwy., at Flamingo Rd., Las Vegas, NV 89122. ☎ **800/634-6371** or 702/456-7777. Fax 702/454-8014. 615 rms, 33 suites. A/C TV TEL. $50–$100 double; $140–$240 suite. Extra person $5. AE, CB, DC, DISC, MC, V. Free parking (self and valet).

Just 5 miles from the Strip (which means it's not precisely near anything, but if you have a car, it's also not far) and Western-themed, Sam's Town is immensely popular with locals and tourists alike. Its friendly atmosphere and nightly laser shows make it a good choice for families. The property occupies 58 acres, with accommodations surrounding one of its biggest selling points: Mystic Falls, a lush 25,000-square-foot indoor park under a nine-story skylight. Here, amid leafy trees, fern gullies, fountains, and flower beds, are meandering streams, rock waterfalls, and wildlife, both real (including a dam-building beaver) and animatronic (chirping birds). Lovely year-round, the park is an especially welcome setting in summer when 100°-plus temperatures make it impossible to spend any time outdoors; in this controlled setting, it's always a comfortable 70°. There are chairs and benches, as well as a log pagoda where you can sit in tranquil comfort and read a book, a novelty in this town.

Large, high-ceilinged accommodations overlooking the park or mountains are also notably appealing, with rustic light-wood furnishings, Native American–motif carpeting, cowhide-shaded lighting fixtures, and Western art on the walls. Each room has a large desk and a cable TV offering pay-movie options, keno, and a hotel-information channel. At night the park is lit by lanterns, and trees are strung with thousands of tiny lights.

Dining/Entertainment: Papamios and **The Great Buffet** are described in chapter 6.

Diamond Lil's, an opulent Old West/Victorian crystal-chandeliered gourmet room, seats diners in plush booths lit by fringe-shaded oil lamps; dinner only. A bar/lounge adjoins.

At **Billy Bob's Steak House and Saloon,** also highlighting steak, prime rib, and seafood, log and stone walls are hung with rusty farm implements and paintings of the Old West. A waterwheel in one room creates a pleasant splashy backdrop; dinner only. The Silver Dollar Bar, embellished by a display of animal horns, adjoins.

Willy and Jose's is a "Mexican cantina" with fading wallpapers and neon beer signs over the bar serving traditional Mexican (not Tex-Mex) fare. Twelve-ounce margaritas are 95¢; dinner only.

Mary's Diner, open for all meals, conforms to the traditions of its genre, complete with counter seating and small jukeboxes adjoining its comfortable red leatherette booths. The menu includes Yankee pot roast, meat loaf with real mashed potatoes, homemade chili, and the like.

Smokey Joe's Cafe and Market is the hotel's 24-hour facility, another Western setting with knotty-pine booths, faux windows overlooking a cowboy town mural, and walls hung with washboards and antique farm implements. Coffee shop fare is supplemented by a full Chinese menu. Great deals here include inexpensive buffets at breakfast and terrific all-you-can-eat salad bars at lunch and dinner, not to mention graveyard specials such as three eggs, a $3/4$-pound ham steak, hash browns, and toast served from 11pm to 11am for $2.95.

Another 24-hour facility is the Final Score Sports Bar, where you'll find pool tables, darts, pinball, air hockey, and a basketball cage; sporting events are aired on more than 30 TV monitors, and there's occasionally live music for dancing. Light fare (burgers, wings, nachos) is available, and there's patio seating overlooking the pool.

Roxy's Saloon, one of 13 bars on the premises, offers live entertainment (C&W) for dancing daily from noon to the wee hours. Rounding out facilities here are: a deli in the race and sports book area, a bowling alley snack bar, a food court, an ice cream parlor, and a rotating bar in the park.

Services: Room service, foreign currency exchange, shoe shine; free shuttle bus to/from the Stardust, MGM, Bally's, Fremont, and California hotels.

Facilities: Casino, two RV parks ($14 a night with complete hook-up), 56-lane bowling alley open 24 hours, 25,000-square-foot Western shop, dance hall, gift/logo shop, sand volleyball court, country dance hall.

9 Downtown

EXPENSIVE

✪ Golden Nugget

129 E. Fremont St., at Casino Center Blvd., Las Vegas, NV 89101. ☎ **800/634-3454** or 702/ 385-7111. Fax 702/386-8362. 1,805 rms, 102 suites. A/C TV TEL. $49–$299 double; $275–$500 suite. Extra person $20. AE, CB, DC, DISC, MC, V. Free parking (self and valet).

The Golden Nugget opened in 1946, the first building in Las Vegas constructed specifically for casino gambling. Steve Wynn took it over as his first major project in Vegas, in 1973. He gradually transformed the Old West/Victorian interiors (typical for downtown) into something more high rent; marble and brass gleams and the whole package seems considerably more resortlike and genuinely luxurious, especially for downtown Vegas. The sunny interior spaces are a welcome change from the Las Vegas tradition of dim lighting. Don't forget their mascot (well, it ought to be): the world's largest gold nugget. The Hand of Faith nugget weighs in at 61 pounds, 11 ounces.

If the decor of the Mirage sounded appealing to you and you want to stay downtown, come here, since the same people own them and the rooms look almost identical. In keeping with the name, the color scheme in the newly refurbished rooms is gold (rather than the beiges of the Mirage), but features they do share include the marble entryways, half-canopy beds, vanity tables with magnifying make-up mirrors, armoires, and marble bathrooms complete with hair dryers. Cable TVs feature pay-movie options. In the North Tower, the rooms are slightly larger than in the South (and also slightly larger than at the Mirage). Suites are done in darker colors, and include a good-sized parlor with a wet bar. Each has two different bathrooms, one for men and one for women (the latter has Jacuzzi jet tubs and potpourri!), each with its own TV. You don't have to walk through the casino to get to your room, but you do have to walk a distance to get to the pool. During the winter, they put up a pavilion over part of the pool deck space to give themselves more interior space.

Dining/Entertainment: The **Carson Street Cafe,** the Nugget's 24-hour restaurant, and its superb buffets and 24-hour Sunday brunch are described in chapter 6.

Stefano's, off a gorgeous marble-floored courtyard, offers a festive setting for northern Italian cuisine, complete with singing waiters. Murals of Venice behind trellised "windows" are designed to look like scenery, and baroque elaboration includes cupids, ornate columns, and gilt-framed mirrors. The wait staff sings Italian opera; dinner only.

The opulent **Lillie Langtry's** is adorned with beveled and gilt-framed mirrors, gilded wood flowers, Chinese art, and a lovely painting of swans. It's a lovely setting, softly lit and enhanced by a backdrop of piano and harp music. The menu is Chinese; dinner only.

This branch of the **California Pizza Kitchen** is a plush precinct with an exhibition kitchen housing an oak-burning pizza oven. In addition to pizzas with trendy toppings the menu offers calzones, salads, pasta, and other entrees. Open for lunch and dinner daily.

In addition, a 24-hour snack bar in the casino offers deli sandwiches, pizza, and light fare, and there are four casino bars including the elegant **Claude's** and the 38 Different Kinds of Beer Bar.

Services: 24-hour room service, shoe shine, concierge.

Facilities: Casino, car-rental desk, full-service unisex hair salon, shops (gifts, jewelry, designer fashions, sportswear, logo items), video-game arcade.

The Nugget's top-rated health club offers a full line of Universal equipment, Lifecycles, StairMasters, treadmills, rowing machines, Gravitron, free weights, steam sauna, tanning beds, and massage. Salon treatments include everything from leg waxing to seaweed-mask facials. Free Sebastian products are available for sprucing up afterward. The spa's opulent Palladian-mirrored foyer is modeled after a salon in New York's Frick Museum.

The entrance to the hotel's immense swimming pool and outdoor whirlpool spa is graced by elegant marble swans and bronze fish sculptures. Fountains, palm trees, and verdant landscaping create a tropical setting, and a poolside bar serves the sundeck.

MODERATE

Days Inn Downtown

707 E. Fremont St., at 7th St., Las Vegas, NV 89101. ☎ **800/325-2344,** 800/325-2525, or 702/388-1400. Fax 702/388-9622. 140 rms, 7 suites. A/C TV TEL. $40–$65 1-bedroom; $45–$80 2-bedroom (rates are for up to 4 people; may be higher during special events). "Super Saver" rate ($39 Sun–Thurs, $50 Fri–Sat) if you reserve 30 days in advance via the toll-free number 800/325-2525 (subject to availability). AE, CB, DC, DISC, MC, V. Free parking (self).

Opened in 1988, this Days Inn still looks quite new. Rooms, in a U-shaped three-story building, are cheerfully decorated and have TVs offering pay movies. On-premises facilities comprise a rooftop pool and sundeck, a few video games, and the Culinary Restaurant, serving coffee-shop fare at all meals.

✪ Fitzgeralds Casino Holiday Inn

301 Fremont St., at 3rd St., Las Vegas, NV 89101. ☎ **800/274-LUCK** or 702/388-2400. Fax 702/388-2181. 638 rms, 14 suites. A/C TV TEL. $40–$85 double, $60–$105 suite. Extra person $10. Children under 19 stay free in parents' room. AE, CB, DC, DISC, MC, V. Free parking (self and valet).

Fitzgeralds recently became a Holiday Inn franchise, and have upgraded all their rooms to fit said chain's code. The result is attractive and received an award for Best Redesign from the Governor's Conference. Outside, a model of Mr. O'Lucky, their very tall (45-foot) leprechaun mascot oversees a new sign; neon coins pour from a rainbow into a pot of gold. (Elsewhere, you can rub a piece of the Blarney stone for luck.) The restaurants have all been given serious facelifts, and a sort of Irish country village walkway, complete with big giant fake tree, leads to the room elevators. Fitzgerald's has the only balcony in downtown from which you can watch the Fremont Street Experience. You can also sit in their McDonald's and gawk at the light show through the atrium windows.

The look in the rooms is clean and comfortable, standard hotel room decor, done in shades of green (no, the leprechaun theme does not follow in here). Because this is the tallest building in downtown (34 stories), you get excellent views; either snow-capped mountains, downtown lights, or the Strip. Jacuzzi tub rooms are $20 more and are slightly larger with wrap-around windows. All offer safes and 25-inch TVs with pay-movie options.

Dining/Entertainment: Limericks, an upscale Irish pub is described in chapter 6.

Vincenzo's is moderately priced, unexciting Italian/seafood restaurant designed to look like a Tuscan village.

Molly's **Country Kitchen** is their coffee shop and looks like an Irish cottage (sort of).

The balcony of the second-floor Lookout Lounge (featuring Irish drinks) is a good

Accommodations Downtown

California Hotel/Casino & RV Park 3
Days Inn Downtown 10
El Cortez Hotel & Casino 9
Fitzgeralds Casino Holiday Inn 8
Four Queens 7
Golden Nugget 4
Jackie Gaughan's Plaza Hotel/Casino 2
Lady Luck Casino Hotel 6
Main Street Station 1
Sam Boyd's Fremont Hotel & Casino 5
Showboat 11

1-0406

vantage point for viewing the Fremont Street Experience. A **McDonald's** and three bars are on the casino floor.

Services: 24-hour room service, complimentary gaming lessons.

Facilities: Casino, tour and show desks, car-rental desk, gift shop, jewelry shop.

✪ Four Queens

202 Fremont St., at Casino Center Blvd., Las Vegas, NV 89101. ☎ **800/634-6045** or 702/385-4011. Fax 702/387-5122. 662 rms, 38 suites. A/C TV TEL. $59–$179 double; $119–$350 suite. Extra person $10. Children under 2 stay free in parents' room. AE, CB, DC, DISC, MC, V. Free parking (self and valet).

Opened in 1966 with a mere 120 rooms, the Four Queens (named for the owner's four daughters) has evolved over the decades into a major downtown property occupying an entire city block. You walk past their glittering lights facade and into their small, but elegant—in a slightly faded, slightly dated way (with mirrors and huge chandeliers)—lobby and you just know you are in old Las Vegas. And are glad. As the staff says, this is the place to stay if you just want to gamble. Their clientele is on the older side (50-plus), who are not coming to Las Vegas for the first time.

Notably nice rooms, decorated in basic hotel room style, are located in 19-story twin towers. Especially lovely are the North Tower rooms, decorated in a southwestern motif and, in most cases, offering views of the Fremont Street Experience. South Tower rooms are done up in earth tones with dark wood furnishings and wallpapers in small floral prints. Minisuites, decorated in traditional styles, have living rooms (separated from the bedrooms by a trellised wall) and dining areas, double-sink baths, and dressing areas. All accommodations offer TVs with in-house information and pay-movie channels. Some rooms are equipped with small refrigerators and coffeemakers.

Dining/Entertainment: Hugo's Cellar is described in chapter 6.

At **Lailani's Island Café,** a whimsical Hawaiian cafeteria with colorful tropical murals on its walls, diners are entertained by island music, a 3-foot talking macaw, dancing flowers in dugout canoes, a five-headed totem pole with eyes that light up, and a fiber-optic light show overhead. Lunch and dinner are served.

Pastina's Italian Bistro is somewhat more traditional, though it, too, has a vaulted fiber-optic ceiling with shooting stars and swirling galaxies. The menu features a choice of pastas and traditional Italian entrees; dinner only.

Magnolia's Veranda, a 24-hour dining facility overlooking the casino, has three sections: a casual plant-filled cafe, an adjoining "courtyard," and a rather elegant crystal-chandeliered dining area adorned with murals of New Orleans. The same menu is offered throughout. Besides the requisite coffee-shop fare, Magnolia's offers Hawaiian specialties. A great deal here is the $4.95 prime rib dinner served from 6pm to 2am.

Hugo's has a cozy lounge with a working fireplace, and two bars serve the casino.

Services: 24-hour room service.

Facilities: Gift shop, car-rental desk, tour and show desks, small video-game arcade, plus a basic workout room that is free.

INEXPENSIVE

California Hotel/Casino & RV Park

12 Ogden Ave., at 1st St., Las Vegas, NV 89101. ☎ **800/634-6255** or 702/385-1222. Fax 702/ 388-2660. 781 rms, 74 suites. A/C TV TEL. Sun–Thurs, $50 double, Fri–Sat, $60; holidays, $70. Extra person $5. Children 12 and under stay free in parents' room. AE, CB, DC, DISC, MC, V. Free parking (self and valet).

This is a hotel with a unique personality. California-themed, it markets mostly in Hawaii, and since 85% of the guests are from the "Aloha State," it offers Hawaiian entrees in several of its restaurants and even has an on-premises store specializing in Hawaiian foodstuff. You'll also notice that dealers are wearing colorful Hawaiian shirts. Of course, everyone is welcome to enjoy the aloha spirit here.

The rooms, however, reflect neither California nor Hawaii. Decorated in contemporary-look burgundy/mauve or apricot/teal color schemes, they have mahogany furnishings and attractive marble baths. In-room safes are a plus, and TVs offer pay-per-view movies and keno channels.

Dining/Entertainment: With its redwood paneling and massive stone fireplace, the **Redwood Bar and Grill,** featuring steak and seafood, looks like an elegant ski lodge. There's piano bar entertainment in the adjoining lounge; dinner only.

The **Pasta Pirate,** themed to suggest a coastal cannery warehouse, has a corrugated-tin ceiling and exposed overhead pipes. Walls are hung with neon signs and historic pages from the *San Francisco Chronicle.* Italian, steak, and seafood entrees are featured; dinner only.

Also evoking San Francisco is the rather charming **Market Street Café,** a 24-hour facility. The menu lists all the expected coffee-shop fare, as well as Hawaiian items and specially marked "heart-smart" choices.

The **Cal Club Snack Bar,** a casual cafeteria/ice-cream parlor, serves sundaes, along with Hawaiian soft drinks (flavors like guava and island punch) and Chinese/ Japanese snack fare.

There are two 24-hour casino bars: the Main Street Bar and the San Francisco Pub.

Dave's Aloha Bar on the mezzanine level is a tropical setting for exotic cocktails, liqueur-spiked coffees and ice-cream drinks, and international beers.

Services: Room service (breakfast only).

Facilities: Casino, car-rental desk, car wash, small rooftop pool, small video-game arcade, shops (gift shop, chocolates). A food store carries items popular with Hawaiians and there are several umbrella tables outside where these snacks can be eaten.

El Cortez Hotel & Casino

600 Fremont St., between 6th and 7th sts., Las Vegas, NV 89101. ☎ **800/634-6703** or 702/ 385-5200. 404 rms, 14 minisuites. A/C TV TEL. $32 double; $40 minisuite. Extra person $3. AE, CB, DC, DISC, JCB, MC, V. Free parking (self and valet).

This small hotel is popular with locals for its casual, "just-folks" downtown atmosphere and its frequent big-prize lotteries (up to $50,000) based on Social Security numbers. The nicest accommodations are the enormous minisuites in the newer, 14-story tower. Some are exceptionally large king-bedded rooms with sofas; others have separate sitting areas with sofas, armchairs, and tables, plus small dressing areas. The rooms in the original building are furnished more traditionally and with less flair, and they cost less. Local calls are just 25¢.

Roberta's Café is an elegant candlelit restaurant featuring charbroiled steaks and seafood; dinner only.

There's also a large 24-hour coffee shop called the **Emerald Room,** where you can enjoy a bacon-and-eggs breakfast with hash browns, toast, and coffee for $1. A "soup-to-nuts" 18-ounce porterhouse steak dinner is $6.45 here. Four bars serve the casino.

On-premises facilities include a small video-game arcade, beauty salon, gift shop, and barbershop.

Under the same ownership is **Ogden House,** just across the street, with rooms that go for just $18 a night.

Jackie Gaughan's Plaza Hotel/Casino

1 Main St., at Fremont St., Las Vegas, NV 89101. ☎ **800/634-6575** or 702/386-2110. Fax 702/386-2378. 876 rms, 161 suites. A/C TV TEL. $40–$120 double; $80–$150 suite. Extra person $8. Children under 12 stay free in parents' room. AE, DC, DISC, MC, V. Free parking (self and valet).

Built in 1971 on the site of the old Union Pacific Railroad Depot, the Plaza, a double-towered, 3-block-long property, permanently altered the downtown skyline. Las Vegas's Amtrak station (currently unused) is right in the hotel, and the main Greyhound terminal adjoins it.

Accommodations are spacious and attractively decorated, with king rooms offering plush sofas.

Dining/Entertainment: The **Center Stage Restaurant,** offering fabulous views of Glitter Gulch and the Fremont Street Experience, is described in chapter 6.

The '50s-motif **Plaza Diner,** open 24 hours a day and agleam with chrome, features red leatherette booths and a Wurlitzer-style jukebox stocked with oldies. Typical diner fare is featured, everything from a BLT to a stack of hotcakes. A noteworthy special is the full roast prime rib dinner for $5.95, available from 10am to midnight (midnight to 10am it's just $4.95).

At the **Back Stage,** comfortable leather booths, walls hung with still-life oil paintings, stained-glass windows, and brass candelabra chandeliers combine to create a warmly inviting ambience. Open for breakfast and lunch, the latter featuring sandwiches, salads, and Cajun specialties.

Other food and beverage facilities include an ice-cream parlor, Coffee and Cravings for gourmet coffees and fresh-baked goods, a 24-hour casino snack bar, several casino cocktail bars, and the Omaha Lounge offering live entertainment in the casino almost around the clock.

Services: Guest-services desk (also handles in-house shows), tour desk.

Facilities: Casino, car-rental desk, shops, a wedding chapel, beauty salon/barbershop. There's a sports deck with a nice-sized swimming pool, a ¼-mile outdoor jogging track, and four Har-Tru tennis courts.

Lady Luck Casino Hotel

206 N. 3rd St., at Ogden Ave., Las Vegas, NV 89101. ☎ **800/523-9582** or 702/477-3000. Fax 702/382-2346. Web site www.lady-luck.com/ladyluck/. 649 rms, 143 suites. A/C TV TEL. $40–$155 double; Sun–Thurs $55–$75 junior suite, Fri–Sat $70–$105. Extra person $8. AE, CB, DC, DISC, JCB, MC, V. Free parking (self and valet).

What is today Lady Luck opened in 1964 as Honest John's, a 2,000-square-foot casino with five employees, five pinball machines, and 17 slots. Today that casino occupies 30,000 square feet, and the hotel, including sleek 17- and 25-story towers, is a major downtown player taking up an entire city block. What it retains from earlier times is a friendly atmosphere, one that has kept customers coming back for decades. Eighty percent of Lady Luck's clientele is repeat business.

Neon tubing overhead around the casino and hotel is color coded to your room key, so you know which way to the particular tower where you are staying. This is good as one of those towers is actually across the street (an over-the-street enclosed walkway takes you there). Tower rooms are decorated in a variety of attractive color schemes, mostly using muted Southwestern hues and handsome oak furnishings. It's all larger, brighter, and lighter than you might expect (though again, a variation on familiar hotel room decor). Rooms also have full length mirrors. The bathroom amenities come in a red plastic, heart-shaped container. All rooms are equipped with small refrigerators and TVs with pay-per-view movie options. Junior suites in the West Tower have parlor areas with sofas and armchairs, separate dressing areas, and baths with whirlpool tubs. The original Garden Rooms are a little smaller and less spiffy-looking in terms of decor; on the plus side, they're right by the pool, which is not heated, by the way (but there aren't a lot of pools in downtown).

Dining/Entertainment: The **Burgundy Room** evokes Paris in the 1930s, with plush velvet-upholstered booths and a display of period art including lithographs and original prints by Erté, Poucette, and Salvador Dalí. Elegantly appointed tables are lit by Venetian hurricane lamps. The menu highlights steak, pasta, and fresh seafood; dinner only.

The **Emperor's Room** is also enhanced by museum-quality paintings, sculpture, and screens from the owner's collection, including an exact replica of a work called "Soldiers of Xian" dating from 2000 B.C. It's an elegant setting, with candlelit tables and a Persian rug on the floor. Cantonese, Mandarin, and Szechuan entrees are offered; dinner only.

At the southwestern-themed, 24-hour **Winners' Café,** a basic coffee-shop menu is augmented by Mexican and Polynesian specialties.

In addition, there are daily buffets (details in chapter 6), and ESPN sports are aired on three TV monitors in the Casino Bar.

Services: 24-hour room service, multilingual front desk, and complimentary airport shuttle.

Facilities: Casino, tour and show desks, car-rental desk, gift shop, unheated swimming pool and sundeck.

✪ Main Street Station

200 N. Main St., between Fremont and I-95, Las Vegas, NV 89101. ☎ **800/465-0711** or 702/

387-1896. Fax 702/388-2660. 392 rms, 14 suites. A/C TV TEL. Sun–Thurs, $45 double, Fri–Sat, $55, holidays and conventions, $65. AE, CB, DC, DISC, MC, V. Free parking (valet and self).

Though not actually on Fremont Street, the Main Street Station is just two short blocks away, barely a 3-minute walk. Considering how terrific it is, this is hardly an inconvenience. Having taken over an abandoned hotel space, the Main Street Station reopened in November 1996 to become, in our opinion, one of the nicest hotels in downtown and one of the best bargains in the city. The overall look is, admittedly as usual for downtown, turn-of-the-century San Francisco. However, unlike everywhere else, the details here are outstanding, producing a beautiful hotel by any measure. Outside, gas lamps flicker on wrought-iron railings and stained glass windows. Inside are hammered tin ceilings, ornate antique-style chandeliers, and lazy ceiling fans. The small lobby is filled with wood panels, long wooden benches, and a front desk straight out of the Old West with an old-timey key cabinet with beveled glass windows. (Check out the painting of a Victorian gambling scene to the left of the front desk.) Even the cashier cages look like antique brass bank teller's cages. Over the casino bar, rattan blade fans rotate horizontally rather than vertically. It's all very Victorian, and even though faux it feels authentic. It's also incredibly appealing and just plain pretty.

Though a small-sized hotel, they pack a lot in. The stylish microbrew pub is described in detail in chapter 7. The setting for both the buffet and the Pullman Grille restaurant are uncommonly pretty, especially for Downtown. And the casino, thanks to some high ceilings, is one of the most smoke-free around. An enclosed bridge connects the hotel with the California across the street, where you will find shopping and a kids' arcade.

The long and narrow rooms are possibly the largest in downtown. The ornate decorating downstairs does not extend up here. White-painted, wooded plantation shutters replace the usual curtains; each room has a very large gilt-framed mirror; the simple but not unattractive furniture is vaguely French provincial, done in medium tone neutrals. It's all clean and in good taste. The bathrooms are small but well appointed. It should be noted that rooms on the north side overlook the freeway, and the railroad track is nearby. The soundproofing seems quite strong—we couldn't hear anything when inside, but then again, we are from Los Angeles. A few guests have complained about noise in these rooms, but the majority have had no problems. If you are concerned, request a room on the south. Each room has Nintendo for a charge and movies for free.

Dining/Entertainment: 777 (Triple 7) Microbrew Pub and Grill is described in detail in chapter 11. The excellent buffet is described in chapter 6.

The **Pullman Grille** is the steak and seafood place, and is much more reasonably priced that similar (and considerably less pretty) places in town. The doors leading to the mahogany dining room are made of massive wood with copper relief figures on them, recycled from a turn-of-the-century mansion, as was the ornate bar and large stone fireplace. Part of the restaurant is a real Pullman train car. It has been turned into the cigar car, where a choice of smokes will be offered guests who are ensconced in cushy Victorian furniture. All the old details are here, including some lovely velvet drapes. Strangely, when empty, the car does not smell like smoke, and it certainly does not trickle into the restaurant proper. (That was the whole idea of having a separate smoking car.)

The **Cascade Cafe** is a 24-hour coffee shop. You order a variety of cheap meals (including some Asian cuisine) at a window.

Services: Dry cleaning and laundry service, in-room massage, safety deposit boxes.

Facilities: Gift shop, show desk, shopping and game room arcade at California Hotel accessible via connecting walkway.

Sam Boyd's Fremont Hotel & Casino

200 E. Fremont St., between Casino Center Blvd. and 3rd St., Las Vegas, NV 89101. ☎ **800/ 634-6182** or 702/385-3232. Fax 702/385-6229. 428 rms, 24 suites. A/C TV TEL. $35–$80 double. Extra person $8. Children under 12 stay free in parents' room. AE, CB, DC, DISC, JCB, MC, V. Free parking (valet).

When it opened in 1956, the Fremont was the first high-rise in downtown Las Vegas. Wayne Newton got his start here, singing in the now-defunct Carousel Showroom. Rooms offer safes and TVs with in-house information channels and pay-movie options.

Dining/Entertainment: The Fremont boasts a gorgeous oak-paneled art deco restaurant called the **Second Street Grill.** Diners are comfortably ensconced in plush leather booths and oversized chairs at candlelit tables. A handsome bar adjoins. The menu, highlighting steaks and seafood, is contemporary American with international overtones; dinner only.

A branch of **Tony Roma's, A Place for Ribs,** offers scrumptious barbecued chicken and smoky, fork-tender baby back ribs, juicy charbroiled steaks, and fresh seafood. A children's menu is a plus. The walls of this handsome plant-filled restaurant are hung with historic photographs of Las Vegas; dinner only.

The **Lanai Cafe** is a comfortable 24-hour coffee shop, with a wide-ranging American and Chinese menu. Specials here include a full prime/rib dinner ($5.95) or a steak and lobster tail dinner ($9.99). The Lanai Express, a tiny cafeteria also featuring American and Chinese fare, adjoins.

The Fremont also has great buffets (see chapter 6 for details). There are bars in the casino, race and sports book, and keno lounge.

Services: Room service at breakfast only.

Facilities: Casino, 24-hour gift shop. Guests can use the swimming pool and RV park at the nearby California Hotel, another Sam Boyd enterprise.

Showboat

2800 Fremont St., between Charleston Blvd. and Mojave Rd., Las Vegas, NV 89104. ☎ **800/ 826-2800** or 702/385-9123. Fax 702/383-9238. 450 rms, 4 suites, 2 executive suites. A/C TV TEL. $29–$139 double; $149–$189 1-bedroom suite, $195–$215 2-bedroom suite. Extra person $10. Children under 12 stay free in parents' room. AE, CB, DC, DISC, MC, V. Free parking (self and valet).

Near to neither the Strip nor downtown, the 40-year-old Showboat is easy to miss, but a recent renovation makes it worth a look, if location isn't an issue. Instead of the "showboat" look of old, it has gone more in a Mardi Gras/old-time Louisiana direction, with Victorian interiors (moldings, distressed paint, and other touches) plus murals of Mississippi plantations and riverboats, and stunning Venetian-glass chandeliers in the lobby. The result is very clean, bright, and pretty. It's a good-looking hotel, with a casino popular with locals. Opened in 1954, it was the first hotel to offer buffet meals and bingo, not to mention bowling alleys. And the bowling alley, North America's largest, hosts major PBA tournaments.

The rooms are small but follow the same New Orleans theme with appropriate wall finish and wallpaper borders. They have dressing areas equipped with cosmetic mirrors. You'll find a hair dryer and extra phone in the bath, and TVs offer pay-movies and hotel-information stations. The medium-size pool is nothing special.

Dining/Entertainment: The **Plantation** keeps to the garden theme. One room evokes a veranda with white porch railings backed by exquisite botanical murals; the other is more elegant, with Palladian windows and ornate Victorian chandeliers.

Together they comprise a lovely setting in which to enjoy mesquite-grilled steaks and seafood specialties; dinner only.

DiNapoli diverges from the New Orleans theme with Roman frescoes, columns, and classical statuary. The menu features California-inspired southern Italian cuisine as well as seafood specialties; dinner only.

And the delightful 24-hour Mardi Gras–themed **Showboat Coffee Shop** extends into the casino with cafe seating.

There's also an adequate buffet here (details in chapter 6), and a snack bar and a bar/lounge are located in the Bowling Center. Several bars serve the casino, including the Mardi Gras Room, which features quality lounge acts and occasional bigger names such as Juice Newton, Sha Na Na, Chubby Checker, and Lacy J. Dalton. When headliners appear, there's a two-drink minimum.

Services: 24-hour room service, shoe shine.

Facilities: Casino, gift shop, beauty salon/barbershop, 24-hour Bowling Center with 106 lanes, bowling pro shop, video-game arcade; Olympic-size swimming pool in a courtyard setting.

10 A Hostel

Las Vegas International Hostel

1208 Las Vegas Blvd. S., between Charleston and Oakey blvds., Las Vegas, NV 89104. ☎ **702/ 385-9955**. Capacity: 60 people. A/C. $14 bed in a dorm room with shared bath accommodating 4 people; $28 private room with shared bath. There's a $2 surcharge for 1-night stays on weekends. AYH and AAIH members receive discounted rates. No credit cards. Free parking (self).

This American Association of International Hostels (AAIH) facility, the only legitimate hostel in town, houses clean but spartan rooms in a two-story building. Upstairs rooms are a tad nicer, with balconies and polished pine floors (ceramic tile downstairs). You get a free sheet and pillowcase and pay $1 for a top sheet, blanket, and towels. Gratis coffee, tea, and lemonade are available in the lounge throughout the day. There are two lounges offering TVs, VCRs (and tapes), stereos, books, and games. Other facilities include barbecue grills, picnic tables, and chaise longues out back; coin-op washers/dryers; a fully equipped kitchen; and bicycle racks and lockup. The host arranges excursions to Hoover Dam; Red Rock Canyon; Mount Charleston; Valley of Fire; and Bryce, Zion, and Grand canyons, and the friendly staff is knowledgeable about local sights and restaurants.

July and August are the busiest months for the hostel, though these are the slowest months elsewhere in town. Hence, if you want to stay here because you like hosteling as a way of life, reserve several weeks in advance. On the other hand, if you're considering a hostel only to save money, try bargaining with Strip hotels in their off-season; you might be able to obtain very low rates.

Note: Although conveniently located (the Sahara Hotel is just a few blocks away), this stretch of Las Vegas Boulevard South is rather seedy. It may not be a good choice for women traveling alone; and it's not wise for anyone to walk around the area alone at night.

6 Dining in Las Vegas

Among the many images that people have of Las Vegas is cheap food deals, bargains so good the food is practically free. They think of the buffets, all a small country can eat, only $3.99!

All that is true, but frankly, eating in Las Vegas is no longer something you don't have to worry about budgeting for. The buffets are certainly there—no good hotel would be without one—as are the cheap meal deals, but you get what you pay for. Some of the cheaper buffets, and even the more moderately priced ones, are mediocre at best, ghastly and inedible at worst. And we don't even want to think about those 69¢ cup of beef stew specials.

Also, in terms of fine dining, for the most part, Vegas is stuck in an unimaginative time warp. A hotel's star restaurant will more than likely be yet another overpriced steak and seafood joint. *Gourmet* here means anything à la orange or flambé. On top of all this, anything cheap (a buffet, a special meal deal) or any place located in a popular hotel-casino will certainly attract a long line. Sometimes you can wait more than an hour for the privilege of paying too much for a disappointing meal.

Which is not to say there isn't hope. Little by little, quality restaurants have been sneaking into Las Vegas. Wolfgang Puck's Spago, Emeril Lagasse's Emeril's New Orleans Fish House (serving stunning Creole seafood), Gatsby's (the MGM Grand's gourmet restaurant, which even hard-core foodie snobs say serves some of the best food they've ever eaten), the Fog City Diner, and Mark Miller's Coyote Cafe all would be standouts in any other major city. Reliable chains such as Lawry's and Il Fornaio have crept in during the last year. The Enigma Cafe, located in the slowly burgeoning Gateway artists district (right between the Strip and downtown so it's accessible to both), offers up healthful, interesting food at prices comparable to some of the best hotel meal deals in town. Best of all, if you look, there are small ethnic joints popping up all over the place. Get off the Strip and go looking for them.

Which is actually part of the problem. Staying on the Strip, if you don't have the mobility of a car, severely limits your food options. Getting outside of those enormous hotel resorts is a major proposition (and don't think that's not done on purpose), which is why so often visitors settle for what the hotel has to offer, long lines, diminished quality, and all. Walking to another hotel—on the Strip, yet another major investment of time—means probably encountering much the same thing. But not always. Once, faced with dismal breakfast choices, we went from the Mirage over to Caesars, landing in their Forum Shops where the Stage Deli stood, largely empty and with considerably better munchie options.

OUR BEST LAS VEGAS RESTAURANT ADVICE

GETTING IN   There are tricks to surviving dining in Vegas. If you can, make reservations in advance, particularly for the better restaurants (you might well get to town, planning to check out some of the better eateries, only to find they are totally booked throughout your stay). Eat as much as you can during off hours, which admittedly are hard to find. But you know that noon to, say, 1:30 or 2 is going to be prime for lunch, and 5:30 to 8:30 (and just after the early shows get out) for dinner. Speaking of time, give yourself plenty of it, particularly if you have to catch a show. We once tried to grab a quick bite in the Riviera, before running up to "La Cage." The only choice was the food court, where long lines in front of all the (fast food chains only) stands left us with about 5 minutes to gobble something decidedly unhealthy.

STAYING HEALTHY   *Unhealthy* is the watchword here; if you don't care about your heart or your waistline, you will do just fine in Vegas. (And really, what says "vacation" more than a cream sauce?) But slowly, salads are making their way silently on to the menus, and some more health-conscious restaurants are opening. You just have to look for them. (The reviews below may give you some hints.) You can always stick to brand names; every fast food restaurant is here, usually in several places, and a number of reliable coffee shop chains are also around. And we certainly don't mean to take away any enjoyment of those extravagant buffets; heck, that's a major part of the fun of Vegas! We insist on eating at at least one during every visit we make. Excess is the watchword here, and what better symbol is there than mounds of shrimp and unlimited prime rib?

SAVING MONEY   The late night specials—a complete steak meal for just a couple dollars—are also an important part of a good, decadent Vegas experience (and a huge boon for insomniacs). And having complained about how prices are going up, you still can eat cheaply and decently (particularly if you are only looking upon food as fuel) all over town. The locals repeatedly say that they almost never cook, because in Vegas, it is always cheaper to eat out. To locate budget fare, see the box on the subject below and check local newspapers (especially Friday editions) and free magazines (such as *Vegas Visitor* and *What's On in Las Vegas*), which are given away at hotel reception desks (sometimes these sources also yield money-saving coupons).

You should also look at the coffeehouses listings in chapter 8, because a number of them serve light and inexpensive food. (Of particular note is the **Jazzed Cafe,** which serves incredibly cheap, incredibly authentic Italian food until 3am.)

ABOUT THEME RESTAURANTS   It shouldn't be too surprising to learn that a town devoted to themes (what hotel worth it's salt doesn't have one, at this point?) is full of virtually every theme restaurant there is (Hard Rock Cafe, All-Star Cafe, Planet Hollywood). For the most part, these establishments glorify some aspect of pop culture; movies, sports, rock music, and so forth. Almost all have prominent celebrity co-owners and tons of "memorabilia" on the walls, which in virtually every case means throwaway items from blockbuster movies, or some article of clothing a celeb wore once (if that) on stage or on the playing field. Almost all have virtually identical menus and have gift shops full of logo items.

This sounds cynical, and it is—but not without reason. Theme restaurants are for the most part noisy, cluttered, overpriced places that are strictly tourist traps. Their celebrity owners pretend they eat there regularly. But given, say, the hectic film production schedules of Bruce Willis and Arnold Schwarzenegger—and the nearly dozen branches of Planet Hollywood worldwide—that seems highly unlikely. (Of course, should said celebs find themselves in Vegas, it is quite likely they would pop into their joint at least once.) But if you eat at one of these places, you've eaten at them all. We don't want to be total killjoys. Fans should have a good time checking out the stuff on the walls of the appropriate restaurant. And while the food won't be the most memorable ever, it probably won't be bad. But that's not really what you go for.

And more are coming. In the near future, expect to see a new **Rainforest Cafe** in the MGM Grand, as well as a **Harley-Davidson Cafe** (3725 Las Vegas Blvd. S.; ☎ 702/740-4555), which, at press time, was expected to open in August 1997.

ABOUT PRICE CATEGORIES   The restaurants in this chapter are arranged first by location, then by the following price categories (based on the average cost of a dinner entree): **Very Expensive,** more than $20; **Expensive,** $15 to $20; **Moderate,** $10 to $15; **Inexpensive,** under $10 (sometimes well under). In expensive and very expensive restaurants, expect to spend no less than twice the price of the average entree for your entire meal with a tip; you can usually get by on a bit less in moderate and inexpensive restaurants. Buffets and Sunday brunches are gathered in a separate category at the end of this chapter.

A FINAL WORD   If you can, get in your car and check out some of the options listed below that are a bit off the beaten track. And be sure to patronize small ethnic places as much as you can. Show Vegas you demand flavor *now*!

1 Best Bets

- **Best Splurge:** It's a toss-up between **Gatsby's** and **Emeril's,** both located in the MGM Grand, and both of which vie for the unofficial "Best Restaurant in Vegas" title. Emeril's features Creole seafood, while Gatsby's is nouvelle and slightly Asian influenced. Both are superb dining experiences. Both offer tasting menus for about $75, not counting a tasting menu of terrific wine. It adds up. Always feeling free to spend your money for you, we can say they are worth it.
- **Best Buffet:** For the Strip, it's **The Mirage.** Not at all the cheapest in town, but the quality goes up accordingly. The salad bar comes loaded with countless possibilities, including a variety of cold salads (when was the last time you saw gefilte fish on a buffet?). And the gigantic mound of shrimp is the right sort of decadent touch you want in a Vegas buffet. In downtown, the new **Main Street Station** has an incredible buffet; all live-action stations, wood-fired brick oven pizzas, fresh lovely salsas and guacamole in the Mexican section, and better than average desserts. Nowhere else in downtown comes even close. (Though they are outstripped on Sundays by the Golden Nugget's Sunday Brunch.)
- **Best Sunday Champagne Brunch:** Bally's lavish **Sterling Sunday Brunch,** where display tables embellished with floral arrangements and ice sculptures are laden with everything from mounds of fresh shrimp to sushi and sashimi, and fancy entrees include the likes of roast duckling with black-currant and blueberry sauce.
- **Best Graveyard Dinner Deal:** **Binion's Horseshoe** offers a complete New York steak dinner served with potato, roll, and salad for just $3 from 10pm to 5:45am.
- **Best Cheap Breakfast:** Make your first stop of the day the **Cyclone Coffee Shop** at the Holiday Inn Casino Boardwalk, where a $1.29 breakfast includes two eggs, bacon or sausage, hash browns, and toast. It's served around the clock.
- **Best Spot for a Romantic Dinner:** The warmly elegant **Fiore,** with its gorgeous interior and arched windows overlooking the palm-fringed pool, is the most

simpatico setting for a leisurely romantic dinner. Brilliant cuisine, a great wine cellar, and superb service combine to create a memorable evening.

- **Best Spot for a Celebration: Mizuno's** teppanyaki grills are ideal for small parties, with the chef's theatrics comprising a tableside show. Additionally, the elegant **Gatsby's** with its superlative food would make a fine spot for a wedding supper.
- **Best Free Show at Dinner:** At Treasure Island's **Buccaneer Bay Club** everyone rushes to the window when the ship battle begins.
- **Best Wine List:** The distinguished cellar at **Gatsby's** houses 600 wines in all price ranges and has a friendly master sommelier on hand to guide you in your selections. Trust him; he knows his stuff.
- **Best View:** See all of Las Vegas from the revolving **Top of the World,** at the Stratosphere, 106 stories up.
- **Best California Cuisine:** Wolfgang Puck's **Spago** didn't invent California cuisine (or did it?) but it might as well have.
- **Best Chinese Cuisine: Chin's,** where piano bar music enhances an ambience of low-key elegance, offers scrumptious and authentic Cantonese fare, including some original creations such as deep-fried battered chicken served with strawberry sauce and fresh strawberries.
- **Best Deli:** The **Stage Deli** in Caesars will give no cause for complaints. You might also try the new deli in **New York New York,** which has been winning raves.
- **Best Healthy/Veggie Conscious:** The **Enigma Cafe** in the Gateway District, which makes it convenient for both the Strip and downtown, offers a large selection of really cheap sandwiches, salads, and smoothies, all fresh and interesting. (They have hummus!) That, plus their enormous menu of coffees and other specialty drinks, and their pretty, relaxing setting make this a great Vegas find.
- **Best Italian Cuisine: Il Fornaio** in New York New York is the best for a moderately priced meal, and **Fiore** in the Rio for something quite a bit more dear.
- **Best New Orleans Cuisine:** One of Las Vegas's newest celebrity chef venues, **Emeril's New Orleans Fish House** at the MGM Grand, offers total authenticity combined with culinary brilliance.
- **Best Southwestern Cuisine:** The fact that it's the only notable southwestern restaurant in town doesn't make the **Coyote Cafe** any less impressive. Superstar Santa Fe chef Mark Miller brings contemporary culinary panache to traditional southwestern cookery, and the results are spicy and spectacular.
- **Best Steak and Seafood: Lawry's The Prime Rib** has such good prime rib, it's hard to ever imagine having any better. And you'll enjoy nothing but the best cuts of beef and the freshest seafood at **The Tillerman,** a gorgeous restaurant with candlelit tables amid an indoor grove of ficus trees and tree-trunk pillars.
- **Best Barbecue: Ware's T Bones Texas BBQ** is a bit out of the way, but the second that meat falls off the bone, or falls apart under your fork, you will be glad you made the drive.

2 Restaurants by Cuisine

AMERICAN

All-American Bar and Grille
(Midstrip, Rio, *M*)
All Star Cafe (South Strip,
Showcase Mall, *M*)

Binion's Horseshoe (Downtown,
Binion's Horseshoe, *I*)
Buccaneer Bay Club (Midstrip,
Treasure Island, *VE*)

Key to abbreviations: *E*=Expensive; *I*=Inexpensive; *M*=Moderate; *VE*=Very Expensive

Carson Street Café (Downtown, Golden Nugget, *I*)

Dive! (North Strip, Fashion Show Mall, *M*)

Fog City Diner (East Las Vegas, *M*)

Hard Rock Cafe (Convention Center/Paradise Road, *M*)

Hippo and the Wild Bunch (Convention Center/Paradise Road, *M*)

Top of the World (North Strip, Stratosphere, *VE*)

ASIAN FUSION

Dragon Noodle Co. (South Strip, Monte Carlo, *M*)

BAGELS

Einstein Bros. Bagels (East Las Vegas, *I*)

BARBECUE

Big Sky (North Strip, Stratosphere, *I*)

Country Star (South Strip, *M*)

Tony Roma's—A Place for Ribs (Downtown, Sam Boyd's Fremont, *M*)

Tony Roma's—A Place for Ribs (North Strip, Stardust, *M*)

Ware's T Bones Texas Style Bar-B-Que (West Las Vegas, *M*)

BUFFETS/BRUNCHES

Bally's Big Kitchen Buffet (Midstrip, *M*)

Bally's Sterling Brunch Buffet (Midstrip, *VE*)

Caesars Palace Palatium Buffet (Midstrip, *M*)

The Circus Circus Buffet (North Strip, *I*)

Excalibur's Round Table Buffet (South Strip, *I*)

Flamingo Hilton Paradise Garden Buffet (Midstrip, *I*)

The Golden Nugget Buffet (Downtown, *M*)

Harrah's Galley Buffet (Midstrip, *I*)

Lady Luck Buffet (Downtown, *I*)

Las Vegas Hilton Buffet of Champions (Convention Center/Paradise Road, *M*)

The Luxor's Pharoah's Pheast Buffet (South Strip, *I*)

Main Street Station Garden Court (Downtown, *I*)

The MGM Grand Oz Buffet (South Strip, *M*)

Mirage Buffet (Midstrip, *M*)

Monte Carlo Buffet (South Strip, *I*)

Rio's Carnival World Buffet (Midstrip, *I*)

Sahara Oasis Buffet (North Strip, *I*)

Sam Boyd's Fremont Paradise Buffet (Downtown, *I*)

Sam's Town, The Great Buffet (East Las Vegas, *I*)

Showboat Captain's Buffet (Downtown, *I*)

Stardust Warehouse Buffet (North Strip, *I*)

Stratosphere Buffet (North Strip, *I*)

Treasure Island Buffet (Midstrip, *I*)

Tropicana Island Buffet (South Strip, *I*)

Tropicana Sunday Brunch Buffet (South Strip, *E*)

CALIFORNIA

Enigma Cafe (West Las Vegas, *I*)

Planet Hollywood (Midstrip, Caesars Palace, *M*)

Spago (Midstrip, Caesars Palace, *VE*)

Wolfgang Puck Café (South Strip, MGM Grand, *E*)

CHINESE

Cathy House (West Las Vegas, *M*)

Chin's (North Strip, Fashion Show Mall, *E*)

The Noodle Kitchen (Midstrip, Mirage, *M*)

CONTEMPORARY CREOLE

Emeril's New Orleans Fish House (South Strip, MGM Grand, *VE*)

CONTINENTAL

Bacchanal (Midstrip, Caesars Palace, *VE*)

Buccaneer Bay Club (Midstrip, Treasure Island, *VE*)

Cafe Nicolle (West Las Vegas, *E*)

Pegasus (Convention Center/
Paradise Road, Alexis Park
Resort, *VE*)
Top of the World (North Strip,
Stratosphere, *VE*)

CUBAN

Rincon Criollo (North Strip, *I*)

DELI

Stage Deli (Midstrip, Caesars
Palace, *M*)

DINER

Green Shack (Convention Center/
Paradise Road, *I*)
Liberty Cafe at the Blue Castle
Pharmacy (North Strip, *I*)
Poppa Gar's (West Las Vegas, *I*)

DONUTS

Ronald's Donuts (West Las
Vegas, *I*)

EURASIAN

Gatsby's (South Strip,
MGM Grand, *VE*)

FOOD COURT

The Food Court (South Strip,
Monte Carlo, *I*)
La Piazza Food Court (Midstrip,
Caesars Palace, *I*)

FRENCH

Andre's (Downtown, *VE*)
Bistro Le Montrachet (Convention
Center/Paradise Road, Las Vegas
Hilton, *VE*)
Monte Carlo Room (North Strip,
Desert Inn, *VE*)
Palace Court (Midstrip, Caesars
Palace, *VE*)
Pamplemousse (Convention Center/
Paradise Road, *E*)

GERMAN/AMERICAN

The Rathskeller (Convention Center/
Paradise Road, *I*)

INDIAN

Shalimar (Convention Center/
Paradise Road, Citibank Plaza, *M*)

INTERNATIONAL

The Garlic Cafe (West Las Vegas, *E*)
Hugo's Cellar (Downtown,
Four Queens, *VE*)

ITALIAN

Fiore (Midstrip, Rio, *VE*)
Papamios (East Las Vegas,
Sam's Town, *M*)
Romano's Macarponi Grill
(West Las Vegas, *M*)

JAPANESE

Ginza (Convention Center/Paradise
Road, *M*)
Mizuno's (South Strip, Tropicana, *E*)

MEDITERRANEAN

Enigma Cafe (West Las Vegas, *I*)
Mediterranean Cafe and Market
(East Las Vegas, *I*)

MEXICAN

Ricardo's (East Las Vegas, *M*)
Viva Mercados (West Las Vegas, *M*)

MOROCCAN

Mamounia (Convention Center/
Paradise Road, *M*)
Marrakech (Convention Center/
Paradise Road, *M*)

PROVENÇALE

Fiore (Midstrip, Rio, *VE*)

PUB FARE

Monte Carlo Pub and Brewery
(South Strip, Monte Carlo, *I*)

SOUTHWESTERN

Chili's Grill and Bar (Convention
Center/Paradise Road, *I*)
Country Star (South Strip, *M*)
Coyote Cafe (South Strip, MGM
Grand, *VE*)
Motown Cafe (South Strip,
New York New York, *M*)

STEAK/SEAFOOD

Center Stage (Downtown,
Jackie Gaughan's, *I*)
Lawry's The Prime Rib (Convention
Center/Paradise Road, *E*)

Limerick's (Downtown, Fitzgeralds, *E*)

Morton's of Chicago (North Strip, Fashion Show Mall, *VE*)

The Palm (Midstrip, Caesars Palace, *VE*)

The Tillerman (East Las Vegas, *VE*)

SWISS/GERMAN

Alpine Village Inn (Convention Center/Paradise Road, *M*)

TEX-MEX

Z Tejas Grill (Convention Center/Paradise Road, *M*)

THAI

Komol (East Las Vegas, *M*)

3 South Strip

VERY EXPENSIVE

✪ Coyote Cafe

The MGM Grand, 3799 Las Vegas Blvd. S. ☎ **702/891-7349**. Reservations recommended for the Grill Room, not accepted for the Cafe. Grill Room main courses $15–$32. Cafe main courses $7.50–$17.50 (many are under $10). AE, CB, DC, DISC, JCB, MC, V. Grill Room daily 5:30–10pm. Cafe daily 8am–11pm. SOUTHWESTERN.

In a town where restaurant cuisine often seems stuck in a 1950s time warp, Mark Miller's Coyote Cafe evokes howls of delight. His robust regional cuisine combines elements of traditional Mexican, Native American, Creole, and Cajun cookery with cutting-edge culinary trends. The main dining room is fronted by a lively cafe/bar, in which an exhibition-cooking area houses a *cazuela* (casserole) oven and *comal* grill under a gleaming ceramic tile hood. The adobe-walled Grill Room offers a more tranquil setting. Tables are candlelit; etched-glass partitions by Santa Fe artist Kit Carson depict whimsical scenes (such as a coyote and a horse dining in a restaurant). A warm glow emanates from innovative sconces that filter light through multicolored Japanese rice paper.

The Grill Room menu changes monthly. If you're lucky, you might find the heavenly "painted soup"—half garlicky black bean, half beer-infused smoked Cheddar—"painted" with chipotle cream and garnished with salsa fresca and de árbol chili powder. A reliable main course is the salmon fillet crusted with ground pumpkin seeds and corn tortillas topped with roasted chile/pumpkin-seed sauce and presented on a bed of spinach-wrapped spaghetti squash studded with pine nuts, corn kernels, scallions, and morsels of sun-dried tomato. Desserts include chocolate banana torte served on banana crème anglaise and topped with a scoop of vanilla ice cream. The wine list includes many by-the-glass selections, including champagnes and sparkling wines, which nicely complement spicy Southwestern fare; Brazilian daiquiris are a house specialty.

The Cafe menu offers similar but somewhat lighter fare. Southwestern breakfasts ($5.95 to $9.50) range from *huevos rancheros* to blue-corn pancakes with toasted pine nuts, honey butter, and real maple syrup.

✪ Emeril's New Orleans Fish House

The MGM Grand, 3799 Las Vegas Blvd. S. ☎ **702/891-7374.** Reservations suggested. Main courses $12–$18 lunch, $18–$28 dinner (more for lobster). AE, CB, DC, DISC, MC, V. Daily 11am–3pm, 5:30–10:30pm. CONTEMPORARY CREOLE.

Tucked into an almost unseen corner of the MGM Grand is one of the very finest restaurants in the city. Chef Emeril Lagasse of New Orleans's Emeril's and NOLA (and an extremely popular TV chef on cable's Food Network) has brought his cuisine to town. The restaurant's quiet and comforting decor provides the stage for creative, exciting, "BAM!" food.

Although Lagasse caters to the tastes of everyone from poultry lovers to vegetarians, seafood is the specialty here, flown in from Louisiana or from anywhere that Chef finds the quality of the ingredients to be the very finest. We started off with the most recent edition of Lagasse's legendary savory "cheesecakes," the Lobster Cheesecake with tomato-tarragon coulis, topped with a dollop of succulent Louisiana choupique caviar. It's a heady, rich appetizer that may be completely unlike anything you've ever had before. Oysters on the half-shell are also a favorite, served with two tangy dipping sauces. And try the barbecue shrimp, which come in a garlic, herb butter sauce that will have you mopping your plate with bread.

Our entrees did not fail to elicit a "Wow!" from everyone at the table. A Creole-seasoned, seared ahi steak was stuffed with Hudson Valley foie gras and served in a bed of Lagasse's famous "smashed" potatoes, creamy and rich, with roasted shallots and a part-shallot reduction—absolutely luxurious. A medley of seafood, from caviar to shrimp to mussels and clams came over pasta in a delicious and very spicy broth. And in a dish that bordered on the sinful, there was a marvelously seasoned filet mignon stuffed with a crawfish dressing and topped with Bordelaise sauce with crawfish tails and sliced andouille sausage. Meat eaters will also be very happy with the utterly tender and flavorful fillet of beef with tasso Hollandaise sauce and homemade Worcestershire.

It would be difficult to recommend one particular dessert from the vast menu since they're all fabulous, but if it's your first visit, a slice of the Banana Cream Pie with banana crust and caramel drizzle is one of the finest desserts you will ever have. And if your capacity for rich food is depleted by the end of your meal, there's a trio of house-made sorbets (mixed berry, apple, and root beer the night we dined there), which provide a lovely finish to your meal without necessarily pushing you over the edge of the abyss. If you're feeling adventurous, don't miss Chef's Degustation, a seven-course tasting menu. It usually features smaller portions (thank heavens) of the most exciting dishes from the regular menu, plus some specials of the evening.

✪ Gatsby's

The MGM Grand, 3799 Las Vegas Blvd. S. ☎ **702/891-7337.** Reservations suggested. Jackets suggested for men. Main courses $28.95–$58. Degustation (tasting) menu $75, $95 with selected wines accompanying each course. AE, CB, DC, DISC, MC, V. Wed–Mon 6–10:30pm. EURASIAN.

This is a very expensive restaurant but on par with the swankiest establishments in more food-oriented cities. Since you're on vacation anyway, set aside some of those blackjack winnings and prepare to discover exactly how exquisite, interesting, and flavorful a meal can be. Gatsby's Chef de Cuisine, Terence Fong, has quite a conundrum to solve: How do you please the generally food-conservative Las Vegas customer and offer an innovative, exciting dining experience that invigorates everyone involved? Provide the expected but don't let it dictate preparation; combine familiar ingredients with more unusual ones to subtly educate the unadventurous; use only fresh, lovely, seasonal items. This means, for example, that Fong's lobster bisque, a rich soup you'll find on many a local menu, presented here with perhaps two lumps of divinely sweet meat and a few bites of equally sugar-rich roasted corn, awakens one to the difference between the ordinary and the extraordinary. It means starting with aromatic yet familiar jasmine and basmati rice, but adding toasted orzo, wheat berries, and quinoa (a rather trendy but very healthful and tasty grain) to produce a delicious confetti of flavors rather than a safe side dish. It means that the gracious wait staff brings

A Frommer's Exclusive

We were so taken with Emeril's delicious Fall River clam chowder, we asked for permission to share the recipe with readers. Here it is:

$^1/_2$ pound unsalted butter
2 cups all-purpose flour
$^1/_2$ pound bacon, medium diced ($^1/_3$-inch squares)
2 cups chopped leeks (about a pound)
2 cups chopped yellow onions
2 cups clam juice
6 cups heavy cream
2 pounds littleneck clams, shucked and chopped
3 bay leaves
1 tablespoon chopped fresh thyme
2 tablespoons finely chopped parsley
salt and pepper

In a sauté pan, melt the butter over medium heat. Stir the flour into the melted butter until smooth. Cook for 6 to 8 minutes to create a blond roux, stirring occasionally. Remove from the heat and set aside. In a stock pot, over medium heat, render the diced bacon for about 5 minutes or until crispy. Add the leeks and onions. Sauté for 3 to 4 minutes or until vegetables are wilted. Stir in the clam juice and cream. Bring the liquid to a simmer. Add the bay leaves and fresh thyme. Season with salt and pepper. Stir in $^1/_2$ cup of the roux at a time, until all the roux is incorporated and the soup is smooth. Simmer for 20 minutes. Stir in the chopped clams and cook for 2 minutes. Add the parsley, and re-season if necessary. Yields about 8 to 10 servings (about 1 gallon).

unexpected treats to tease diners into anticipation, such as tiny cilantro crepe purses of beluga caviar and vodka crème fraîche, or perfectly smoked salmon on 50¢-sized blini.

Anything from this kitchen that includes foie gras is worth ordering. This delicacy might show up on the menu in more than one guise, accompanied with pan-roasted stuffed quail and a lentil-corn salad, or with Perigourd truffles and organic greens dressed in a port wine vinaigrette. Maine lobster might be simply sautéed and served with lobster-ginger butter to gild the already sumptuous meat; ahi tuna gets an Asian preparation with a sesame seed crust and a spicy wasabi butter. Fans of exotic meats, or anyone curious to try ostrich or buffalo, are in the right place. The grilled domestic ostrich, bathed in a red wine-shallot reduction and served with wild mushroom risotto, is a lovely dish, tender and as not the least bit gamy. Duck is well treated here, as well. It's slow roasted, so the slices are as tender and lean as possible, garnished with an Asian-style sauce and pretty little vegetables. Vegetarians will find dinner just as lush. Along with the chef's vegetable plate, replete with couscous or risotto or that wonderful rice confetti and lots of recently plucked delicacies, vegetable broth-based soups, a couple of salads, and appetizers such as the vegetable spring rolls will profoundly satisfy your appetite and expectations.

It's painful to recall the dessert menu, living so far from the source. Melanie Bonnano, the pastry chef, takes great delight in whimsical presentations like a Cup of Java, a treat that fulfills coffee and chocolate lovers on a number of levels. Her coffee-and-cream granita-laden chocolate cup will have you examining your freezer in a new light. Soufflés available in five flavors are a house specialty, but chocolate

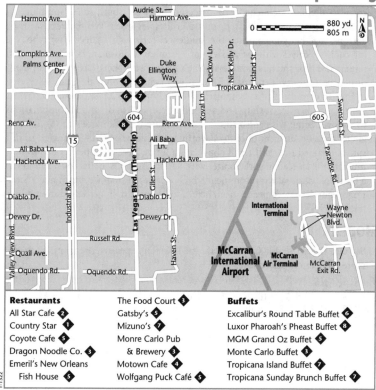

cake mysteriously filled with fresh raspberries and wrapped in filo pastry is a feast for the eyes and tongue.

Everything, from the lavish crackers and bread to the sorbets presented in the center of ice flowers, is made in-house. If you are curious to see the kitchen, a special chef's table sits in a little room separated from the activity by glass windows—when you make reservations, you can request this spot, although it's hard to concentrate on conversation when you're craning your neck to watch the pastry chef. It's also possible to request a special tasting menu ($75), which will truly give you a sense of the restaurant's possibilities. For an extra $30, the enthusiastic sommelier will pair wines from the luxuriously stocked cellar with each course. While spending a few hundred dollars on dinner for two may seem extravagant, the experience is worth that and more. At Gatsby's, unlike most places in Las Vegas, there's no possible way to lose.

EXPENSIVE

Mizuno's

Tropicana Resort and Casino, 3801 Las Vegas Blvd. S. ☎ **702/739-2222.** Reservations suggested. Full Samurai dinners mostly $14.95–$19.95, Shogun combination dinners $24.95–$38.95. AE, CB, DC, MC, V. Daily 5–10:30pm. JAPANESE.

This stunning, marble-floored restaurant is filled with authentic Japanese artifacts, among them an ancient temple bell, a 400-year-old vase from Tokyo, and antique scrolls and shoji screens. One of the latter depicts the restaurant's theme, the exchange of cultures between the East and West as exemplified by the silk and tea trade. A meandering glass "stream" is lit by tiny twinkling lights to suggest running water, and cut-glass dividers are etched with graceful cherry blossoms, irises, and plum trees. Food is prepared at marble teppanyaki grill tables where you're seated with other patrons; together you comprise the "audience" for a highly skilled chef, who, wielding cooking knives with the panache of a samurai swordsman, rapidly trims, chops, sautés, and flips the food onto everyone's plates. This being Las Vegas, his dazzling display of dexterity is enhanced by a flashing light show over the grill.

Entrees comprised of tasty morsels of New York strip steak, filet mignon, shrimp, lobster, chicken, or shrimp and vegetable tempura, and various combinations of the above, come with miso soup or consommé (get the tastier miso), salad with ginger dressing, an array of crispy flavorful vegetables stir-fried with sesame seeds and spices, steamed rice, and tea. Though it's a lot of food, an appetizer of shrimp and mushrooms sautéed in garlic butter with lemon soy sauce merits consideration. And a bottle of warm sake is recommended. Ginger or red bean ice cream make for a fittingly light dessert. A great bargain here: a full early bird dinner served from 5 to 6pm for just $9.95.

MODERATE

See also the listing for **Coyote Cafe** (p. 110), an expensive restaurant fronted by a more moderately priced cafe.

All Star Cafe

3785 Las Vegas Blvd. S., at Tropicana Ave (in the Showcase Mall, right next to the MGM Grand). ☎ **702/795-8326**. Reservations for parties of 10 or more only. Main courses $6–$18. DC, DISC, JCB, MC, V. Sun–Thurs 11am–12pm, Fri–Sat 11am–1pm. AMERICAN.

This is the sports theme restaurant, filled with memorabilia from hundreds of different sports legends, covering just about every sport you can imagine. Buffs should be pleased. The co-owners are Vegas resident Andre Agassi, Monica Seles, Wayne Gretsky, Ken Griffey Jr., Joe Montana, Shaquille O'Neal, and new wunderkind Tiger Woods (who recently joined as an investor). The menu is "All American" and includes pasta specialties, salads, and the usual hamburgers and hot dogs.

Country Star

3724 Las Vegas Blvd. S., at Harmon Ave. ☎ **702/740-8400**. Reservations for large parties only. Main courses $5.95–$21.95 (most under $14). AE, CB, DC, DISC, MC. V. Sun–Thurs 11am–10pm, Fri–Sun 11am–11pm. BARBECUE /SOUTHWESTERN.

This would be the country music entry, attempting to cash in on the success of the Hard Rock. Restaurant principals include Reba McEntire, Vince Gill, Tracy Lawrence, Neal McCoy, Lorianne Crook, and Charlie Chase. Music memorabilia (Merle Haggard's boots, a Minnie Pearl hat with dangling price tag, Dolly Parton's wedding dress, gold records, Grand Ole Opry posters). It's more low key and friendly than, say, Hard Rock or Planet Hollywood. Dozens of video monitors, including several embedded in the entranceway floor, play nonstop C&W music videos. Actually, the food here is pretty good. The barbecue sauce is terrific (bottles are on the tables).

Dragon Noodle Co.

Monte Carlo Resort, 3770 Las Vegas Blvd. S., between Flamingo Rd. and Tropicana Ave. ☎ **702/730-7777**. Main courses $5.50–$16.95 (many items under $10). Sun–Thurs 11am–11pm, Fri–Sat 11am–midnight. AE, CB, DC, DISC, MC, V. ASIAN FUSION.

Dragon Noodle was designed according to the complex principles of *Feng Shui* (pronounced fung shway), the ancient Chinese art of geomancy used in planning building interiors to maximize prosperity and positive energy. At its opening, a Buddha Lion (harbinger of good luck) danced among the diners accompanied by drums, gongs, and crashing cymbals, while exploding firecrackers drove away evil spirits. The resulting casual, minimalist interior suggests a marketplace, with displays of Asian foodstuffs and sacks of rice on the floor. Along the back wall is a noteworthy exhibit of Asian teapots and other kitchen antiques. Classical piano music creates a soothing audio backdrop.

Order up a platter of pan-seared potstickers and create your own dipping sauce by mixing hoisin sauce, hot sauce, and vinegar. Other notable dishes here are spicy, wok-seared Mongolian beef served over crispy rice-stick noodles with scallion shreds, crisp-skinned roast duck, and Thai-style barbecued chicken scented with lemongrass, ginger, hot chili, and a hint of curry (it's served with spicy peanut and shallot sauces). With any of the above, we like to order steamed buns and make little sandwiches; try it. Dragon Noodle's extensive selection of teas (equivalent to a carefully crafted wine list) are served in exquisite pots. Other beverage options include more than a dozen wines by the glass, Asian beers, specialty iced teas, and fresh-squeezed juices. Among the Asian-nuanced desserts is a rich coconut cake layered with cream cheese frosting and topped with toasted coconut.

Motown Cafe

New York New York Hotel, 3790 Las Vegas Blvd. S., at Tropicana. ☎ **702/740-6440.** Reservations not accepted. Main courses $6–$17. AE, DISC, MC, V. Sun–Thurs 7am–11pm, Fri–Sat 7am–12am. SOUTHWESTERN.

The menu at this tribute to Motown record label artists features light Southwestern cuisine (jambalaya, shrimp Creole) probably because no one could figure out what the indigenous cuisine of Detroit was. (This is in addition to the basic burgers and so forth). They also offer a breakfast buffet. And as we all know, Motown music is just about the best there is for dancing, and so the Cafe stays open until 3am on weekdays, and 4am on weekends for dancing.

✪ Wolfgang Puck Café

MGM Grand, 3799 Las Vegas Blvd. S. ☎ **702/895-9653.** Reservations not accepted. Main courses $9–$14.95. AE, MC, V. Sun–Thurs 8am–11pm, Fri–Sat 8am–midnight. CALIFORNIA.

A brightly colored riot of mosaic tiles and other experiments in geometric design, the Wolfgang Puck Café stands out in the MGM Grand. It's more or less Spago Lite: downscaled salads, pizzas, and pastas, all showing the Puck hand, and while perhaps a little more money than your average cafe, the food is comparably better, if sometimes not *that* special. However, it's all very fresh nouvelle cuisine, which makes a nice change of pace. The specialty pizzas are fun; constructed on crusts topped with fontina and mozzarella cheeses, they're brushed with pesto and layered with embellishments such as spicy jalapeño-marinated sautéed chicken, leeks, and cilantro. (And no, it's not just like eating the Puck brand sold in the frozen food section.) It's always a thrill to get a good salad in Vegas, and there are quite a few on this menu. Worth noting is the signature Chinois chicken salad tossed with crispy fried wontons, julienned carrots, cabbage, and green onions in a Chinese honey-mustard sauce. For something cheap, try the surprisingly large baby greens salad with the goat cheese toast—that and the very fine herb bread that comes gratis is $4.95, which fills you up in a fairly healthy way for not a lot of money. Desert highlights include a caramel cheesecake, a warm chocolate soufflé, and a hot chocolate truffle cake with chocolate sauce. There does tend to be a line, particularly after EFX lets out just across the casino.

INEXPENSIVE

✪ The Food Court

Monte Carlo Resort and Casino, 3770 Las Vegas Blvd., between Flamingo Rd. and Tropicana Ave. ☎ **702/730-7777.** Main courses $2–$10. Cash only. Daily 6am–3am. FOOD COURT.

Food courts are a dime a dozen in Vegas, but the one in the Monte Carlo has some surprisingly good options. Sure, there is the always reliable **McDonald's,** and for sweets there is **Häagen-Dazs,** but they also have a branch of **Nathan's Hot Dogs,** New York's finest. **Golden Bagel** offers another New York staple, big and tasty enough to satisfy even picky natives. **Sbarro** offers enticing pizza slices. It's much more attractively decorated than your usual mall food courts, and with those extended hours (each stand has its own, but they all fall within the listed parameters), there remains little time for anyone to go hungry. If you want a good cheap meal on the Strip and wish to avoid some of those dubious Night Owl specials, come here.

Monte Carlo Pub & Brewery

Monte Carlo Resort, 3770 Las Vegas Blvd. S., between Flamingo Rd. and Tropicana Ave. ☎ **702/730-7777.** Main courses $5.95–$7.95. AE, CB, DC, DISC, MC, V. Sun–Thurs 11am–1am, Fri–Sat 11am–3am. PUB FARE.

When the Monte Carlo opened in summer 1996, this large and lively pub immediately became a favorite lunch spot and after-work hangout for local businesspeople. A working microbrewery (you can view the copper holding tanks and vats through large windows), it has a high-ceilinged warehouse/industrial interior, with exposed-brick and rusty corrugated-tin walls, track lighting, and a network of exposed pipes overhead. An ornate mahogany backbar with beveled mirrors adds a note of elegance. The Pub is cigar-friendly (maintaining a humidor), and rock videos blare forth from a large screen and 40 TV monitors around the room. This is no place for a romantic rendezvous.

The menu features somewhat sophisticated versions of pub fare, doled out in enormous portions. We like the pizza topped with lamb, grilled eggplant, and goat cheese. Other choices include penne pasta with wild mushrooms in garlic cream sauce, a sample platter of sausages served with warm potato salad and whole-grain mustard, sandwiches, burgers, and barbecued baby back ribs. A microbrew with your meal (or a sampler of five) is de rigueur. Desserts include bread pudding with butterscotch rum sauce and creamy peanut butter pie. After 9pm, only pizza is served, and dueling pianos provide dance music and entertainment.

4 Mid-Strip

VERY EXPENSIVE

Bacchanal

Caesars Palace, 3570 Las Vegas Blvd. S., just north of Flamingo Rd. ☎ **702/731-7110.** Reservations essential. Fixed-price $69.50, plus tax and gratuity. AE, CB, DC, DISC, MC, V. Tues–Sat 6–11pm with seatings at 6, 6:30, 9, and 9:30pm. CONTINENTAL.

Its pedimented doorways guarded by golden lions, Bacchanal is an archetypal Las Vegas experience—an imperial Roman feast with comely "wine goddesses" performing sinuous belly dances, decanting wine from shoulder height into ornate silver chalices, and, believe it or not, massaging male diners and feeding them grapes! When not performing, the goddesses repose gracefully around a fountained pool centered on a bronze Venus. The setting is palatial: White-columned walls are backed by murals of ancient Rome; an azure ceiling suggests an open sky, with a grape arbor looping from beam to beam and crystal torches provide romantic lighting. The dramatic focus of the evening is a thunder and lightning storm produced by Zeus to announce the arrival of Caesar and Cleopatra. Caesar makes a short speech, and the royal pair tour the room greeting diners. Abandon all reality, ye who enter here.

Dinner is a sumptuous multicourse feast, including unlimited wine and champagne. The menu changes a bit seasonally. Dinner begins with a selection of crudités served with creamy roasted garlic-chive dip. This is followed by a smoked roma tomato soup and a salad of field greens with champagne vinaigrette dressing.

A choice of five entrees might range from roast rack of lamb to oven-roasted wild salmon fillet. The dramatic finale—a flaming dessert of vanilla ice cream topped with liqueur-soaked fresh fruits—will be accompanied by petits fours and tea or coffee. The food falls short of haute gourmet standards, but there's plenty of it, and the elaborate presentation (not to mention the wine) justifies the price.

✪ Buccaneer Bay Club

Treasure Island, 3300 Las Vegas Blvd. S. ☎ **702/894-7350.** Reservations required. Main courses $16–$26. AE, CB, DC, DISC, JCB, MC, V. Nightly 5–10:30pm. AMERICAN/CONTINENTAL.

This is a little-known gem (at least, outside of Treasure Island guests) that features a laudable menu more innovative than the standard found at other equivalent hotel restaurants. And it's certainly considerably cheaper.

A meandering layout creates a series of intimate dining nooks (perfect for quiet conversations) all done in a posh pirate theme with a low-beamed ceiling and stucco walls adorned with daggers and pistols. Treasure chests are displayed in wall niches along with a veritable museum of artifacts including a Spanish conquistador's helmet. The whole thing overlooks the hotel's "bay" where a pirate battle is waged every 90 minutes. This probably isn't the best place to view it from (the windows are smallish, and you're behind the action), but the wait staff does notify you at show time and will hold your food service until it's through if you have chosen to watch. It's fun to watch everyone rush to the windows when they announce, "Pirates are on!"

Speaking of the service, it is among the best we've experienced, with an efficient team of friendly, knowledgeable, and almost prescient servers at every table (they anticipated a woman's desire for another glass of wine before she even had finished wistfully vocalizing it).

Appetizers come in both hot (shrimp Jamaica, escargot brioche) and cold (shrimp cocktail, Parma prosciutto) varieties with the savory celery root flan and the quail being the true standouts. Regarding the latter, it was not on the menu, so be sure to ask about specials. Entrees run the gamut from poultry (chicken, duck, pheasant) to beef (filet mignon, prime rib, steak) to seafood (sea bass, lobster, salmon). Favorites here are the Pheasant Charles, which comes with pan-seared, thyme-roasted wild mushroom risotto and is served in a Merlot lingonberry sauce. There's also Colorado Buffalo Prime Rib, which is roasted and grilled over mesquite wood and served with creamy horseradish potatoes. It's hard to get over the thought of eating a buffalo at first, but if you can, it'll be one of the best pieces of cow-based meat you'll ever taste. Desserts include apple binets, white chocolate cheesecake with raspberry sauce, and the house specialty apricot or harlequin (Grand Marnier, white and dark chocolate) minisoufflés.

Fiore

Rio Suite Hotel, 3700 W. Flamingo Rd., at I-15. ☎ **702/252-7702.** Reservations recommended. Main courses $26–$48. AE, CB, DC, DISC, MC, V. Nightly 5pm–11pm. ITALIAN/PROVENÇALE.

Fiore offers a deliciously simpatico setting for the brilliantly innovative cuisine of chef Kolachai Ngimsangaim. In his spacious, mahogany-ceilinged dining room, with arched windows overlooking a palm-fringed pool, tables are exquisitely appointed with fine silver, flowers, and Villeroy and Boch china in diverse floral patterns. Flower- and fruit-motif carpeting furthers the "fiore" motif, while an exhibition kitchen aglow with wood-burning pizza ovens (nine different hardwoods are used for grilling here) adds warmth and theatricality. We love the interior space, but it's also tempting to dine alfresco on the flower-bordered flagstone terrace (heated in winter, mist-cooled in summer). Light jazz provides a pleasant musical backdrop.

Ngimsangaim's seasonally changing menus complement the culinary elegance of northern Italy with the earthy exuberance of southern France. For an appetizer we've had the sautéed herb-crusted prawns in a buttery mustard/anise sauce. This was followed by an entree of barbecued Atlantic salmon in honeyed hickory sauce, served with grilled polenta, portobello mushrooms, roasted roma tomatoes, and grilled asparagus spears. Fiore's thoughtful list of more than 400 wines in several price ranges is international in scope and includes 45 premium by-the-glass selections. Consult knowledgeable sommelier Barrie Larvin for suggestions. Dine slowly, and consider including a cheese course—excellent cheeses are served with seasonal fruits. But do save room for dessert—perhaps a warm chocolate torte on crème anglaise embellished with raspberry stars and chocolate hearts. In addition to an extensive listing of cognacs, ports, and dessert wines, hand-rolled cigars elegantly presented in a mahogany humidor are a postprandial option on the terrace.

Palace Court

Caesars Palace, 3570 Las Vegas Blvd. S., just north of Flamingo Rd. ☎ **702/734-7110.** Reservations essential. Main courses $29–$55. AE, MC, V. Nightly 6, 6:30, 9, 9:30. FRENCH.

The Palace Court has long been considered one of the best restaurants in town, but word from those who know is that it has declined somewhat in quality. While alumni are cooking up delicious storms at other restaurants, the Palace Court recently (as of this writing) had lost both its long-time chef and its pastry chef. This doesn't bode well for improvements; on the other hand, once the new staff is settled in, a recovery might follow. It would be worth asking around before spending a bundle here.

In case you want to see the world.

At American Express, we're here to make your journey a smooth one. So we have over 1,700 travel service locations in over 120 countries ready to help. What else would you expect from the world's largest travel agency?

do more ®

Travel

http://www.americanexpress.com/travel

In case you want to be welcomed there.

We're here to see that you're always welcomed at establishments everywhere. That's why millions of people carry the American Express® Card – for peace of mind, confidence, and security, around the world or just around the corner.

do more®

AMERICAN EXPRESS

Cards

In case you're running low.

We're here to help with more than 118,000 Express Cash locations around the world. In order to enroll, just call American Express before you start your vacation.

do more

Express Cash

And just in case.

We're here with American Express® Travelers Cheques and Cheques *for Two.*® They're the safest way to carry money on your vacation and the surest way to get a refund, practically anywhere, anytime.

Another way we help you...

do more

Travelers Cheques

But if you do go, here is what you can expect. Reached via a crystal-ceilinged bronze elevator or a brass-balustraded spiral staircase, the circular Palace Court is as opulent as a Venetian palazzo. The centerpiece of the room—a towering stained-glass domed skylight, 36 feet in diameter—shelters a grove of ficus trees flanked by classical statuary and flower beds. White-lattice windows draped with peach balloon curtains overlook the hotel's swimming pool and the mountains beyond. On the opposite wall is a charming mural of the French countryside. Tables are elegantly appointed (with gold and white Lenox china, vermeil flatware, and hand-blown crystal) and softly lit by shaded brass candle lamps.

Menus change seasonally. A recent one offered appetizers of poached champagne-glazed Long Island oysters (embellished with Beluga caviar, smoked salmon, and julienned leeks) and ravioli stuffed with minced pink prawns, mushrooms, and truffles in lobster bisque sauce. Sorbets are served between courses in frosted glass lilies. Among the entrees, Maine lobster was served with coral (lobster roe) butter and steamed broccoli, and chateaubriand came with peppery red wine/game sauce, a mousseline of spinach, poached pears, and dauphinois potatoes.

There's an extensive wine list, with 12 by-the-glass selections; consult the sommelier for assistance.

Petit-fours and chocolate truffles are served gratis at the conclusion of your meal. However, that doesn't mean you should forgo dessert. Choices include ambrosial soufflés and a totally satisfying flourless chocolate truffle cake topped with homemade hazelnut ice cream. *Note:* A fixed-price pretheater special (soup or salad, entree, and dessert) is served Sunday to Thursday from 6 to 7pm; it costs $34.50.

End your evening over après-dinner drinks in the romantic adjoining piano bar/lounge. Overlooking the pool, this plushly furnished venue has a stained-glass skylight that retracts for a view of open starlit sky. Off the lounge is an intimate crystal-chandeliered European-style casino for high-stakes players only.

The Palm

The Forum Shops at Caesars Palace, 3500 Las Vegas Blvd. S. ☎ **702/732-7256.** Reservations recommended. Main courses $8.50–$14 lunch, $15–$35 dinner. AE, CB, DC, MC, V. Daily 11:30am–11pm. STEAK/SEAFOOD.

Grandsons of New York's original Palm owners John Ganzi and Pio Bozzi have parlayed the family business into a nationwide restaurant empire. Hence, this Las Vegas branch. In the Palm tradition, signature pine-wainscoted ecru walls are plastered with celebrity caricatures of everyone from Wayne Newton to Walt Kelly's Pogo. Diners are comfortably seated in roomy mahogany booths upholstered in dark green leather. A star-studded clientele includes everyone from Tony Curtis (who celebrated a birthday here) to George Foreman (who got a standing ovation from fellow diners).

Another Palm tradition is a bare-bones menu that austerely offers up appetizers (such as shrimp cocktail, clams casino, melon and prosciutto) and entrees (filet mignon, lamb chops, salmon fillet, broiled crab cakes, linguine with clam sauce, prime rib of beef) without descriptive frills. By contrast, a listing for string beans *aglio e olio* (in garlic and oil) seems positively lyrical. Food preparation is simple (nothing is drizzled, infused, or nuanced here). Rather, the emphasis is on fresh fish and seafood, top-quality cuts of meat, and salads using the ripest, reddest, and juiciest tomatoes—all served up in satisfying, large portions. Side dishes of cottage fries and creamed spinach are recommended. The wine list nicely complements the menu, and desserts include big wedges of cheesecake and chocolate pecan pie. At lunch you can choose a $12 fixed-price meal, which includes an entree (perhaps prime rib or batter-fried shrimp), salad, cottage fries, and tea or coffee.

✪ Spago

The Forum Shops at Caesars Palace, 3500 Las Vegas Blvd. S. ☎ **702/369-6300.** Reservations recommended for the dining room; not accepted at the cafe. Dining room main courses $14–$28. Cafe main courses $8.50–$16.50. AE, CB, DC, DISC, MC, V. Dining room Sun–Thurs 6–10:30pm, Fri–Sat 5:30–11pm. Cafe daily 11am–1am. CALIFORNIA.

Wolfgang Puck's landmark L.A. restaurant provides a rare foodie oasis in Vegas. However, though one of the few truly innovative restaurants in Vegas, Spago has been riding a bit on its reputation. While anything you get here is going to be better and more interesting than what you'd get at the vast majority of Vegas restaurants, you get the feeling they've been far ahead of the pack for just long enough to get comfortable. Which is not to say Spago is not worth the splurge—it just means that others have caught up with them (and in some cases, though it may be considered heresy to say it, may have surpassed Puck's baby), and they are no longer the only foodie game in town.

But it's still an experience going there—call it California casual elegance. The postindustrial interior is the very model of a modern major restaurant, while the exterior cafe on the Forum Shops is more relaxed, and provides an opportunity for people watching as fine as at any European sidewalk cafe. It's probably not as star-heavy as the celebrated L.A. original, but it's safe to say that any Hollywood muck-a-muck in town would probably be inclined to eat here.

When Nomi Malone, who appeared in the film *Showgirls,* came to eat at the cafe, she peevishly said she didn't "know what any of this stuff is." She must not get out much; the cafe menu features such familiar items as meat loaf and pizza, although glamorized versions—this isn't Country Kitchen, and so this pizza features smoked salmon. Not to mention crème fraîche. It sounds like an unholy hybrid of Italian and deli, but it's sublime. Other cafe specialties include Puck's signature Chinois chicken salad and a superb mesquite-fried salmon served with a tangy toss of soba noodles and cashews in a coconut-sesame-chili paste vinaigrette nuanced with lime juice and Szechuan mustard. The inside menu changes seasonally; examples of potential choices include scallops with a divine basil risotto, an appetizer of tuna sashimi in hot olive oil and sesame, or porcini mushrooms with a truffle sauce. The "signature" dish is a Chinese-style duck, moist but with a perfectly crispy skin. It's about as good as duck gets. It was served with a doughy steamed bun and Chinese vegetables. Deserts range from fresh fruit sorbets in surprising flavors (cantaloupe, honeydew), to a luscious brownie topped with homemade chocolate, whipped cream, and ice cream. The wine list is impressive, but the house wine was a disappointment and possibly not worth the cost.

MODERATE

See also the listing for **Spago** (above), an expensive restaurant fronted by more moderately priced cafe.

All-American Bar & Grille

Rio Suite Hotel, 3700 W. Flamingo Rd., at I-15. ☎ **702/252-7767.** Reservations not accepted. Main courses $5.95–$13.75 at lunch (most under $10), $11.95–$23.95 at dinner. AE, CB, DC, DISC, MC, V. Daily 11am–11pm. AMERICAN.

This warmly inviting balconied restaurant has two themes: sports and Americana. Mahogany-paneled walls are hung with snowshoes, golf clubs, oars, and croquet mallets; there's a portrait of George Washington and a torch-bearing Statue of Liberty; vintage American flags fly from lofty mahogany rafters; and the wait staff is in flag-motif shirts. You can also eat in a lively sunken bar area filled with athletic memorabilia (Roger Staubach's football jersey, and the like), while watching sporting events aired on eight TV monitors.

At lunch, the menu features burgers, salads, and sandwiches. Dinner options include steaks, seafood, and a choice of 27 domestic beers and selected wines by the glass.

A typical meal here might begin with an order of Blue Point oysters, followed by filet mignon and lobster tails (served with soup or salad, warm sourdough bread and butter, grilled vegetables, and a baked potato), with a finale of peach cobbler topped with homemade vanilla ice cream.

The Noodle Kitchen

Mirage, 3400 Las Vegas Blvd. S., between Flamingo Rd. and Sands Ave. ☎ **800/456-4564.** Reservations not accepted. Main courses $7.95–$22.75 (many under $10). AE, CB, DC, DISC, MC, V. Daily 11am–4am. CHINESE.

The Mirage designed The Noodle Kitchen to serve its sizable clientele of Asian high rollers, a clientele desirous of authentic, non-Americanized Chinese fare. Most of the diners here are Asian, but American and European food aficionados will also appreciate the Kitchen's high-quality cuisine. It's really not so much a separate establishment as a section of the hotel's lushly tropical Caribe Café.

Start off with clear soup, flavored with Chinese cilantro and replete with thin egg noodles and dumplings filled with minced shrimp and ear mushrooms. A combination plate of soy chicken slices, roast pork, and tender crisp-skinned roast duck with plum sauce makes a marvelous entree choice, especially when accompanied by delicious al dente steamed vegetables (Chinese broccoli or choy sum) in oyster sauce. If you like to spice things up, you'll find three hot sauces on the table. There are Asian desserts (such as red bean ice delight), but as these are an acquired taste, you might prefer fresh-baked cakes and pies from the Caribe Café menu. Or skip dessert altogether in favor of sweet Vietnamese iced coffee mixed with condensed milk, coconut milk, and shaved ice. All bar drinks, including Chinese and Japanese beers, are available.

Planet Hollywood

Forum Shops at Caesars Palace, 3500 Las Vegas Blvd. S. ☎ **702/791-STAR.** Reservations not accepted. Main courses $7.95–$19.95 (most under $13). AE, DC, MC, V. Sun–Thurs 11am–midnight, Fri–Sat 11am–1am. CALIFORNIA.

Arnold, Sly, Bruce, and Demi joined forces with some finance buddies to create a movie version of the Hard Rock. It was an instant success and a sure sign of the decline of Western civilization. Some of the objects displayed are worthless, others are sort of amusing—Barbara Eden's genie bottle, chariot wheels from *Ben Hur*, the side of beef Stallone sparred with in *Rocky*, the *Star Trek* control tower. Video monitors are everywhere, showing trailers for soon-to-be-released movies, themed video montages, and footage of Planet Hollywood grand openings around the world (which isn't the least bit self-indulgent and promotional, oh, no). The restaurant is also the scene of frequent autograph signings. Further reluctant credit is given for the more imaginative than average theme-restaurant menu; blackened shrimp served with Creole mustard sauce; linguine tossed with Thai shrimp, peanuts, and julienned vegetables in spicy sweet chili sauce; white chocolate bread pudding drenched in whiskey sauce and topped with white chocolate ice cream. There's a walkway here directly from the Strip.

Stage Deli

Forum Shops at Caesars Palace, 3500 Las Vegas Blvd. S. ☎ **702/893-4045.** Reservations accepted for large parties only. Main courses $9.95–$13.95, sandwiches $5.95–$13.95. AE, DC, DISC, JCB, MC, V. Sun–Thurs 7:30am–10:30pm, Fri–Sat 7:30am–midnight. DELI.

New York City's Stage Deli—a legendary hangout for comedians, athletes, and politicians—has been slapping pastrami on rye for more than half a century. Its Las

Vegas branch retains the Stage's brightly lit, Big Apple essence. Walls are embellished with subway graffiti and hung with Broadway theater posters, bowls of pickles grace the white Formica tables, and, in the New York tradition, comics like Buddy Hackett and Henny Youngman drop by whenever they're in town.

The deli is often not crowded. In addition to being handy for Caesars guests, if you are staying next door at the Mirage, it's easy to pop over, making it a satisfying breakfast alternative (to often overcrowded, overpriced, and not very good hotel breakfast joints in the area). The huge (we mean it) menu means finding something for even the pickiest of eaters.

Most of the fare—including fresh-baked pumpernickel and rye, meats, chewy bagels, lox, spicy deli mustard, and pickles—comes in daily from New York. The Stage dishes up authentic 5-inch-high sandwiches stuffed with pastrami, corned beef, brisket, or chopped liver. Maybe overstuffed is a better description. Unless you have a hearty appetite, are feeding two, or have a fridge in your room for leftovers, you might want to try the half sandwich and soup or salad combos. Other specialties here include matzo ball soup, knishes, kasha varnishkes, cheese blintzes, kreplach, pirogen, and smoked fish platters accompanied by bagels and cream cheese. Or you might prefer a full meal consisting of pot roast and gravy, salad, homemade dinner rolls, potato pancakes, and fresh vegetables. Desserts run the gamut from rugelach cheesecake to Hungarian-style apple strudel, and available beverages include wine and beer, milk shakes, Dr. Brown's sodas, and chocolate egg creams.

INEXPENSIVE

La Piazza Food Court

Caesars Palace, 3570 Las Vegas Blvd. S., just north of Flamingo Rd. ☎ **702/731-7110.** Complete meals are $7–$15. AE, DC, DISC, MC, V. Sun–Thurs 8:30am–11pm, Fri–Sat 9am–midnight. FOOD COURT.

Essentially an upscale version of a cafeteria, this is a great choice for families. Food stations are located along an attractive arched walkway lit by pink neon, and the brass-railed dining area, under massive domes, is rather elegant, with gold-topped columns and comfortable upholstered seating. The food is top quality—terrific deep-dish pizzas, an excellent salad bar, fresh-baked pies and cakes, sushi, smoked fish, immense burritos, Chinese stir-fry, rotisserie chicken, and a New York style deli, **Häagen-Dazs** bars, and a selection of beverages that includes herbal teas, wine, beer, espresso, and cappuccino. Just about any single beverage you can think of, from virtually all over the world, you can find it here. There's something for every dining mood. Waffle cones are baked on the premises, creating a delicious aroma.

5 North Strip

VERY EXPENSIVE

The Monte Carlo Room

Desert Inn, 3145 Las Vegas Blvd. S., between Desert Inn Rd. and Sands Ave. ☎ **702/733-4444.** Reservations recommended. Jackets for men required. Main courses $28–$80. AE, CB, DC, DISC, JCB, MC, V. Thurs–Mon 6–11pm. FRENCH.

The delightful Monte Carlo Room is equally renowned for its sublime setting and fine French cuisine. The romantic main dining room has charming murals of Greek youths and nymphs lolling in a classical setting framed by rose bowers and Palladian windows overlooking the palm-fringed pool. The ceiling is painted with cupids frolicking amid fluffy clouds. Diners are comfortably ensconced in tapestried banquettes at tables illuminated by white taper candles or pink-shaded crystal lamps.

Great Meal Deals

We've already alluded to the rock-bottom-budget meals and graveyard specials available at casino hotel restaurants. For your convenience, some of the best buys are assembled below. Quality not assured and Pepto-Bismol not provided. You'll find addresses and phone numbers for these hotels in chapter 5. Keep your eyes open as you travel through town, as hotels tend to advertise their specials on their marquees. (For example, **Ellis Island Restaurant** was advertising a $3.95 prime rib special when we last went by.)

- **Binion's Horseshoe Coffeeshop:** A 16-ounce T-bone steak complete with salad, corn, and a baked potato, $6.25; served 5pm to 9:45pm.
- **California Hotel:** A top sirloin and two baby lobster tails plus salad and a glass of wine for $10.95.
- **The El Cortez, Emerald Room:** A soup-to-nuts dinner with an 18-ounce porterhouse steak is $6.45, and a dollar will buy a breakfast of bacon and eggs with hash browns, toast, and coffee, both 24 hours.
- **Fitzgeralds, Molly's Country Kitchen:** Round the clock, enjoy a roast turkey dinner with sage dressing and giblet gravy, soup or salad, and choice of potato for $4.95.
- **Golden Nugget, Carson City Cafe:** From 4 to 11pm, a 10-ounce prime rib dinner (with baked potato and a vegetable) is $9.95. And from 11pm to 7am an 8-ounce grilled ham steak with eggs, hash browns, and toast costs $3.95.
- **Holiday Inn Casino Boardwalk, Cyclone Coffee Shop:** Round-the-clock standouts include a hearty hobo stew of beef, potatoes, carrots, and gravy served in a pound loaf of freshly baked bread for $2.99; an all-you-can-eat fish fry with coleslaw and fries for $2.49; and a breakfast of two eggs, bacon, or sausage, hash browns and toast for $1.29 (the same price will buy you all the pancakes you can eat!). Wednesdays from 4 to 10pm, an 8-ounce prime rib dinner is $3.49.
- **Imperial Palace, Coffee Shop:** They have a night owl prime rib special, quite possibly the cheapest in town, $2.95; open 11pm to 7am.
- **Jackie Gaughan's Plaza, Plaza Diner:** Between 11pm and 11am, a graveyard special features a 16-ounce ham steak with two eggs, hash browns, toast, and coffee for $1.95.
- **The Luxor, Pyramid Café:** A sirloin steak and eggs breakfast with hash browns and toast is $2.99 Thursday to Tuesday from 11pm to 6am.
- **The Rio, Beach Café:** A 10-ounce T-bone steak with eggs, potatoes, and toast is $2.99 between 11pm and 7am.
- **Sam Boyd's Fremont, Lanai Cafe:** Specials here include a full prime rib dinner (with baked potato, vegetable, and salad) for $5.95, served 4pm to 2am; a steak-and-lobster-tail dinner (same side dishes) for $9.99, served 9pm to 2am; and a pound of Alaskan crab legs with rice and coleslaw for $7.77, served 11pm to 6am.
- **Sam's Town, Smokey Joe's Cafe:** From 11pm to 11am, a hearty breakfast including a $3/4$-pound ham steak, three eggs, hash browns, and toast is $2.95, for the same meal with steak instead of ham you'll pay $3.95.

Excellent appetizer choices include seafood ravioli with champagne-caviar sauce or a terrine of fresh goose liver. We also love the thick, velvety, cognac-laced lobster bisque, full of rich flavor, served in a scooped-out round loaf of bread. For your entree, consider a classic French entrecôte au poivre or duck à l'orange served with apple- and pine nut—studded wild rice. A mélange of vegetables and a potato dish (perhaps pommes soufflés) accompany entrees. There's an extensive wine list; consult the sommelier for suggestions. Flaming tableside preparations are a specialty, including desserts such as crêpes Suzette and cherries jubilee.

Morton's of Chicago

3200 Las Vegas Blvd. S., in the Fashion Show Mall (take Spring Mountain Rd. off the Strip, make a right at Fashion Show Dr., and follow the signs). ☎ **702/893-0703.** Reservations recommended. Main courses $18–$30. AE, CB, DC, JCB, MC, V. Mon–Sat 5:30–10:30pm, Sun 5–9:30pm. STEAK/SEAFOOD.

This famous gourmet steak chain has a warm, clublike interior. Ecru walls are hung with LeRoy Neiman prints and photographs of celebrity diners, rich mahogany paneling adds a note of substantial elegance, and much of the seating is in roomy, gold leather booths. An exhibition kitchen gleams with copper pots, and wines are stored in a brick-walled rack. Frequent power diners here include most hotel/casino owners as well as Strip entertainers Siegfried and Roy. Robert de Niro and Joe Pesci came in frequently during the filming of *Casino,* and, one night, Tony Curtis joined the wait staff in singing "Happy Birthday" to a guest.

Start off with an appetizer, perhaps a lump crabmeat cocktail with mustard-mayonnaise sauce. Entree choices include succulent prime Midwestern steaks prepared to your exact specifications, plus lemon oregano chicken, lamb chops, Sicilian veal, grilled swordfish, whole baked Maine lobster, and prime rib with creamed horseradish. Side orders such as flavorfully fresh al dente asparagus served with hollandaise or hash browns are highly recommended. Portions are bountiful; plan to share. A loaf of warm onion bread on every table is complimentary. Leave room for dessert, perhaps a Grand Marnier soufflé. There's an extensive wine list, and you may want to retreat to a sofa in the cozy mahogany-paneled bar/lounge for after-dinner drinks.

Top of the World

Stratosphere Las Vegas Hotel, 2000 Las Vegas Blvd. S., between St. Louis St. and Baltimore Ave. ☎ **702/380-7711.** Reservations required. Main courses $13–$21 lunch, $21–$29 dinner. AE, CB, DC, DISC, JCB, MC, V. Daily 11am–3:45pm; Sun–Thurs 4–11pm, Fri–Sat 4pm–midnight. AMERICAN/CONTINENTAL.

Okay, revolving restaurants are the very definition of kitsch. But you know what? We like 'em. And when you've got views like these, well, there is a difference between having good taste and being made of stone.

Because you are 869 feet in the air, Vegas is stretched out before you in a glittering palette. Who knew this town could be so beautiful? This proves the Stratosphere is good for something. The Top of the World restaurant may not have the best food in Vegas (though some things are actually pretty good), but it has hands down the best view. (It takes about an hour for one revolution.) You will be so busy admiring the Strip, noticing that Vegas goes on much further than you thought, wondering which casino that particular cluster of lights is, and trying to spot your hotel, that you won't even notice what you are eating. It's one of the most romantic spots in town to dine.

But it's expensive, and the entrees, at least, not worth the cost. Having anticipated that customers might want to fill up tables just ordering a small snack, there is a $15 per person minimum. Here's what you do: Order only the generous-sized appetizers and desserts. You won't be disappointed, and you can easily make the minimum. The menu changes, but recent appetizers included Southwestern spring rolls (think of a cross between an egg roll and a fajita) filled with chicken and veggies, slightly deep fried to a nice crunch, and served with a fine guacamole. It's tart, crunchy, messy, and fattening, which means it has to be good. There was also an oversized (to the point of silliness) bruschetta (chopped tomato, basil, and garlic covered in olive

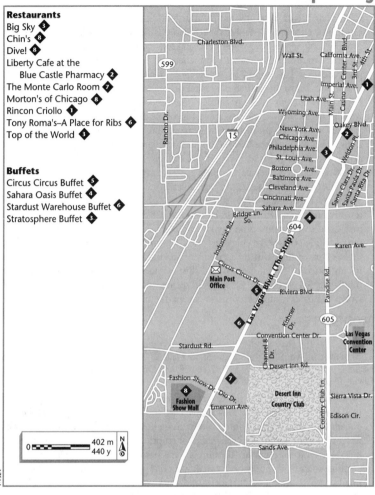

Restaurants
Big Sky ❸
Chin's ❽
Dive! ❾
Liberty Cafe at the
    Blue Castle Pharmacy ❷
The Monte Carlo Room ❼
Morton's of Chicago ❽
Rincon Criollo ❶
Tony Roma's–A Place for Ribs ❻
Top of the World ❸

Buffets
Circus Circus Buffet ❺
Sahara Oasis Buffet ❹
Stardust Warehouse Buffet ❻
Stratosphere Buffet ❸

oil on huge toasted slices of bread) that was tasty if hard to eat. The salads are over-priced and overly fussy, while the entrees are not terribly imaginative. (The fillet of almond-crusted salmon did get a thumbs up on an earlier visit.) The desserts were stellar, with the stand-out being the expensive ($9) but easily shared by two (it's huge and rich) Chocolate Stratosphere Tower. Yep, a chocolate replica of the very building you are sitting in; the top part is filled with a terrific chocolate mousse, and the whole thing gets covered in chocolate sauce, poured by your waiter with great ceremony. It's a gimmick, but chocolate lovers will be thrilled. Additional happiness came with towering *vacherin,* layers of hazelnut meringue filled with Bavarian cream, garnished with fresh berries, and served with crème anglaise and kiwi and raspberry sauces. The service was also impeccable.

EXPENSIVE

✪ Chin's

3200 Las Vegas Blvd. S., in the Fashion Show Mall (turn at the Frontier sign). ☎ **702/ 733-8899.** Reservations recommended. Main courses $9.95–$11.95 lunch, $10–$29.50 dinner. AE, MC, V. Mon–Sat 11:30am–10pm, Sun noon–10pm. CHINESE.

Chin's has been a Vegas fixture for nearly 20 years and is consistently voted by locals in the *Las Vegas Review* as their favorite Chines restaurant. It is certainly a surprise for anyone who knows Chinese food solely through take-out or strip malls. The simple, stark decor produces an ambience of low-key elegance. The prices will surprise you, too. This is not $1 Chinese food. But as owner Mr. Chin points out, Chinese food takes so much time to prepare (all that chopping, dicing, splicing, and what not) and to present in the traditionally stylish way (no steam trays here) that it's a wonder anyone would ever charge just a couple dollars for a dish.

Chin is justly proud of his achievements, but he adds as much to his restaurant as the food. You will see him moving from table to table, greeting regulars by name; do try to have him visit with you, if you can. He's full of stories, like how Jerry Lewis and Neil Sedaka are regulars, with a special dish created just for the latter (shrimp with lobster in lobster sauce, no vegetables).

However, anyone with broad experience with Chinese food won't find anything terribly surprising here. Experiments with more radical dishes failed (too timid tourists?), and so the menu is on the safe side. Which is not to say it isn't good. Standouts include strawberry chicken (think lemon chicken but with a different fruit; Chin's created this twist on a familiar dish, and other local restaurants have copied it); an appetizer of sinful deep-fried shrimp puffs (stuffed with minced shrimp and mildly curried cream cheese); splendid spring rolls; and barbecue pork fried rice that strikes that tricky, careful balance between dry and greasy.

MODERATE

Dive!

3200 Las Vegas Blvd. S., in the Fashion Show Mall. ☎ **702/369-DIVE.** Reservations for large parties only. Main courses $6.95–$13.95. AE, CB, DC, DISC, MC. V. Sun–Thurs 11:30am–10pm, Fri–Sat 11:30am–11pm. AMERICAN.

Notable for being one of the few theme restaurants not devoted to memorabilia, DIVE! was partly created by Steven Spielberg and movie exec Jeffrey Katzenberg. The outside is admittedly quite fun: yellow submarine crashing through a 30-foot wall of water that cascades into an oversized pool erupting with depth-charge blasts. Its gunmetal-gray interior replicates the hull of a submarine with vaulted cylindrical ceilings, porthole-shaped (albeit neon-accented, since this is Vegas) windows, exposed conduits that burst with steam, sonar screens, and working periscopes. Every hour a high-tech show projected on a 16-cube video wall (and 48 additional monitors throughout the restaurant) simulates a fantasy submarine dive. And overhead, a luxury ocean liner, a manta ray research vessel, exotic fish, a fighting shark, and model subs circumnavigate the room on a computerized track. It's all whimsical and imaginative. Surprise— they serve submarine sandwiches (among other choices). Kids should love it and adults will find it slightly less annoying than, say, Chuck E. Cheese (and with somewhat more sophisticated food).

Tony Roma's—A Place for Ribs

Stardust Resort and Casino, 3000 Las Vegas Blvd. S., at Convention Center Dr. ☎ **702/732-6111.** Reservations not accepted. Main courses $8.25–$12.95. Children's portions $4.95. AE, CB, DC, DISC, MC, V. Sun–Thurs 5–11pm, Fri–Sat 5pm–midnight. BARBECUE.

Tony Roma's is a deservedly popular national chain, and the company has voted this Stardust location the very best of its 140 franchises in terms of service, food quality, and cleanliness. It's a comfortable place, and a tub with brass faucets sits outside, so you can wash your sticky fingers on exiting.

This is a great choice for family dining. The house specialty is meaty, fork-tender baby back ribs barbecued in tangy sauce, but you can also order big, juicy beef ribs, honey-and molasses-basted, Carolina-style pork ribs, or spicy Cajun ribs. A sampler plate is available. There are also hearty platters of barbecued shrimp or chicken, burgers, the catch of the day, steaks, and salads. Do consider a side order of onion rings (served in a loaf). Entrees come with coleslaw and a choice of baked potato, french fries, or ranch-style beans. The children's menu lists a choice of four meals in a basket—ribs, burgers, chicken fingers, or chicken drumstick and thighs, all served with fries. For dessert there are fresh-baked chocolate, coconut, and banana cream pies, and all bar drinks are available. There is another Tony Roma's downtown, at Sam Boyd's Fremont Hotel and Casino, 200 E. Fremont St.

INEXPENSIVE

Big Sky

Stratosphere Las Vegas Hotel, 2000 Las Vegas Blvd. S., between St. Louis St. and Baltimore Ave. ☎ 702/780-7777. All-you-can-eat dinner $12.99, free for children under 6. AE, CB, DC, DISC, JCB, MC, V. Sun–Thurs 5–11pm, Fri–Sat 5pm–midnight. BARBECUE.

Food bargains abound in Las Vegas, and this is one of the best. Big Sky features murals depicting the Old West, oil paintings of cowboys, log handrails, lasso-motif carpeting, and a cashier housed in a chuck wagon. All of this provides a suitably rustic setting for hearty all-you-can-eat family style feasts. Country music helps set the tone, and service is down home and friendly.

Entree choices include prime rib with creamed horseradish sauce and a barbecue combination (beef brisket, St. Louis ribs, Carolina pulled pork, and fried chicken). At press time, there was talk of adding steaks as well. Whatever you select, it will come with a huge salad, scrumptious corn muffins (don't fill up on them; there's lots more food coming), corn on the cob, seasoned steak fries, coleslaw, Texas toast, and baked beans with pork. And when you've eaten your fill, you can waddle over to the dessert table and help yourself to apple cobbler, fresh berries and cream, and bread pudding with rum sauce. There's a full bar.

✪ Liberty Cafe at the Blue Castle Pharmacy

1700 S. Las Vegas Blvd. ☎ 702-383-0101. Reservations not accepted. Nothing over $6.50. Cash only. 24 hours. DINER.

You can go to any number of retro soda fountain replicas (such as Johnny Rockets) and theme restaurants that pretend to be a cheap diners, but why bother when the (admittedly, decidedly unflashy) real thing is just past the end of the Strip? The soda fountain/lunch counter at the Blue Castle Pharmacy was Las Vegas's first 24-hour restaurant, and it has been going strong for 60 years. Plunk down at the counter, and watch the cooks go nuts trying to keep up with the orders. The menu is basic comfort food: standard grill items (meat loaf, ground round steak, chops), fluffy cream pies, and classic breakfasts served "anytime"—try the biscuits and cream gravy at 3am. They also serve gyros and the like. But the best bet is a $^1/_3$-pound burger and "thick creamy shake," both the way they were meant to be and about as good as they get. At around $5, this is half what you would pay for a comparable meal at the Hard Rock Cafe. And as waitress Beverly says, "This is really real." Places like this are a vanishing species—it's worth the short walk from the Stratosphere.

Rincon Criollo

1145 Las Vegas Blvd. S. ☎ 702-388-1906. Reservations not accepted. Main courses $6.50–$9.95, paella (for 3) $20. AE, DISC, MC, V. CUBAN

Located beyond the wedding chapels on Las Vegas Boulevard, Rincon Criollo has all the right details for a good, cheap ethnic joint: full of locals and empty of frills. It's not the best Cuban food ever, but it gets the job done. The main courses (featuring

Cuban pork and chicken specialties) are hit and miss; try the marinated pork leg or, better still, ask your server for a recommendation. Paella is offered, but only for parties of three or more (and starts at $20). The side-course *chorizo* (a spicy sausage) is excellent, and the Cuban sandwich (roast pork, ham, and cheese on bread, which is then pressed and flattened out) is huge and tasty. For only $3.50, the latter makes a fine change of pace meal.

6 Convention Center/Paradise Road/Sahara Avenue

VERY EXPENSIVE

Bistro Le Montrachet

Las Vegas Hilton, 3000 Paradise Rd. ☎ **702/732-5111.** Reservations suggested. Main courses $23–$46. AE, CB, DC, DISC, JCB, MC, V. Wed–Mon 6–10:30pm. FRENCH.

This ultraelegant French restaurant seats diners under a dome bathed in a flattering pink light, an effect enhanced by the discreet glow emanating from shaded Chinese lamps. The room centers on a templelike circle of massive walnut columns wherein a large floral arrangement graces an ornate marble table. Rich, mahogany-paneled walls are hung with landscapes and still-lifes; a crystal chandelier and beveled mirrors add sparkle.

Dishes are exquisitely presented and prepared. You might begin with chilled duck foie gras served on toast points. Also noteworthy are creamy lobster bisque and the salad "Le Montrachet," a refreshing mélange of Belgian endive, watercress, julienned beets, and enoki mushrooms in a Gorgonzola/walnut oil dressing. Entree choices range from roasted breast of Muscovy duck (served with white and black beans and currants in a crème de cassis sauce) to broiled live Maine lobster removed from the shell and served atop herbed Moroccan couscous with crab dressing and drawn butter. Among desserts, we're partial to the rich crème brûlée complemented by seasonal fruits, berries, and petits fours. The restaurant's wine cellar stocks more than 400 wines from vineyards spanning the globe.

Pegasus

Alexis Park Resort, 375 E. Harmon Ave., between Koval Lane and Paradise Rd. ☎ **702/796-3300.** Reservations recommended. Main courses $13.50–$39. AE, DC, MC, V. Nightly 6–11pm. CONTINENTAL.

This low-key luxury resort attracts many visiting celebrities and Strip headliners, and its premier restaurant is a fitting venue for such an upscale clientele. Its splashing fountains and mist of diffused lighting playing on etched mirrors make us feel like we're dining in an underwater kingdom. Planters of greenery, pots of ferns, and a large floral centerpiece further beautify this serene setting, as does a wall of arched windows overlooking a fountain-splashed rock garden.

Flambé dishes are featured, and sorbets are served between courses. You might begin with a quail egg and mandarin orange salad tossed with sweet mustard dressing. Among the soups, a splendid choice is the velvety cognac-laced lobster bisque. And fresh-shucked oysters Rockefeller here elevate this dish to its delicate apogee. The featured entree is Maine lobster sautéed with black truffles in a Madeira/bordelaise sauce; crowned with almond meringue baked to a golden brown, it is dramatically presented in a flaming veil of fire. A daily game special is offered each evening, perhaps ostrich with fresh seared foie gras. Desserts include bananas Foster and cherries jubilee along with pastries and cakes from the cart. There's an extensive wine list (mostly French and Californian) with choices in varying price ranges.

🎪 Family-Friendly Dining

Buffets *(see p. 147)*   Cheap meals for the whole family. The kids can choose what they like, and there are sometimes make-your-own sundae machines.

DIVE! *(see p. 126)*   Housed in a submarine and featuring a zany high-tech show every hour projected on a video wall, this is the most fun family oriented spot of all.

Hard Rock Cafe *(see p. 132)*   Kids also adore this restaurant, which throbs with excitement and is filled with rock memorabilia.

Hippo and the Wild Bunch *(see p. 133)*   A cartoonlike decor and wild party atmosphere (sometimes balloon artists are on hand making hats and animals for diners) makes this a favorite with kids. Adults will be thrilled with the high quality of the food.

Planet Hollywood *(see p. 121)*   This popular chain houses a veritable museum of movie memorabilia, and the action on numerous video monitors keeps kids from getting bored.

Pink Pony   This bubble-gum pink circus-motif 24-hour coffee shop at Circus Circus will appeal to kids. And mom and dad can linger over coffee while the kids race upstairs to watch circus acts and play carnival games.

Sherwood Forest Cafe   Kids love to climb on the lavender dragons fronting this 24-hour coffee shop at Excalibur, and they also enjoy numerous child-oriented activities while you're on the premises.

EXPENSIVE

✪ Lawry's The Prime Rib

4043 Howard Hughes Pkwy. at Flamingo (between Paradise and Koval). ☎ **702/893-2223.** Reservations recommended. Main courses $18.95–$29.95. AE, DC, DISC, JCB, MC, V. Sun–Thurs 5pm–10pm, Fri–Sat 5–11pm. STEAK/SEAFOOD.

If you love prime rib, come here. If you could take or leave prime rib, Lawry's will turn you into a believer. Because Lawry's does one thing, and it does it better than anyone else. Lawry's first opened in Los Angeles in 1938 and still remains a popular tradition. Originally, all Lawry's offered was prime rib, which they did perfectly and with tremendous style. Over the years, they have added three branches, the most recent landing in Las Vegas at the beginning of 1997. Yes, you can get prime rib all over town for under five bucks. But that's a tuna fish sandwich to Lawry's caviar (if one might mix food metaphors.)

Eating at Lawry's is a ceremony, with all the parts played the same for the last 60 years. Waitresses in brown and white English maid uniforms, complete with starched white cap, take your order. For side dishes, that is. The real decision, what cut of rib you are going to have, comes later. Actually, that's the only part of the tradition that has changed. Lawry's has added fresh fish (halibut, salmon, or swordfish, depending on the evening) to its menu. Anyway, you tell the waitress what side dishes you might want (sublime creamed spinach, baked potato) for an extra price. Later, she returns with a spinning salad bowl (think salad preparation as Busby Berkeley musical number). The bowl, resting on crushed ice, spins as she pours Lawry's special dressing in a stream from high over her head. Tomatoes garnish. Applause follows. Eventually, giant metal carving carts (designed after the original ones) come to your table, bearing the meat. You name your cut (the regular Lawry's, the extralarge Diamond Jim Brady, only for serious carnivores, and the wimpy thin English cut), rare, medium, well. It comes with terrific Yorkshire pudding, nicely browned and not soggy, and some creamed horse radish that is combined with fluffy whipped cream, simultaneously sweet and tart.

Flavorful, tender, perfectly cooked, lightly seasoned, this will be the best prime rib you will ever have. Okay, maybe that's going too far, but the rest is accurate, honest. It just has to be tasted to be believed. You can finish off with a rich dessert (English trifle is highly recommended), but it almost seems pointless. Incidentally, the other Lawry's are decorated English manor style, but the Vegas branch has instead tried to recreate a 1930s restaurant, with art deco touches all around and big band music on the sound system.

Pamplemousse

400 E. Sahara Ave., between Santa Paula and Santa Rita drives, just east of Paradise Rd. ☎ **702/733-2066.** Reservations essential. Main courses $17.50–$24.50. AE, CB, DC, DISC, MC, V. Two seatings nightly at 6–6:30pm and 9–9:30pm. FRENCH.

Evoking a cozy French countryside inn, Pamplemousse is a catacomb of low-ceilinged rooms and intimate dining nooks with rough-hewn beams. Copperware and provincial pottery adorn the walls; candlelit tables, beautifully appointed with Villeroy and Boch show plates and fresh flowers, are draped in pale-pink linen; and classical music or light jazz plays softly in the background. It's all very charming and un-Vegasy. There's additional seating in a small garden sheltered by a striped tent. The restaurant's name, which means grapefruit, was suggested by the late singer Bobby Darin, one of the many celebrity pals of owner Georges La Forge. Strip headliners Wayne Newton, Robert Goulet, Siegfried and Roy, and Englebert Humperdinck are regulars.

The menu, which changes nightly, is recited by your waiter. The meal always begins with a large complimentary basket of crudités (about 10 different crisp, fresh vegetables), a big bowl of olives, and, a nice country touch, a basket of hard-boiled eggs. From there, you might proceed to an appetizer of lightly floured bay scallops sautéed in buttery grapefruit sauce, followed by an entree of crispy duck breast and banana in a sauce of orange honey, dark rum, and crème de banane. Filet mignon, New York steak, and rack of lamb are always featured. For dessert, perhaps there'll be homemade dark chocolate ice cream with pralines in a sabayon sauce. An extensive, well-rounded wine list complements the menu.

MODERATE

Alpine Village Inn

3003 Paradise Rd., between Riviera Blvd. and Convention Center Dr. ☎ **702/734-6888.** Reservations recommended. Fixed-price dinners $9.95–$19.50; children's portions (under 12 only) about half price. AE, CB, DC, DISC, MC, V. Sun–Thurs 5–10pm, Fri–Sat 5–11pm. SWISS/GERMAN.

A Las Vegas tradition since 1950, this extremely popular family restaurant doesn't subscribe to the less-is-more theory of interior design. Walls are painted with murals of snowy Alpine scenery, an effect echoed by snow-covered chalet roofing, twinkling Christmas tree lights, and miniature ski lifts on cables strung across the ceiling. There are Swiss and Austrian cowbells, mounted deer heads, and window boxes filled with geraniums. And the very efficient wait staff is in Tyrolean costume.

Dinner is a multicourse feast beginning with a big pewter bowl of crudités served with herbed cottage cheese dip. A steaming bowl of savory Bavarian chicken soup is followed by a salad, and a basket of fresh-baked breads includes scrumptious hot cinnamon rolls. For your entree, I recommend the roast duckling with sausage stuffing served over wild and brown rice (it comes with orange and cherry sauces) or roast tender chicken with chestnut stuffing. These are accompanied by an array of

Dining East of the Strip

Alpine Village Inn **5**
Bistro Le Montrachet **6**
Chili's Grill & Bar **4**
Einstein Bros. Bagels **17**
Fog City Diner **11**
Ginza **2**
Hard Rock Cafe **13**
Hippo & the Wild Bunch **14**
Komol **3**
Lawry's The Prime Rib **10**
Mamounia **16**
Marrakesh **9**
Mediterranean Café & Market **15**

Pamplemousse **1**
Papamios **18**
Pegasus **12**
The Rathskeller **5**
Ricardo's **20**
Shalimar **8**
The Tillerman **19**
Ware's T Bones Texas Style Bar-B-Que **18** **21**
Z Tejas Grill **7**

Buffets
Las Vegas Hilton Buffet of Champions **6**
Sam's Town, The Great Buffet **18**

vegetables and choice of crisp potato pancakes, a baked potato, or Swiss *Rösti* potatoes (shredded potato mixed with onion, bacon, eggs, and spices, fried in a pancake, and garnished with grated Parmesan). If you'd like more than one of the above selections, the waiters generally comply. The finale: homemade apple or peach strudel, served warm (topped with vanilla ice cream if you so desire). Tea or coffee is included. The wine list offers wines by the glass and a large selection of beers, 19 varieties of schnapps, and exotic cocktails.

After dinner, if you can still move, check out the adjoining gift shop's selection of cuckoo clocks, crystal, beer steins, music boxes, cowbells, and Hummel figures. There's also a bar/lounge and a separate downstairs restaurant called the Rathskellar (details below).

Ginza

1000 E. Sahara Ave., between State St. and Maryland Pkwy. ☎ **702/732-3080.** Reservations for large parties only. Main courses $12.55–$17.50. AE, MC, V. Tues–Sun 5pm–1am. JAPANESE.

For almost 2 decades, this charming little restaurant has attracted a devoted clientele of local Japanese and Japanese food aficionados. There's a sushi bar in the front room, and the main dining area has shoji screen–covered windows, tables sheltered by shingled eaves, rice paper lighting fixtures, and cream walls adorned with Japanese fans, paintings, and prints. Four spacious, red leather booths are the sole concession to Las Vegas style.

You might begin with a shared appetizer of tempura shrimp and vegetables. Entrees such as beef, chicken, or salmon sprinkled with sesame seeds in a thick teriyaki sauce come with soup (miso or egg flower), salad, and green tea. Sushi is a highlight, and there are about 30 à la carte selections from which to choose. Be sure to try an appetizer or entree portion of Ginza's unique Vegas rolls: salmon, tuna, yellowtail, and avocado rolled with seaweed in sesame-studded rice and quickly deep-fried so the sesame seeds form a crunchy crust. It's served with lemon soy sauce. Also delicious are seaweed-wrapped California rolls. The fish is extremely fresh, and everything here is made from scratch. A bottle of sake is recommended. For dessert there's lemon sherbet or ginger and green tea ice creams.

Hard Rock Cafe

4475 Paradise Rd., at Harmon Ave. ☎ **702/733-8400.** Reservations not accepted. Main courses $8.95–$13.95; burgers and sandwiches $5.50–7.95. AE, DC, MC, V. Sun–Thurs 11am–11:30pm, Fri–Sat 11am–midnight. AMERICAN.

The original Hard Rock Cafe opened in London as a meeting place for American expatriates and homesick exchange students dying for a good burger. T-shirts then simply said "Hard Rock Cafe," with no identifying city. No need for one. Now that Hard Rocks are everywhere (can it be long before there is one in Tibet?), the cachet is gone.

But this is the only Hard Rock (so far) attached to a hotel and a truly extraordinary casino, so let's cut this branch some slack. Allegedly, some stars do eat here; it's not out of the question because if a big rock act is playing in town, they will be playing at the Hard Rock. And staying there. So it is not at all uncommon to see them wandering the lobby or getting dealt a hand at the blackjack tables. Eating there? Well, sure, maybe. Sheryl Crow, Michael Keaton, the Ramones, Pat Benatar, and Eddie Van Halen have been spotted there over time.

The menu offers some good salads in addition to the burgers. An inexpensive children's menu is a plus for families. Don't be frightened by the line outside—it's usually not for the restaurant but the on-premises Hard Rock merchandise store. The Hard Rock Hotel and Casino is next door (see chapter 5).

✪ Hippo & the Wild Bunch

4503 Paradise Rd., at Harmon Ave., just across from the Hard Rock Hotel. ☎ **702/731-5446.**
Main courses $5.95–$13.95; children's menu $1.75–$2.95. AC, CB, DC, DISC, MC, V. Sun–Thurs
11am–3am, Fri–Sat 11am–5am. AMERICAN.

Georges La Forge, owner of the cozily romantic Pamplemousse (see description above), surprised everyone when he opened this wildly whimsical restaurant in 1995. Its kooky-cluttery interior includes cartoonlike animal sculptures (such as a hippo in a tree house), a tangle of vines strung overhead, and walls painted with bright jungle foliage. There are balloons tied to many chairs, and often a balloon artist is on the scene creating twisty animals and hats for guests. There are usually several exuberant parties going on (only some of them children's parties), and the chaotic ambience is exacerbated by loud rock music, a wait staff on roller skates, a bustling exhibition kitchen, and TV monitors over the bar airing sporting events. Tuesday to Sunday from 8pm to 3am, a DJ plays music for dancing.

Hippo's "party-on" atmosphere notwithstanding, the food is superb. Come at lunch to enjoy it without all the hoopla; at dinner, weather permitting, you might sit out on the quieter, tree-bordered patio. Noteworthy items on La Forge's eclectic menu include delicious potstickers with chili oil/soy dipping sauce, a classic salad Niçoise, pizzas, and spicy Southwestern ravioli in a red pepper sauce topped with diced vegetables. Burgers here are as good as burgers get, char-grilled and served on fresh-baked buns (ask for garlic mashed potatoes instead of fries). There's a dynamite tiramisu for dessert, and beverages, including a full bar, range from fresh-squeezed juices to coffee specialties.

Romano's Macaroni Grill

2400 W. Sahara Ave., 2 blocks west of I-15 (on your right, directly across from Palace Station, if you're coming from the Strip). ☎ **702/248-9500** for priority seating. Main courses $4.95–$9.25 at lunch, $6.50–$16.95 at dinner (most under $12). AE, CB, DC, DISC, MC, V. Sun–Thurs 11am–10pm, Fri–Sat 11am–11pm. ITALIAN.

The Macaroni Grill is a stellar exception to the general mediocrity of chain restaurants. The first thing you'll notice is its cheerful interior, with arched stone walls, shuttered windows, colorful murals of Venice, and lights festively strung from rafters overhead. This warmly welcoming ambience is enhanced by the glow from an oak-burning pizza oven tended by white-toqued chefs; strolling opera singers (there's recorded Italian music at other times); and aesthetic displays of foodstuff, Chianti, flowers, and desserts.

But the big surprise is the food. Everything is made from the freshest ingredients, and the quality of cuisine would be notable at twice the price. Thin-crust pizzas (order one topped with pancetta, ricotta, Gruyère, smoked mozzarella, and sun-dried tomatoes) are scrumptious, as are pastas such as farfalle (bow ties) tossed with grilled chicken, pancetta, and red and green onions in Asiago cream sauce. Equally good: an entree of sautéed chicken with mushrooms, artichoke hearts, capers, and pancetta in lemon butter, served with spaghettini. There are fresh-baked breads—focaccia and ciabatta (a crusty country loaf) for sopping up sauces or dipping in extra virgin olive oil. And desserts keep to the same lofty standard, especially an apple custard torte with hazelnut crust and caramel topping. Macaroni Grill has a full bar, premium wines are sold by the glass, and a children's menu offers an entree and beverage for just $3.25.

✪ Shalimar

3900 S. Paradise Rd. (in the Citibank Plaza). ☎ 702/796-0302. Reservations suggested. Lunch buffet $6.95; dinner main courses $10.50–$15.95. AE, DISC, MC, V. Mon–Fri 11:30am–2:30pm, 5:30pm–10:30pm; Sat–Sun 5:30pm–10:30pm. INDIAN

Have You Heard the One About the Belly Dancer?

If you have never tried Moroccan food, you should. Not only are you in for some new taste treats, but the action-packed presentation and gluttonous portions are very appropriate to Vegas. A full Moroccan feast (which is what most U.S. Moroccan restaurants feature) is an event. Vegas has two notable Moroccan establishments: **Marrakech**, 3900 Paradise Rd., at Howard Hughes Dr. (☎ 702/737-5611), where a six-course meal will cost you $23.95 per person (reservations recommended; AE, DISC, DC, MC, V accepted; open Monday to Sunday 5:30 to 11pm); and **Mamounia**, 4632 S. Maryland Pkwy., between Harmon and Tropicana avenues (☎ 702/597-0092), where a Moroccan feast will set you back $22.95 per person (reservations recommended; AE, DISC, DC, MC, V accepted; open Monday to Sunday 5pm to 11pm.Moroccan Feast $22.95).

Both rooms are covered, floor to ceiling, with Moroccan (or Moroccan style) rugs, furnished with low tables made of intricately inlaid wood (from the town of Essaouria). There is some simple tile work on the walls at Marrakech. It all adds up to that Arabian nights den of thieves feel. Diners sit on cushions on the floor or on very low cushioned benches.

Oh, and you eat with your fingers. Yep, that's part of the fun. A waiter comes out and pours water into a brass bowl so you can wash your hands and passes out huge towels for your lap. You then start a multicourse feast, beginning with a trio of cold salads: marinated carrots, eggplant and tomato and cucumber. Use the bread supplied from a big basket to scoop it up. The salads sound and are relatively simple, and are supremely tasty. This is followed by shrimp in a garlic sauce that seems more Italian than Moroccan (peculiarly, both restaurants feature this out-of-place item). But if you like garlic and shrimp, you won't complain too much. Next is *b'stilla*, a truly amazing dish if done right. Layers of filo are interspersed with chicken, eggs, and nuts; the whole thing is topped by powdered sugar and cinnamon. The uninitiated raise their eyebrows at it, while their more informed companions dig in. After you try it, you will fight for more than your fair share too. The final course is some kind of fowl (chicken or Cornish game hen), usually in a wonderful lemon and olive sauce. You finish up with some sweet mint tea, poured with great ceremony. All of this adds up to way too much food, so those cushions come in handy as you roll on the floor, holding your stomach and moaning. But what's that sound? It's the belly dancer, come out to dazzle you with her gravity defying shimmy skills, get the crowd going in a conga line (or, unfortunately, the Macarena), and accept a tip or two.

This experience is roughly the same at the two restaurants (though it's a lot more fun when the establishment is full; when the belly dancer emerges, a party atmosphere follows), but the food at Marrakech is considerably better. However, they found that the b'stilla was too strange for many patrons, so they turned it into a dessert with a fruit filling; they will make it with chicken if you ask when ordering; trust us and do. In its favor, the Mamounia offers à la carte items (Marrakech is considering this), so you can try other Moroccan specialties such as tajines, which are delicious stews cooked in clay pots.

In a town full of buffet deals, it's hard to get excited about another one, but on the other hand, all those other buffet deals offer pretty much the identical food: carving stations, various cafeteria hot dishes, and so forth. Here at Shalimar, a lunch buffet means about two dozen different North Indian–style dishes. All for about seven bucks. It's not as colorful or huge (in fact, it's just a table covered with steam trays) as those buffets up the street, but it is far more interesting and different. It's also a great deal and one of the first places to run to if you are sick of Strip food. Just ask the locals who vote it their favorite ethnic restaurant in the *Las Vegas Review Journal's* annual poll.

The buffet usually includes *tandoori* (chicken marinated in spiced yogurt cooked in a clay oven), *marsala* (tandoori in a curry sauce), *naan* (the flat Indian bread), and various vegetable dishes. (Vegetarians will find plenty to eat here—they offer special veggie dishes daily.) One stand-out at a recent visit was the *Bengan Bharta* (eggplant diced fine and cooked with onions, tomatoes and spices). There was also a yellow squash curry that was outrageously good. The tandoori chicken was perfect, tender, and moist. (Tandoori, by the way, is a very low-fat way of preparing chicken.) In the evening, a full Indian menu, with *vindaloo* (an especially hot curry where the meat is marinated in vinegar), flavored naans (try the garlic or onion) and other Indian specialties are offered à la carte. They will spice to order: mild, medium, hot, or very hot. If you make a mistake, you can always order *raita* (yogurt mixed with mild spices and cucumber); it cools your mouth nicely.

The restaurant has managed to spruce up its strip mall corner nicely, thanks to some Indian-style metal hanging lamps and peaked archways.

Z Tejas Grill

3824 Paradise Rd., between Twain Ave. and Corporate Dr. ☎ **702/732-1660.** Reservations recommended. Main courses $7.25–$11.95 at lunch, $9.75–$16.95 at dinner. AE, CB, DC, DISC, JCB, MC, V. Daily 11am–11pm. TEX-MEX.

This Austin, Texas-based restaurant's rather odd name came about because its original chef, a Frenchman, kept referring to it as "zee" Tejas Grill. We're partial to its sleek, split-level knotty-pine interior, with oak shutters separating dining areas, pine beams overhead, muted turquoise and peach walls hung with large abstract paintings, and cactus-motif central chandelier. During the day sunshine streams in through large windows (especially on the plant-filled enclosed patio); at night, soft lighting and candlelit tables make this a good choice for romantic dinners.

A unique, and very tasty, appetizer here is the Navajo roll: crisp-fried Mexican cheeses, seasoned fresh lump crabmeat, and vegetables wrapped in herb bread and topped with fried spinach and cornmeal crumbs. Follow it with spicy grilled Jamaican jerk chicken, nuanced with lime and served with peanut sauce and rum-spiked coconut-banana ketchup; it comes with two side dishes, perhaps roasted garlic/skin-on mashed potatoes and mixed vegetables. Swig down a few of the Grill's excellent made-from-scratch margaritas with your meal, but do leave room for some graham cracker-crusted praline cheesecake smothered with pecans. During Happy Hour (4 to 7pm weekdays), stop by for half-priced appetizers and 50¢ off on drinks.

INEXPENSIVE

Chili's Grill & Bar

2590 S. Maryland Pkwy., between Sahara and Karen aves., in the Sahara Town Square Shopping Center. ☎ **702/733-6462.** Main courses mostly $4.99–$10.29. AE, CB, DC, DISC, MC, V. Mon–Thurs 11am–10pm, Fri–Sat 11am–11pm, Sun 11:30am–10pm. Free parking. SOUTHWESTERN.

Chili's is a national chain, based in Texas, offering superior "bowls of red" and other Southwestern specialties. This branch is a sunny, brick-floored restaurant with many plants flourishing in the light streaming in through numerous windows. Seating is in comfortable upholstered booths, ceramic-tiled tables are situated beneath hanging lamps made from old copper chili pots, and walls are adorned with framed posters and photographs of chili cook-offs. This is a great choice for family dining.

Chili is, of course, a specialty, available with or without beans. Equally popular are the fabulous half-pound burgers, made from fresh-ground beef and served with home-style fries and various toppings (we like cheese and chili). Or order up a sizzling platter of steak or chicken fajitas. Lighter items include a grilled chicken Caesar salad or a plate of steamed vegetables. Similarly, desserts run the gamut from a brownie topped with ice cream, hot fudge, chopped walnuts, and whipped cream to low-fat frozen yogurt. A children's menu, listed on a place mat with games and puzzles, offers full meals for $2.79, including "bottomless fountain drinks."

The Rathskellar

3003 Paradise Rd., between Riviera Blvd. and Convention Center Dr. ☎ **702/734-6888.** Reservations recommended. Burgers and sandwiches $4.25–$7.50; main courses $8.75–$11.95. AE, CB, DC, DISC, MC, V. Sun–Thurs 5–10pm, Fri–Sat 5–11pm. GERMAN/AMERICAN.

The Rathskellar is a rollicking downstairs adjunct to the Alpine Village Inn (see above), a cozy beer hall, with red-and-white checkered tablecloths and a floor strewn with peanut shells (there are bowls of peanuts on every table). A pianist and singer entertain nightly, and everyone sings along. Choices here include a sauerbraten sandwich on pumpernickel rye served with German potato salad; a hot, open-faced turkey sandwich served with mashed potatoes, cranberry sauce, and gravy (salad bar included); barbecued pork ribs with baked beans; half-pound burgers; and beer-battered deep-fried buffalo wings with french fries. For dessert, there's apple or peach strudel à la mode. An extensive children's menu makes this a popular choice for family dining.

7 East Las Vegas/Flamingo Road

VERY EXPENSIVE

✪ The Tillerman

2245 E. Flamingo Rd., at Channel 10 Dr. (just west of Eastern Ave.). ☎ **702/731-4036.** Reservations not accepted. Main courses $15.95–$36.95. AE, CB, DC, DISC, MC, V. Nightly 5–11pm, bar/lounge until midnight. STEAK/SEAFOOD.

Ask any local for a list of favorite restaurants, and you can be sure the Tillerman in east Las Vegas will be on it. Its verdant, plant-filled interior is under a lofty, beamed cathedral ceiling with retractable skylights. Candlelit dining areas offer seating amid a grove of ficus trees, and the woodsy ambience is furthered by exquisite oak paneling and tree-trunk pillars. A circular stained-glass window provides a lovely focal point. There's additional seating on the mezzanine level, where diners enjoy treetop views. All the top Strip performers are regular Tillerman customers.

Your meal here begins with a relish tray and a basket of delicious, oven-fresh breads. Also complimentary is a Lazy Susan salad bar served at your table with a choice of homemade dressings, including a memorable chunky blue cheese. Portions are immense, so appetizers are really not necessary, but then again, they're too good to pass up. Especially notable: ultrafresh, plump red medallions of yellowfin tuna blackened and served almost rare in spicy mustard sauce. Meat entrees include prime center-cut New York strip steak, fork-tender filet mignon, and a center-cut veal chop. And there are at least a dozen fresh seafood specials each night; we've had a memorable piece of snowy white halibut, charcoal-broiled and brushed with pecan pesto. Entrees come with a white and wild rice mixture tossed with slivered almonds and chives and fresh vegetables. Homemade desserts, such as Bavarian cream with strawberries and bananas, change nightly. The wine list highlights California selections.

Note: Since the Tillerman doesn't take reservations, arrive early to avoid waiting, or else plan a predinner cocktail in the cozy, oak-paneled lounge with a working fireplace.

MODERATE

✪ Fog City Diner

325 Hughes Center Dr., off Flamingo Rd. at Howard Hughes Pkwy. (between Koval Lane and Paradise Rd.) ☎ **702/737-0200.** Reservations recommended. Main courses $6.50–$13.95. AE, CB, DC, DISC, MC, V. Sun–Thurs 11:30am–10pm, Fri–Sat 11:30am–11pm. AMERICAN.

San Francisco transplant Fog City Diner (it was featured in a Visa commercial for years) is one of the better dining choices in Las Vegas. It's not fancy food, per se— meat loaf, clam chowder and so forth—but it's all prepared with impeccable taste with new, clever gourmet twists on familiar Blue Plate Specials. In other words, this is not your mother's meat loaf. (No offense to your mother.) Here, it comes blackened and with a tomato chutney gravy that is out of this world. The menu changes seasonally, but with a constant emphasis on extremely fresh fish. They are very proud of said fish, which is trucked in every day from Los Angeles; they claim it is the freshest and most marvelously prepared of anywhere in Las Vegas. Even antifish folk might find their minds changed by the aforementioned clam chowder and their Pacific Northwest oysters. A section on the menu has a variety of small dishes; they call it "American dim sum," a variety of portions for grazing. These might include mu-shu pork burritos (which are more mu-shu than burrito—that's just the shape) or seared butter-soft ahi tuna with tomato chow chow. Making a meal by grazing on a selection of these is worth considering. Entrees are often accompanied by hearty portions of garlic mashed potatoes. They also carry La Brea Bakery bread (the much famed Los Angeles bakery), and though it's not cheap, the garlic/leek/basil bread is hard to pass up. For dessert, they will strongly urge you to try the moist chocolate chile tart in orange rind sauce, topped with a scoop of Häagen-Dazs coffee ice cream. Yes, chile and chocolate. It sounds extremely weird, but our waiter correctly described the spice of the chile as something that simply tickles the back of your throat as you swallow a bite. It's unusual and well worth trying.

The restaurant itself is part diner, part train car, with leather booths and an *Orient Express*–style interior. It's more casual than anything else. You can also eat at the even more informal onyx oyster bar facing the open kitchen. Don't miss the jokes scattered about (signs saying "no crybabies" or referring to "those silly clove cigarettes").

Komol

953 E. Sahara (in the Commercial Center). ☎ **702/731-6542.** Reservations accepted. Main courses $5.59–$10.95. AE, DISC, MC, V. 11am–10pm Mon–Sun. THAI.

Locals feel this is the best Thai restaurant in town. It certainly is a hole-in-the-wall dive, like all good ethnic places. The menu is pretty large, divided up into different sections for poultry, beef, and pork, plus a separate section for vegetarian dishes, plus many rice and noodle selections. They will spice to your specifications. Unless you know your spicy Asian food, it might be best to play it on the safe side. While we don't want things bland, too much heat can overwhelm all other flavors. The mild to medium packs enough of a kick for most people.

Among the items tried during a recent visit was a vegetarian green curry and the *Pud-kee-mao* (flat rice noodles stir fried with ground chicken, mint, garlic and hot peppers). *Nam Sod* is ground pork done with a hot and sour sauce, ginger, and peanuts, all of which you wrap up in lettuce leaves. Sort of an Asian burrito. Sort of. The Thai iced tea was particularly good; just the right amount of sweetness and tea taste for a drink that is often overly sweet.

Worth noting, the Commercial Center also has any number of other ethnic (mostly Asian) restaurants, including Korean barbecue.

Papamios

Sam's Town, 5111 Boulder Hwy., at Flamingo Rd. ☎ **702/454-8041.** Reservations recommended. Main courses $8.95–$12.95; pizzas $7.45–$9.95. Weekend brunch $13.95. AE, CB, DC, DISC, MC, V. Sun 4:30pm–10:30pm, Mon–Thurs 5–10pm, Fri–Sat 5–11pm; Sun brunch 9am–2pm. ITALIAN.

Make dinner or brunch here an occasion to visit Sam's Town, and, if possible, snag a table on the festive veranda overlooking verdant Mystic Falls Park, the enclosed atrium with fern gullies, babbling brooks, and gushing waterfalls. You don't have to worry about the weather; in this vast climate-controlled park, it's always 70°. The veranda is a great venue for viewing nightly laser shows. And Papamios's interior is also appealing—casually elegant, with dining areas defined by Corinthian-colonnaded archways, checker-clothed tables lit by oil lamps, and strings of colored lights suspended overhead.

An appetizer of roasted mushrooms and fried polenta topped with buffalo mozzarella makes a great beginning. Entrees, served with salad, include shrimp scampi on a bed of angel hair pasta; veal marsala with spinach and tiger-striped mushroom ravioli; and linguini tossed with shrimp, mussels, and lobster in lemon/champagne Alfredo sauce with fresh tomato garnish. Tiramisu is the house specialty dessert. More than a dozen wines are offered by the glass.

Weekend brunches here are also lovely. They feature bountiful buffets (with shrimp and crab, salads, fruits, and breakfast pastries), a glass of champagne, and a choice of entrees ranging from grilled baby lamb chops with pineapple relish to huevos rancheros.

Ricardo's

2380 Tropicana Ave., at Eastern Ave. (northwest corner). ☎ **702/798-4515.** Reservations recommended. Main courses $7.50–$12.95; lunch buffet $6.95; children's plates $2.95–$3.95, including milk or soft drink with complimentary refills. AE, CB, DC, DISC, MC, V. Mon–Thurs 11am–10pm, Fri–Sat 11am–11pm, Sun 11am–10pm. MEXICAN.

This hacienda-style restaurant is a great favorite with locals. It has several stucco-walled dining rooms separated by arched doorways—all of them lovely, with candlelit oak tables and booths upholstered in Aztec prints. One room is a plant-filled greenhouse, another a garden room under a lofty pine-beamed ceiling. Yet a third dining area has a ceramic-tiled fireplace (ablaze in winter) and a dark wood coffered ceiling. Strolling Mexican musicians entertain at night.

Start off with an appetizer of deep-fried battered chicken wings served with melted cheddar (ask for jalapeños if you like your cheese sauce hotter). Nachos smothered with cheese and guacamole are also very good here. For an entree, you can't go wrong with chicken, beef, or pork fajitas served sizzling on a hot skillet atop sautéed onions, mushrooms, and peppers; they come with rice and beans, tortillas, a selection of salsas, guacamole, and tomato wedges with cilantro. All the usual taco/enchilada/tamale combinations are also listed. A delicious dessert is *helado* Las Vegas: ice cream rolled in corn flakes and cinnamon, deep-fried, and served with honey and whipped cream. Be sure to order a pitcher of Ricardo's great margaritas. The same menu is available all day, but a buffet is offered at lunch. The kids' menu on a place mat with games and puzzles features both Mexican and American fare.

INEXPENSIVE

Einstein Bros. Bagels

4624 S. Maryland Pkwy., between Harmon and Tropicana aves. in the University Gardens Shopping Center. ☎ **702/795-7800.** All items under $6. MC, V. Mon–Sat 6am–8pm (till 6pm in summer), Sun 7am–5pm. BAGELS.

You may not like digging into an enormous buffet first thing in the morning, and continental breakfast in a hotel is usually a rip-off. A welcome alternative is a fresh-baked bagel, of which there are 15 varieties here—everything from onion to wild blueberry. Cream cheeses also come in many flavors, anything from sun-dried tomato to vegetable and jalapeño. Einstein's is a pleasant place for the morning meal, with both indoor seating and outdoor tables cooled by misters. Service is friendly, and four special blend coffees are available each day.

Note: Bagel buffs might also want to check out the nearby **Bagelmania** at 855 Twain Ave. (☎ **702/369-3322**). It has the advantage (or disadvantage, depending on your point of view) of not being a chain like Einstein, but the bagels are sometimes chilled for freshness, which is heresy. Avoid this problem by catching them early in the morning, when their extensive selection is hot and fresh.

✪ Mediterranean Café & Market

4147 S. Maryland Pkwy., at Flamingo Rd., in the Tiffany Square strip mall. ☎ **702/731-6030.** Main courses $3.99–$8.49 (all sandwiches under $5). AE, MC, DISC, V. Daily 8am–10pm. MEDITERRANEAN.

It is an immeasurable thrill to find this totally authentic, mom-and-pop Middle Eastern restaurant in Las Vegas, where high-quality ethnic eateries are scarce. When the weather's cool, it's pleasant to sit out front under the umbrellas. Inside, tables are covered with fruit-motif plastic cloths, walls adorned with Mediterranean landscapes (paintings and photographs) and Persian miniatures; a plastic grape arbor girds the room, and shelves are cluttered with inlaid ivory boxes, hookahs, and brassware. Background music is Greek, Turkish, and Arabic.

Everything here is homemade and delicious. You might order up a gyro (slivers of rotisseried beef and lamb enfolded into a pita with lettuce and tomato). Other good choices are a phyllo pie layered with spinach and feta cheese, served with hummus; skewers of grilled chicken and vegetable kabobs with lavash bread and hummus; and a combination platter of hummus, tabouli, stuffed grape leaves, and felafel. All entrees come with pita bread and salad. Try a side order of *bourrani* (creamy yogurt dip mixed with steamed spinach, sautéed garlic, and slivered almonds). Finish up with baklava and rich Turkish coffee. Wine and beer are available. You can also come by in the morning for Middle Eastern breakfasts. A Mediterranean market adjoins.

8 West Las Vegas

EXPENSIVE

Cafe Nicolle

4760 W. Sahara at Decatur (in the Sahara Pavilion). ☎ **702/870-7675.** Reservations recommended for large parties. Main courses $6.95–$14.95 at lunch, $15.95–$24.95 at dinner. AE, MC, V. Mon–Sat 11am–10:30pm. CONTINENTAL

Cafe Nicolle is a local favorite, a place to go for either a special occasion (we noted at least one preprom couple) or just to hang out on the lovely patio, which features a cooling mist on hot summer nights. (That patio dining is particularly unique for Vegas, and the space is just charming.) Even the waitstaff will eat here on their off nights, which is a mighty fine recommendation. Inside, it's airy, though unimaginatively decorated ('80s black lacquer), with tables set far enough apart for a pleasant buzz but not enough for your neighbor to eavesdrop.

There are no surprises on the menu—pastas, crepes, chicken, veal—but everything is prepared beautifully and served attractively with generous portions. They have extremely good, fresh fish, presented very simply, but so the fish's own flavor is able to shine, as opposed to overwhelming it with a sauce or two. The Florentine crepe is made with lots of fresh spinach and not too much cheese in the sauce. Be sure to dip your fresh bread in the excellent garlic and rosemary olive oil found on the table.

Cafe Nicolle is not all that different from restaurants found on the Strip, but if you need a break from the hubbub and it's sometimes suffocating crush of people there or just want a chance to dine in a restaurant with windows and breathe some fresh air, this is worth the short drive.

The Garlic Cafe

3650 S. Decatur Blvd., at Spring Mountain Rd. ☎ **702/221-0266.** Reservations recommended. Main courses $9.25–$27.95. AE, DC, MC, V. Daily 5pm–10pm. INTERNATIONAL.

If you don't like garlic, there is no reason to read further. If you do like garlic, head toward the Garlic Cafe right now. Garlic is the food of the gods, and Warren, the owner/chef/creator of this cafe understands that. Unlike similar ventures (the Stinking Rose in San Francisco, for example) this is a more international menu. Warren found that garlic was a unifying theme around the world, so here are dishes from Thailand, Jamaica, Japan, Hungary, and so on. You can decide on the level of garlic in your dish. Their garlic scale usually runs from 1 to 5 (each level is one head of garlic, so a "5" equals five whole heads), and they will go as high as you want. The current record holder is up to 60. The waiters will help you decide what level is best for any given dish; certain ones (like the duck) would get overwhelmed by too much of our favorite seasoning.

Everyone gets a roast *skordalia* (partly pureed garlic) and bagel chip appetizer, but you can order still others; the choices differ nightly but will always include a perfectly roasted head of garlic. The entree portions are huge (which makes up for the somewhat high prices), and they very nicely presented. Not to mention imaginatively—okay, incredibly eccentrically—named. Like the Salmon in Garfunkel Crust (a fillet of salmon in a garlic-basil cracker crust with béarnaise sauce) or Grandpa Murray in a Hurry "Don't Worry!" Chicken Curry. If you are nice, maybe they will let you take the menu home so you don't have to try to remember what you ate. Finish it off with some garlic ice cream. It's not as weird as it sounds, a very good vanilla with just a hint of garlic that somehow works in a sweet and sour kind of way. The real fun comes with the chocolate-covered (roasted) garlic clove.

The food is not the most utterly memorable ever, but it is competently made and the garlic works as well as you would like. Plus, it's all just a lot of fun, as is imagining the poor soul next to you later at the blackjack tables. No, they don't hand out Breath Assure when you leave. Strangely enough, this restaurant has not yet caught on too much with the tourists, despite having a theme.

MODERATE

Cathy House

5300 W. Spring Mountain Rd. (in Spring Valley). ☎ **702/876-3838.** Reservations recommended. Main courses $6.75–$13.75. AE, MC, V. Daily 11am–10:30pm. CHINESE.

Las Vegas actually has a Chinatown—a very large strip mall (naturally) on Spring Mountain Road near Wynn. There are several Asian restaurants there, including the average **Plum Tree Inn,** and **Pho Vietnam,** a Vietnamese place. The Plum Tree Inn serves dim sum, but ask locals who look like they know, and they will send you instead farther up Spring Mountain Road to the Cathy House (on the opposite side of the street). This only looks far from the Strip on a map; it's really about a 7-minute drive from Treasure Island.

Ordering dim sum, if you haven't experienced it, is sort of like being at a Chinese sushi bar, in that you order many individual, tasty little dishes. Of course, dim sum itself is nothing like sushi. Rather, it's a range of potstickers, panfried dumplings, *baos*

Lorenzi Park

95

Canyon Dr.
Lantern Ln.
Rancho Cir.
Alta Dr.
Palomino Ln.
Campbell Dr.
Lacy Ln.
Rancho Ln.

Martin Luther King Blvd.

15

3rd Pl.
3rd St.
4th St.
California St.
Colorado Ave.
S. Main St.
604

Valley View Blvd.

Charleston Blvd.
Ashby Ave.
Silver Ave.
Westwood Dr.

Cragin Park

New York Ave.
Chicago Ave.
Philadelphia Ave.
St. Louis Ave.
Boston Ave.
Baltimore Ave.
Cleveland Ave.
Cincinnati Ave.

Oakey Blvd.

Rancho Dr.

Highland Dr.

Decatur Blvd.

Sahara Ave.

Industrial Rd.

Circus Circus Dr.

Las Vegas Blvd. (The Strip)

15

Stardust Rd.

Valley View Blvd.

Meade Ave.

Pennwood Ave.

Westwood Dr.

Fashion Show Dr.

Fashion Show Mall

Sirius Ave.

Desert Inn Rd.

604

Decatur Blvd.

Spring Mountain Rd.

Twain Ave.

Viking Rd.

Flamingo Rd.

15

Jones Blvd.

Harmon Ave.
Naples Dr.
Polaris Ave.

Saddle Ave.

1-1326

Cafe Nicolle 3
Cathy House 5
Enigma Cafe 1
The Garlic Cafe 6
Poppa Gar's 2
Romano's Macaroni Grill 4
Viva Mercados 7

0   .75 mi.
     1.2 km

(soft, doughy buns filled with meat like barbecued pork), translucent rice noodles wrapped around shrimp, sticky rice in lotus leaves, chicken feet, and so forth. Some of it's steamed, some is fried—for that extra good grease! You can make your own dipping sauce by combining soy sauce, vinegar, and hot pepper oil. The Chinese eat this for breakfast; the rest of us probably can't handle it until a bit later in the day. The waitstaff pushes steam carts filled with little dishes; point, and they will attempt to tell you what each one is. Better, just blindly order a bunch and dig in. Each dish ranges from approximately $1 to $3; each server makes a note of what you just received, and the total is tallied at the end. (For some reason, it almost always works out to about nine dollars a person.) Dim sum is usually available only until mid-afternoon.

The stand-out at the Cathy House was a vegetable bao that included Chinese glass noodles. Lightly browned and not overly doughy like many baos, it was slightly sweet and utterly delicious. The shrimp wrapped in rice noodles were big and plump, while anything that was fried was so good we decided to ignore our arteries for awhile. Cathy House (which features quite a good view through the windows on one side) also has a full dinner menu, which includes the strawberry chicken invented by Chin's; it's considerably cheaper here.

Viva Mercados

6182 W. Flamingo, at Jones. ☎ **702/871-8826.** Main courses $7.95–$16.95. AE, DISC, V, MC. Sun–Thurs 11am–10pm, Fri–Sat 11am–11pm. MEXICAN.

Ask any local about Mexican food in Vegas, and almost certainly they will point to Viva Mercados as the best in town. That recommendation, plus the restaurant's health-conscious attitude toward food preparation makes this worth the roughly 10-minute drive from the Strip.

Given all those warnings lately about Mexican food and its heart attack–inducing properties, Viva Mercados's approach to food is nothing to be sniffed at. No dish is prepared with or cooked in any kind of animal fat. Nope, the lard so dear to Mexican cooking is not found here. The oil used is an artery-friendly canola. Additionally, this makes the place particularly appealing to vegetarians, who will also be pleased by the regular veggie specials. Everything is quite fresh, and they do particularly amazing things with seafood. Try the Maresco Vallarta, which is orange roughy, shrimp, and scallops cooked in a coconut tomato sauce, with capers and olives. They have all sorts of noteworthy shrimp dishes, and 11 different salsas, ranked 1 to 10 for degree of spice. (Ask for advice, first.) The staff is friendly (try to chat with owner Bobby Mercado) and the portions hearty.

✪ Ware's T Bones Texas Style Bar-B-Que

2740 N. Green Pkwy., at Sunset (inside Swizzle Stick Lounge). ☎ **702/435-5937.** Sandwiches $3.95–$5.25; main courses $9.25–$14.95. Cash only. Daily 9am–10pm. BARBECUE.

William Ware hails from Alabama but went to culinary school in New York City. He opened up the Hard Rock Cafe in Los Angeles but has since gone on to operate his own restaurants. Las Vegas was incredibly lucky the day he decided to leave Los Angeles and come here. His first outlet was so popular he recently opened a second. Neither is near anything that you might call a beaten path, though the Flamingo Road restaurant (the complete address is at the end of this review) is virtually in the lap of **Sam's Town**. Guests staying there, and those with a car, should come here immediately.

Especially if you like barbecue. Ware uses his own recipe for salad dressings and for the barbecue sauce, which is more sweet than hot (which may be a drawback for those who figure it's not barbecue unless you've seared your mouth). It's a light, tasty sauce that puts the heavy, gloppy stuff they serve in chains (and throughout most

A Donut Delight

Not that there aren't lots of donut places around town—actually, there aren't that many. But still, the ones you find are the chain variety, fine if you have a yen on the spot, but in reality, you might as well be eating frosted foam rubber. If you are a connoisseur with a car or happen to be checking out the restaurants in the Chinatown area on Spring Mountain Road, go to **Ronald's Donuts,** 4600 Spring Mountain, at Dectaur (☎ **702/873-1032**). Some have called them celestial. You decide.

Vegas locales) to shame. And what it is covering is superb. The meat is blackened but tender perfection. Pick up a pork or beef rib and watch the meat slide right off. The brisket is buttery soft—you won't need a knife to cut it, as it falls apart under your fork.

Just about everything is good (including the sides of corn muffins and slaw), but be sure to check out the barbecue chicken salad. It's available as an entree, but rather than waste the stomach space (so you can leave room for those pork ribs), sweetly ask if you can have a small serving as an appetizer. Not only is the chicken dynamite, but it's covered with Ware's own honey mustard dressing (an original tart/sweet creation totally unlike anything else you've had with that name) and tossed with apples and walnuts. It will make your mouth sing. Note also the "Feast for Two" special: For $24.95, you get two half chickens, three beef ribs, six pork ribs, half a pound of brisket, a pint of slaw, a pint of beans, and two corn muffins. This meal could easily feed three rather than two. Ware's also serves hearty country breakfasts until 4pm.

Ware's second outlet is at 4734 E. Flamingo Rd., at Mountain Vista and Boulder Highway (in Albertson's Shopping Center) (☎ **702/435-5937**).

INEXPENSIVE

✪ Enigma Cafe

918-¹/₂ S. Fourth St., at Charleston. ☎ **702/386-0999.** No items over $6. Mon 7am–3pm, Tues–Fri 7am–midnight, Sat–Sun 9am–midnight. Cash only. CALIFORNIA/MEDITERRANEAN

Finding the Enigma Cafe is almost as good as finding a breeze on a really hot Vegas day. Or maybe it's more like suddenly finding yourself transported out of Vegas and into California. Owners Julie and Len have taken two 1930s-era cottages and turned them into a cafe/coffeehouse/art space that, during the day, is a restful, garden patio setting (orders are taken inside one house, inside the other is the art gallery, with more seating) with folk and classical music playing. At night the space blooms with candles, live music, and poetry readings.

The menu is a huge relief: healthful, interesting sandwiches ("Mossy Melt" is tuna salad "revived up with" horseradish and havarti, toasted open face) and familiar ones (ham and Swiss, but well garnished), salads (again with a range from the ordinary green variety to "Dr. Bombay's" curried chicken breast with veggies) to hummus burritos and the "Tippy Elvis Supreme" (named after a local polka band/art project), which is peanut butter and bananas (what else?). You can get a side platter of hummus, feta cheese, veggies, and pita, or have a thick fruit smoothie. And that doesn't even begin to cover their wide range of coffee drinks. Best of all, it's cheap. Considering the soothing affect it has on your mind, spirit, wallet, and stomach, Enigma is like a vacation from your vacation. This is actually very close to both the Strip and downtown, particularly the latter, where good (and healthful) food is hard to find.

9 Downtown

VERY EXPENSIVE

Andre's

401 S. 6th St., at Lewis Ave., a few blocks south of Fremont St. ☎ **702/385-5016**. Reservations required. Main courses $19.75–$33. AE, CB, DC, MC, V. Nightly from 6pm; closing hours vary. FRENCH.

Owner-chef Andre Rochat has created a rustic country-French setting in a converted 1930s house in downtown Las Vegas. Low ceilings are crossed with rough-hewn beams, and wainscoted stucco walls (embedded with straw) are hung with provincial pottery and copperware. Soft lighting emanates from candles and sconces. In addition to a catacomb of cozy interior rooms, there's a lovely, ivy-walled garden patio under the shade of a mulberry tree. This is a major celebrity haunt where you're likely to see Strip headliners. One night, Tom Hanks, Steven Spielberg, and James Spader were all spotted joining some pals for a bachelor party.

The menu changes seasonally. On a recent visit, appetizers included jumbo sea scallops rolled in a crunchy macadamia nut crust with citrus beurre blanc and red beet coulis. And among the entrees, a fan of pink, juicy slices of sautéed duck came with a confit of port wine and onions. A medley of vegetables—perhaps pommes lyonnaise, asparagus, broccoli hollandaise, and baby carrots—accompanies each entree, and sorbets are served between courses. For dessert, there is Andre's classic fruit tarts, flaky butter crusts layered with Grand Marnier custard and topped with fresh, plump berries. An extensive wine list (more than 900 labels) is international in scope and includes many rare vintages; consult the sommelier.

Hugo's Cellar

Four Queen's, 202 Fremont St., at Casino Center Blvd. ☎ **702/385-4011**. Reservations required. Main courses $24–$35. AE, DC, DISC, MC, V. Nightly 5:30pm–10:30pm. INTERNATIONAL.

Hugo's Cellar is indeed in a cellar, or at least below street level in the Four Queen's Hotel. No, they aren't ashamed of it—quite the opposite. This is their gourmet

---

Two Classic Vegas Restaurants

In a world gone mad—and that's the way Vegas seems sometimes—it's good to know some things never change. The following two restaurants don't serve the best food in town, but they've been around forever. And that should be rewarded. Besides, both are classically Las Vegas, a rapidly vanishing species. Go for the experience.

Green Shack, 2504 E. Fremont, 1 block south of Charleston (☎ **702/383-0007**), is just a little dive, but more importantly, it's the oldest continuously operating restaurant in Las Vegas. That should count for something. It's menu hasn't changed a bit over the years. Try the fried chicken.

Poppa Gar's, 1624 W. Oakey, near Industrial (☎ **702/384-4513**), is a classic diner with counter and booths that sport plaques with the names of patrons who have been long forgotten, except maybe by Poppa Gar himself. A genuine character, he shot all those dead animals whose heads decorate the place. (He used to serve wild game that he shot himself. Or you could bring in your own and he would cook it for you.) Rumor has it he secretly runs this town, and given the number of city government types who jam the place at lunch, you do have to wonder.

Andre's **9**
Binion's Horshoe
  Coffee Shop **4**
Carson Street Café **3**
Center Stage **1**
Green Shack **11**
Hugo's Cellar **5**
Limerick's **8**
Main Street Station
  Garden Court **2**
Buffets
Golden Nugget
  Buffet **3**
Lady Luck Banquet
  Buffet **7**
Sam Boyd's Fremont
  Paradise Buffet **6**
Showboat
  Captain's Buffet **10**

restaurant, and it's highly regarded by the locals. You pass through a small, dark (romantic, not creepy) bar with a few tables and a friendly bartender, perfect for a little quiet tête-à-tête between hands at the poker tables. Each female guest is given a red rose when she enters the restaurant—the beginning of a series of nice touches. The restaurant space proper is dimly lit, lined with dark wood and brick. It's fairly intimate, but if you really want to be cozy, ask for one of the curtained booths against the wall.

The meal is full of ceremony, perfectly delivered by a well-trained and cordial wait staff. Salads, included in the price, are prepared at your table, from a cart full of choices. (In Vegas style, though, most choices are on the calorie-intensive side.) A tiny cup with palate-cleansing sorbet prepares you for the main course. Unfortunately, despite the high regard, the main courses are not all that novel (various cuts of meat, seafood, chicken prepared different ways) and can be disappointing. Promising choices include the Chicken "Hugo" (with basil and pine nuts prepared in a cream sauce), or the Rack of Lamb Indonesian with Indonesian spices. Vegetables are included, as is a finish of chocolate-dipped fruits with cream.

The service is impeccable (you have little to no wait between courses), and it really makes you feel pampered. That salad, the small dessert, and so forth are included, making an initially hefty-seeming price tag appear a bit more reasonable, especially when compared to Strip establishments that aren't much better and can cost nearly twice as much. While the main food is not spectacular, the salads and desserts were fine. It is not worth going out of your way for the food, but it perhaps is for the whole package.

EXPENSIVE

Limerick's

Fitzgerald's Casino Holiday Inn, 301 Fremont St., at 3rd St. ☎ **702/388-2400**. Reservations recommended. Main courses $13.95–$21. AE, MC, V, D. Nightly 5:30–10:30pm. STEAK/SEAFOOD.

An extensive renovation a year ago turned a down-at-the-heels eatery into a posh steakhouse. Decorated in the classic Olde English gentlemen's club style, Limerick's is meant to be an oasis of gracious dining away from hectic casino life, and the overall effect is comforting and moderately womb-like, particularly in the cozy booths at the back. Unfortunately, casino "ca-chings" still creep in, but it's not overly bothersome. The menu is classic, upscale steakhouse: beef, chops, some lobster, and chicken. The portions are Vegas-sized (the small prime rib was 14 ounces), so bring an appetite (and a love of red meat), or take your leftovers back to the room to feed the kids for a couple days. The filet mignon was tender enough to cut with a fork, while the lamb chops came with a pecan mustard glaze. Patrons who don't eat red meat might want to try the apricot chicken. Appetizers are mostly seafood, though there is a fine sounding baked brie with strawberry preserves. "Chef's choice" desserts change nightly, and the wine list is good and extensive.

INEXPENSIVE

Binion's Horseshoe

Binion's Horseshoe, 128 E. Fremont St., at Casino Center Blvd. ☎ **702/382-1600**. Main courses $4.25–$14.95 (most under $8). AE, CB, DC, DISC, MC, V. Daily 24 hours. AMERICAN.

Down a flight of steps from the casino floor, this is no humble hotel coffee shop. It's heralded by a gorgeous stained-glass dome and entered via doors embellished with antique beveled glass panels. The interior is equally impressive, with a magnificent, pressed copper ceiling, rich oak paneling, walls hung with original oil paintings you'll wish you owned, and displays of antiques, turn-of-the-century magazine covers, and black-and-white photographs of the Old West. Notice, too, an exhibit of vintage playing cards that depict real kings and queens (Henry VIII and Anne Boleyn).

The menu lists all the traditional Las Vegas coffee-shop items: sandwiches, burgers, Southern-fried chicken, steak and seafood entrees, along with breakfast fare. And you can't beat Binion's specials: two eggs with an immense slab of grilled ham, home fries, toast, and tea or coffee ($2.99 from 6am to 2pm); a 10-ounce New York steak dinner with baked potato, salad, and roll and butter ($3.99 from 10pm to 5:45am); a 7-ounce New York steak with eggs, home fries, and toast ($2.99 from 10pm to 5:45am); 10-ounce prime rib dinner, including soup or salad, potato, and vegetables ($5.25 from 5 to 9:45pm)—$6.25 for a 16-ounce T-bone steak instead of prime rib. All bar drinks are available, and there's peanut butter cream pie for dessert.

Carson Street Café

Golden Nugget, 129 E. Fremont St. between 1st St. and Casino Center Blvd. ☎ **702/ 385-7111**. Main courses mostly $5.95–$14.95. AE, CB, DC, DISC, MC, V. Daily 24 hours. AMERICAN.

Las Vegas has many delightful 24-hour hotel restaurants. The Golden Nugget's is reminiscent of an elegant street cafe on the Champs-Elysées, albeit one overlooking a gorgeous hotel lobby instead of a Paris street. Its jewel-toned interior, under a white-fringed green awning, has murals of park scenes and topiary, white latticing, and seating amid potted orange trees and planters of greenery—it couldn't be lovelier.

And the food is notably excellent. A wide-ranging menu offers terrific salads (such as Oriental chicken), overstuffed deli sandwiches, burgers, Mexican fare (chicken burritos, fajita sandwiches), numerous breakfast items, and entrees running the gamut from filet mignon to country fried steak with mashed potatoes and vegetables. From 4 to 11pm, a 10-ounce prime rib dinner (with baked potato and a vegetable) is $9.95. And from 11pm to 7am an 8-ounce grilled ham steak with eggs, hash browns, and toast costs $3.95. There's a full bar. Desserts options include fresh-baked eclairs, strawberry shortcake, and hot fudge or butterscotch sundaes.

Center Stage

Jackie Gaughan's Plaza Hotel Casino, 1 Main St., at Fremont St. ☎ **702/386-2110.** Reservations essential. Main courses $5.95–$16 (many under $10). AE, DISC, MC, V. Nightly 5–11pm. STEAK/SEAFOOD.

The aptly named Center Stage offers a dramatic vantage point, the best in town for viewing the Fremont Street Experience. The restaurant occupies a second-story glass dome, with a windowed wall directly facing Fremont Street. Seating is in semicircular booths, all of which provide good to excellent views of downtown's nightly laser-light show, the music for which is piped into the restaurant. This is both a comfortable and attractive dining room, done up in aesthetically pleasing shades of green with planters of lush faux foliage.

It's a thrilling place to be. What's less than thrilling—though the menu is extremely low priced—is the lackluster performance in the kitchen. Best bet is to stick to the most basic menu items. Order the prime rib au jus, served with onion soup or salad (take the salad), warm sourdough bread and butter, a vegetable, and baked potato, rice, or fettuccine Alfredo (take the potato). It's just $7.95, and you get to see the show. Be sure to make reservations and arrive early to snag one of the best seats.

10 Buffets & Sunday Brunches

Lavish, low-priced buffets are a Las Vegas tradition, designed to lure you to the gaming tables and make you feel like you got such a bargain for your meal you can afford to drop more money. They're a gimmick, and we love them. Something about filling up on too much prime rib and shrimp just says "Vegas" to us. Of course, there is a quite a range, from some perfunctory steam table displays and salad bars heavy on iceberg lettuce, to unbelievably opulent spreads with caviar and free-flowing champagne. Some are quite beautifully presented, as well. Some of the food is awful, some of it merely works as fuel, some of it is memorable.

No trip to Las Vegas is complete without trying one or two buffets. Of the dozens, the most noteworthy are described below. Mind you, almost all buffets have some things in common. Unless otherwise noted, every one listed below will have a carving station, a salad bar (quality differs), and hot main courses and side dishes. We will try only to point out when a buffet has something original or notable.

Note: Buffet meals are extremely popular, and reservations are usually not taken (we've indicated when they are accepted, and in all those cases, they are highly recommended). Arrive early (before opening) or late to avoid a long line, especially on weekends.

SOUTH STRIP
EXPENSIVE

✪ **Tropicana Sunday Brunch Buffet**

3801 Las Vegas Blvd. S. ☎ **702/739-2376.** $25.95 adults, $15.95 children 10 and under. Sunday only 9:30am–2pm.

This elaborate spread is served in the elegant El Gaucho Steak House (see description under hotel listing in chapter 5). Tables are elegantly appointed, and food displays are embellished with an ice sculpture and a cascade of fresh fruit. Try to get a seat by the wall of windows that overlooks a flamingo pond in the pool area. On one visit, this impressive feast was comprised of sushi, ceviche, raw oysters, cold shrimp, smoked seafood (trout, salmon, whitefish, and sable), caviar, a carving station that can also include rack of lamb, salmon Florentine, and roast pork, a waffle and omelet station, a full complement of breakfast meats and potato dishes, cheeses and cold cuts, an extensive salad bar, steak and tuna tartare, fresh vegetables, pasta dishes, numerous entrees (stuffed Maine lobster, filet mignon in burgundy sauce, roast chicken breast stuffed with fruit, red snapper in dill butter sauce, and roast pork with mustard sauce, among others), unlimited champagne, and dozens of desserts (including bananas Foster).

MODERATE

The MGM Grand Oz Buffet

3799 Las Vegas Blvd. S. ☎ **702/891-7777.** Brunch $5.95, dinner $7.95; reduced prices for children under 10, free for children under 4. Daily 7am–2:30pm and 4–10pm.

This rather average buffet does feature a fresh Belgian waffle station at breakfast. Dinner also has all-you-can-eat shrimp and an all-you-can-eat shrimp and prime rib option. Also available: low-fat, sugar-free desserts! And at all meals you get a full pot of coffee on your table.

INEXPENSIVE

✪ Excalibur's Round Table Buffet

3850 Las Vegas Blvd. S. ☎ **702/597-7777.** Breakfast $3.99, lunch $4.99, dinner $5.99. Daily 7–11am, 11am–4pm, and 4–10pm.

This strikes the perfect balance of cheap prices, mandatory, tacky decor, and adequate food. This is what you want in a cheap Vegas buffet. But on a recent trip they didn't have mashed potatoes or macaroni salad, which are essential for an archetypal buffet. The plates are large, so you don't have to make as many trips to the buffet tables.

✪ The Luxor Pharaoh's Pheast Buffet

3900 Las Vegas Blvd. S. ☎ **702/262-4000.** Breakfast $4.49, lunch $5.49, dinner $7.49. Daily 7–11am, 11am–4pm and 4–11pm.

Located on the lower level, where the Luxor showroom used to be, this huge new buffet looks like it was set in the middle of an archaeological dig, complete with wood braces holding up the ceiling, pot shards, papyrus, and servers dressed in khaki dig outfits. It's a unique and fun decor—be sure to avoid tripping on the mummies and their sarcophagi sticking half up out of the ground. The food is better than most cheap buffets, including a Mexican station with some genuinely spicy food, Chinese stir-fry, and different Italian pastas. Desserts were disappointing. A beer and wine cart makes the rounds. Word has probably gotten out, unfortunately, because the lines are always enormous.

Monte Carlo Buffet

3770 Las Vegas Blvd. S. ☎ **702/730-7777.** Breakfast $5.49, lunch $6.59, dinner $8.49. Daily 7–11am, 11am–4pm & 4–10pm.

A "courtyard" under a painted sky, the Monte Carlo's buffet room has a Moroccan market theme, with murals of Arab scenes, Moorish archways, Oriental carpets, and walls hung with photographs of, and artifacts from, Morocco. Dinner includes a rotisserie (for chicken and pork loin or London broil), a Chinese food station, a taco/fajita bar, a baked potato bar, numerous salads and more than a dozen desserts plus frozen yogurt and ice cream machines. Lunches are similar. At breakfast, the expected fare is supplemented by an omelet station, and choices include crepes, blintzes, and corned beef hash. Fresh-baked New York–style bagels are a plus.

Tropicana Island Buffet

3801 Las Vegas Blvd. S. ☎ **702/739-2222.** Brunch $9.95, dinner $10.95. Daily 7am–1pm and 5pm–10pm.

This buffet is served in a large and delightful dining room, lushly planted with tropical flowers and foliage. There are coral-reef aquariums at the entrance, and the appealing interior keeps to the island theme. Big semicircular booths backed by mirrored walls are separated by bead curtains, and, on the lower level, floor-to-ceiling windows overlook the Trop's stunning palm-fringed pool. Dinners here feature an extensive salad bar and peel-and-eat-shrimp.

MID-STRIP
VERY EXPENSIVE

✪ Bally's Sterling Sunday Brunch

3645 Las Vegas Blvd. S. ☎ **702/739-4111.** Reservations recommended. Brunch is $49.95. Sunday only 9:30am–2:30pm.

This brunch is served in the clubby elegant precincts of Bally's Steakhouse. Flower arrangements and ice sculptures grace lavish buffet spreads tended by white-hatted chefs. There's a waffle and omelet station, a sushi and sashimi bar, and a brimming dessert table. You might choose smoked fish with bagels and cream cheese or help yourself from a mound of fresh shrimp. Entrees vary weekly. On a recent visit the possibilities included rolled chicken stuffed with pistachios and porcini mushrooms, beef tenderloin, steak Diane, seared salmon with beet butter sauce and fried leeks, roast duckling with black currant and blueberry sauce, and penne Florentine with pine nuts, and smoked chicken in vodka sauce. Of course, there are deli and breakfast meats, vegetables and scrumptious salads, cheeses, raw bar offerings, seasonal fruits and berries, and side dishes such as stuffed potatoes with caviar and sour cream. Champagne flows freely.

MODERATE

✪ Bally's Big Kitchen Buffet

3645 Las Vegas Blvd. S. ☎ **702/739-4111.** Breakfast $8.95, brunch $9.95, dinner $12.95. Daily 7am–11am, 11am–2:30pm and 4:30–10pm.

This gorgeous spread is served in a carpeted and crystal-chandeliered dining room with comfortably upholstered armchair seating. Everything is extremely fresh and of the highest quality. There's always a bountiful salad bar, a good choice of fruits and vegetables, entrees (perhaps seafood casserole in a creamy dill sauce, baked red snapper, pork chops sautéed in Cajun spices, barbecued chicken, and broiled steak in peppercorn sauce), pastas, rice and potato dishes, cold cuts, and a vast array of fresh-baked desserts. The brunch buffet includes breakfast fare and all-you-can-eat shrimp, while the dinner buffet adds Chinese selections.

✪ Caesars Palace Palatium Buffet

3570 Las Vegas Blvd. S. ☎ **702/731-7110.** Breakfast $7.95, lunch $9.95, dinner $16.95; Sat brunch $14.95; Sun brunch $16.95 adults, children 4 to 12 half price, under 3 free (includes unlimited champagne). Mon–Fri 8–11:30am and 11:30am–3:30pm; daily 4:30–10pm; Sat–Sun 8:30am–3:30pm.

Named for the 2nd-century meeting place of Rome's academy of chefs, this elegant dining room is adorned with murals of ancient Rome and fronted by an imposing colonnaded pediment. Selections at lunch and dinner include elaborate salad bars, fresh-baked breads, and much, much more. The evening meal includes a cold seafood station. Especially lavish are weekend brunches with omelet stations (in addition to egg dishes), breakfast meats, fresh-squeezed juices, potatoes prepared in various ways, pastas, rice casseroles, carved meats, cold shrimp, smoked salmon, and a waffle and ice-cream sundae bar in addition to two dessert islands spotlighting cakes and pastries. That's not the half of it.

✪ Mirage Buffet

3400 Las Vegas Blvd. S. ☎ **702/791-7111.** Breakfast $7.50, lunch $8.95, dinner $12.95; Sun brunch $13.95; reduced prices for children ages 4 to 10, children under 4 free. Mon–Sat 7–10:45am, 11am–2:45pm, and 3–9:30pm; Sun 8am–9:30pm.

The Mirage offers lavish spreads in a lovely garden-themed setting with palm trees, a plant-filled stone fountain, and seating under verdigris eaves and domes embellished with flowers. You pay somewhat more here than at other buffets, but you certainly get what you pay for. The salad bars alone are enormous, filled with at least 25 different choices such as Thai beef, seafood, salad Niçoise, tabbouleh, Chinese chicken, Creole rice, and tortellini. At brunch champagne flows freely, and a scrumptious array of smoked fish is added to the board, along with such items as fruit-filled crepes and blintzes. And every meal features a spectacular dessert table (the bread pudding in bourbon sauce is noteworthy). For healthful eating there are many light items to choose from, including sugar- and fat-free puddings. And on Sundays a nonalcoholic sparkling cider is a possible champagne alternative.

INEXPENSIVE

Flamingo Hilton Paradise Garden Buffet

3555 Las Vegas Blvd. S. ☎ **702/733-3111.** Breakfast $6.50, lunch $7.50, dinner $9.95 (includes 2 glasses of wine). Daily 6am–noon, noon–2:30pm, and 4:30–10pm.

The buffet here occupies a vast room, with floor-to-ceiling windows overlooking a verdant tropical landscape of cascading waterfalls and a pond filled with ducks, swans, and flamingos. The interior, one of the most pleasant in Las Vegas, is equally lush, though its palm trees and tropical foliage are faux. At dinner, there is an extensive international food station (which changes monthly) presenting French, Chinese, Mexican, German, or Italian specialties. A large salad bar, fresh fruits, pastas, vegetables, potato dishes, and a vast dessert display round out the offerings. Lunch is similar, featuring a mix of international cuisines as well as a stir-fry station and a soup/salad/pasta bar. At breakfast, you'll find all the expected fare, including a made-to-order omelet station, and fresh-baked breads.

Harrah's Galley Buffet

3475 Las Vegas Blvd. S. ☎ **702/369-5000.** Breakfast $4.99, lunch $5.99, dinner $8.55. Daily 7–11am, 11am–4pm, and 4–11pm (taxes not included).

The buffet at Harrah's is served in a very pleasant riverboat-themed room with murals of Mississippi paddle wheelers and vintage signs from shipping companies on the wall. A lavish food display under a stained-glass skylight features a full panoply of hot entrees (perhaps braised beef burgundy, teriyaki chicken, stuffed grape leaves, baked cod, pastas, barbecued chicken, and buffalo wings), an array of fresh vegetables and potato dishes, an Asian food station, a fresh fruit and salad bar, and a make-your-own sundae station in addition to a variety of homemade desserts. There's an omelet station at breakfast.

Note: Harrah's is still planning to remodel its buffet. Plans call for a Fresh Market Square Buffet room that will feature international foods and interactive cooking stations.

✪ Rio's Carnival World Buffet

3700 W. Flamingo Rd. ☎ **702/252-7777.** Breakfast $5.55, lunch $7.77, dinner $9.99; weekend brunch $7.99 (champagne is $1 per glass). Mon–Fri 7–10:30am and Mon–Fri 11am–3pm; daily 3:30–10pm; Sat–Sun 7am–3:30pm.

The buffet here is located in a festively decorated room with variegated wide, sequined ribbons looped overhead and seating amid planters of lush, faux tropical blooms. Chairs and booths are upholstered in bright hues—green, purple, red, orange, and turquoise. This is an excellent buffet with cheerfully decorative food booths set up like stations in an upscale food court. A barbecued chicken and ribs station offers side dishes of baked beans and mashed potatoes. Other stations offer stir-fry (chicken, beef, pork, and vegetables), Mexican taco fixings and accompaniments, Chinese fare, a Japanese sushi and teppanyaki grill, a Brazilian mixed grill, Italian pasta and antipasto, and fish and chips. There's even a diner setup for hot dogs, burgers, fries, and milk shakes. All this is in addition to the usual offerings of most Las Vegas buffets. A stunning array of oven-fresh cakes, pies, and pastries (including sugar-free and low-fat desserts) are arranged in a palm-fringed circular display area, and there's also a make-your-own sundae bar. A full cash bar is another Rio plus. Everything is fresh and beautifully prepared and presented.

Treasure Island Buffet

3300 Las Vegas Blvd. S. ☎ **702/894-7111.** Breakfast $5.39, lunch $6.99, dinner $8.99; Sun brunch $8.99. Mon–Sat 7–10:45am and 11am–3:45pm; daily 4–10:30pm; Sun 7:30am–3:30pm.

The buffet is served in two internationally themed rooms. The American room, under a central rough-hewn beamed canopy hung with the flags of the 13 colonies, re-creates New Orleans during the era of Jean Lafitte. And the Italian room, modeled after a Tuscan villa overlooking a bustling piazza, has strings of festival lights overhead and food displays under a striped awning. Both rooms are filled with authentic antiques and artifacts typical of their locales and time periods. And both also serve identical fare, including extensive American breakfasts. Dinners offer a Chinese food station, peel-and-eat shrimp, a salad bar, potato and rice side dishes, cheeses and cold cuts, fresh fruits and vegetables, breads, and a large choice of desserts. Lunch is similar, and Sunday brunch includes unlimited champagne.

NORTH STRIP
INEXPENSIVE

The Circus Circus Buffet

2880 Las Vegas Blvd. S. ☎ **702/734-0410.** Breakfast $2.99, lunch $3.99, dinner $4.99. Daily 6–11:30am, noon–4pm, and 4:30–11pm.

Here's a choice: the cheapest buffet on the Strip, versus the worst buffet food in town. Here you'll find 45 items of typical cafeteria fare, and none of them all that good. Kids love it, some adults find it inedible. If food is strictly fuel for you, you can't go wrong here. Otherwise, trundle off to another buffet.

Sahara Oasis Buffet

2535 Las Vegas Blvd. S. ☎ **702/737-2111.** Breakfast $2.49, brunch $3.49, dinner $5.49. Daily 6–11am, 11:30am–3:30pm, and 4–10pm.

This buffet is a vast spread served in an attractive room with a wall of windows overlooking the pool and brass palm trees shading the food display tables. It's not fancy fare, but it is abundant, fresh, and tasty.

Stardust Warehouse Buffet

3000 Las Vegas Blvd. S. ☎ **702/732-6111**. Breakfast $4.95, lunch $5.95, dinner $8.51; Sun brunch $6.95. Mon–Sat 7–10:30am and 10:30am–3pm; daily 4–10pm; Sun 7am–3:30pm.

This buffet features, as the name suggests, a raftered warehouse decor, with big restaurant cans of olive oil and chili, sacks of flour, crates of apples, and other provender on display. Tables are covered in laminated burlap potato sacking. It's a pleasant setting for very good buffet meals, featuring a carving station (roast beef, ham, and turkey). You can also pump your own frozen yogurt.

Stratosphere Buffet

2000 Las Vegas Blvd. S. ☎ **702/380-7711**. Breakfast $5.99, lunch $7.99, dinner $9.99. Daily 7am–11am and 11am–4pm; Sun–Thurs 4–10pm, Fri–Sat 4–11pm.

In a cheerful World's Fair–themed buffet room—with a hot air balloon motif adorning murals, columns, and carpeting—the Stratosphere sets out fresh-looking fare and plenty of it. Breakfast is average at best, disappointing at worst. Lunch and dinner have stations for Mexican, Chinese, and kosher-style fare; daily changing international stations (perhaps Jamaican, Creole, or Italian); and a station for picnic food such as fried chicken and hot dogs. Desserts are supplemented by a make-your-own-sundae frozen-yogurt bar and a flambé dessert station turning out bananas Foster and cherries jubilee.

CONVENTION CENTER/PARADISE ROAD
MODERATE

✪ Las Vegas Hilton Buffet of Champions

3000 Paradise Rd. ☎ **702/732-5111**. Breakfast $7.99, lunch $8.99, dinner $12.99; weekend brunch $11.99 (includes unlimited champagne). Children 12 and under half price. Mon–Fri 7–10am and 11am–2:30pm; daily 5–10pm; Sat–Sunday 8am–2:30pm.

This buffet is served in a beautiful gardenlike dining room with pristine white trellises, big planters of flowers, and magnificent white wrought-iron chandeliers and sconces. As the name implies, the room, located near the casino entrance to the race and sports SuperBook, is sports themed. Cream walls are adorned with attractive murals and photographs of hockey, football, boxing, and horse racing, and there are bookshelves stocked with sporting literature. All in all, it's one of the loveliest buffet rooms in town. And the fare is fresh and delicious. Dinner additionally features all-you-can-eat crab and shrimp.

EAST LAS VEGAS/FLAMINGO ROAD
INEXPENSIVE

✪ Sam's Town, The Great Buffet

5111 Boulder Hwy. ☎ **702/456-7777**. Breakfast $4.99, lunch $6.99, dinner $8.99 (Fri seafood buffet $12.99); Sun brunch $6.99; all buffets half price for children 6 and under. Mon–Sat 8–11am and 11am–3pm; Sun–Thurs 4–9pm Fri–Sat 4pm–10pm; Sun 8am–3pm.

Friendly service and good food have made Sam's Town's buffets extremely popular. About 70% of their clientele consists of local folks, not tourists. The buffet room is as homey as your living room, with fruit-motif carpeting, gaslight-style brass chandeliers, and planters of foliage creating intimate dining niches. Dinners includes a

Chinese stir-fry station, a burger grill, and a wide array of side dishes and fresh fruits and vegetables. For dessert, numerous pies and cakes are supplemented by frozen yogurt with homemade fudge, homemade candies, caramel apples, and fruit cobbler. Tuesday nights Cajun seafood entrees are featured. But best of all are the Friday seafood buffets, offering paella, deep-fried oysters, crawfish étouffée, Cajun red snapper, steamed Dungeness crab with drawn butter, shrimp scampi with pasta, raw oysters, peel-and-eat shrimp, and much more. Sunday champagne brunches offers extensive breakfast and lunch fare, including blintzes, Mexican breakfast tortes, a carving station, Southern and Cajun specialties, and unlimited champagne.

DOWNTOWN
MODERATE

✪ The Golden Nugget Buffet
129 E. Fremont St. ☎ **702/385-7111.** Breakfast $5.75, lunch $7.50, dinner $10.25; Sun brunch $10.25. Mon–Sat 7–10:30am, 10:30am–3pm and 4–10pm; Sun 8am–10pm.

This buffet has often been voted number one in Las Vegas. Not only is the food fresh and delicious, but it's served in an opulent dining room with marble-topped serving tables amid planters of greenery and potted palms. Mirrored columns, beveled mirrors, etched glass, and brass add sparkle to the room, and swagged draperies provide a note of elegance. Most of the seating is in plush booths. The buffet tables are also laden with an extensive salad bar (about 50 items), fresh fruit, and marvelous desserts including Zelma Wynn's (Steve's mother) famous bread pudding. Every night fresh seafood is featured. Most lavish is the all-day Sunday champagne brunch, which adds such dishes as eggs Benedict, blintzes, pancakes, creamed herring, and smoked fish with bagels and cream cheese. *Note:* This stunning buffet room is also the setting for a $2.99 late-night meal of steak and eggs with home fries and biscuits with gravy; it's served 11pm to 4am.

✪ Main Street Station Garden Court
200 N. Main Street. ☎ **702/787-1896.** Breakfast $4.99, lunch $6.99, dinner $8.99; Fri seafood buffet $12.99; Sun champagne brunch $7.99, Children 3 and under free. Daily 7am–10:30am, 11am–3pm, and 4pm–10pm; Sun 7am–3pm.

Set in what is truly one of the prettiest buffet spaces in town (and certainly in downtown), with very high ceilings and tall windows bringing in much-needed, actual natural light, the Main St. Station Garden Court buffet is one of the best in town, much less in downtown. Featuring nine live-action stations (meaning you can watch your food being prepared), including a wood-fired brick oven pizza (delicious), many fresh salsas at the Mexican station, a barbecue rotisserie, fresh sausage at the carving station, Chinese, Hawaiian, and a selection of southern specialties (soul food and the like). On Friday nights, they have all this plus countless kinds of seafood all the way up to lobster.

INEXPENSIVE

Lady Luck Banquet Buffet
206 N. 3rd St. ☎ **702/477-3000.** Breakfast $4.99, lunch $5.49, dinner $7.77. Daily 6–10:30am, 10:30am–2pm, and 4–10pm.

This buffet is served in a pretty garden-themed room. Dinner includes all-you-can-eat prime rib, and, frequently, there are Chinese, Polynesian, and Italian specialties as well. Offerings additionally include an extensive salad bar, a make-your-own-sundae bar, an array of fresh-baked pies and cakes, and beverages.

✪ Sam Boyd's Fremont Paradise Buffet

200 E. Fremont St. ☎ **702/385-3232.** Breakfast $4.95, lunch $5.95, dinner $8.95 ($13.95 for Seafood Fantasy); Sun brunch $7.95. Mon–Sat 7–10:30am & 11am–3pm; Mon, Wed, Thurs 4–10pm (Sat until 11pm); Seafood Fantasy Sun and Tues 4–10pm (Fri until 11pm); Sun 7am–3pm.

This buffet is served in an attractive, tropically themed room. Diners sit in spacious booths amid lush jungle foliage—birds of paradise, palms, and bright tropical blooms—and the buffet area is surrounded by a "waterfall" of Tivoli lighting under a reflective ceiling. Island music, enhanced by bird calls and the sound of splashing waterfalls, helps set the tone. Meals here are on the lavish side.

Sunday, Tuesday, and Friday nights the buffet is renamed the Seafood Fantasy, and food tables, adorned with beautiful ice sculptures, are laden with lobster claws, crab legs, shrimp, raw oysters, smoked salmon, clams, and entrees such as steamed mussels, shrimp scampi, and scallops Provençale—all in addition to the usual meat carving stations and a few nonseafood entrees. It's great! And finally, the Fremont has a delightful champagne Sunday brunch served by "island girls" in colorful Polynesian garb. It includes not only unlimited champagne, but a full carving station, lox with bagels and cream cheese, an omelet station, and desserts.

Showboat Captain's Buffet

2800 Fremont St. ☎ **702/385-9123.** Lunch $4.95, dinner $6.45. Mon–Fri 10am–3:30pm; daily 4:30–10pm.

This buffet occupies a cheerful New Orleans garden themed room. Wednesday is all-you-can-eat New York strip steak night. They have added a taco and a pizza bar. The Showboat initiated Las Vegas hotel buffets.

What to See & Do in Las Vegas

You aren't going to lack for things to do in Las Vegas. More than likely, you have come here for the gambling, which should keep you pretty busy (we say with some understatement). But you can't sit at a slot machine forever. (Or maybe you can.) In any event, it shouldn't be too hard to find ways to fill your time between poker hands.

Just walking on the Strip and gazing at the gaudy, garish, absurd wonder of it all can occupy quite a lot of time. This is the number-one activity we recommend in Vegas; at night, it is a mind-boggling sight like no other. And of course, there are shows and plenty of other nighttime entertainment. But if you need something else to do, or if you are trying to amuse yourself while the rest of your party gambles away, this chapter will guide you. Don't forget to check out the free attractions, such as the Mirage's volcano and white tiger exhibit, Treasure Island's pirate battle, and the new Masquerade Show at the Rio Hotel.

You might also consider using a spa at a major hotel; they are too pricey (as high as $20 a day) to fill in for your daily gym visit, but spending a couple of hours working out, sweating out Vegas toxins in the steam room, and generally pampering yourself will leave you feeling relaxed, refreshed, and ready to go all night again.

There are also plenty of sightseeing options, like Hoover Dam (a major tourist destination) and Red Rock Canyon, along with excursions to the Grand Canyon.

In this chapter, all sightseeing options are described in detail. Check them out, along with the side trips listed in chapter 11 and perhaps even a trip to southern Utah, which is outlined in chapter 12, and plan an itinerary that suits your interests.

Be sure to take a look at attractions listed for children, many of which may also interest adults.

SUGGESTED ITINERARIES

The itineraries outlined here are for adults. If you're traveling with kids, incorporate some of the suggestions "Especially for Kids" listed below. The activities mentioned briefly here are described more fully later in this chapter.

If You Have 1 Day

Spend most of the day casino-hopping. These are buildings like no other, thank goodness. Each grandiose interior tops the last. Be sure

Fun Fact

Fremont Street was hub of Las Vegas for almost 4 decades before the first casino hotel, El Rancho, opened on the Strip in 1941.

to see the Mirage (including the white tigers), Treasure Island, Caesars Palace (including the Forum Shops and the talking statues), New York New York, the MGM Grand, Luxor, and Excalibur. Then at night, take a drive (if you can) down the Strip. As amazing as all this is during the day, you can't believe it at night. Aside from just the Strip itself, there is the pirate battle at Treasure Island (consider watching it from the Battle Bar) and the volcano explosion next door at the Mirage. Eat at a buffet (details in chapter 6), and have a drink at the top of the Stratosphere, goggling at the view from the tallest building west of the Mississippi. Oh, and maybe you should gamble a little, too.

If You Have 2 Days

Do more of the above since you may well have not covered it all. Make sure you do something really Vegasey and visit the Liberace Museum. The Dolphin Habitat at the Mirage is worth a look. Or you can rest your feet at the Caesars OMNIMAX theater and their giant screen films. At night, take in a show. We think *Mystère*, the production from the avant-garde Cirque de Soliel, is the finest in Vegas, but there are plenty to chose from. Be sure to leave some time to go Downtown to check out the casinos in the classic Glitter Gulch and the Fremont Street Experience light show.

If You Have 3 Days

By now you've spent 2 days gambling and gawking. So take a break and drive out to Red Rock Canyon. The panoramic, 13-mile Scenic Loop Drive is best seen early in the morning when there's little traffic. If you're so inclined, spend some time hiking here. Have lunch at nearby Bonnie Springs Ranch. After lunch enjoy a guided trail ride into the desert wilderness (see chapter 11 for details). Return to town to experience dinner and a show at Caesars Magical Empire, an interactive theater experience that is thoroughly entertaining (details in this chapter).

If You Have 4 Days or More

Plan a tour to Hoover Dam. Leave early in the morning, returning to Las Vegas after lunch via Valley of Fire State Park, stopping at the Lost City Museum in Overton en route (see chapter 11 for details). Alternatively, you can rest up by spending the day by the hotel pool, or going to the hotel spa and possibly consuming a healthful salad or smoothie at the Engima Cafe. At night, presumably refreshed and toxins purged, hit the casinos and/or catch another show. If you aren't tired of magic, Lance Burton is a wonderful show for a reasonable price, or there is EFX if you feel like splurging, or Jubliee! if your trip won't be complete without a topless revue. You can also splurge on dinner. Gatsby's or Emeril's, both in the MGM Grand, are two of the best restaurants, but if you also want a good dinner with a great free show, go to Treasure Island's Buccaneer Bay Club, which overlooks the pirate battle.

As you plan any additional days, consider excursions to other nearby attractions such as Mount Charleston, Goodsprings, or the Grand Canyon. Inquire about interesting tours at your hotel sightseeing desk.

Las Vegas Attractions

To Salt Lake City
& Valley of Fire

To Reno
& Mt. Charleston

95
93
95

Bonanza Rd.

515

To Hoover Dam

Ogden Ave.

Fremont St.

DOWNTOWN

To Laughlin

582

599

Bonnieville
Ave.

Charleston
Blvd.

Casino Center Blvd.

Gateway
District

To
Red Rock
Canyon

Rancho Dr.

Main St.

Las Vegas Blvd. (The Strip)

Maryland Pkwy.

Stratosphere

15

Sahara Ave.

604

Karen Ave.

605

Circus
Circus Dr.

Circus Circus

NORTH STRIP

Las Vegas
Country Club

Convention
Center Dr.

Las Vegas
Convention Center

Stardust Rd.

Debbie
Reynolds

Desert Inn Rd.

Desert Inn
Country Club

Sands Ave.

Industrial Rd.

Swenson Ave.

Twain Ave.

Mirage

MID-STRIP

Tropicana Wash

Imperial
Palace

Caesars
Palace

Flamingo Rd.

Koval Ln.

University
of Nevada
Las Vegas

Eastern Ave.

Excalibur

Harmon Ave.

Flamingo Wash

Paradise Rd.

Las Vegas Blvd. (The Strip)

MGM
Grand

Luxor

Reno Ave.

Tropicana Ave.

To Hoover Dam

SOUTH STRIP

Hacienda Ave.

605

15

Russell Rd.

McCarran
International
Airport

Russell Rd.

0   1 mi
1.61 km

N

To Los Angeles

Caesars Magical Empire ⑫
Caesars Omnimax Theatre ⑫
An Evening in Vienna ⑱
Fremont Street Experience ④
Grand Slam Canyon ⑦
Hollywood Movie Museum ⑩
Imperial Palace Auto Collection ⑬
King Tut's Tomb ⑲
Las Vegas Motor Speedway ①
Las Vegas Natural History
    Museum ③
Liberace Museum ⑳
Lied Discovery Children's
    Museum ②
Luxor IMAX Theatre/
    Secrets of the Luxor Pyramid ⑲
Magic & Movie Hall of Fame ⑭
MGM Grand Adventures
    Theme Park ⑰
MGM Grand Youth Center ⑯
Mirage Dolphin Habitat ⑪
Scandia Family Fun Center ⑨
Secret Garden of Siegfried
    & Roy ⑪
Star Trek:
    The Experience ⑧
Stratosphere Thrill Rides ⑤
Sunset Stampede ⑮
Wet 'n' Wild ⑥

1-0409

Sin City Inverted

If you want to get away from the glitz and kitsch or just go where most of the tourists don't go, here are ten "Un-Vegasey" things to do, kindly supplied by James P. Reza, Geoff Carter, and the editors of *Scope* magazine.

- **Enigma Garden Café** (see also the listings in chapters 6 and 10). Open around the clock, this wonderful garden cafe draws an intriguing mix of local artists, musicians, strippers, lawyers, and many other colorful characters. As close to a true oasis as you'll ever find.

- **Double Down Saloon** (see also the listing in chapter 10). Sin City's coolest bar, hands down. Enjoy cocktails, plug songs into the world's wildest jukebox, admire the bizarre mural work by Vegas artists, or just mingle with local characters and the occasional celebrity.

- **Utopia** (see also the listing in chapter 10). This two-story discotheque is not only the best nightclub in town, but may also have a lock on the entire Southwest. Dance to techno, rave, acid jazz, and rare groove while watching people feel each other up.

- **West Sahara Library Fine Arts Museum** (9002 W. Sahara Ave., ☎ 702/228-1940). Don't laugh. Las Vegas has its very own gala art museum, ensconced in the most impressive new building built in the Valley since Wayne Newton set up residence. Built to Smithsonian specs, the museum is one of the few urban buildings in Vegas that lends a sense of space and quality to the surrounding stucco.

- **Retro Vintage Couture** (906 S. Valley View, ☎ 702/877-8989). Melina Crisostomo's vintage clothing boutique is one of no kind we're aware of. Try out entire wardrobes from the '40s to the '70s, assisted by the wonderful staff.

- **Contemporary Arts Collective** (103 E. Charlesteon no. 102, ☎ 702/382-3886). Las Vegas's premier artist collective maintains a gallery inside the "Arts Factory" art compound. The CAC's unique vision of this town is too good to miss.

- **Jazzed Cafe and Vinoteca** (see also the listing in chapter 10). Run by professional dancers Kirk Offerle and Connie Chambers, this tiny, elegant bistro stays open till the wee hours, lit by candles and the brilliance of the clientele. Great java, terrific wine list.

- **Floyd Lamb State Park** (I-95 North; exit at Durango). This huge former working ranch once served as a forerunner of those trendy "desert spas" so popular in Scottsdale. Today you'll find acres and acres of grassy picnic areas, walking, hiking, biking, and horse trails, huge shade trees, and two lakes. Wanna be a true native? Always call it "Tule Springs."

- **Chinatown Mall** (4255 Spring Mountain Rd.). The Occident meets the Orient in a big way. A prodigious meeting of great restaurants, interesting shops, and unique amenities, all with roots buried deep in the Far East.

- **Huntridge Theater for the Performing Arts** (1208 E. Charleston, ☎ 702/477-7703). This 50-year-old theater has played host to the likes of Abbott and Costello, Judy Garland, Nine Inch Nails, Sarah McLachlan, and Beck.

1 Attractions in Las Vegas

✪ Caesars Magical Empire

Caesars Palace, 3570 Las Vegas Blvd. S. ☎ **800/445-4544** or 702/731-7333. Reservations necessary. Admission (including a three-course meal and wine; gratuities extra) $65–$75. Daily 4:30–11:30pm. Children must be at least 10 years of age.

Caesars spent a lot of money constructing this facility, and it shows. It's an impressive place of tunnels, grottos, revolving rooms, theaters, and so forth, with a surprise around every corner. Upon arrival, you are assigned to a group of no more than 24, which is escorted through catacombs by Centurian guards to a private dining room. There, you are treated to an intimate magic show by your own private magician. Assisted by some very funny wait staff, there is usually a little story played out as you eat your dinner. Up close magic is performed between courses. Afterwards, you are taken through the rest of the Cavern (beware the Forbidden Crypt of Ramses if you have anything even remotely resembling motion sickness—they ask only if you have "balance problems"); you'll end up in a seven-story dome, with massive Egyptian columns and sculptures, where you can see several other magic shows ranging in size. Here, you can experience Lumineria, a 5-minute show combining smoke, dancing fire, and high-tech lighting effects (cover your eyes before the finale—it's nearly blinding), or chat with some skeletons (Habeas and Corpus) on the walls and, best of all, request songs from "Invisibella," the player piano ghost with a nearly unlimited repertoire and a great sense of humor. All throughout are additional spots with some kind of trick to them; be sure to ask the bartenders for advice. (And look for ghosts in the bathroom mirrors.) The idea for the concept was L.A.'s Magic Castle; Caesars has put its own ancient civilization stamp on it, and the place is truly impressive.

The three-course dinner isn't bad (salad and dessert were pretty good, main course average, though it featured a tasty polenta), and the whole experience is playful and genuinely fun. You can stay as long as you want, even after you have seen all the shows (though that could take awhile as they rotate performers in the venues). There are two different bars inside, with video poker in case you are jonesing. You could hang out for hours in the Grotto Bar, making requests to Invisibella. As you are assigned one of the 10 dining rooms by lottery, you could go several nights in a row and see a different show with a different magician (and presumably, story) each time. Remember, this is interactive theater, so if your magician tries to get you involved, play along as your fun factor will increase if you are a good sport.

Allow yourself at least 3 hours to see everything once. Considering how much show, spectacle, food and just plain entertainment you get, this is one of the best values in the city.

Note: While you're at Caesars, check out the talking statues at the Forum Shops and catch an OMNIMAX movie (the latter described below).

Caesars OMNIMAX Theatre

Caesars Palace, 3570 Las Vegas Blvd. S. ☎ **800/634-6698** or 702/731-7901. Admission $7 adults; seniors, children 2–12, hotel guests, and military personnel $5. Show times vary. You must purchase tickets at the box office (open daily 9am–11pm) on the day of the performance.

If you've never seen one of these 3-D-like films, you're in for a treat. The OMNIMAX Theatre here is housed in a geodesic dome, a space-age environment with 368 seats that recline 27°, affording a panoramic view of the curved 57-foot screen. The movies, projected via 70mm film (which is 10 times the frame size of ordinary 35mm film), offer an awesome visual display enhanced by a state-of-the-art sound system

(89 speakers engulf the audience in sound). Depending on the film being shown, viewers might soar over the Rocky Mountains, plummet down steep waterfalls, ride the rapids, travel into outer space, or perch at the rim of an erupting volcano. Shows change frequently, but whatever you see will be stupendous.

✪ An Evening in Vienna

Excalibur Hotel, 3850 Las Vegas Blvd. S. ☎ **702/597-7600.** Admission $7.95 adults, $5.95 for children under 12 and seniors (including tax). Mon–Thurs 2pm, Sat–Sun 2pm. Dark Fri. Seating is on a first-come, first-served basis. Tickets can be purchased up to 3 days in advance at Excalibur ticket booths.

This is not your average, glitzy, high-production-value Vegas show—quite the opposite. In fact, it's so low key it almost comes as a shock to the system. The magnificent white Lipizzaner stallions hail originally from Spain, but were developed at the Spanish Riding School in Vienna. The horses are trained in the elegant and graceful movements of dressage and hautécole. But the real attraction is the "airs above the ground," gravity defying, seemingly physically impossible leaps the stallions perform naturally for play. They have been shown for centuries in Vienna (Disney made a movie about them), and a touring company has set up permanent residence at the Excalibur. The company re-creates what the Vienna show would be like, with riders in formal uniforms, and the horses performing to classical music. (Watch as the complicated dressage footwork by the horses is choreographed so well to the music that it appears the horse is dancing.) Obviously, it lacks the grand air the real thing would have, and it really suffers in comparison to the extravaganzas performed everywhere else. These comparisons are unfair; the stuff you see here is performed without tricks of lighting or mirrors, and unlike other white mammals on the Strip, these horses are really doing something. Narration explaining the history of the Lippizaners could use a little punching up. If you have a kid who loves horses—or if you love horses—this is a must-see. Children with short attention spans, used to MTV and other barrages of images, may be bored. But the price makes this the best bargain show in town, and, frankly, after the constant sensory bombardment that is Las Vegas (particularly Vegas shows), spending an hour here is a great relief.

✪ Fremont Street Experience

Fremont St., between Main St. and Las Vegas Blvd. in downtown Las Vegas. Shows nightly. Free admission.

For some years, downtown Vegas has been losing ground to the Strip. But thanks to a $70 million revitalization project, that is starting to change. Fremont Street, the heart of "Glitter Gulch," has been closed off and turned into a pedestrian mall. The Fremont Street Experience is a 5-block open-air pedestrian mall, a landscaped strip of outdoor cafes, vendor carts, and colorful kiosks purveying food and merchandise. Overhead is a 90-foot-high steel-mesh "celestial vault"; at night, it is the Sky Parade, a high-tech light and laser show (the canopy is equipped with more than 2.1 million lights) enhanced by a concert hall quality sound system, which takes place four times nightly. But there's music between shows as well. Not only does the canopy provide shade, it cools the area through a misting system in summer and warms you with radiant heaters in winter. The difference this makes cannot be overemphasized; what was once a ghost town of tacky, rapidly aging buildings, in an area with more undesirables than not, is now a bustling (at least at night), friendly, safe place (they have private security guards who hustle said undesirables away). It's a place where you can stroll, eat, or even dance to the music under the lights. The crowd it attracts is more upscale than in years past, and of course, it's a lot less crowded than the hectic Strip. Some rightly mourn the passing of cruising Glitter Gulch, gawking at the original lights. It does indeed mean the end of classic Las Vegas, but on the other hand, classic

Las Vegas was dead and nearly buried anyway. This has given a second life to a deserving neighborhood.

And in a further effort to retain as much of classic Las Vegas as possible, the **Neon Museum** is installing vintage hotel and casino signs along the promenade. The first installation is the horse and rider from the old Hacienda, which presently rides the sky over the intersection of Fremont and Las Vegas Boulevard. (Eventually, the Neon Museum hopes to have an indoor installation on the Fremont Street Experience, to showcase some of the smaller signs they have collected.) *Note:* A good place to view the light show is from the balcony at Fitzgerald's Hotel.

Hollywood Movie Museum
Debbie Reynolds Hotel, 305 Convention Center Dr. ☎ **702/7-DEBBIE.** Admission $7.95 adults, $5.95 children 3–12. Mon–Fri 10am–10pm, with tours every hour on the hour.

Debbie Reynolds has been buying up Hollywood memorabilia for decades. Her $30 million collection, comprising items from more than a half century of American movies, celebrates Hollywood's Golden Age. Changing exhibits showcase some 3,000 costumes, including the famous white dress worn by Marilyn Monroe in *The Seven Year Itch,* Elizabeth Taylor's Cleopatra headdress, Vivien Leigh's hats from *Gone with the Wind,* Doris Day's mermaid outfit from *Glass Bottom Boat,* the sequined royal-blue swimsuit Esther Williams wore in *Deep in My Heart,* a pair of Judy Garland's ruby slippers from *The Wizard of Oz,* and the dancing shoes of Fred Astaire and Cyd Charisse, among them. Additionally, props, artifacts, and furnishings from classic films (she has a 36,000-square-foot warehouse filled with them) include the dagger used by Errol Flynn in *The Adventures of Don Juan,* Yul Brynner's bullwhip and throne from *The King and I,* Winchester rifles from *Annie Get Your Gun,* and the Ark of the Covenant from *The Ten Commandments.* Museum displays are enhanced by a 35-minute multimedia show presented in a high-tech 80-seat theater that re-creates the intimate ambience of a Hollywood screening room. Guests are greeted by Debbie (on screen), who narrates a nostalgic overview of Hollywood's classic and epic motion pictures. A 30-foot revolving stage, two 10-foot revolving platforms, and lighted dioramas on the side walls permit the dramatic display of film clips, sets, and costumes.

Imperial Palace Auto Collection
Imperial Palace Hotel, 3535 Las Vegas Blvd. S. ☎ **702/731-3311.** Admission $6.95 adults, $3 seniors and children under 12, free for children under 5 and AAA members. Daily 9:30am–11:30pm.

If you're not a "car person," don't assume you won't be interested in this premier collection of antique, classic, and special-interest vehicles. There's more here than just cars and trucks. Check out the graceful lines and handsome sculpture of one of the 43 Model J Dusenbergs (the largest collection in the world valued at over $50 million). The craftsmanship and attention to detail make these cars, and others here, true works of art.

There's also a great deal of history. Take a walk down President's Row where you can see JFK's 1962 "bubbletop" Lincoln Continental, Lyndon Johnson's 1964 Cadillac, Eisenhower's 1952 Chrysler Imperial 20-foot-long parade car, Truman's 1950 Lincoln Cosmopolitan with gold-plated interior, FDR's unrestored 1936 V-16 Cadillac, and Herbert Hoover's 1929 Cadillac. Directly opposite this tribute to democracy, in both location and political theory, is the dictator section. Here you will see Adolf Hitler's armored, bulletproof, and mineproof 1936 Mercedes-Benz 770K, Emperor Hirohito's 1935 Packard, Czar Nicholas II's 1914 Rolls-Royce, former Mexican president Lazaro Cardena's black 1939 V-12 Packard (armor-plated to resist 50-caliber machine gun bullets), and Argentinean strongman Juan Peron's 1939 straight-8 Packard (no pictures of Evita anywhere). The Imperial Palace owner, who came under fire some years ago for throwing a birthday party for Hitler, claims he is not a Fascist, just a buff, but you do have to wonder.

Commercial vehicles of bygone days include antique buses, military transports, taxis (among them, the 1908 French model that appeared in the movie version of *My Fair Lady*), gasoline trucks, fire engines, delivery trucks and vans, dump trucks, and pickup trucks. Other highlights are Al Capone's 1930 V-16 Cadillac, Elvis Presley's powder blue 1976 Cadillac Eldorado, Liberace's pale-cream 1981 Zimmer (complete with candelabra), W.C. Fields's black 1938 Cadillac V-16 touring sedan with built-in bar, Caruso's 1920 green and black Hudson, Howard Hughes's 1954 Chrysler (because of his phobia about germs, Hughes installed a special air-purification system that cost more than the car itself!), and a 1947 Tucker (one of only 51 manufactured before the company went out of business).

King Tut's Tomb & Museum

Luxor Las Vegas, 3900 Las Vegas Blvd. S. ☎ **702/262-4000.** Admission $4. Sun–Thurs 9am–11pm, Fri–Sat 9am–11:30pm.

Note: At press time this exhibit was closed during the Luxor remodeling. Plans are to reopen it in a new location within the hotel.

This full-scale reproduction of King Tutankhamen's Tomb includes the antechamber, annex, burial chamber, and treasury housing replicas (all handcrafted in Egypt by artisans using historically correct gold leaf and linens, pigments, tools, and ancient methods) of the glittering inventory discovered by archaeologists Howard Carter and Lord Carnarvon in the Valley of Kings at Luxor in 1922. All items have been meticulously positioned according to Carter's records. It's hardly like seeing the real thing, but if you aren't going to Egypt any time soon, perhaps checking out reproductions isn't a bad idea. A 20-minute audio tour (available in English, French, Spanish, and Japanese) is preceded by a 4-minute introductory film.

Las Vegas Motor Speedway

7000 Las Vegas Blvd. N., directly across from Nellis Air Force base (take I-15 north to Speedway exit 54). ☎ **702/644-4443** for ticket information. Tickets $10–$75 (higher prices for major events).

This 107,000-seat facility, the first new superspeedway to be built in the southwest in over 2 decades, opened with a 500K Indy Racing League event. A $100 million state-of-the-art motor sports entertainment complex, it includes a 1.5-mile superspeedway, a 2.5-mile FIA-approved road course, paved and dirt short-track ovals, and a 4,000-foot drag strip. Also on the property are facilities for Go-Kart, Legends Car, Sand Drag, and Motocross competition. The new speedway is accessible via shuttle buses to and from the Imperial Palace hotel, though some of the other major hotels have their own shuttles to the Speedway.

✪ Liberace Museum

1775 E. Tropicana Ave., at Spencer St. ☎ **702/798-5595.** Admission $6.50 adults, $4.50 seniors over 60, $3.50 students, $2 children 6–12, free for children under 6. Mon–Sat 10am–5pm, Sun 1–5pm.

You can keep your Louvres and Vaticans and Smithsonians; *this* is a museum. Housed, like everything else in Vegas, in a strip mall, this is a shrine to the glory and excess that was the art project known as Liberace. You've got your costumes (bejeweled), your many cars (bejeweled), your many pianos (bejeweled), and many jewels (also bejeweled). It just shows what can be bought with lots of money and no taste. The thing is, Liberace was in on the joke (we think). The people who come here largely aren't. Many of these guests would not have liked him living next door to them if his name was, say, Bruce Smith, but they idolize the man-the-myth. Not found here is any reference to AIDS or chauffeurs who had plastic surgery to look more like him. But you will find a Czar Nicholas uniform with 22-karat-gold braiding and a blue velvet cape styled after the coronation robes of King George V and covered with $60,000 worth of rare chinchilla. Not to mention a $50,000 50.6-pound rhinestone, the world's largest, presented to him by the grateful (I'll bet they were) Austrian firm that supplied all his costume stones. The gift shop has plenty of rhinestone-covered objects plus countless Liberace knickknacks of increasing tackiness. This is a one-of-a-kind place. Unless you have a severely underdeveloped appreciation for camp or take your museum going very seriously, you shouldn't miss it. The museum is 2^1/$_2$ miles east of the Strip on your right.

Luxor IMAX Theater/Secrets of the Luxor Pyramid

Luxor Las Vegas, 3900 Las Vegas Blvd. S. ☎ **702/262-4000.** Admission $7 for IMAX 2-D, $8.50 for 3-D; for "Secrets" Episode One $4, Episode Two $5. A combined ticket, including both episodes of "Secrets of the Luxor Pyramid" (described below), is $9. Sun–Thurs 10am–11pm, Fri–Sat 10am–11:30pm. Show times vary depending on the length of the film.

This is a state-of-the-art theater that projects the film on a seven-story screen. There are two different films running, one in standard two dimensions, the other 3-D. The glasses for the latter are really cool headsets that include built-in speakers, bringing certain sounds right into your head. The movies change periodically, but always include some extraordinary special effects. If you have a fear of heights, make sure to ask for a seat on one of the lower levels.

"Secrets of the Luxor Pyramid" is a two-part adventure. In "Episode One" you become part of the audience for a live broadcast that begins a tabloid TV talk show. The topic is the mysterious happenings below the pyramid. The guests are a militaristic government agent, Colonel Calggert, and Mac MacPherson (the good guy). Parts of this are in 3-D, and it sets up the story for "Episode Two."

"Episode Two" is a motion-simulator ride in which technology is used to create an action adventure involving a chase sequence inside a pyramid. In a rapidly plummeting elevator (the cable has broken!) you'll descend to an ancient temple 2 miles beneath the Luxor pyramid. Against the orders of Colonel Claggert, you'll accompany MacPherson and Carina Wolinski (the love interest) in their search for a mysterious crystal obelisk containing the secrets of the universe. In a thrill ride through the temple's maze, you'll experience an explosive battle with evil forces, rescue Carina from the clutches of Dr. Osiris, and narrowly escape death before returning to the surface. You have an option to take a different route if you have motion sickness, which means you won't get the best special effects. Otherwise, it's a standard thrill ride with interesting touches.

Magic and Movie Hall of Fame

O'Shea's Casino, 3555 Las Vegas Blvd. S., between Sands Avenue and Flamingo Road. ☎ **702/ 737-1343.** Admission $9.95 adults, $3 children under 12 accompanied by an adult. Tues–Sat 10am–6pm. Magic shows at 11:30am and 1:30, 3, and 4:30pm.

The price of entry here is very reasonable, considering you can almost always get a $5 discount coupon out front or in the casino's food court. Admission includes a half-hour show in the Houdini Theatre (note performance hours above) featuring magician/ventriloquist Valentine Vox.

After the performance, visitors tour a vast museum that houses props and artifacts of famous magicians such as Houdini (bound with ropes and shackled in leg irons and handcuffs, Houdini once had himself lowered into the East River in a wood packing case that was nailed shut and weighed down with 200 pounds of lead;

Siegfried & Roy's House

When they aren't on stage, they are just plain (okay, nothing is plain with them) Siegfried Fischbacher and Roy Horn. And they live in a house at 1639 Valley on the corner of Vegas Drive (right across from the golf course). We aren't giving much away; if you want to be anonymous, you don't put a big gold "S R" on all your gates. Which by the way are huge and gilt. White lions top the massive white stucco wall which lines the property. You can't see any of the fabulous wonders inside (there is a book on sale at the Mirage, complete with many photos of their house, over-decorated, stuffed-within-an-inch-of-its-life with objects from around the world, tigers roaming freely), but you can see the bits of the vaguely Spanish mission-style dwelling peeking over the top of the walls. Across the street are much smaller houses, also sporting the gold "SR" on their gates. These have been purchased by the Austrian magicians, as guest houses, turning the whole block into a sort of compound. Drive by with the windows down and maybe you can hear lions and tigers (and bears) roar.

he freed himself in just 57 seconds!), levitation master Harry Kellar, Sevais Le Roy (who "cremated" a girl on stage), Thurston (his spike cabinet is on display), the Mephistophelian Dante (who popularized the phrases "hocus-pocus" and "abracadabra"), and Carter the Great (Houdini was his assistant as a teenager).

Exhibits are enhanced by dozens of video clips of actual performances. Modern-day practitioners are also included; a highlight is a behind-the-scenes video tour with illusionists Siegfried and Roy. Another section contains antique automata, mechanical devices, Gypsy fortune telling booths, vintage arcade games, Nickelodeons, and music boxes, some of them operable by visitors. You'll learn about the history of ventriloquism, which dates back to the 5th century B.C. and was used by ancient diviners to imitate the voices of the dead. Hundreds of antique and modern dummies are on display, and there's entertaining video footage of the greats—Edgar Bergen with Charlie McCarthy and Mortimer Snerd, Arthur Prince with Jim (Prince smoked a cigar while he did his dummy's voice), Valentine Vox (who you've seen in the show), Paul Winchell with Jerry Mahoney, and others. You can attempt ventriloquism yourself in a how-to booth equipped with a dummy and instructions. Movie costumes, such as a dress Liz Taylor wore in *Cleopatra* and Clark Gable's jacket from *Gone With the Wind*, are displayed in another area, along with tableaux of famous movie scenes. The tour winds up in a gift shop where a magician demonstrates many of the wares (magic tricks, juggling equipment) on sale, providing further entertainment.

The Secret Garden of Siegfried and Roy and ✪ Mirage Dolphin Habitat

Mirage Hotel, 3400 Las Vegas Blvd. S. ☎ **702/791-7111.** Admission $10, free for children under 11. Mon–Sun 10am–5:30pm. (Dolphin exhibit only on Wed $5, when the Secret Garden is closed.) Hours subject to change.

Siegfried and Roy's famous white tigers have long had a free exhibit in the Mirage. They still do, but now they have an additional space, a gorgeous area behind the dolphin exhibit. Here, the white tigers are joined by white lions, Bengal tigers, an Asian elephant, a panther, and a snow leopard. (Many of these are bred by Siegfried & Roy and are also in their nightly show.) It's really just a gloried zoo, featuring only the big-ticket animals; however, it is a very pretty place, with plenty of foliage and some bits of Indian- and Asian-themed architecture. Zoo purists will be horrified at the smallish spaces the animals occupy, but all are rotated between here and their more lavish digs at the illusionist team's home. What this does allow you to do is get very up close with a tiger, which is quite a thrill—those paws are massive indeed. Visitors are given little portable phonelike objects on which they can play a series of programs, listening to Roy and Mirage owner Steve Wynn discuss conservation or the attributes of each animal and deliver anecdotes.

The Dolphin habitat is more satisfying. It was designed to provide a healthy and nurturing environment and to educate the public about marine mammals and their role in the ecosystem. Specialists worldwide were consulted in creating the habitat, which was designed to serve as a model of a quality, secured environment. The pool is more than eight times larger than government regulations require, and its 2.5 million gallons of man-made seawater are cycled and cleaned once every 2 hours. It must be working, as the adult dolphins here are breeding regularly. The Mirage displays only dolphins already in captivity—no dolphins will be taken from the wild. You can watch the dolphins frolic both above and below ground through viewing windows, in three different pools. (There is nothing quite like the kick you get from seeing a baby dolphin play.) The knowledgeable staff, who surely have the best job in Vegas, will answer questions. If they aren't already, ask them to play ball with the dolphins; they toss large beach balls into the pools, and the dolphins hit them out with their noses, leaping out the water cackling with dolphin glee. You catch the ball, getting nicely wet, and toss it back to them. If you have never played ball with a dolphin, shove that happy child next to you out of the way and go for it. There is also a video of a resident dolphin (Duchess) giving birth (to Squirt) underwater. You can stay as long as you like, which might just be hours.

STAR TREK: THE EXPERIENCE

Las Vegas Hilton, 3000 Paradise Rd. ☎ **702-732-5111.** Admission will be about $10. Hours not yet available.

Trekkers take note: Opening by 1998, STAR TREK: The Experience promises to "boldly go where no entertainment experience has gone before." Visitors will become Starfleet crew members on an intergalactic journey that utilizes simulator rides, interactive videos, morphing, and virtual-reality stations, holograms, and state-of-the-art computer games. Your voyage will begin in a "history-of-the-future" museum filled with authentic Star Trek costumes, weaponry, and props. From the Starfleet Gallery Room, you'll be "beamed up" to the Bridge of the Starship Enterprise and board a shuttlecraft for a simulated journey through the universe. Upon successful completion of your mission, you'll disembark at Deep Space Nine to play (there's a state-of-the-art video-game room), dine, shop, and encounter aliens in the 24th century. A Cardassian-style restaurant will serve futuristically named foods, such as Glop-on-a-Stick, and, in the lounge, you'll order food and drinks from machines equipped with voice-recognition capabilities.

Stratosphere Thrill Rides

Stratosphere, 2000 Las Vegas Blvd. S. ☎ **702/380-7777.** Admission for either ride is $5, plus $5 to ascend the tower (if you dine in the buffet room or Top of the World, there's no charge to go up to the tower). Sun–Thurs 10am–midnight, Fri–Sat 10am–2am. Minimum height requirement for both rides is 48 inches.

Atop the 1,149-foot Stratosphere Tower are two marvelous thrill rides. The **Let It Ride High Roller** (the world's highest roller-coaster) was recently revamped to go at even faster speeds as it zooms around a hilly track that is seemingly suspended in midair. Even more fun is the **Big Shot,** a breathtaking free-fall ride that thrusts you 160 feet in the air along a 228-foot spire at the top of the tower, then plummets back down again. Sitting in an open car, you seem to be dangling in space over Las Vegas. We have one relative, a thrill ride enthusiast, who said he never felt more scared than when he rode the Big Shot. After he survived, he promptly put his kids on it, who loved it.

Sunset Stampede

Sam's Town, 5111 Boulder Hwy., at Flamingo Rd. ☎ **702/456-7777.** Free admission. Daily shows at 2, 6, 8, and 10pm.

This 10-minute laser-light and water spectacular takes place four times daily in the lush and lovely 25,000-square foot Mystic Falls Park. The evening shows have even more thrilling lighting effects. The show begins with jets of steam over the park's waterfall, which is bathed in purple light. Soon a mist envelops the entire garden. An animatronic wolf howls at the top of the mountain as the show begins. Water shoots up in a lofty geyser, enhanced by high-tech lighting effects and laser wildlife creatures racing across the "great plains." The musical backdrop is dramatic and enchanting. To signal the end of the show, the wolf howls once again. If you don't have a car, free bus transport is available to and from the Strip; call for details.

2 Getting Married

This is one of the most popular things to do in Las Vegas. Why? It's very easy to get married here. Too easy. See that total stranger standing next to you? Grab him or her, head down to the **Clark Country Marriage License Bureau** (200 S. 3rd at Briger Avenue; ☎ 702/455-3156; open Monday to Sunday from 8am to midnight, 24 hours legal holidays) to get your license, find a wedding chapel (not hard since they line the north end of the Strip—Las Vegas Blvd. S.), and tie the knot. Just like that. No blood test, no waiting period—heck, not even an awkward dating period.

But even if you have actually known your intended for some time, Las Vegas is a great place to get married. The ease is the primary attraction, but there are a number of other appealing reasons. You can have any kind of wedding you want, from a big, traditional production number, to a small, intimate affair, to a spur-of-the-moment "just the happy couple in blue jeans" kind of thing, to Elvis in a pink Cadillac at a drive-up window. (Oh, yes. More on that later.) The wedding chapels take care of everything; usually they will even provide a limo to take you to the license bureau and back. Most offer all the accessories, from rings to flowers to a videotape memory of the event.

We personally know several very happy couples who opted for the Vegas route. Motivations differed, with the ease factor heading the list (though the Vegas-ness of the whole thing came in a close second), but one and all reported having great fun. Really, what more romantic way to start off your life together than in gales of laughter?

In any event, the more than 100,000 couples who take advantage of all this can't be wrong. If you want to follow in the footsteps of Elvis and Priscilla (at the Aladdin Hotel), Michael Jordan, Joan Collins, Bruce Willis and Demi Moore, the following is a list of the most notable wedding chapels on or near the Strip. There are many more in town, and almost all the major hotels offer a chapel as well; though the latter are cleaner and less tacky than some of the Strip chapels, they do tend to be without any personality at all. (One exception might be the chapel at the Excalibur Hotel, where you can dress in medieval costumes.)

With regard to decor, there isn't a radical difference between the major places, though some are decidedly more spiffy and less sad than others. Attitude certainly makes a difference with several. (In passing, standing outside a wedding chapel for a couple hours makes for interesting people-watching, as you see brides in full white gowns accompanied by a whole retinue, pregnant brides in ordinary dresses, or happy couples wearing sweats, all ready to march down that aisle.)

You can also call **Las Vegas Weddings and Rooms** (☎ 800/488-MATE), a one-stop shop for wedding services. They'll find a chapel or outdoor garden that suits your taste (not to mention such only-in-Vegas venues as the former mansions of Elvis Presley and Liberace), book you into a hotel for the honeymoon, arrange the ceremony, and provide flowers, a photographer (or videographer), wedding cake, limo, car rental, music, champagne, balloons, and a garter for the bride. Basically they can arrange anything you like. Theme weddings are a specialty. They even have a New Age minister on call who can perform a Native American ceremony. And yes, you can get married by an Elvis impersonator. Let Las Vegas Weddings arrange your honeymoon stay—sightseeing tours, show tickets, and meals, as well.

Be aware that Valentine's Day is a very popular day to get married in Vegas. Some of the chapels perform as many as 80 services.

But remember, you also don't have to plan ahead. Just show up, get your paperwork, close your eyes, and pick a chapel. And above all, have fun. Good luck and best wishes to you both.

ABOUT THE PRICES   Weddings can be very cheap in Vegas: A license is about $35, and a basic service not much more. Even a full blown shebang package—photos, music, some flowers, video, cake, other doodads—will run only about $500 total. We haven't quoted any prices here since the ultimate cost depends entirely on how much you want to spend. Go cheap, and the whole thing will put you back maybe $100, including the license (maybe even somewhat less); go elaborate, and the price is still reasonable by today's wedding price standards. Be sure to remember that there are often "hidden" charges, such as expected gratuities for the minister, and so forth. If you're penny-pinching, you'll want to keep those in mind.

Chapel of the Bells

2233 Las Vegas Blvd. S. ☎ **800/233-2391** or 702/735-6803. Mon–Thurs 10am–9pm, Fri–Sat 10am–midnight. They stay open as late as they need to on holidays.

Sporting perhaps the largest and gaudiest sign on the Strip, this chapel also shares a parking lot with the bright pink Fun City Motel. We won't make any jokes. The chapel has wood paneling, sage carpeting, and gilt trim up by the pulpit. Electric candles light the walls. It only seats about 25. They prefer advance booking but can do same-day ceremonies if called for.

Chapel of Love

1431 Las Vegas Blvd. S. ☎ **800/922-5683** or 702/387-0155. Mon–Thurs 8am–10pm, Fri–Sat 8am–midnight, Sun 9am–9pm.

A friendly place largely run by women (men take the photos and are the limo drivers), featuring four different chapels. None are very big; the Lavender and Peach Chapels hold only 16. (And yes, the difference would be in the modest floral themes on the wallpaper and at the pulpit and the stained glass windows.) The Rose Chapel holds 50, and the Rainbow Chapel (no, it's not done in rainbows, thank heavens, though there is one on the window under the kissing doves) holds 35. Obviously, some of these rooms are downright tiny and the decor not the most memorable (though the wallpaper adds a touch of individuality; so many of the other chapels just have white walls with wood paneling). But this is a pretty place and very affordable. There is a also a reception room for a cold buffet or hot hors d'oeuvres. Their packages are quite reasonable, and they put all the "hidden" charges (such as suggested gratuities for the minister and so forth) right in their brochure so there are no surprises.

An Elvis Impersonator's Top 10 Reasons to Get Married in Las Vegas

Jesse Garon has appeared in numerous Las Vegas productions as "Young Elvis." He arrives at any special event in a 1955 pink, neon-lit Cadillac. Jesse Garon is available for weddings, receptions, birthdays, conventions, grand openings, and so on. Video and print support also available. For all your Elvis impersonator needs, call ☎ **702/474-9227.**

1. The only place in the world where Elvis will marry you, at a drive-up window, in a pink Cadillac—24 hours a day.

2. Chances are you'll never forget your anniversary.

3. Where else can you treat all your guests to a wedding buffet for only 99¢ a head?

4. Four words: One helluva bachelor party.

5. On wedding night, show spouse that new "watch me disappear" act you learned from Siegfried and Roy.

6. Show your parents who's boss—have your wedding your way.

7. Wedding bells ring for you everywhere you go. They just sound like slot machines.

8. You can throw dice instead of rice.

9. Easy to lie about age on the marriage certificate—just like Joan Collins did!

10. With all the money you save, it's dice clocks for everyone!

✪ Cupid's Wedding Chapel

827 Las Vegas Blvd. S. ☎ **800/543-2933** or 702/598-4444. Sun–Thurs 10am–10pm, Fri–Sat 10am–1am.

"The little chapel with the big heart." Well, they just might be. The manager explains that, unlike other chapels on the Strip, they schedule weddings an hour apart. This gives them time for the full production number; they pride themselves on offering "a traditional church wedding at a chapel prices." This includes a bridal processional, dimmed lights as the minister introduces the happy couple, and then a tape of the couple's favorite song, so they can have their first dance right there at the pulpit after their "first" kiss. They also offer family weddings for those couples blending preexisting ones; the children become a part of the service, and as their parents exchange rings with each other, the kids are given their own small token, to let them know the parents are marrying them as well. "I am a diehard romantic," said the manager, "I want huggin', kissin', and I don't care if they faint—a wedding is a place for romance." You just know she cries at each and every service they perform. The chapel is pleasantly low-frills and down to earth, with white walls and pews, and modern stained glass with doves and roses. (Kitsch-phobes will be pleased to know the cupids are only in the lobby.) It seats 60 to 70. And, yes, if they don't have something already scheduled, they will take walk-ups. There is a restaurant (Thai) right next door that was closed as of this writing, but if it has reopened, there's your reception!

Graceland Wedding Chapel

619 Las Vegas Blvd. S. ☎ **800/824-5732** or 702/474-6655. Sun–Thurs 9am–9pm, Fri–Sat 9am–midnight.

Housed in a landmark building that is one of the oldest wedding chapels in Vegas, the Graceland bills itself as "the proverbial Mom and Pop outfit. We offer friendly, courteous service, and are willing to go that extra step." No, there is no Elvis connection; one of the owners was friends with Elvis and asked his permission to use the name. This is a tiny New England church building with a small bridge and white picket fence out front. Inside is a 33-seat chapel; burgundy and white walls with a large, modern stained glass window of doves and roses behind the pulpit. The pews are dark blonde wood. It is not the nicest of the chapels. Jon Bon Jovi and Lorenzo Lamas got married here, though not to each other.

Little Chapel of the Flowers

1717 Las Vegas Blvd. S. ☎ **800/843-2410** or 702/735-4331. Mon–Sun 8am–10pm.

This is another miniature old-fashioned church building with a very tiny garden and gazebo. They have two chapels off their pretty and comfortable lobby (mock-antique look). The Victorian chapel, which holds only 30, has white walls and dark wood pews and doesn't look very Victorian at all. The Heritage Chapel holds 70 and adds rose-colored drapes and electric candle chandeliers. They also offer a medium size reception room and live organ music on request. It's a pretty, friendly place, but not particularly special in terms of look (though it is not shabby as some chapels are). They do not allow rice or confetti throwing.

The Little White Chapel

1301 Las Vegas Blvd. S. ☎ **800/545-8111** or 702/382-5943. Open 24 hours.

This is arguably the most famous of the chapels on the Strip, maybe because they have the big sign saying Michael Jordan and Joan Collins were married there (again, not to each other), maybe because they were the first to do the drive-up window. It is indeed little and white. However, they feel like a factory line, processing wedding after wedding after wedding, 24 hours a day. Move 'em in and move 'em out. (No wonder they put in that drive-up window!) The staff, dressed in hot pink smocks, was brusque, hasty, and had a bit of an attitude (though we know one couple who got married here and had no complaints). They do offer full wedding ceremonies, complete with candlelight service and traditional music. There are two chapels, the smaller of which has a large photo of a forest stream. They also have a gazebo for outdoor services, but since that is right on the Strip, it's not as nice as it sounds. If you want something special, there are probably better choices, but for a true Vegas wedding experience, this is Kitsch Wedding Central.

Mission of the Bells

1205 Las Vegas Blvd. S. ☎ **800/634-6277** or 702/366-0646. Mon–Fri 9am–6pm, Sat 12pm–8pm, Sun 10am–6pm.

This is the largest wedding chapel on the Strip; the chapel holds 125. The outside is like an adobe mission (hence the name) topped by a large bell, and so the inside carries through on the Southwestern theme, with wood benches, fake adobe wall at the altar, Native American design stained glass windows, a very tall cathedral ceiling, and Western Indian style chandeliers. It is large and warm, not claustrophobic. It's recently come under new management. Across the street is Slightly Sinful "a romantic boutique," in case you need a trousseau or otherwise stock up for the wedding night.

✪ A Special Memory Wedding Chapel

800 S. Fourth St., at Gass. ☎ **800/9-MARRYU** or 702/384-2211. Sun–Thurs 8am–10, Fri–Sat 8am–12am.

This is a terrific new wedding chapel, particularly when compared to the rather tired facades of the classics on the Strip. This is absolutely the place to go if you want a traditional, big production wedding; you won't feel in the least bit tacky or in any other way like you got married in Vegas. It's a New England church-style building, complete with steeple. The interior looks like a proper church (well, a plain one—don't think ornate gothic cathedral) with a peaked roof, pews with padded red seats, modern stained glass windows of doves and flowers, and lots of dark wood. It is all very clean and new and seats about 87 comfortably. There is a short staircase leading to an actual bride's room; she can make an entrance coming down it or through the double doors at the back. The area outside the chapel is like a mini-mall of bridal paraphernalia stores. Should all this just be too darn nice and proper for you, they also offer a drive-up window (where they do about 300 weddings a month!). It costs you $25—just ring the buzzer for service. They have a photo studio on site and will do small cake, cold cuts, and champagne receptions. There is a gazebo for outside weddings, and they sell T-shirts!

San Francisco Sally's Victorian Chapel

1304 Las Vegas Blvd. S. ☎ **800/658-8677** or 702/385-7777. Sun–Thurs 10am–4pm, Fri–Sat 10am–8pm.

An extremely tiny wedding chapel bursting at the seams with Victorian frills (fringed lamps, swags of lace curtains). They basically offer "an Olde Tyme Parlor Wedding." This is perfect if you want a very intimate wedding—like you, your intended, and someone to officiate. It literally can't hold more than six people. (And the space at the back of the room opens for an even tinier reception area—it can barely fit the cake!) But if you love Victoriana, or you want to play dress up at your wedding, this is the place. The shop rents out dresses and costumes, so you can wear a Scarlett O'Hara antebellum outfit or some other period number for your big day. (It's all fantasy anyway, so why not go whole hog?) They specialize in extras without extra charges like altering and whatnot. The women who run it refer to themselves as "a bunch of mother hens," are delightful, and will pamper you to within an inch of your life. (One couple drops in every year just to say hi.) Some may find it a bit cutesy, but it really is quite charming and has its own distinct personality, unlike most of the other chapels in the area (where the interiors all start to blur together after awhile.) This is decidedly a special place that might be just right depending on your wedding desires and fantasies.

Silver Bell Chapel

607 Las Vegas Blvd. S. ☎ **800/221-8491** or 702/382-3727. Web site: http://www.tricks.corn/silverball. Sun–Thurs 8am–midnight, Fri–Sat 24 hours.

Let's call this the Little Chapel Lined in Neon, at least at night. It's slightly chapel-shaped on the outside, with a small garden including a very little stream and bridge out front. Only 35 people can fit in the small, white walled chapel, seated on white wood pews. They are opening an outside wedding and reception garden and should have a drive-through window by 1998.

Wee Kirk O'the Heather

231 Las Vegas Blvd. S. ☎ **702/382-9830.** Mon–Sun 10am–midnight.

This is the oldest wedding chapel in Las Vegas (it's been here since 1940) and the one at the very end of the Strip, right before downtown (and thus even closer to the license bureau). It would be declared a historic landmark, except some renovations in the past moved just enough interior walls to alter it enough to keep it from being official. It had been closed for 2 years and is in the middle of some remodeling, so it was unclear at press time how it would look. The planned changes should still keep the look simple, and they plan to have fresh flowers (unlike the artificial ones everywhere else) to match the season. They have an organ as well.

3 Attractions in Nearby Henderson

About 6 miles from the Strip in the town of Henderson are four factories in fairly close proximity to one another. All offer free tours to the public. It's best to see them on a weekday when they're fully operative. To get to Henderson, drive east on Tropicana Avenue, make a right on Mountain Vista, then go 2 miles to Sunset Way; turn left into Green Valley Business Park. You will soon see Ethel M Chocolates, a good place to begin. Use the map in this section to find your way to the other three facilities.

Cranberry World West

1301 American Pacific Dr., Henderson. ☎ **702/566-7160.** Free admission. Daily 9am–5pm.

At this Ocean Spray juice processing and distribution plant, the message is that cranberries are more than a Thanksgiving side dish. Visitors view a 7-minute film about cranberry history, harvesting, and the manufacturing processes. Ocean Spray, you'll learn, is also the leading grapefruit grower in the country. The film is followed by a self-guided tour with interactive exhibits, a look at the plant from a view station, and a visit to the juice bar and test kitchen for a free sampling of 10 Ocean Spray juice drinks, cranberry-studded baked goods, and other products from the company's gourmet line (cranberry mustard, salsa, and others). The tour winds up in the gift shop where you can purchase Ocean Spray products.

Ethel M Chocolates

2 Cactus Garden Dr., just off Mountain Vista and Sunset Way in the Green Valley Business Park. ☎ **702/433-2500** for recorded information, or 702/458-8864. Free admission. Daily 8:30am–7pm. Closed Christmas.

Just 6 miles from the Strip is the Ethel M Chocolate Factory and Cactus Garden, a tourist attraction that draws about 2,000 visitors a day. Ethel Mars began making fine chocolates in a little candy kitchen around the turn of the century and her small enterprise evolved to produce not only dozens of varieties of superb boxed chocolates but some of the world's most famous candies: M&Ms, Milky Way, 3 Musketeers, Snickers, and Mars bars.

On a self-guided tour of the plant, you'll see the candy-making process from a glass-enclosed viewing aisle. All of the equipment is marked to aid visitor comprehension. "Kitchen" procedures include the cooking of buttery cream fillings in immense copper kettles, the hand-sorting of nuts, grinding of fresh peanut butter, and fudge making. In one production-line process, little creamy centers are bathed in chocolate and decorated with Ethel M's trademark swirls. On another line, chocolate is deposited into molds, vibrated to eliminate air bubbles, cooled, filled (with nuts, creams, and/or liqueurs), and hand boxed. There are actually employees whose job involves the "arduous" task of tasting for quality control. Depending on what's being made the day you visit, you may observe all or little of the above; however, you will see it all in informative video presentations shown along the aisle. The tour winds up in an attractive gift shop where you can sample a free piece of chocolate candy (my favorite is almond butter krisp) and hand-dipped ice cream; here, you can also purchase chocolates and have them shipped anywhere in the United States.

Also on the premises is a 2.5-acre garden displaying 350 species of rare and exotic cacti with signs provided for self-guided tours. It's best appreciated in spring when the cacti are in full bloom. Behind the garden, also with a self-guided tour, is Ethel M's "Living Machine," a natural wastewater treatment and recycling plant that consists of aerated tanks, ecological fluid beds, a constructed wetlands, reed beds, and a storage pond.

Going Vegas

If you're looking for a quintessential Las Vegas experience, try these suggestions from James P. Reza, Geoff Carter, and the editors of *Scope* magazine.

- **Peppermill's Fireside Lounge** (see also the listing in chapter 10). This lounge is so evocative of the Me Decade, it's impossible not to love it. Dark, cozy, sexy, and somewhat kitschy, a great place for romantic encounters. Try to sit by the year-round fire pit, if you can stand the heat.

- **Binion's Horseshoe** (see also the listing in chapter 5). This downtown hotel/casino proffers the greatest souvenir in Sin City, if not the entire US of A: a free picture of you taken in front of a million dollars worth of paper currency. Did we mention it was free?

- **Movie and Magic Hall of Fame** at O'Shea's (see also the listing earlier in this chapter). Curator Valentine Vox has assembled an amazing collection of magic and ventriloquism memorabilia, representing everyone from Houdini to Edgar Bergen.

- **GameWorks** (3769 Las Vegas Blvd. S., ☎ **702/432-4263**). This multilevel entertainment center gives visitors a chance to wreak digitized havoc on the latest video game creations. A few brave souls try the 75-foot climbing wall; most just hang in the lounge and shoot pool.

- **Cheetah's** (see also the listing in chapter 10). How could you possibly visit Sin City and not sample the ubiquitous lap dance? Couples are welcome at Cheetah's, the site of Paul Verhoven's laughably overdone film *Showgirls*. More quality, less silicone, and a VIP lounge that has hosted lap dances for Wilt Chamberlain, Sting, and Drew Barrymore.

- **The Forum Shops at Caesars Palace** (see the listing in chapter 9). The most unique shopping experience in the world. Take Rodeo Drive, marry it to Rome, douse the whole thing in Spielberg, and you're still nowhere near this elegant retail space.

- **Sky Lounge at the Polo Towers** (see the listing in chapter 10). Hidden on the 19th floor of a time-share condominium complex, this lounge offers a far more engaging view than the Stratosphere Tower, absolutely free of charge. Watch out for kamikaze tour groups.

- **Hard Rock Hotel** (see also the listing in chapter 5). Everything about this hotel/casino—the bars, the Joint showroom, Mr. Lucky's 24/7—manages to evoke classic Vegas, a city that was built for young hipsters, not fanny-pack–wielding families.

- **Love Shack** (various locations, check local listings). Our vote for Sin City's best lounge act. Covering the music of the '70s and '80s with tenacious fervor, Love Shack is nothing short of a funky riot in 6-inch heels and mascara.

- **Red Rock Canyon** (see chapter 11 for complete details). Providing needed respite from the neon jungle, Red Rock is as beautiful as the desert gets. This haven for hikers and rock-climbers gets a bit overrun at times, but it is still worth the trip. *Note:* Don't feed the wild burros. Unlike the entertainers at Cheetah's, they bite.

To Las Vegas

N

Mountain Vista

Cactus Garden Dr.

Sunset Rd. Sunset Way

95

To Boulder Hwy.

Sunset Rd.

Marks

Warm Springs Rd.

Stephanie

Gibson

American Pacific Rd.

Gallagher Crest

Marshmallow Ln.

Mary Crest

Cranberry World
West ❸
Ethel M Chocolates ❶
Kidd's Marshmallow
Factory ❹
Ron Lee's World
of Clowns ❷

15

Lake Mead Drive

To Boulder City
& Hoover Dam

Kidd's Marshmallow Factory

1180 Marshmallow Lane, Henderson. ☎ **800/234-2383** or 702/564-3878. Free admission. Mon–Fri 9am–4:30pm, Sat–Sun 9:30am–4:30pm.

This factory has a delicious aroma. Here you can observe the marshmallow manufacturing process via large windows—cornstarch being rolled smooth on a conveyer belt, then cut into marshmallow shapes that are bounced in a drum, bagged, and boxed into cartons. Signs along the way explain the process. The tour ends in a gift shop where you'll receive free samples and can purchase marshmallow products and logo items. Kidd and Company was founded in Chicago in the 1880s.

Ron Lee's World of Clowns

330 Carousel Parkway, Henderson. ☎ **800/829-3928** or 702/434-3920. Free admission. Daily 8am–5:30pm.

In this 30,000-square-foot factory, manufacturer Ron Lee creates collector figurines of Hobo Joe and other clowns, as well as Disney and Warner Brothers characters. Visitors can tour the factory, and, via large windows, observe workers making models and rubber molds, soldering parts together, deburring, painting, finishing, and shipping. The procedures are explained on videotapes overhead. Also on the premises are a carousel, a museum of Ringling Bros. costumes and props, a display of about 600 hand-painted eggs depicting famous clowns, a large gift shop, and displays of clown sculptures and mechanical miniature carousels and Ferris wheels. The Carousel

Cafe on the premises offers gourmet coffees, sandwiches, and fresh-baked desserts. There's seating inside and on a terrace cooled by misters.

4 Especially for Kids

Like much of the rest of the world, you may be under the impression that Las Vegas has evolved from an adults-only fantasyland into a vacation destination suitable for the entire family. The only explanation for this myth is that Las Vegas was referred to as "Disneyland for adults" by so many and for so long that the town became momentarily confused and decided it actually was Disneyland. Some of the gargantuan hotels then spent small fortunes on redecorating in an attempt to lure families with vast quantities of junk food and a lot of hype. They now vehemently deny that any such notion ever crossed their collective minds, and, no, they don't know how that roller coaster got into the parking lot.

To put things simply, Las Vegas makes money—lots and lots of money—by promoting gambling, drinking, and sex. These are all fine pursuits if you happen to be an adult, but if you haven't reached the magical age of 21, you really don't count in this town. In any case, the casinos and even the Strip itself are simply too stimulating, noisy, and smoky for young kids.

Older progeny may have a tolerance for crowds and the incessant pinging of the slot machines, but they will be thoroughly annoyed with you when casino security chastises them if they so much as stop to tie their shoe laces anywhere near the gaming tables. Since you can't get from your hotel room to the parking lot without ambling through a casino, you can't reasonably expect a teenager to be in a good mood once you stagger outside. And those amusement parks and video halls that haven't yet been purged are expensive places to park your kids for an afternoon or evening, assuming they are old enough to be left unsupervised.

Nevertheless, you may have a perfectly legitimate reason for bringing your children to Las Vegas (like grandma was busy, or you were just stopping through on your way from somewhere else), so here are some places to take the children both on and off the Strip.

Circus Circus (see p. 81) has ongoing circus acts throughout the day, a vast video game and pinball arcade, and dozens of carnival games on its mezzanine level. Behind the hotel is Grand Slam Canyon, detailed below. **Excalibur** (see p. 52) also offers video and carnival games, plus thrill cinemas and free shows (jugglers, puppets, etc.). At **Caesars Palace,** both the Magical Empire (for kids 12 and older only, see p. 159) and OMNIMAX movies (see p. 159) are a thrill for everyone in the family; a video-game arcade adjoins the OMNIMAX Theater. Animated talking statues in the **Forum Shops** are also a kick. The ship battle in front of **Treasure Island** (see p. 68) is sure to please, as will the erupting volcano and the Secret Garden of Siegfried and Roy and dolphin habitat at the **Mirage** (see p. 164); while you're here, see the tigers and the sharks. Ditto the various attractions at the **Luxor Las Vegas** (the Imax Theater, p. 163; King Tut's Tomb, if it has reopened after the current renovation, p. 162; and Secrets of the Luxor Pyramid, p. 163).

Kids will enjoy **The Magic and Movie Hall of Fame** (see p. 163), but they'll want to leave before you do.

Of moderate interest to youngsters are the quartet of **factory tours in Henderson** (see p. 171), especially Ethel M Chocolates and Kidd's Marshmallow Factory, where free samples sweeten the learning experience.

Appropriate shows for kids include King Arthur's Tournament at Excalibur (see p. 227), An Evening in Vienna (this is the name for the show starring the extraordinary Lippizaner stallions (see p. 160), Siegfried and Roy at the Mirage (see p. 229), Lance Burton at the **Monte Carlo** (see p. 227), Starlight Express at the **Hilton** (see p. 230), EFX at the **MGM Grand** (see p. 223), and Cirque du Soleil's Mystère at Treasure Island (see p. 220). As a general rule, early shows are less racy than late-night shows.

Beyond the city limits (see chapter 11 for details on all of these) is **Bonnie Springs Ranch/Old Nevada,** with trail and stagecoach rides, a petting zoo, old-fashioned melodramas, stunt shoot-outs, a Nevada-themed wax museum, crafts demonstrations, and more. **Lake Mead** has great recreational facilities for family vacations. Finally, organized tours (see chapter 11) to the Grand Canyon and other interesting sights in southern Nevada and neighboring states can be fun family activities. Check your hotel sightseeing desk.

Specifically kid-pleasing attractions are described below.

Grand Slam Canyon Theme Park

2889 Las Vegas Blvd. S., behind Circus Circus Hotel. ☎ **702/734-3939.** Free admission; pay per ride. Park hours vary; call ahead.

This isn't a half-bad place to spend a hot afternoon, especially now that Circus Circus, the casino/hotel that built this indoor amusement park, has undergone a facelift. The glass dome that towers overhead lets in natural light, a solace to those of us who look peaked under the glow of the artificial kind. A double-loop roller coaster careens around the simulated Grand Canyon, and there's the requisite water flume, a laser tag area, and a modest number of other rides for kids of all ages. A dinosaur-bone excavation area will provide a good time for preschoolers and a place to rest for the supervising adults. Video games and an arcade are separate from the attractions, cutting down just a tad on the noise level. Jugglers and magicians provide impromptu entertainment. Our only caveat is don't leave kids here alone. They could easily get lost.

Las Vegas Natural History Museum

900 Las Vegas Blvd. N., at Washington. ☎ **702/384-3466.** Admission $5 adults; $2.50 children 4–12. Mon–Sun 9am–4pm

Conveniently located across the street from the Lied Discovery Children's Museum (described below), this humble temple of taxidermy harkens back to elementary school field trips circa 1965, when stuffed elk and brown bears forever protecting their kill were as close as most of us got to exotic animals. Worn around the edges but very sweet and relaxed, the museum is enlivened by a hands-on activity room and two life-sized dinosaurs that roar at one another intermittently. A small boy was observed leaping toward his dad upon watching this display, so you might want to warn any sensitive little ones that the big tyrannosaurs aren't going anywhere. Surprisingly, the gift shop here is particularly well stocked with neat items you won't mind too terribly buying for the kids.

Lied Discovery Children's Museum

833 Las Vegas Blvd. N., a half-block south of Washington, across the street from Cashman Field. ☎ **702/382-5437.** Admission $5 for adults, $4 for kids 12–17, $3 for kids 3–11. Wed–Sat 10am–5pm, Sun 12pm–5.

A hands-on science museum designed for curious kids, the bright, airy, two-story Lied makes an ideal outing for toddlers and young children. With lots of interactive exhibits to examine, including a miniature grocery store, a bubble tube for encasing oneself inside a soap bubble, a radio station, and music and drawing areas, you'll soon forget your video poker losses. Clever, thought-inducing exhibits are everywhere. Learn how it feels to be handicapped by playing basketball from a wheelchair. Feed a wooden "sandwich" to a cut-out of a snake, and to a human cut-out and see how much nutrition each receives. See how much sunscreen their giant stuffed mascot needs to keep from burning. On weekend afternoons from 1pm until 3pm, free drop-in art classes are offered, giving you a bit of time to ramble around the gift store or read the fine print on the exhibit placards. The Lied also shares space with a city library branch, so after the kids run around you can calm them back down with a story or two.

MGM Grand Adventures

Behind the MGM Grand Hotel, 3799 Las Vegas Blvd. S. ☎ **702/891-7777.** Admission only (no rides): $2. Admission with unlimited rides: hotel guests $9, everyone else $11. Sky Screamer: one person $22.20, two people $17.50 each, three people $12.50 each. Open daily (hours vary seasonally).

This theme park, slapped together without a great deal of thought on a former parking lot, looks as if some Hollywood set designers dropped off a variety of hokey movie facades and then, unburdened, cheerfully rode off into the sunset. The attractions, such as a clothes-soaking log flume and kiddie bumper cars, are sparsely scattered among a great many food and T-shirt emporiums. It leaves one with the impression that fun has a lot to do with the contents of one's pocketbook and/or stomach. For some peculiar reason, the park sports three tiny boxing arenas where you and a friend can suit up like samurai and duke it out. This is also home of the Sky Screamer, a combination bungee jump/swing that will thrill kids old enough (and daring enough) to give it a try. There is a separate charge for this ride on top of park admission, although you can pay $2 for park entrance alone, a better deal if you only wish to fly through the air. It's also fun just to sit on a bench and watch people on this contraption.

MGM Grand Youth Center

MGM Grand Hotel, 3799 Las Vegas Blvd. S. ☎ **702/892-3200.** For children 3–12 (no diaper wearers). Daily 10am–midnight. Costs vary, depending upon season and whether or not you are a guest of the hotel (call ahead to get more information).

This is the sole child-care center on the Strip, and according to the genial manager, it's booked solid summers and holidays. MGM Grand hotel guests get first priority to leave their youngsters in a warren of brightly decorated and well-supervised, albeit windowless, rooms. Arts and crafts compete with Nintendo and videos for kids' attention, and there are no organized activities (although they do serve meals). You can pay through the nose to have a counselor accompany your child to the theme park (4 hours/$50), but it might be cheaper to bring along a baby-sitter. If we were children and our parents left us here on a family vacation, we'd never let them forget it.

Scandia Family Fun Center

2900 Sirius Ave., at Rancho Dr. between Sahara Ave. and Spring Mountain Rd. off-ramps. ☎ **702/364-0070.** Free admission, but there's a fee for each game or activity. Super Saver Pass $10.95 (includes 1 round of miniature golf, 2 rides, and 5 game tokens); Unlimited Wristband Package $14.95 (includes unlimited bumper boat and car rides, unlimited miniature golf, and 10 tokens for batting cages or arcade games). Sept to early June: Sun–Thurs 10am–11pm, Fri–Sat until midnight; mid-June to August: Sun–Thurs 10am–midnight, Fri–Sat until 1am.

This family amusement center just a few blocks off the Strip offers three 18-hole miniature golf courses ($5.50 per game, children under 6 free), a state-of-the-art video arcade with 225 machines, miniature car racing and bumper boats ($3.95 per ride, small children ride free with an adult), and automated softball- and baseball-pitching machines for batting practice ($1.25 for 25 pitches). A snack bar is on the premises.

Wet 'n' Wild

2601 Las Vegas Blvd. S., just south of Sahara Ave. ☎ **702/878-7811.** Admission $21.95 adults, half-price seniors over 55, $15.95 children under 10, free for children under 3. Daily early

May–Sept 30, 10am–6 or 8pm (sometimes later). Season and hours vary somewhat from year to year, so call ahead.

When temperatures soar, head for this 26-acre water park right in the heart of the Strip and cool off while jumping waves, careening down steep flumes, and running rapids. Among the highlights: Royal Flush, a thrill ride that washes you down a precipitous chute into a saucerlike bowl at 45 miles per hour, then flushes you into a bottomless pool; Surf Lagoon, a 500,000-gallon wave pool; Banzai Banzai, a roller-coasterlike water ride (aboard a plastic sled, you race down a 45°-angled 150-foot chute and skip porpoiselike across a 120-foot pool); Der Stuka, the world's fastest and highest water chute; Raging Rapids, a simulated white-water rafting adventure on a 500-foot-long river; Lazy River, a leisurely float trip; Blue Niagara, a dizzying descent inside intertwined looping tubes from a height of six stories; Willy Willy (a hydra-hurricane that propels riders on inner tubes around a 90-foot-diameter pool at 10 miles per hour); Bomb Bay (enter a bomblike casing 76 feet in the air for a speedy vertical flight straight down to a pool target); and the Black Hole (an exhilaratingly rapid space-themed flume descent in the dark enhanced by a bombardment of colorful fiber-optic star fields and spinning galaxy patterns en route to splashdown). There are additional flumes, a challenging children's water playground, and a sun-bathing area with a cascading waterfall, as well as video and arcade games. Food concessions are located throughout the park, and you can purchase swimwear and accessories at the Beach Trends Shop. Also, be on the lookout for discount coupons. Many Las Vegas packages include a free admission (sometimes partial-day).

5 Organized Tours

Just about every hotel in town has a sightseeing desk offering a seemingly infinite number of tours in and around Las Vegas. You're sure to find a tour company that will take you where you want to go.

Gray Line (☎ **702/384-1234**) offers a rather comprehensive roster, including:

- 8¹/₂-hour city tours, including visits to Ethel M Chocolates and Cranberry World, the view from the Stratosphere Tower, and the Fremont Street Experience.
- Full-day excursions to Laughlin, Nevada, an up-and-coming mini–Las Vegas 100 miles south with casino hotels on the banks of the Colorado River.
- Half- and full-day excursions to Hoover Dam and Lake Mead (see chapter 11 for details).
- A full-day excursion to Red Rock Canyon and Mt. Charleston.
- An 8-hour excursion to the Valley of Fire that includes lunch at a Lake Mead resort and a drive by Wayne Newton's Ranch.
- A full-day river-rafting tour on the Colorado River from the base of Hoover Dam through majestic Black Canyon.
- A morning or afternoon air tour (and you thought they only had buses) of Grand Canyon.
- A 10-hour Grand Canyon excursion that includes "flightseeing" and river rafting on the Colorado.
- An overnight trip to Grand Canyon.

Call for details or inquire at your hotel sightseeing desk, where you'll also find free magazines with coupons for discounts on these tours.

GRAND CANYON TOURS   Generally, tourists visiting Las Vegas don't drive 300 miles to Arizona to see the Grand Canyon, but there are dozens of sightseeing tours departing from the city daily. In addition to the Gray Line tours described above, the major operator, **Scenic Airlines** (☎ **800/634-6801** or 702/638-3200), runs deluxe, full-day guided air-ground tours for $189 per person ($149 for children 2 to 11); the price includes a bus excursion through the national park, a flight over the canyon, lunch, and a screening of the IMAX movie Grand Canyon: The Hidden Secrets. All scenic tours include "flightseeing." The company also offers both full-day and overnight tours with hiking. And though all Scenic tours include hotel pickup and drop-off, if you take the Premium Deluxe Tour ($229 for adults, $179 for children) you'll be transported by limo.

Scenic also offers tours to other points of interest and national parks, including Yellowstone and Grand Teton. Ask for details when you call.

INDIVIDUALIZED TOURS A totally different type of tour is offered by Char Cruze of **Creative Adventures** (☎ **702/361-5565**). Char, a charming fourth-generation Las Vegan (she was at the opening of the Flamingo), spent her childhood riding horseback through the mesquite and cottonwoods of the Mojave Desert, discovering magical places you'd never find on your own or on a commercial tour. Char is a lecturer and storyteller as well as a tour guide. She has extensively studied southern Nevada's geology and desert wildlife, its regional history and Native American cultures. Her personalized tours, enhanced by fascinating stories about everything from miners to mobsters, visit haunted mines, sacred Paiute grounds, ghost towns, canyons, and ancient petroglyphs. Depending on your itinerary, the cost is about $100 a day if you use your own car (more, depending on the number of people, if rental transportation is required). It's a good idea to make arrangements with her prior to leaving home.

6 Playing Golf

There are dozens of local courses, including very challenging ones—the Sheraton Desert Inn Country has hosted many PGA tournaments. Beginner and intermediate golfers might prefer the other courses listed.

Angel Park Golf Club
100 S. Rampart Blvd., between Charleston Blvd. and Westcliff St. ☎ **888/446/5358** or 702/254-4653.

This 36-hole par-70/71 public course, was designed by Arnold Palmer. In addition to the 18-hole Palm and Mountain Courses, Angel Park offers a night-lit Cloud 9 course (12 holes for daylight play, 9 at night), where each hole is patterned after a famous par-3. **Yardage:** Palm Course 6,438 championship, 5,721 regular, 4,565 ladies; Mountain Course 6,783 championship, 6,272 regular, 5,143 ladies. **Facilities:** pro shop, night-lit driving range, 18-hole putting course, restaurant, snack bar, cocktail bar, beverage cart.

Black Mountain Golf & Country Club
500 Greenway Rd., in nearby Henderson. ☎ **702/565-7933.**

Two new greens have recently been added to this 18-hole, par-72 semiprivate course, which requires reservations 4 days in advance. **Yardage:** 6,541 championship, 6,223 regular, 5,478 ladies. **Facilities:** pro shop, putting green, driving range, restaurant, snack bar, and cocktail lounge.

Craig Ranch Golf Club
628 W. Craig Rd., Losee Rd. and Martin Luther King Blvd. ☎ **702/642-9700.**

This is an 18-hole, par-70 public course. **Yardage:** 6,001 regular, 5,221 ladies. **Facilities:** driving range, pro shop, PGA teaching pro, putting green, and snack bar.

Desert Inn Golf Club

3145 Las Vegas Blvd. S. ☎ **702/733-4290.**

The Desert Inn course gets the nod from champions. It's an 18-hole, par-72 resort course. **Yardage:** 7,150 championship, 6,715 regular, 5,800 ladies. **Facilities:** driving range, putting green, pro shop, and restaurant. You can reserve 90 days in advance for Sunday through Thursday, 2 days in advance for Friday and Saturday. This is the most famous and demanding course in Las Vegas. Golf Digest calls it one of America's top resort courses. The driving range is open to Desert Inn and Caesars guests only; anyone can play the course, but nonguests pay a higher fee.

Desert Rose Golf Club

5483 Clubhouse Dr., 3 blocks west of Nellis Blvd., off Sahara Ave. ☎ **702/431-4653.**

This is an 18-hole, par-71 public course. **Yardage:** 6,511 championship, 6,135 regular, 5,458 ladies. **Facilities:** driving range, putting and chipping greens, PGA teaching pro, pro shop, restaurant, and cocktail lounge.

Las Vegas Hilton Country Club

1911 Desert Inn Rd., between Maryland Pkwy. and Eastern Ave. ☎ **702/796-0016.**

This is an 18-hole, par-72 public course. **Yardage:** 6,815 championship, 6,418 regular, 5,741 ladies. **Facilities:** pro shop, golf school, driving range, restaurant, and cocktail lounge. Hilton guests enjoy preferred tee times and rates.

7 Staying Active

Bring your sports gear to Las Vegas. The city and surrounding areas offer plenty of opportunities for active sports. In addition to many highly rated golf courses (described above), just about every hotel has a large swimming pool and health club, and tennis courts abound. All types of water sports are offered at Lake Mead National Recreation Area, there's rafting on the Colorado, horseback riding at Mount Charleston and Bonnie Springs, great hiking in the canyons, and much, much more. Do plan to get out of those smoke-filled casinos and into the fresh air once in a while. It's good for your health and your finances.

Note: When choosing a hotel, check out its recreational facilities, all listed in chapter 5.

BICYCLING   Escape the City Streets (☎ 702/596-2953) rents 21-speed mountain bikes and offers free delivery to all downtown and Strip hotels. Rates are $26 for the first day, $20 for a half day or consecutive days, $90 for a full week. You must show a major credit card (American Express, MasterCard, or VISA). Inquire about bike trips to Red Rock Canyon and other good biking areas.

BOWLING   The Showboat Hotel & Casino, 2800 E. Fremont St. (☎ 702/385-9153), is famous for housing the largest bowling center in North America—106 lanes—and for being the oldest stop on the Professional Bowlers Tour. A major renovation a few years back made its premises bright and spiffy. Open 24 hours.

BUNGEE JUMPING   At A.J. Hackett Bungy, 810 Circus Circus Dr. between Las Vegas Boulevard South and Industrial Road (☎ 702/385-4321), an elevator in the shape of a rocket takes you to the top of a 175-foot tower, the base for an exhilarating plunge toward a large swimming pool below. The price is $61 for your first jump includes a membership and T-shirt ($81 with a videotape), $25 for the second and third jumps; the fourth is free. Students and military with ID should inquire about discounts. If you're under 18, you must be accompanied by a parent. Owner A.J. Hackett, who claims to have been the first commercial developer of bungee jumping

---

Desert Hiking Tips

Hiking in the desert is exceptionally rewarding, but it can be dangerous. Some safety tips:

1. Do not hike alone.

2. Carry plenty of water and drink it often. Don't assume spring waters are safe to drink. A gallon of water per person, per day is recommended for hikers.

3. Be alert for signs of heat exhaustion (headache, nausea, dizziness, fatigue, and cool, damp, pale, or red skin).

4. Gauge your fitness accurately. Desert hiking may involve rough or steep terrain. Don't take on more than you can handle.

5. Check weather forecasts before starting out. Thunderstorms can turn into raging flash floods, which are extremely hazardous to hikers.

6. Dress properly. Wear sturdy walking shoes for rock scrambling, long pants (to protect yourself from rocks and cacti), a hat, sunscreen, and sunglasses.

7. Carry a small first-aid kit.

8. Be careful when climbing on sandstone, which can be surprisingly soft and crumbly.

9. Don't feed or play with animals, such as wild burros in Red Rock Canyon.

10. Be alert for snakes and insects. Though they're rarely encountered, you'll want to look into a crevice before putting your hand into it.

11. Visit park or other information offices before you start out and acquaint yourself with rules and regulations and any possible hazards. It's also a good idea to tell them where you are going, when you will return, how many are in your party, and so on. Some park offices offer hiker-registration programs.

12. Follow the hiker's rule of thumb: Take only photographs, and leave only footprints.

(in New Zealand), has overseen more than 500,000 jumps without an accident. Call for hours.

FISHING   One doesn't usually think of fishing in the desert, but there are lakes and large ponds. Closest to Las Vegas are the ponds in **Floyd R. Lamb State Park,** 9200 Tule Springs Rd. (☎ **702/486-5413**). The park is about 15 miles from the Strip. To get there take I-15 to U.S. 95 north, get off at the Durango exit and follow the signs. You can fish here for catfish, trout, bluegill, sunfish, and large-mouth bass. You will need your own gear, bait, and tackle, as well as a Nevada fishing license, which is available at any sporting goods store (check the Las Vegas yellow pages). There's also fishing at Lake Mead (see listing in chapter 11 for details).

HEALTH CLUBS   Almost every hotel in Las Vegas has an on-premises health club. The facilities, of course, vary enormously. Descriptions are given of each club in hotel facilities listings in chapter 5.

But none offers the amazing range of facilities you'll find at the **Las Vegas Sporting House,** 3025 Industrial Rd., right behind the Stardust Hotel (☎ **702/733-8999**). Opened in 1978, this 65,000-square-foot club is ultraluxurious. UNLV teams and many athletes and Strip headliners (including Siegfried and Roy) work out here. Facilities include: 10 racquetball/handball courts, two squash courts, two outdoor tennis courts (lit for night play), a full gymnasium for basketball and volleyball, an outdoor pool and sunbathing area, a 25-meter indoor pool for lap swimming, indoor and outdoor jogging tracks, treadmills, Lifecycles, Virtual Reality bikes, stair machines, and free weights. In addition, there are full lines of Cybex, Universal, and Paramount machines, along with some Nautilus equipment; sauna, steam, and Jacuzzi; a pro shop; men's and women's skin care and hair salons; massage; free babysitting service while you work out; restaurant, bar, and lounge. Aerobics classes are given at frequent intervals throughout the day, and you can try "spinning," a new workout technique that burns 800 calories in 40 minutes! Cost for a single visit is $15 to $20 (depending on the club's arrangement with your hotel); reduced weekly rates are available. Open daily 24 hours.

HORSEBACK RIDING   The **Mt. Charleston Riding Stables** (☎ **800/955-1314** or 702/872-5408), under the auspices of the Mount Charleston Resort, offer glorious scenic trail rides to the edge of the wilderness. They depart from stables on Kyle Canyon Road. Since the schedule varies, it's best to call in advance for details. Cost is $45 for 2 hours, $60 for 3. The stables also offer sleigh rides in winter and hayrides in summer. Riding stables at **Bonnie Springs Ranch** (☎ **702/875-4191**) also offer guided trail rides daily. Rates are $18 per hour.

HIKING   Except in summer, when the temperature can reach 120° in the shade, the Las Vegas area is great for hiking. The best hiking season is November through March. Great locales include the incredibly scenic Red Rock Canyon, Valley of Fire State Park, and Mount Charleston (see individual headings in chapter 11 for details).

JET-SKIING   **Las Vegas Adventure Tours (LVAT)** (☎ **800/553-5452** or 702/564-5452) offers jet-ski rides on Lake Mead. Call LVAT, too, about horseback riding, hot-air ballooning, Grand Canyon flightseeing, and all-terrain-vehicle desert tours.

RACQUETBALL   There are courts in several locations around town. The **Las Vegas Athletic Club East,** 1070 E. Sahara Ave., at Maryland Parkway (☎ **702/733-1919**), has seven courts open 24 hours a day, 7 days a week. Rates are $10 per person, per day; $25 per week. Call to reserve a court.

The **Las Vegas Athletic Club West,** 3315 Spring Mountain Rd., between I-15 and Valley View Boulevard (☎ **702/362-3720**), has eight courts open weekdays 5am to 11pm; weekends 8am to 8pm. Rates are $10 per person, per visit; $25 per week.

The **Las Vegas Sporting House,** 3025 Industrial Rd., right behind the Stardust Hotel (☎ **702/733-8999**), has 10 racquetball/handball courts open 24 hours a day, 7 days a week. Rates are $15 per visit if you're staying at a local hotel.

The **University of Nevada, Las Vegas (UNLV),** 4505 Maryland Pkwy., just off Swenson Street (☎ **702/895-3150**), has eight racquetball courts open weekdays 6am to 9:45pm, Saturdays 8am to 5:30pm, Sundays 10am to 5:30pm. Hours may vary somewhat each semester. Rates are $2 per person, per hour. Call before you go to find out if a court is available. You must pick up a guest pass in the Physical Education Building.

RIVER RAFTING   **Black Canyon Inc.** (☎ **800/696-RAFT** or 702/293-3776) offers daily raft trips on the Colorado River from February 1 through the end of November. As an authorized concessionaire, Black Canyon can get into otherwise restricted areas at the base of the dam. Trips include 3 hours of scenic rafting and lunch. You'll see waterfalls gush from majestic canyon walls, pass tranquil coves, spy bighorn sheep on sheer cliffs, and spot blue herons, cormorants, and falcons. Knowledgeable guides provide a lot of fascinating area history and geology. Each raft is piloted by an experienced navigator. Rates, including Las Vegas hotel pickup and return, are $74.95 per person, $64.95 if you drive to and from the expedition depot.

ROCK CLIMBING   Red Rock Canyon, just 19 miles west of Las Vegas, is one of the world's most popular rock-climbing areas. In addition to awe-inspiring natural beauty, it offers everything from boulders to big walls. If you'd like to join the big-horn sheep, Red Rock has more than 1,000 routes to inaugurate beginners and challenge accomplished climbers. Experienced climbers can contact the visitor center (☎ 702/363-1921) for information.

If you're interested in learning or improving your skills, an excellent rock-climbing school and guide service called **Sky's the Limit** (☎ 800/733-7597 or 702/363-4533) offers programs for beginning, intermediate, and advanced climbers. No experience is needed. The school is accredited by the American Mountain Guides Association.

TENNIS   Tennis buffs should choose one of the many hotels in town that have tennis courts.

Bally's (☎ 702/739-4598) has eight night-lit hard courts. Fees per hour range from $10 to $15 for guests, $15 to $20 for nonguests. Facilities include a pro shop. Hours vary seasonally. Reservations are advised.

The **Flamingo Hilton** (☎ 702/733-3444) has four outdoor hard courts (all lit for night play), and a pro shop. It is open to the public Monday to Friday from 7am to 8pm, Saturday and Sunday from 7am to 6pm. Rates are $20 per hour for nonguests, $12 for guests. Lessons are available. Reservations are required.

The **Riviera** (☎ 702/734-5110) has two outdoor hard courts (both lit for night play) that are open to the public, subject to availability; hotel guests have priority. It is open 24 hours. There is no charge for guests; nonguests pay $10 per hour. Reservations are required.

The **Desert Inn** (☎ 702/733-4557) has five outdoor hard courts (all lit for night play) and a pro shop. They are open to the public. Hours are daybreak to 10pm. Rates are $10 per person for a daily pass (you book for an hour but can stay longer if no one is waiting); they are free for guests. Reservations are necessary.

In addition to hotels, the **University of Nevada, Las Vegas (UNLV),** Harmon Avenue just east of Swenson Street (☎ 702/895-0844) has a dozen courts (all lit for night play) that are open weekdays from 6am to 9:45pm, on weekends from 8am to 9pm. Rates are $5 per person, per day on weekdays; $10 weekends. You should call before going to find out if a court is available.

8 Spectator Sports

Las Vegas isn't known for its sports teams. Except for minor league baseball and hockey, the only consistent spectator sports are those at UNLV. The **Las Vegas Motor Speedway** (described in detail earlier in this chapter) is a major new venue for car racing and should draw major events to Las Vegas.

But since the city has several top-notch sporting arenas, there are important annual events that take place in Las Vegas, details for which can be found in the "Las Vegas Calendar of Events" in chapter 2. The **PBA Invitational Bowling Tournament** is held in the Showboat's massive bowling center each January. The **PGA Tour Las Vegas Senior Classic** is held each April in nearby Summerlin, and **Las Vegas Invitational** in Las Vegas each October. The **National Finals Rodeo** is held in UNLV's Thomas and Mack Center each December. From time to time, you'll find NBA exhibition games, professional ice skating tournaments, or gymnastics exhibitions. Then there are the only-in-Vegas spectaculars, such as Evel Knievel's ill-fated attempt to jump the fountains in front of Caesars.

Now that you know your way around, let's move on to something simple.

For card and collect calls.

1 800 CALL ATT is the only number you need to know when you're away from home. Dial it from any phone, anywhere* and your calls will always go through to AT&T.
*Available in U.S. and Canada. © 1997 AT&T

AT&T

Finally, Las Vegas is well known as a major location for boxing matches. These are held in several Strip hotels, most often at Caesars or the MGM Grand, but sometimes at the Mirage or Aladdin. Tickets are hard to come by and quite expensive.

BASEBALL

The **Las Vegas Stars,** a AAA baseball team, play from April through August at the 10,000-seat **Cashman Field Center,** 850 Las Vegas Blvd. N. (☎ **702/386-7200** for tickets and information). Tickets are priced at $4 to $7.

BASKETBALL

The Thomas and Mack Center, also on the UNLV campus at Tropicana Avenue and Swenson Street (☎ **702/895-3900**), is an 18,500-seat facility used for a variety of sporting events. It is home to the **UNLV's Runnin' Rebels,** who play 16 to 20 games during a November-to-March season. Other events here include major boxing tournaments, NBA exhibition games, and rodeos. For information and to charge tickets, call the stadium number or Ticketmaster (☎ **702/474-4000**).

FOOTBALL

The Sam Boyd Stadium at the University of Nevada, Las Vegas (UNLV), Boulder Highway and Russell Road (☎ **702/895-3900**), is a 32,000-seat outdoor stadium. The **UNLV Rebels** play about six football games here each year between September and November. And the stadium is also used for motor sports and supercross events, truck and tractor pulls, high school football games, and the Las Vegas Bowl in December. For information and to charge tickets, call the above number or Ticketmaster (☎ **702/474-4000**).

HOCKEY

Las Vegas Thunder (International Hockey League) plays about 40 games at UNLV's Thomas and Mack Center (Tropicana Avenue and Swenson Street) between October and early April (call ☎ **702/798-PUCK** for information).

MAJOR SPORTS VENUES IN HOTELS

The **Aladdin's** 7,000-seat **Theatre for the Performing Arts,** 3667 Las Vegas Blvd. S. (☎ **800/637-8133** or 702/736-0240), is occasionally used for professional boxing matches.

Caesars Palace (☎ **800/634-6698** or 702/731-7110) has a long tradition of sporting events, from Evel Knievel's attempted motorcycle jump over its fountains in 1967 to Grand Prix auto races. Mary Lou Retton has tumbled in gymnastic events at Caesars, and Olympians Brian Boitano and Katarina Witt have taken to the ice, as has Wayne Gretzky (he led the L.A. Kings to victory over the New York Rangers in a preseason exhibition game). And well over 100 world-championship boxing contests have taken place here since the hotel opened. In the spirit of ancient Rome, Caesars awards riches and honors to the "gladiators" who compete in its arenas.

The **MGM Grand's Garden Events Arena** (☎ **800/929-1111** or 702/891-7777) is a major venue for sporting events: professional boxing matches, rodeos, tennis, ice-skating shows, World Figure Skating Championships, and more.

The **Mirage** (☎ **800/627-6667** or 702/791-7111) also features occasional championship boxing matches.

8 About Casino Gambling

What? You didn't come to Las Vegas for the Liberace Museum? We are shocked. *Shocked.*

Yes, there are gambling opportunities in Vegas. We've noticed this. You will, too. The tip-off will be the slot machines in the airport as soon as you step off the plane. Or the slot machines in the convenience stores as soon as you drive across the state line. Let's not kid ourselves, gambling is what Vegas is about. The bright lights, the shows, the showgirls, the food—it's all there just to lure you in and make you open your wallet. (The free drinks certainly help ease the latter as well.)

You can disappoint them if you want, but what would be the point? *This is Las Vegas.* You don't have to be a high roller. You would not believe how much fun you can have with a nickel slot machine. You won't get rich, but neither will most of those guys playing the $5 dollar slots, either. Of course, that's not going to stop anyone from trying. Almost everyone plays in Vegas with the hopes of winning The Big One. That only a few ever do doesn't stop them from trying again and again and again. That's how the casinos make their money, by the way.

It's not that the odds are stacked so incredibly high in their favor—though the odds are in their favor, and don't ever think otherwise. Rather, it's that if there is one constant in this world, it's human greed. Look around in any casino, and you'll see countless souls who, having doubled their winnings, are now trying to quadruple them, and are losing it all back again. And then trying to recoup their initial bankroll and losing still more in the process. See that chandelier up there? Enjoy it—you paid for it.

Which is not meant to dissuade you from gambling. Just be sure to look at it as recreation and entertainment, *not* as an investment or money-making opportunity. Spend only as much as you can afford to lose and not a penny more. It doesn't matter if that's $10 or $100,000. You can have just as good a time with either. (Though if you can afford to lose $100,000, we would like to meet you.)

Remember also that there is no system that is sure to help you win. We all have our own system and our own ideas. Reading books and listening to others at the tables will help you pick up some tips, but if there were a surefire way to win, the casinos will have taken care of it (and we will leave you to imagine just what that might

Stilled forever is the click of the roulette wheel, the rattle of dice, and the swish of cards.
—Short-sighted editorial in the *Nevada State Journal*
after gambling was outlawed in 1910

entail). Try to have the courage to walk away when your bankroll is up, not down. Remember, your children's college fund is just that, and not a gambling budget supplement.

The first part of this chapter is a contribution from James Randi, a master magician, who looks at the four major fallacies people bring with them to the gaming tables in Las Vegas; it's fascinating, and we thank him for this contribution. The second part tells you the basics of betting. Knowing how to play the games not only improves your odds but makes playing more enjoyable. In addition to the instructions below, you'll find dozens of books on how to gamble at all casino hotel gift shops, and many casinos offer free gaming lessons on the premises. The third part of this chapter describes all the major casinos in town. Remember that gambling is supposed to be entertainment; picking a gaming table where the other players are laughing, slapping each other on the back, and generally enjoying themselves tends to make for considerable more fun than a table where everyone is sitting around in stony silence, morosely staring at their cards. Unless you really need to concentrate, pick a table where everyone seems to be enjoying themselves, and you will too, even if you don't win. Maybe.

1 The Four Most Pervasive Myths About Gambling

by James Randi

James Randi is a world-class magician (as the Amazing Randi), now involved in examining supernatural, paranormal and occult claims. He is the author of 11 books on these subjects, and the president of the James Randi Educational Foundation in Fort Lauderdale, Florida. The JREF offers a prize of $1,100,000 to any person who can produce a demonstration of any paranormal activity. His Web site is **http://www.randi.org**, *where details of the offer can be found.*

Most of us know little, if anything, about statistics. It's a never-never land we can live without, something for those guys in white coats and thick glasses to mumble over. And because we don't trouble to learn the basics of this rather interesting field of study, we sometimes find ourselves unable to deal with the realities that the gambling process produces.

I often present my audiences with a puzzle. Suppose that a mathematician, a gambler, and a magician are walking together on Broadway, and come upon a small cluster of people who are observing a chap standing at a small table set up on the sidewalk. They are told that this fellow has just tossed a quarter into the air and allowed it to fall onto the table, nine times. And that has produced nine "tails" in a row. Now the crowd is being asked to bet on what the next toss of the coin will bring. The question: How will each of these three observers place their bets?

The mathematician will reason that each toss of the coin is independent of the last toss, so the chances are still exactly 50/50 for heads or tails. He'll say that either bet is okay, and that it doesn't make any difference which decision is made.

The gambler will go one of two ways; either he'll reason that there's a "run" taking place here—and that a bet on another tail will be the better choice—or he'll opine that it's time for the head to come up—and he'll put his wager on that likelihood. He's torn between two popular fallacies of gambling practice.

The magician? He has the best chance of winning, because he knows that there is only one chance in 512 that a coin will come up tails nine times in a row—*unless there's something wrong with that coin!* He'll bet tails, and he'll win!

The reasoning of the mathematician is quite correct, that of the gambler is quite wrong (in either one of his scenarios), but just as long as that isn't a double-tailed coin. The point of view taken by the magician is highly specialized, but human nature being what it is, that view is probably the correct one.

In professional gambling centers like Las Vegas, great care is taken to ensure that there are no two-tailed quarters or other purposeful anomalies that enable cheating to take place. The casinos make their percentages on the built-in mathematical advantage, clearly stated and available to any who ask, and though that is a very tiny "edge, "it's enough to pay for the razzle-dazzle that is offered the customers. It's volume that supports the business. The scrutiny that is applied to each and every procedure in Vegas is everywhere evident.

So, **Fallacy Number One** is: Cheating of some sort is necessary for an operation to prosper. It isn't.

Fallacy Number Two: Some people just have "hunches" and "visions" that enable them to win at the slots and tables. Sorry folks, it just ain't so. The science of parapsychology, which has studied such claims for many decades now, has never come up with evidence that any form of clairvoyance ("clear-seeing," the supposed ability to know hidden data, such as the next card to come up in a deal or the next face on the dice) or telepathy ("mind-reading") actually exists. It's remarkably easy for us to imagine that we have a hot streak going, or that the cards are falling our way, but the inexorable laws of chance prevail and always will.

Fallacy Number Three: There are folks who can give us systems for winning. Now, judicious bet-placing is possible, and there are mathematical methods of minimizing losses, it's true. But the investment and base capital needed to follow through with these methods makes them a rather poor investment. The return percentage can be earned much more easily by almost any other form of endeavor, at less risk and less expenditure of boring hours following complicated charts and equations. The best observation we can make on the "systems" is: Why do the inventors sell something that they themselves could use to get rich, which is what they say you can do with it? Think about that!

Of course, the simplest of all the systems is bet-doubling. It sounds great, in theory, but an hour spent tossing coins in your hotel room, or at the gaming tables, will convince you that theory and practice are quite different matters. Bet-doubling, as applied to heads-or-tails (on a fair coin!), consists of placing a unit bet on the first coin toss, then pocketing the proceeds if you win, but doubling your bet on the next toss if you lose. If you get a lose, lose, win sequence, that means you will have lost three units (one plus two) and won four. You're up one unit. You start again. If you get a lose, lose, lose, win sequence, you've put out 15 units, and brought in 16. Again, you're only up one unit. And no matter how long your sequences go, you'll *always* be up only one unit at the end of a sequence. It requires you to make that "unit" somewhat sizable if you want to have any significant winnings at all, and that may mean going bankrupt by simply running out of capital before a sequence ends—and if you hang on, you'll only have been able to end up *one* unit ahead, in any case. Not a good investment, at all.

Fallacy Number Four: Studying the results of the roulette wheels will provide the bettor with useful data. We're peculiar animals in that we constantly search for meaning in all sets of observations. That's how subjects of Rorschach tests find weird faces, figures, and creatures in ink blots that are actually random patterns with single symmetry. Similarly, any set of roulette results are, essentially, random numbers; there are no patterns to be found there that can give indications of probable future spins of the wheels. Bearing in mind that those wheels are carefully monitored to detect any biases or defects, we should conclude that finding clues in past performances is futile.

I recall that when I worked in Wiesbaden, Germany, just after World War II, I stuck around late one night after closing at the "Spielbank" and watched as an elderly gentleman removed all the rotors of the 12 wheels they had in operation, wrote out the numbers 1 to 12 on separate scraps of paper, and reassembled the wheels according to the random order in which he drew each slip of paper from a bowl. He was ensuring that any inconsistencies in the wheels would be essentially nullified. Yet, as he told me, the front desk at the casino continued to sell booklets setting out the results of each of the wheels, because patrons insisted on having them, and persisted in believing that there just had to be a pattern there, if only it could be found.

We're only human. We can't escape certain defects in our thinking mechanism, but we can resist reacting to them. When we see Penn and Teller, Ayala, Siegfried and Roy, or Lance Burton doing their wonders, we smile smugly and assure ourselves that those miracles are only illusions. But if we haven't solved those illusions, and we haven't, how can we assume that we aren't being fooled by our own self-created delusions? Let's get a grip on reality and enjoy Las Vegas for what it really is: a grand illusion, a fairyland, a let's-pretend project, but not one in which the laws of nature are suspended or can be ignored.

Enjoy!

2 The Games

BACCARAT

The ancient game of baccarat, or *chemin de fer,* is played with eight decks of cards. Firm rules apply, and there is no skill involved other than deciding whether to bet on the bank or the player. Any beginner can play, but check the betting minimum before you sit down as this tends to be a high-stakes game. The cards are shuffled by the croupier and then placed in a box that is called the "shoe."

Players may wager on "bank" or "player" at any time. Two cards are dealt from the shoe and given to the player who has the largest wager against the bank, and two cards are dealt to the croupier acting as banker. If the rule calls for a third card (see rules on chart shown here), the player or banker, or both, must take the third card. In the event of a tie, the hand is dealt over.

The object of the game is to come as close as possible to the number 9. To score the hands, the cards of each hand are totaled and the *last digit* is used. All cards have face value. For example: 10 plus 5 equals 15 (score is 5); 10 plus 4 plus 9 equals 23 (score is 3); 4 plus 3 plus 3 equals 10 (score is 0); and 4 plus 3 plus 2 equals 9 (score is 9). The closest hand to 9 wins.

Each player has a chance to deal the cards. The shoe passes to the player on the right each time the bank loses. If the player wishes, he or she may pass the shoe at any time.

Note: When you bet on the bank and the bank wins, you are charged a 5% commission. This must be paid at the start of a new game or when you leave the table.

Baccarat Rules

Player's Hand
Having
0-1-2-3-4-5   Must draw a third card.
6-7   *Must stand.*
8-9   Natural. Banker cannot draw.

Banker's Hand

Having	**Draws** When giving Player 3rd card of:	**Does Not Draw** When giving Player 3rd card of:
3	1-2-3-4-5-6-7-9-10	8
4	2-3-4-5-6-7	1-8-9-10
5	4-5-6-7	1-2-3-8-9-10
6	6-7	1-2-3-4-5-8-9-10
7	*Must stand.*	
8-9	Natural. Player cannot draw.	

If the player takes no third card, the banker must stand on 6. No one draws against a natural 8 or 9.

BIG SIX

Big Six provides pleasant recreation and involves no study or effort. The wheel has 56 positions on it, 54 of them marked by bills from $1 to $20 denominations. The other two spots are jokers, and each pays 40 to 1 if the wheel stops in that position.

All other stops pay at face value. Those marked with $20 bills pay 20 to 1; the $5 bills pay 5 to 1; and so forth.

BLACKJACK

The dealer starts the game by dealing each player two cards. In some casinos they're dealt to the player faceup, in others facedown, but the dealer always gets one card up and one card down. Everybody plays against the dealer. The object is to get a total that is higher than that of the dealer without exceeding 21. All face cards count as 10; all other number cards except aces count as their number value. An ace may be counted as 1 or 11, whichever you choose it to be.

Starting at his or her left, the dealer gives additional cards to the players who wish to draw (be "hit") or none to a player who wishes to "stand" or "hold." If your count is nearer to 21 than the dealer's, you win. If it's under the dealer's, you lose. Ties are a push and nobody wins. After all the players are satisfied with their counts, the dealer exposes his or her facedown card. If his two cards total 16 or less, the dealer must "hit" (draw an additional card) until reaching 17 or over. If the dealer's total goes over 21, he or she must pay all the players whose hands have not gone "bust." It is important to note here that the blackjack dealer has no choice as to whether he or she should stay or draw. A dealer's decisions are predetermined and known to all the players at the table.

HOW TO PLAY   Here are eight "rules" for blackjack.

1. Place the amount of chips that you want to bet on the betting space on your table.
2. Look at the first two cards the dealer starts you with. If your hand adds up to the total you prefer, place your cards *under your bet money*, indicating that you don't

wish any additional cards. If you elect to draw an additional card, you tell the dealer to "hit" you by making a sweeping motion with your cards, or point to your open hand (watch your fellow players).

3. If your count goes over 21, you go "bust" and lose, even if the dealer also goes "bust" afterward. Unless hands are dealt faceup, *you then turn your hand faceup on the table.*

4. If you make 21 in your first two cards (any picture card or 10 with an ace), you've got blackjack. *You expose your winning hand immediately,* and you collect 1 1/2 times your bet, unless the dealer has blackjack, too, in which case it's a push and nobody wins.

5. If you find a "pair" in your first two cards (say, two 8s or two aces) you may "split" the pair into two hands and treat each card as the first card dealt in two separate hands. *Turn the pair faceup on the table,* place the original bet on one of these cards, then place an equal amount on the other card. *Split aces are limited to a one-card draw on each.*

6. You may double your original bet and make a one-card draw after receiving your initial two cards. *Turn your hand faceup* and you'll receive one more card facedown.

7. Anytime the dealer deals himself or herself an ace for the "up" card, you may insure your hand against the possibility that the hole card is a 10 or face card, which would give him or her an automatic blackjack. To insure, you place an amount up to one-half of your bet on the "insurance" line. If the dealer does have a blackjack, you do not lose, even though he or she has your hand beat, and you keep your bet and your insurance money. If the dealer does not have a blackjack, he or she takes your insurance money and play continues in the normal fashion.

8. *Remember:* The dealer *must* stand on 17 or more and *must* hit a hand of 16 or less.

PROFESSIONAL TIPS   Advice of the experts in playing blackjack is as follows.

1. *Do not* ask for an extra card if you have a count of 17, 18, 19, 20, or 21 in your cards, no matter what the dealer has showing in his or her "up" card.

2. *Do not* ask for an extra card when you have 12, 13, 14, 15, 16, or more if the dealer has a 2, 3, 4, 5, or 6 showing in his or her "up" card.

3. *Do ask* for an extra card or more when you have a count of 12 through 16 in your hand if the dealer's "up" card is a 7, 8, 9, 10, or ace.

There's a lot more to blackjack-playing strategy than the above, of course. So consider this merely as the bare bones of the game.

A final tip: Avoid insurance bets; they're sucker bait!

CRAPS

The most exciting casino action is always at the craps tables. Betting is frenetic, play fast-paced, and groups quickly bond yelling and screaming in response to the action.

THE TABLE   The craps table is divided into marked areas (Pass, Come, Field, Big 6, Big 8, and so on), where you place your chips to bet. The following are a few simple directions.

PASS LINE   A "Pass Line" bet pays even money. If the first roll of the dice adds up to 7 or 11, you win your bet; if the first roll adds up to 2, 3, or 12, you lose your bet. If any other number comes up, it's your "point." If you roll your point again, you win, but if a 7 comes up again before your point is rolled, you lose.

DON'T PASS LINE   Betting on the "Don't Pass" is the opposite of betting on the Pass Line. This time, you lose if a 7 or an 11 is thrown on the first roll, and you win if a 2 or a 3 is thrown on the first roll.

If the first roll is 12, however, it's a push (standoff), and nobody wins. If none of these numbers is thrown and you have a point instead, in order to win, a 7 will have to be thrown before the point comes up again. A "Don't Pass" bet also pays even money.

COME   Betting on "Come" is the same as betting on the Pass Line, but you must bet *after* the first roll or on any following roll. Again, you'll win on 7 or 11 and lose on 2, 3, or 12. Any other number is your point, and you win if your point comes up again before a 7.

DON'T COME   This is the opposite of a "Come" bet. Again, you wait until after the first roll to bet. A 7 or an 11 means you lose; a 2 or a 3 means you win; 12 is a push, and nobody wins. You win if 7 comes up before the point. (The point, you'll recall, was the first number rolled if it was none of the above.)

FIELD   This is a bet for one roll only. The "Field" consists of seven numbers: 2, 3, 4, 9, 10, 11, and 12. If any of these numbers is thrown on the next roll, you win even money, except on 2 and 12, which pay to 2 to 1 (at some casinos 3 to 1).

BIG 6 AND 8   A "Big 6 and 8" bet pays even money. You win if either a 6 or an 8 is rolled before a 7.

ANY 7   An "Any 7" bet pays the winner five for one. If a 7 is thrown on the first roll after you bet, you win.

"HARD WAY" BETS   In the middle of a craps table are pictures of several possible dice combinations together with the odds the casino will pay you if you bet and win on any of those combinations being thrown. For example, if 8 is thrown by having a 4 appear on each die, and you bet on it, the bank will pay 10 for 1; if 4 is thrown by having a 2 appear on each die, and you bet on it, the bank will pay 8 for 1; if 3 is thrown, the bank pays 15 for 1. You win at the odds quoted if the *exact* combination of numbers you bet on comes up. But you lose either if a 7 is rolled or if the number you bet on was rolled any way other than the "Hard Way" shown on the table. In-the-know gamblers tend to avoid "Hard Way" bets as an easy way to lose their money. And note that the odds quoted are *not* 3 to 1, 4 to 1, or 8 to 1; here the key word is *for*—that is, 3 for 1 or 8 for 1.

ANY CRAPS   Here you're lucky if the dice "crap out"—if they show 2, 3, or 12 on the first roll after you bet. If this happens, the bank pays for 8 for 1. Any other number is a loser.

PLACE BETS   You can make a "Place Bet" on any of the following numbers: 4, 5, 6, 8, 9, and 10. You're betting that the number you choose will be thrown before a 7 is thrown. If you win, the payoff is as follows: 4 or 10 pays at the rate of 9 to 5; 5 or 9 pays at the rate of 7 to 5; 6 or 8 pays at the rate of 7 to 6. "Place Bets" can be removed at any time before a roll.

SOME PROBABILITIES   Because each die has six sides numbered from 1 to 6, and craps is played with a pair of dice, the probability of throwing certain numbers has been studied carefully. Professionals have employed complex mathematical formulas in searching for the answers. And computers have data-processed curves of probability.

Impressions

The most exciting thing in craps is to win. The next most exciting thing is to lose.
                                                                    —Nick the Greek

Suffice it to say that 7 (a crucial number in craps) will be thrown more frequently than any other number over the long run, for there are six possible combinations that make 7 when you break down the 1 to 6 possibilities on each separate die. As to the total possible number of combinations on the dice, there are 36.

Comparing the 36 possible combinations, numbers, or point combinations, run as follows:

2 and 12 may be thrown in *1 way* only.

3 and 11 may be thrown in *2 ways.*

4 and 10 may be thrown in *3 ways.*

5 and 9 may be thrown in *4 ways.*

6 and 8 may be thrown in *5 ways.*

7 may be thrown in *6 ways.*

So 7 has an advantage over all other combinations, which, over the long run, is in favor of the casino. You can't beat the law of averages. Players, however, often have winning streaks, a proven fact in ESP studies, and that's when the experts advise that it's wise to increase the size of bets. But when a losing streak sets in, stop playing!

KENO

This is one of the oldest games of chance. Originating in China, the game can be traced back to a time before Christ, when it operated as a national lottery. Legend has it that funds acquired from the game were used to finance construction of the Great Wall of China.

Keno was first introduced into the United States in the 1800s by Chinese railroad construction workers. Easy to play, and offering a chance to sit down and converse between bets, it is one of the most popular games in town—despite the fact that *the house percentage is greater than that of any other casino game!*

To play, you must first obtain a keno form, available at the counter in the keno lounge and in most Las Vegas coffee shops. In the latter, you'll usually find blank keno forms and thick black crayons on your table. Fill yours out, and a miniskirted keno runner will come and collect it. After the game is over, she'll return with your winning or losing ticket. If you've won, it's customary to offer a tip, depending on your winnings.

Looking at your keno ticket and the keno board, you'll see that it is divided horizontally into two rectangles. The upper half (in China the yin area) contains the numbers 1 through 40, the lower (yang) half contains the numbers 41 through 80. You can win a maximum of $50,000, even more on progressive games, though it's highly unlikely (the probability is less than a hundredth of a percent). Mark up to 15 out of the 80 numbers; bets range from about 70¢ on up. A one-number mark is known

PRICE PER WAY	PRICE PER GAME

$50,000.00 LIMIT TO AGGREGATE PLAYERS EACH GAME

MARK NUMBER OF SPOTS OR WAYS PLAYED

NO. OF GAMES	TOTAL PRICE

1	2	3	4	5	6	7	8	9	10
11	12	13	14	15	16	17	18	19	20
21	22	23	24	25	26	27	28	29	30
31	32	33	34	35	36	37	38	39	40

WE PAY ON MACHINE ISSUED TICKETS - TICKETS WITH ERRORS NOT CORRECTED BEFORE START OF GAME WILL BE ACCEPTED AS ISSUED.

41	42	43	44	45	46	47	48	49	50
51	52	53	54	55	56	57	58	59	60
61	62	63	64	65	66	67	68	69	70
71	72	73	74	75	76	77	78	79	80

WE ARE NOT RESPONSIBLE FOR KENO RUNNERS TICKETS NOT VALIDATED BEFORE START OF NEXT GAME.

as a one-spot, a two-number selection is a two-spot, and so on. After you have selected the number of spots you wish to play, write the price of the ticket in the right hand corner where indicated. The more you bet, the more you can win if your numbers come up. Before the game starts, you have to give the completed form to a keno runner or hand it in at the keno lounge desk, and pay for your bet. You'll get back a duplicate form with the number of the game you're playing on it. Then the game begins. As numbers appear on the keno board, compare them to the numbers you've marked on your ticket. After 20 numbers have appeared on the board, if you've won, turn in your ticket immediately for a payoff before the next game begins. Otherwise, you will forfeit your winnings, a frustrating experience to say the least.

On a straight ticket that is marked with one or two spots, all of your numbers must appear on the board for you to win anything. With a few exceptions, if you mark from 3 to 7 spots, 3 numbers must appear on the board for you to win anything. Similarly, if you mark 8 to 12 spots, usually at least 5 numbers must come up for you to win the minimum amount. And if you mark 13 to 15 spots, usually at least 6 numbers must come up for a winning ticket. To win the maximum amount ($50,000), which requires that all of your numbers come up, you must select at least

8 spots. The more numbers on the board matching the numbers on your ticket, the more you win. If you want to keep playing the same numbers over and over, you can replay a ticket by handing in your duplicate to the keno runner; you don't have to keep rewriting it.

In addition to the straight bets described above, you can split your ticket, betting various amounts on two or more groups of numbers. To do so, circle the groups. The amount you bet is then divided by the number of groups. You could, if you so desired, play as many as 40 two-spots on a single ticket. Another possibility is to play three groups of four numbers each as eight spots (any two of the three groups of four numbers can be considered an eight spot). It does get a little complex, since combination betting options are almost infinite. Helpful casino personnel in the keno lounge can help you with combination betting.

POKER

Poker is *the* game of the Old West. There's at least one sequence in every Western where the hero faces off against the villain over a poker hand. In Las Vegas poker is a tradition, although it isn't played at every casino.

There are lots of variations on the basic game, but one of the most popular is Hold 'Em. Five cards are dealt face up in the center of the table and two are dealt to each player. The player uses the best five of seven, and the best hand wins. The house dealer takes care of the shuffling and the dealing and moves a marker around the table to alternate the start of the deal. The house rakes 1% to 10% (it depends on the casino) from each pot. Most casinos include the usual seven-card stud and a few have hi-lo split.

If you don't know how to play poker, don't attempt to learn at a table. Find a casino that teaches it in free gaming lessons.

Pai gow poker (a variation on poker) has become increasingly popular. The game is played with a traditional deck plus one joker. The joker is a wild card that can be used as an ace or to complete a straight, a flush, a straight flush, or a royal flush. Each player is dealt seven cards to arrange into two hands: a two-card hand and a five-card hand. As in standard poker, the highest two-card hand is two aces, and the highest five-card hand is a royal flush. The five-card hand *must* be higher than the two-card hand (if the two-card hand is a pair of sixes, for example, the five-card hand must be a pair of sevens or better). Any player's hand that is set incorrectly is an automatic lose. The object of the game is for both of the player's hands to rank higher than both of the banker's hands. Should one hand rank exactly the same as the banker's hand, this is a tie (called a "copy"), *and the banker wins all tie hands.* If the player wins one hand but loses the other, this is a "push," and no money changes hands. The house dealer or any player may be the banker. The bank is offered to each player, and each player may accept or pass. Winning hands are paid even money, less a 5% commission.

ROULETTE

Roulette is an extremely easy game to play, and it's really quite colorful and exciting to watch. The wheel spins, and the little ball bounces around, finally dropping into one of the slots, numbered 1 to 36, plus 0 and 00. You can bet on a single number, a combination of numbers, or red or black, odd or even. If you're lucky, you can win as much as 35 to 1 (see the table). The method of placing single-number bets, column bets, and others is fairly obvious. The dealer will be happy to show you how to "straddle" two or more numbers and make many other interesting betting combinations. Each player is given different-colored chips so that it's easy to follow the numbers you're on.

Roulette Chart Key	Odds	Type of Bet
		Straight Bets
A	35 to 1	*Straight-up:* All numbers, plus 0 and 00.
B	2 to 1	*Column Bet:* Pays off on any number in that horizontal column.
C	2 to 1	*First Dozen:* Pays off on any number 1 through 12. Same for second and third dozen.
D	Even Money	
		Combination Bets
E	17 to 1	*Split:* Pays off on 11 or 12.
F	11 to 1	Pays off on 28, 29, or 30.
G	8 to 1	*Corner:* Pays off on 17, 18, 20, or 21.
H	6 to 1	Pays off on 0, 00, 1, 2, or 3.
I	5 to 1	Pays off on 22, 23, 24, 25, 26, or 27.

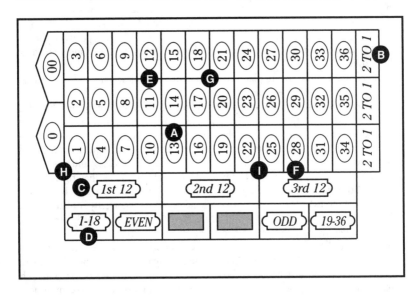

A number of typical bets are indicated by means of letters on the roulette layout depicted here. The winning odds for each of these sample bets are listed. These bets can be made on any corresponding combinations of numbers.

SLOTS

You put the coin in the slot and pull the handle. What, you thought there was a trick to this?

Actually, there is a bit more to it. But first, some background. Old-timers will tell you slots were invented to give wives something to do while their husbands gambled. Slots used to be stuck at the edges of the casino and could be counted on one hand, maybe two. But now they *are* the casino. The casinos make more from slots than from craps, blackjack, and roulette combined. There are 115,00 slot machines (not including video poker) in the county alone. Some of these are at the airport, steps from you as you deplane. It's a just a matter of time before the planes flying into Vegas feature slots that pop up as soon as you cross the state line.

But in order to keep up with the increasing competition, the plain old machine, where reels just spun, has become nearly obsolete. Now, they are all computerized, and have added buttons to push, so you can avoid carpel tunnel syndrome yanking the handle all night. (The handles are still there on many of them.) The idea is still simple: Get three (sometimes four) cherries (clowns, sevens, dinosaurs, whatever) in a row, and you win something. Each machine has its own combination; some will pay you something with just one symbol showing; on most the more combinations there are, the more opportunities for loot. Some will even pay if you get three blanks. Study each machine to learn what it does.

The **payback** goes up considerably if you bet the limit (from two to as many as 45 coins). But while the payoff can be much bigger, the odds *against* winning also go up when you put in the limit. (So if you hit something on a machine and realize your $25 win would have been $500 had you only put in more money, take a deep breath, stop kicking yourself, and remember you might not actually have hit that winning combination so easily had you bet the limit.)

Progressive slots are groups of machines where the jackpot gets bigger every few moments (just as lottery jackpots build up). Bigger and better games keep showing up; for example, there's Anchor Gaming's much-imitated **Wheel of Gold,** wherein if you get the right symbol, you get to spin a roulette wheel, which guarantees you a win of a serious number of coins. **Totem Pole** is the Godzilla of slot machines, a behemoth that allows you to spin up to three reels at once (provided you put in the limit). And of course, there's our personal favorite, **Piggy Bankin'.** This has a LED display on which a silly tune plays and a pig cavorts (at erratic times, he trots across the screen, oinks, giggles when you lose and imitates Elvis, among other playful actions). It's so much fun to watch you start putting in the coins just to get the pig to move, forget about the money. But meanwhile, money is building up in the piggy bank, an extra bonus you win if you hit the right symbol.

Other gimmick machines include **Clear Winner,** where you can satisfy your curiosity about the inner workings of a slot machine, and **Rockin' Reels,** which looks like a jukebox. And of course, there are always those **Big Giant Slot** machines, gimmicky devices found in almost every casino. They may not win as often as regular slots (though there is no definite word on it one way or the other), but not only are they just plain fun to spin, they often turn into audience participation gambling, as watchers gather to cheer you on to victory.

Are there surefire ways to win on a slot machine? No. But you can lose more slowly. The slots are on computer timers, and there are times when they are hitting and times when they are not. A bank of empty slots probably (but not certainly) means they aren't hitting. Go find a line where lots of people are sitting around with trays full of money. (Of course, yours will be the one that doesn't hit.) A good rule of thumb is that if your slot doesn't hit something in four or five pulls, leave it and go find another. It's not as though you won't have some choice in the matter. Also, each casino has some bank of slots that they advertise as more loose or with a bigger payback. Try these. It's what they want you to do, but what the heck.

SLOT CLUBS

If you play slots or video poker, it definitely pays to join a slot club. These so-called clubs are designed to attract and keep customers in a given casino by providing

If you aim to leave Las Vegas with a small fortune, go there with a large one.
                                                    —Anonymous American saying

incentives—meals, shows, discounts on rooms, gifts, tournament invitations, discounts at hotel shops, VIP treatment, and (more and more) cash rebates. Of course, your rewards are greater if you play just in one casino, but your mobility is limited.

When you join a slot club (inquire at the casino desk), you're given something that looks like a credit card, which you must insert into an ATM-like device whenever you play. (Don't forget to retrieve your card when you leave the machine, as we sometimes do—though that may work in your favor if someone comes along and plays the machine without removing it.) The device tracks your play and computes bonus points.

Which slot club should you join? Actually, you should join one at any casino where you play, since even the act of joining usually entitles you to some benefits. It's convenient to concentrate play where you're staying; if you play a great deal, a casino hotel's slot-club benefits may be a factor in your accommodations choice. Consider, though, particularly if you aren't a high roller, the slot clubs downtown. You get more bang for your buck, because you don't have to spend as much to start raking in the goodies.

One way to judge a slot club is by the quality of service when you enroll. Personnel should politely answer all your questions (for instance, is nickel play included? or is there a time limit for earning required points?) and be able to tell you exactly how many points you need for various bonuses.

To maximize your slot-club profits and choose the club that's best for you is a complex business. If you want to get into it in depth, order a copy of Jeffrey Compton's *The Las Vegas Advisor Guide to Slot Clubs* ($9.95 plus shipping), which examines just about every facet of the situation (☎ **800/244-2224**). Compton gives high ratings to the clubs at Caesars Palace, the Desert Inn, the Mirage, Treasure Island, the Flamingo Hilton, the Rio, the Sahara, Sam's Town, the Four Queens, the Golden Nugget, and Lady Luck.

SPORTS BOOKS

Most of the larger hotels in Las Vegas have sports book operations—they look a lot like commodities-futures trading boards. In some, almost as large as theaters, you can sit comfortably and watch ball games, fights, and, at some casinos, horse races on huge TV screens. To add to your enjoyment, there's usually a deli/bar nearby that serves sandwiches, hot dogs, soft drinks, and beer. As a matter of fact, some of the best sandwiches in Las Vegas are served next to the sports books. Sports books take bets on virtually every sport.

VIDEO POKER

Rapidly coming up on slots in popularity, video poker works the same way as regular poker, except you play against the machine. You are dealt a hand, you pick which cards to keep and which to discard, and then get your new hand. And, it is hoped, collect your winnings. Somewhat more of a challenge and more active than slots because you have some control (or at least illusion of control) over your fate, and they are easier than playing actual poker with a table full of folks who probably take it very seriously.

There are a number of varieties of this machine, with **Jacks are Better, Dueces Wild,** and so forth. Be sure to study your machine before you sit down. (The best returns are offered on the **Jacks are Wild** machines, when the payback for a pair of Jacks or better is 2 times your bet, and 3 times for three of a kind.) Some machines offer Double Down: After you have won, you get a chance to draw cards against the machine, with the higher card the winner. If you win, your money is doubled and you are offered a chance to go again. Your money can increase nicely during this time, and you can also lose it all very fast, which is most annoying. Technology is catching up with Video Poker, too. Now they even have touch screens, which offer a variety of different poker games, blackjack, and video slots—just touch your screen and choose your poison.

3 The Casinos

Casino choice is a personal thing. Some like to find their lucky place and stick with it, while others love to take advantage of the nearly endless choices Vegas offers. Everyone should casino-hop at least once to marvel (or get dizzy) at the decor/spectacle and the sheer excess of it all. But beyond decoration, there isn't too much difference. You've got your slot machines, gaming tables, big chandeliers.

Virtually all casinos make sure they have no clocks or windows—they do not want you to interrupt your losing streak by realizing how much time has passed. Of course, we've all heard the legend that Vegas casinos pump in fresh oxygen to keep the players from getting tired and wanting to pack it in. The veracity of this is hard to confirm, but we can only hope it's true, especially when we think of that time we looked up after a long stretch of gambling and discovered it was Thursday.

Don't be a snob, and don't be overly dazzled by the fancy casinos. Sometimes you can have a better time at one of the older places downtown, where stakes are lower, pretensions are nonexistent, and the clientele are often friendlier.

What follows is description of most of the major casinos in Vegas, including a claustrophobia rating, whether or not they have a Big Giant Slot Machine (it's a sucker bet, but we love them), and a completely arbitrary assessment based on whether or not we won there.

BALLY'S LAS VEGAS   Bally's casino is one of the most clean and well lit and definitely has that high-rent appeal. It's large (the size of a football field) with lots of colorful signage. The big ceiling makes for a low claustrophobia level. There's a Most Valuable Player Slot Club, offering members cash rebates, room discounts, free meals and show tickets, and invitations to special events, among other perks. The casino hosts frequent slot tournaments, and free gaming lessons are offered. Gaming facilities include a keno lounge, a state-of-the-art race and sports book, blackjack tables, craps, roulette, baccarat, minibaccarat, Caribbean stud (Bally's innovated this now popular Las Vegas game), pai gow, a Big Six wheel, Let-It-Ride tables, and slot/video poker machines. There are also blackjack tables and slot/video poker machines in Bally's Avenue Shoppes. There is not, however, a Big Giant Slot machine. For shame.

BARBARY COAST   The Barbary Coast has a cheerful 1890s-style casino ornately decorated with $2 million worth of gorgeous stained-glass skylights and signs, as well as immense crystal-dangling globe chandeliers over the gaming tables. It's worth stopping in just to take a look around when you're in the central "four corners" area of the Strip. The casino has a free Fun Club for slot players; participants earn points toward cash and prizes. Gaming facilities include a race and sports book, keno, blackjack tables, craps, roulette, minibaccarat, Let-It-Ride, pai gow poker, and slot/video poker machines.

The World's Series, Las Vegas Style

Binion's Horseshoe is internationally known as the home of the World Series of Poker. It was "Nick the Greek" Dondolos who first approached Benny Binion in 1949 with the idea for a high-stakes poker marathon between top players. Binion agreed, with the stipulation that the game be open to public viewing. The competition, between Dondolos and the legendary Johnny Moss, lasted 5 months with breaks only for sleep. Moss ultimately won about $2 million. As Dondolos lost his last pot, he rose from his chair, bowed politely, and said, "Mr. Moss, I have to let you go."

In 1970, Binion decided to re-create the battle of poker giants, which evolved into the annual World Series of Poker. Johnny Moss won the first year, and went on to snag the championship again in 1971 and 1974. Thomas "Amarillo Slim" Preston won the event in 1972 and popularized it on the talk-show circuit. Last year, there were more than 4,000 entrants from 22 countries, and total winnings were in excess of $11 million (more than $93 million in prize money has been distributed since the tournament began). A Poker Hall of Fame wall in the casino honors great players (running the gamut from Edmond Hugh, who created the rules, to Wild Bill Hickok).

BINION'S HORSESHOE   Professionals who know say that "for the serious player, the Binions *are* this town." Benny Binion could neither read nor write, but boy, did he know how to run a casino. His venerable establishment has gotten eclipsed over the years, but it claims the highest betting limits in Las Vegas on all games (probably in the entire world, according to a spokesperson). It offers single-deck blackjack and $2 minimums, 10-times odds on craps, and high progressive jackpots. We especially like the older part of the casino here, which—with its flocked wallpaper, gorgeous lighting fixtures, and gold-tasseled burgundy velvet drapes—looks like a turn-of-the-century Old West bordello. Unfortunately, all this adds up to a very high claustrophobia level. Gaming facilities include a keno lounge, race and sports book, a 500-seat bingo parlor, blackjack, craps, roulette, baccarat, minibaccarat, pai gow poker, Let-It-Ride, Caribbean stud, Big Six, and slot and video poker machines. They have two Big Giant Slot machines, at least one of which has been very very good to us. Binion's is located downtown at 128 E. Fremont St. between Casino Center Boulevard and First Street.

While you're visiting Binion's casino, be sure to see the display of $1 million (comprised of 100 $10,000 bills) encased in a gold horseshoe-shaped vault. If you'd like a photograph of yourself with all that moolah, you can get one taken free from 4pm to midnight daily.

CAESARS PALACE   Caesars casino is simultaneously the ultimate in gambling luxury and the ultimate in Vegas kitsch. Cocktail waitresses in togas parade about, as you gamble under the watchful gaze of faux marble Roman statues. The very high ceiling makes for a very low claustrophobia level, especially thanks to the recent facelift, which has lightened up the paint and made the whole casino much brighter. A notable facility in the latter is the state-of-the-art Race and Sports Book, with huge electronic display boards and giant video screens. (Caesars pioneered computer-generated wagering data that can be communicated in less than half a second and sophisticated satellite equipment that can pick up virtually any broadcast sporting event in the world.) The domed VIP slot arena of the Forum Casino (minimum bet is $5, but you can wager up to $1,500 on a single pull!) is a plush, crystal-chandeliered precinct with seating in roomy, adjustable chairs. Slot players can accumulate bonus points toward cash back, gifts, gratis show tickets, meals, and rooms by joining the Emperors Club. Club membership also lets you in on grand-prize drawings, tournaments, and parties.

Most upscale of Caesars's gaming rooms is the intimate, European-style casino adjoining the **Palace Court** restaurant. Total facilities in all three casinos contain craps tables, blackjack, roulette, baccarat, minibaccarat, Let-It-Ride, Caribbean stud, pai gow poker, two Big Six wheels, slot/video poker machines, and a keno lounge. It's a gorgeous and elegant place to gamble, but we've never won there, so we hate it.

CALIFORNIA HOTEL/CASINO   The California is a festive place filled with Hawaiian shirts and balloons. This friendly facility actually provides sofas and armchairs in the casino area—an unheard-of luxury in this town. Players can join the Cal Slot Club and amass points toward gifts and cash prizes or participate in daily slot tournaments. Gaming facilities include a keno lounge, sports book, blackjack tables, craps, roulette, minibaccarat, pai gow poker, Let-It-Ride, Caribbean stud, and slot and video poker machines. This is the first place we found our favorite Piggy Bankin' machines.

CIRCUS CIRCUS   This vast property has three full-size casinos that, combined, comprise one of the largest gaming operations in Nevada (more than 100,000 square feet). More importantly, they have an entire circus midway set up throughout, so you are literally gambling with trapeze stunts going on over your head. The other great gimmick is the slot machine carousel—yep, it turns while you spin the reels. The Ringmaster Players Club offers slot/video poker and table players the opportunity to earn points redeemable for cash, discounted rooms and meals, and other benefits. Circus Bucks progressive slot machines here build from a jackpot base of $500,000, which players can win on a $2 pull. Gaming facilities include a 10,000-square-foot race and sports book with 30 video monitors ranging from 13 to 52 inches, 40-seat and 89-seat keno lounges, poker tables, blackjack, craps, roulette, a Big Six wheel, Let-It-Ride, pai gow poker, dice, Caribbean stud poker, and slot and video poker machines. Unfortunately, it is crowded, noisy, and there are lots of children passing through. That, plus some low ceilings (not in the Big Top, obviously), make for a very high claustrophobia rating. Although the recent upgrades and remodeling aim to improve matters.

DESERT INN   Possibly the most genuinely elegant casino in Vegas, it's also one of the smallest for a major hotel. They don't care—they are looking for one good James Bond figure, rather than the masses. Crystal chandeliers here replace the usual neon glitz, and gaming tables are comfortably spaced. The ambience is reminiscent of intimate European gaming houses, and is downright quiet. Some might find this almost creepy. Others may find it a huge relief. Since there are fewer slot machines here than at most major casinos, there's less noise in ringing bells and clinking coins. Most table games have a $5 minimum. Facilities include a race and sports book, poker, blackjack, Spanish 21 (like blackjack, but there are no 10s in the deck), craps, pai gow, pai gow poker, Let-It-Ride, Caribbean stud, minibaccarat, baccarat, roulette, and slot/video poker machines. A sophisticated casino lounge is a plus. The very high ceiling gives it a nonexistent claustrophobia rating.

EL CORTEZ   This friendly downtown casino features frequent big-prize drawings (up to $50,000) based on your Social Security number. It's also popular for low limits (10¢ roulette and 25¢ craps). Gaming facilities include a race and sports book, keno, blackjack, craps, roulette, minibaccarat, and slot/video poker machines.

EXCALIBUR   As you might expect, the Excalibur casino is replete with suits of armor, stained-glass panels, knights, dragons, and velvet and satin heraldic banners, with gaming action taking place beneath vast iron and gold chandeliers fit for a medieval castle fortress. This all makes it fine for kitsch-seekers, but anyone hating crowds or sensitive to noise will hate it. The overall effect is less like a castle and more like a dungeon. A popular feature here is Circus Bucks, a progressive slot machine that builds from a jackpot base of $500,000; players can win on a $3 pull. Excalibur's 100,000-plus square feet of gaming facilities also include a race and sports book, a keno lounge, a poker room, blackjack, minibaccarat, Caribbean stud, Let-It-Ride, casino war (like the game you played as a kid), craps, roulette, pai gow poker, Big Six, and slot/video poker machines. A nonsmoking area is a plus. One of us won a lot of money here and refused to share it with the other, so our final judgment about the casino is, well, mixed.

FITZGERALDS   They recently redid their casino in greens and golds, and the overall effect is not quite as tacky as you might expect. In fact, it's rather friendly, and with a medium to low claustrophobia level. The casino is actually two levels: From the upstairs part you can access a balcony from which you get an up-close view of the Fremont St. Experience. Their mascot, Mr. O'Lucky (a costumed leprechaun), roams the casino. You don't have to be nice to him. Blackjack, craps, and keno tournaments are frequent events here. Slot machines that paid back over 100% the previous week are marked with a Mr. Lucky sign. The Fitzgerald Card offers slot players gifts, meals, and other perks for accumulated points. Several slot machines have cars as prizes, fun books provide two-for-one gaming coupons, and there are $1 minimum blackjack tables. Facilities include a sports book, a keno lounge, blackjack, craps, Let-It-Ride, roulette, Spanish 21 (see the Desert Inn above), "21" Superbucks, Caribbean stud, and slot and video poker machines. They have dollar Piggy Bankin' machines.

FLAMINGO HILTON   If you've seen the movie *Bugsey,* you won't recognize this as Mr. Seigel's baby. The Flamingo is in the middle of redoing its casino area, which is just as well, because right now, it is overly crowded in feel, thanks to overall tight confines. It sprawls across a large space, meandering around corners, so it is very difficult to get out of. Actual daylight does stream in from windows and glass doorways on the Strip, however. There are slots here offering Cadillacs and Continentals as jackpots. Players Club slot bettors qualify for free meals, shows, rooms, and other play-based incentives. Free gaming lessons are offered weekdays. Gaming facilities include a keno lounge, a state-of-the-art race and sports book, poker room, Caribbean stud, blackjack, Let-It-Ride, "double down" poker, craps, roulette, minibaccarat, pai gow poker, *sic bo,* Big Six, and slot/video poker machines. One of our favorite slot machines is here, but we won't tell you which one to save it for ourselves. Sorry.

FOUR QUEENS   New Orleans's themed, with turn-of-the-century-style globe chandeliers, which make for good lighting and a low claustrophobia level. It's small, but the dealers are helpful, which is one of the pluses of gambling in the more manageable sized casinos. The facility boasts the world's largest slot machine; more than 9 feet high and almost 20 feet long; six people can play it at one time! It's the Mother of all Big Giant Slot machines, and frankly, it intimidates even us. Here is also the world's largest blackjack table (it seats 12 players). The Reel Winners Club offers slot players bonus points toward cash rebates. Slot, blackjack, and craps tournaments are frequent events, and there are major poker tournaments every January and September. The casino also offers exciting multiple-action blackjack (it's like playing three hands at once with separate wagers on each). Gaming facilities include a keno lounge, sports book, blackjack, craps, roulette, pai gow poker, Caribbean stud, Let-It-Ride, and slot/video poker machines.

GOLD COAST   Adjacent to the Rio, this casino is not only well lit, but totally unique in Vegas: It has windows! It's a little thing, but it made us really excited. They also had a higher ratio of video poker machines to slot machines, rather than the other way around. The Gold Coast is located at 4000 W. Flamingo.

GOLDEN GATE   This is one of the oldest casinos downtown, and though its age is showing, it's still fun to go there. As you might expect from the name, old San Francisco (think earthquake time) artifacts and decor abound. At one end of the narrow casino is the bar, where a piano player performs ragtime jazz, which is better than the homogenized pap offered in most casino lounges. Unfortunately, the low ceiling, dark period wallpaper, and small dimensions give this a high claustrophobia level. Golden Gate is at 1 Fremont St.

GOLDEN NUGGET   Frankly, this is not the standout that other casino properties owned by Steve Wynn are. It goes for luxury, of course, but so much is crammed into so little space that the only feeling that emerges is one of overcrowding. That's not to say we didn't like it, because we won a lot of money there. And compared to most other downtown properties, this is the most like the Strip. It is much cleaner and fresher feeling, in an area filled with dingy, time-forgotten spaces. Slot players can earn bonus points toward complimentary rooms, meals, shows, and gifts by joining the 24 Karat Club. Gaming facilities include an attractive and comfortable keno lounge, a race and sports book, blackjack ($1 minimum bet), craps, roulette, baccarat, pai gow, pai gow poker, red dog, Big Six, and slot/video poker machines.

GOLD SPIKE   Okay, we just criticized dingy, time-forgotten spaces (see above) in downtown, and the Gold Spike certainly lands in that category. So what? Here, everyone is equal, and everyone is having a good time, or at least they can sincerely join you in your misery. Think 1970s shag carpeting, faux wood paneling, and a best-not-thought-too-hard-about 49¢ shrimp cocktail. Best of all, they have penny slots! (Not very many, to be sure, and getting a seat at one can require patience.) Hey tightwads, take a buck, and spend a few hours. The Gold Spike is at 400 Ogden at Las Vegas Boulevard, downtown.

HARD ROCK HOTEL & CASINO   Where Gen X goes to gamble. The Hard Rock has certainly taken casino decor to a whole new level. The attention to detail and the resulting playfulness is admirable, if not incredible. Gaming tables have piano keyboards at one end; some slots have Fender guitar fret boards as arms; gaming chips have band names and/or pictures on them; slot machines are similarly rock themed (check out the Jimi Hendrix machine!); and so it goes. The whole thing is set in the middle of a circular room, around the outskirts of which is various rock memorabilia in glass cases. Rock blares over the sound system, allowing boomers to boogie while they gamble. A bank of slots makes gambling an act of charity: Environmentally committed owner Peter Morton (the Hard Rock's motto is "Save the Planet") donates profits from specified slots to organizations dedicated to saving the rain forests. A Back Stage Pass allows patrons to rack up discounts on meals, lodging, and gift shop items while playing slots and table games. The race and sports book here provides comfortable seating in leather-upholstered reclining armchairs. Gaming facilities (with selected nonsmoking tables) include blackjack, roulette, craps, Caribbean stud, minibaccarat, Let-It-Ride, pai gow poker, and slot/video poker machines. All this is genuinely amazing, but the noise level is above even that of a normal casino and we just hated it. It's worth looking at anyway.

HARRAH'S Confetti carpeting and fiber-optic fireworks overhead combine with murals and an overall Mardi Gras theme to make a festive environment. Does it help you win more? Who knows. But the different, better energy that has resulted from this recent, costly face-lift certainly couldn't hurt. Don't miss the "party pits," gaming table areas where dealers are encouraged to wear funny hats, celebrate wins, and otherwise break the usual stern dealer facade. Singing, dancing, and the handing out of party favors have all been known to break out. Gambling is supposed to be fun, so enjoy it. Slot and table game players can earn bonus points toward complimentary rooms, meals, and show tickets by acquiring a Harrah's Gold Card in the casino. Facilities include a sports book, keno lounge, poker room, blackjack, craps, roulette, minibaccarat, pai gow poker, red dog, casino war (in the Party Pit), Let-It-Ride, Big Six, and slot and video poker machines. There are nonsmoking areas, and free gaming lessons are offered weekdays.

IMPERIAL PALACE The 75,000-square-foot casino here reflects the hotel's pagoda-roofed Asian exterior with a dragon-motif ceiling and giant wind-chime chandeliers. There is a nonsmoking slot machine area separate from the main casino (as opposed to just another part of the room, at best, in other casinos), and a Breathalizer for voluntary alcohol limit checks on your way to the parking lot (useful since there are nine bars on the casino premises). Visitors can get free Scratch Slotto cards for prizes up to $5,000 in cash (cards and free passes to the auto collection are distributed on the sidewalk out front). A gaming school offers lessons in craps and blackjack, and slots tournaments take place daily. The Imperial Palace boasts a 230-seat race and sports book, attractively decorated with oil murals of sporting events; the room is tiered like a grandstand, and every seat has its own color monitor. Other gaming facilities include a keno lounge, blackjack, craps, roulette, minibaccarat, pai gow poker, Caribbean stud, Big Six, and slot/video poker machines. One Big Giant Slot machine is red white and blue; try singing the National Anthem to it, and see if you win more money.

JACKIE GAUGHAN'S PLAZA HOTEL/CASINO This is old Vegas, with an attempt at '60s glamour (think women in white go-go boots). Now it's a little worn. Gaming facilities include a keno lounge (featuring double keno), race and sports book, blackjack, craps, roulette, baccarat, Caribbean stud, pai gow poker, poker, pan, Let-It-Ride, and slot/video poker machines. Cautious bettors will appreciate the $1 blackjack tables and penny slots here.

LADY LUCK Even though it's an older casino with the anticipated drop in glamour, it's surprisingly cheerful and with a low to medium claustrophobia level. Decorations give it a festive quality, and cocktail waitresses push drink carts, to mix you up something right on the spot. The Mad Money Slot Club offers scrip, cash, meals, accommodations, and prizes as incentives. Liberal game rules are attractive to gamblers. You can play "fast action hold 'em" here—a combination of 21, poker, and pai gow poker. Other gaming facilities include a keno lounge, blackjack, craps, roulette, minibaccarat, pai gow poker, and slot/video poker machines.

LAS VEGAS HILTON Austrian crystal chandeliers add a strong touch of class to the Hilton's 67,000-square-foot casino. It's actually on the medium size, but it does have an enormous sports book—at 30,500 square feet, the world's largest race and sports book facility. It, too, is a luxurious precinct equipped with the most advanced audio, video, and computer technology available, including 46 TV monitors, some as large as 15 feet across. In fact, its video wall is second in size only to NASA's. The casino is adjacent to the lobby, but neither are especially loud nor frantic. Especially

Memories of a Longtime Dealer

Lou has been a part of the gaming industry for 40 years, the first 20 of which he spent as a dealer in Las Vegas.

"My favorite places were the Flamingo, the Sands, and the Desert Inn. That's when the corporations weren't there. That's when the other folks were in. The mob guys—I never knew it, but that's what they were. I was just a kid. Bugsey had just gotten killed when I went to work at the Flamingo. The sands was my very first favorite. That was the hotel of all hotels. They had the very best management team. They took care of their help. Their benefits were better than any union. It was the place.

Years ago you had great entertainment. You could go to a lounge and catch better acts than in the showroom. Major stars were in the lounges, or they would come in and sit in with the acts after the showroom closed. Don Rickles: Sinatra would get up with him once in awhile. Sinatra gave me my first $100 tip. He was playing blackjack. Then he said, "Do you want to play it or keep it?" I wanted to be polite, so I said, "Bet it." And he lost. In those days when the stars would appear on stage, between shows they would come out into the casinos. Sinatra and Sammy would deal. They would blow money, but the casinos didn't care. It was a fun fun place. The casinos were run the way they were supposed to be run—for the customer, not so corporate-minded. In those days, you could go to Vegas, get your room very reasonable, your food was practically free, your shows were practically free, you would spend $500 in the casino, but you would come back and be happy because gaming was a form of entertainment. When they ran the casinos you would have a ball, come home and be happy. They were very happy if the restaurants and shows lost money—you still lost that $500. Now it would cost you $100 to stay at a hotel, and food is much more expensive, and to get a ticket to one of these shows is ridiculous. Now you gamble only $150 and you aren't as happy when you come home, because you don't feel like you've been treated to anything. It all goes into the same pocket—what difference does it make? It gives the customer the same hours and more fun. They don't understand that. It's not the same industry as when they ran it. And it shows."

LOU THE DEALER'S GAMING TIPS: If you are a craps shooter, just look around at the tables where they have the most chips. Find the guy with the most chips, and do what he does. Follow him along.

For **blackjack,** everybody will tell you in all your books to try to play single and double decks. I don't agree with that and I never will. The average player goes in to enjoy himself and to win a few dollars. So he is not a professional card counter. Play a shoe. If that shoe is going bad, and you catch a run, you will make a lot more money than with a single deck.

Look at gaming as a form of entertainment. Look at that $100 that you might have spent on dinner or a club, where we laughed and had a few drinks and had a good time. Think of it that way.

If you double your money, quit. Not quit gambling, but quit that table. Go have a sandwich or watch a show. And *then* come back. The odds aren't that tremendously in favor of the casinos. How they make their money is through greed; gamblers doubling their money then trying to quadruple it and losing it all, and more.

Try to survive. Don't try to win the hotel. Just to win a few dollars. Then stop and enjoy it.

plush are the vast 6,900-square-foot baccarat room—with gorgeous crystal chandeliers, silk-covered walls, and velvet-upholstered furnishings—and the VIP slot area where personnel are attired in tuxedos. Both areas offer gracious service to players. Because so many conventioneers stay here, the crowd is more changeable than at most casinos. By joining Club Magic, a slot club, you can amass bonus points toward cash prizes, gifts, and complimentary rooms, meals, and show tickets. In addition to the above, gaming facilities include a keno lounge, blackjack, craps, roulette, baccarat, pai gow, pai gow poker, Caribbean stud, Big Six, and slot/video poker machines.

Note: When STAR TREK: The Experience opens shortly at the Hilton, its gateway will be the futuristic new 22,000-square-foot Spacequest Casino. Overhead, "space windows," will offer a constantly changing vista of planets, stars, and space ships; the casino's ceiling will appear to separate to make way for a projectile launch; and stars will glitter brightly in the night sky.

LUXOR LAS VEGAS   More accessible than ever thanks to the addition of the air-conditioned people mover from Excalibur, Luxor has been completed remodeled and, in our opinion, improved immeasurably. You enter through a giant temple gateway flanked by massive statues of Ramses. Gone is the space-wasting center area that used to contain the bathrooms, cashiers, and casino offices. This additional space gives the casino a much more airy feel, which makes gives it a low claustrophobia level—in parts you can see all the way up the inside of the pyramid. King Tut heads and sphinxes adorn slot areas. There's a nonsmoking slot area. The Gold Chamber Club offers rewards of cash, merchandise, meals, and special services to slot and table players. And sports action unfolds on 17 large-screen TVs and 128 personalized monitors in Luxor's race and sports book. Additional gaming facilities include a keno lounge, blackjack, craps, roulette, poker, baccarat, minibaccarat, pai gow, Big Six, Caribbean stud, and slot/video poker machines. We already felt inclined to like this casino thanks to a good run at blackjack, but the redesign has made it even more inviting.

MAIN STREET STATION   Part of a long-closed old hotel that has been recently renovated and reopened to great success, this is the best of the downtown casinos, at least in terms of comfort and pleasant environment. Even the Golden Nugget, nice as it is, has more noise and distractions. The decor here is, again, classic Vegas/old timey (Victorian-era) San Francisco, but with extra touches (check out the old-fashioned fans above the truly beautiful bar) that make it work much better than other attempts at the same. Strangely, it seems just about smoke-free, perhaps thanks in part to a very high ceiling. The claustrophobia level is zero. Gaming facilities include a keno lounge, blackjack, craps, roulette, Caribbean stud, Let-It-Ride, pai gow poker, and slot/video poker machines.

MAXIM   This friendly, but dimly lit, facility (with some of the '70s frills) is the neighborhood bar of casinos. They have a racetrack game where you can place bets on little mechanical horse and jockeys—kind of a kid's toy for adults. Pick up a fun book here for a free $1,000 slot pull. Gaming facilities include a keno lounge, sports book, blackjack, craps, roulette, Caribbean stud, Let-It-Ride, pai gow poker, and slot/video poker machines.

MGM GRAND   The world's largest casino—at 171,500 square feet, we've been to countries that were smaller!—is divided into four themed areas, in a futile attempt to make it seem smaller. Much of the Wizard of Oz decorations have been removed, but spend an hour in here and you might well feel like Dorothy after she got hit by the twister. One section features a high-roller slot area with machines that operate on coins valued at $100 and $500! The sports casino houses a big poker room, a state-of-the-art race and sports book, and the Turf Club Lounge. And the French Riviera–themed Monte Carlo casino has a luxurious marble-columned and gold-draped private high-end gaming area. Carousels of progressive slots unique to the MGM Grand include the very popular Majestic Lions high-frequency $1 slot machines that pay out more than $1 million daily and Lion's Share $1 slots capable of jackpots exceeding $1 million each at any time. And since Chrysler is a resort sponsor, there are several win-a-car slots. The MGM Grand Director's Club offers guests prizes ranging from comps and gifts to cash rebates. Additional gaming facilities include a keno lounge, blackjack, craps, roulette, baccarat, minibaccarat, pai gow, pai gow poker, Caribbean stud, Let-It-Ride, Casino War, Big Six, and slot/video poker machines.

THE MIRAGE   Gamble in a Polynesian village in one of the prettiest casinos in town. It has a meandering layout, and the low ceiling makes for a medium claustrophobia level, but neither of these things is overwhelming. This remains one of our favorite places to gamble. Facilities include a separate poker room and a plush European-style *salon privé* for high rollers at baccarat, blackjack, and roulette; an elegant dining room serves catered meals to gamblers there. Slot players can join the Club Mirage and work toward bonus points for cash rebates, special room rates, complimentary meals and/or show tickets, and other benefits. The elaborate race and sports book offers theater stereo sound and a movie theater-size screen. Other gaming facilities here: a keno lounge, 75 blackjack tables, craps, roulette, baccarat, minibaccarat, pai gow, pai gow poker, Big Six, and slot and video poker machines. It's one of the most pleasant, and popular, casinos in town so it more often than not crowded.

MONTE CARLO   All huge ceilings and white-light interiors: Obviously, they are trying to evoke gambling in Monaco. While the decor shows lots of attention, it perhaps had too much attention. Bulbs line the ceiling, and everywhere you look is some detail or other. It's busy on both your eyes and your ears. So despite the effort put in, it's not a pleasant place to gamble. There's a large and comfortable race and sports book area, with its own cocktail lounge. And you can win a BMW sports car at a bank of 25¢ "Rich and Famous" slots. The Club Monte Carlo offers slot players cash rebates, merchandise, rooms, and meals for accumulated points. Other gaming facilities include a keno lounge, bingo room, poker room, blackjack, craps, roulette, baccarat, minibaccarat, Let-It-Ride, Caribbean stud, pai gow, pai gow poker, Big Six, and slot and video poker machines.

NEW YORK NEW YORK   Another theme-run-wild place: tuxes on the backs of gaming chairs, change carts that look like yellow cabs, and so forth, all set in a miniature New York City. It's all fabulous fun, but despite a low claustrophobia level (thanks to an unusually high ceiling), it is a major case of sensory overload akin to the reaction elicited by a first-time look at the Strip. This may prove distracting. On the other hand, we won there, so we love it. And it is, if one can say this about anything in Vegas with a straight face, in spots quite beautiful. Serious gamblers understandably may sniff at it all and prefer to take their business to a more seemly casino,

---

Impressions

What I like most about gambling is that it does not make sense. The hobby of gambling, even at my wimpy betting level, allows me to believe things that I know are not true. It gives me a chance to apply the most Byzantine rules and structures to my most ordinary actions, all in search of that compelling fiction known as luck.

—Edward Allen, *Penny Ante*

but everyone else should have about the most Vegasey time they can. Additional gaming facilities include a keno lounge, blackjack, craps, roulette, baccarat, minibaccarat, pai gow, pai gow poker, Caribbean stud, Let-It-Ride, Casino War, Big Six, and slot/video poker machines.

ORLEANS This is not a particularly special gambling space, though it has a low claustrophobia level, but over the sound system they play Cajun and Zydeco music, so you can two-step while you gamble, which can make losing somewhat less painful. It has all the needed tables—blackjack, craps, and so forth—plus plenty of slots, including a Wheel of Fortune machine that works like those other roulette wheel slots, but in this case, actually plays the theme song from the TV show. It will even applaud for you if you win.

THE RIO This Brazilian-themed resort's 85,000-square-foot casino is, despite the presence of plenty of glitter and neon, very dark. It has about the highest claustrophobia rating of the major casinos. Its sports book feels a little grimy. The waitresses wear scanty costumes (particularly in the back), probably in an effort to distract you and throw your game off. Do not let them. The part of the casino in the new Masquerade Village is considerably more pleasant (the very high ceilings help) though still crowded, plus the loud live show adds still more noise. In an area called Jackpot Jungle, slot machines come equipped with TV monitors that present old movies and in-house information while you play. And in the high-end slot area ($5 to $100 a pull), guests enjoy a private lounge and gratis champagne. There are nonsmoking slot and gaming table areas. Facilities include a keno lounge, race and sports book, blackjack, craps, roulette, baccarat, minibaccarat, pai gow, Caribbean stud, survival dice, Let-It-Ride, Big Six, and slot and video poker machines.

THE RIVIERA The Riviera's 100,000-square-foot casino, one of the largest in the world, means that there are plenty of opportunities to get lost and cranky. A wall of windows lets daylight stream in (most unusual), and the gaming tables are situated beneath gleaming brass arches lit by recessed, pink neon tubing. The casino's Slot and Gold (seniors) clubs allow slot players to earn bonus points toward free meals, rooms, and show tickets. The race and sports book here offers individual monitors at each of its 250 seats, and this is one of the few places in town where you can play the ancient Chinese game of *sic bo* (a fast-paced dice game resembling craps). Additional facilities include a large keno parlor, blackjack, craps, roulette, baccarat, pai gow poker, Caribbean stud, Let-It-Ride, Big Six, and slot/video poker machines.

THE SAHARA The Sahara is in the process of changing its casino's look and adding a large new area, so it might be worth checking out. This is one place where there seem to be more tables than slots and video poker machines, but that might change with the new addition. When we were last there, they had a whole row of Piggy Bankin' machines that were all paying off, so we were happy. The Sahara runs frequent slot tournaments and other events, and its slot club, Club Sahara, offers cash rebates and other perks. Gaming facilities include a race and sports book, keno lounge, blackjack, craps, roulette, poker, Let-It-Ride, pai gow poker, Caribbean stud, a Big Six wheel, and slot/video poker machines. *Note:* This is the only Strip casino that offers pan, a card game.

SAM BOYD'S FREMONT HOTEL & CASINO This 32,000-square-foot casino offers a relaxed atmosphere and low gambling limits ($2 blackjack, 25¢ roulette). It's also surprisingly open and bright for a downtown casino. Just 50¢ could win you a Cadillac or Ford Mustang here, plus a progressive cash jackpot. Casino guests can accumulate bonus points redeemable toward cash by joining the Five Star Slot Club, and take part in frequent slot and keno tournaments. Gaming facilities include two keno lounges, a race and sports book, blackjack, craps, roulette, Caribbean stud, Let-It-Ride, pai gow poker, and slot/video poker machines. No Big Giant Slot machine, though.

SAM'S TOWN   In its three immense floors of gaming action (153,083 square feet, second only to the MGM Grand in size), Sam Town's maintains the friendly, just-folks ambience that characterizes the entire property. The casino is adorned with Old West paraphernalia (horseshoes, Winchester rifles, holsters, and saddlebags), and country music plays nonstop. If you don't like country music, don't go here. Sam's Town claims its friendliness extends to looser slots. The casino gives away a house (with a car and $10,000 in cash) every 3 months and offers 10-times odds on craps and single-deck blackjack. Join the Sam's Town Slot Club to earn points towards rooms, meals, and cash rebates. Free gaming lessons are offered weekdays from 11am to 4pm, poker lessons at other times. Gaming facilities include a race and sports book with more than 60 monitors, 2 keno lounges, a 590-seat bingo parlor, blackjack, craps, roulette, poker, pai gow poker, Caribbean stud, and slot/video poker machines (including a nonsmoking slot area).

SHOWBOAT   The Showboat's casino, recently renovated, has a Mardi Gras/Bourbon Street theme. It's not the most elaborate in town, but it is certainly clean, friendly, and comfortable. At night, a jazz band plays from an open pavilion. The Showboat's enormous 24-hour bingo parlor is a facility also noted for high payouts. Slot players can join a club to accumulate bonus points toward free meals, rooms, gifts, and cash prizes. And if you're traveling with kids ages 2 to 7, you can leave them at an in-house baby-sitting facility free for 3 hours while you gamble. Older kids can be dropped at the Showboat's 106-lane bowling center. In addition to bingo, gaming facilities include a keno lounge, race and sports book, blackjack (including single deck "21"), craps, roulette, Let-It-Ride, pai gow, Caribbean stud, and slot and video poker machines.

THE STARDUST   Always mobbed, this popular casino features 90,000 square feet of lively gaming action, including a 250-seat race and sports book with a sophisticated satellite system and more than 50 TV monitors airing sporting events and horse racing results around the clock. Adjacent to it is a sports handicapper's library offering comprehensive statistical information on current sporting events. Stardust Slot Club members win cash rebates, with credit piling up even on nickel machines; free rooms, shows, meals, and invitations to special events are also possible bonuses. Other gaming facilities include: a large, well-lit keno lounge, a poker room, an elegant baccarat lounge, blackjack, craps, roulette, minibaccarat, pai gow poker, Caribbean stud, Let-It-Ride, Big Six, and slot and video poker machines. If you're a novice, avail yourself of gratis gaming lessons. We usually do well there, so even though it's a little loud we like it. Check out those $1 slots just inside the front door—they've been very good to us.

THE STRATOSPHERE   Originally set up to evoke a world's fair, but ending up more like a circus, the Stratosphere redid the whole area in order to make it more appealing for the many adults who were staying away in droves. The newly redone facility aims for class, but doesn't necessarily achieve it. It's not that it fails, it just no longer has any identity at all. They heavily advertise their high payback on certain slots and video poker: 98% payback on dollar slots and 100% payback on quarter video poker (if you bet the maximum on each). We can't say we noticed a difference, but other people around us were winning like crazy. There's a test area for new slot games, a Harley slot area with motorcycle-seat stools, and a high-roller slot room ($5 minimum bet) where chairs move up and down and can vibrate to give you a back

Impressions

I am, after all, the best hold 'em player alive. I'm forced to play this tournament, you understand, to demonstrate this fact.

—Once and future casino owner Bob Stupak on why he entered
Binion's Horseshoe World Series of Poker

massage while you play. The Stratosphere Players Club sponsors frequent tournaments, and its members can earn points towards gifts, VIP perks, discounted room rates, meals, and cash rebates. Other facilities include a keno lounge, a sports book, bingo, blackjack (with new rules that allow for more wins, supposedly), craps, roulette, poker, minibaccarat, pai gow, pai gow poker, Caribbean stud, Let-It-Ride, Big Six, and slot and video poker machines.

TREASURE ISLAND Treasure Island's huge casino is highly themed. If you have ever gone to Disneyland's Pirates of the Caribbean and thought, "Gee, if only this were a casino," this is the place for you. Kids seem to be everywhere, because they are dazzled by the pirate stuff. Many people complain they don't like the atmosphere here, possibly because that very theme backfires. Especially luxurious are a high-limit baccarat/blackjack area (where players enjoy a buffet of hot hors d'oeuvres) and a high-limit slot area. Slot club members can earn meals, services, show tickets, and cash rebates. Throughout the casino there is something called Slot 2000. Hit a button, and a video screen pops up showing a (female) casino worker, to whom you can talk. She will answer questions, send someone over with drinks, make reservations, and otherwise help make your time there better. If you win a jackpot, she will come on and congratulate you. No, she can't see you, so don't try to flirt. There are nonsmoking gaming tables in each pit. A race and sports book boasts state-of-the-art electronic information boards and TV monitors at every seat as well as numerous large-screen monitors. Other facilities include a keno lounge, over 50 blackjack tables, craps, roulette, poker, minibaccarat, pai gow, pai gow poker, Caribbean stud, Let-It-Ride, Big Six, and slot and video poker machines.

TROPICANA The Trop casino is quite good-looking, and, yes, highly tropical, with gaming tables situated beneath a massive, stained-glass archway and art nouveau lighting fixtures. In summer it offers something totally unique: swim-up blackjack tables located in the hotel's stunning 5-acre tropical garden and pool area. Slot and table game players can earn bonus points toward rooms, shows, and meals by obtaining an Island Winners Club card in the casino. A luxurious high-end slot area has machines that take up to $100 on a single pull. Numerous tournaments take place here, and free gaming lessons are offered weekdays. Facilities include a sports book, keno lounge, poker room, blackjack, craps, roulette, baccarat, pai gow poker, Let-It-Ride, Caribbean stud, minibaccarat, pai gow, and slot and video poker machines.

WESTWARD HO HOTEL & CASINO This small but centrally located strip casino hosts many slot tournaments, and slot players who obtain Preferred Customer cards can amass credits toward complimentary rooms, meals, and shows, among other benefits. Gaming facilities include blackjack, craps, roulette, Big Six, and slot/video poker machines.

Las Vegas Shopping

Unless you're looking for souvenir decks of cards, Styrofoam dice, and miniature slot machines, Las Vegas is not exactly a shopping mecca. It does, however, have several noteworthy malls that can amply supply the basics. And many hotels also offer comprehensive, and sometimes highly themed, shopping arcades, most notably Caesars Palace (details below). You might consider driving Maryland Parkway, which runs parallel to the Strip on the east, and has just about one of everything: Target, Toys R Us, several major department stores, Tower Records, major drug stores (in case you forgot your shampoo and don't want to spend $8 on a new one in your hotel sundry shop), some alternative culture stores (tattoo parlors and hip clothing stores), and so forth. It goes on for blocks.

1 The Malls

Boulevard Mall

3528 S. Maryland Pkwy., between Twain Ave. and Desert Inn Rd. ☎ **702/732-8949.** Mon–Fri 10am–9pm, Sat 10am–8pm, Sun 11am–6pm.

The Boulevard is the largest mall in Las Vegas. Its 144-plus stores and restaurants are arranged in arcade fashion on a single floor occupying 1.2 million square feet. Geared to the average consumer (not the carriage trade), it has anchors like Sears, JC Penney, Woolworth, Macy's, Dillard's, and Marshalls. Other notables include The Disney Store, The Nature Company, a 23,000-square-foot Good Guys (electronics), The Gap, Gap Kids, The Limited, Victoria's Secret, Colorado (for outdoor clothing and gear), Howard and Phil's Western Wear, and African and World Imports. There's a wide variety of shops offering moderately priced shoes and clothing for the entire family, books and gifts, jewelry, and home furnishings, plus more than a dozen fast-food eateries. In short, you can find just about anything you need here. There's free valet parking.

Fashion Show Mall

3200 Las Vegas Blvd. S., at the corner of Spring Mountain Rd. ☎ **702/369-8382.** Mon–Fri 10am–9pm, Sat 10am–7pm, Sun noon–6pm.

This luxurious and centrally located mall, one of the city's largest, opened in 1981 to great hoopla. Designers Adolfo, Geoffrey Beene, Bill Blass, Bob Mackie, and Pauline Trigere were all on hand to display their fashion interpretations of the "Las Vegas look."

Impressions

Tip Number 3: Win a bunch of money. I can't recommend this too highly. If it hasn't occurred to you, win $1,200 and see for yourself. It's very energizing and really adds to your Vegas fun.

—Merrill Markoe, *Viva Las Wine Goddesses!*

The mall comprises more than 130 shops, restaurants, and services. It is anchored by Neiman-Marcus, Saks Fifth Avenue, Macy's, Robinsons-May, and Dillard's. Other notable tenants: Abercrombie and Fitch, The Disney Store, The Walt Disney Gallery, The Discovery Channel Store, Lillie Rubin (upscale women's clothing), The Gap, Benetton, Uomo, Banana Republic, Victoria's Secret, Caché, Williams-Sonoma Grand Cuisine, The Body Shop, Mondi (upscale women's clothing), Waldenbooks, Louis Vuitton, and Sharper Image. There are several card and book shops, a wide selection of apparel stores for the whole family (including large sizes and petites), 9 jewelers, 21 shoe stores, and gift and specialty shops. There are dozens of eating places (see chapter 6 for specifics). Valet parking is available, and you can even arrange to have your car hand washed while you shop.

Galleria at Sunset

1300 W. Sunset Rd., at Stephanie St. just off I-515 in nearby Henderson. ☎ **702/434-0202.** Mon–Sat 10am–9pm, Sun 11am–6pm.

This upscale 1 million-square-foot shopping center, 9 miles southeast of downtown Las Vegas, opened in 1996, with performing Disney characters on hand to welcome shoppers and a nighttime display of fireworks. The mall has a southwestern motif, evidenced in the use of terra-cotta stone, interior landscaping, cascading fountains, and skylights; eight 20-foot hand-carved pillars flank the main entrance. Anchored by four department stores—Dillard's, JC Penney, Mervyn's California, and Robinsons-May—the Galleria's 110 emporia include branches of The Disney Store, The Gap/Gap Kids/Baby Gap, The Limited and The Limited Too, Eddie Bauer, Miller's Outpost, Ann Taylor, bebe, Caché, Compagnie International, Lane Bryant, Lerner New York, Victoria's Secret, The Body Shop, B. Dalton, and Sam Goody. In addition to shoes and clothing for the entire family, you'll find electronics, eyewear, gifts, books, home furnishings, jewelry, and luggage here. Dining facilities include an extensive food court and two restaurants.

The Meadows

4300 Meadows Lane, at the intersection of Valley View and U.S. 95. ☎ **702/878-4849.** Mon–Fri 10am–9pm, Sat–Sun 10am–6pm.

Another immense mall, the Meadows comprises 144 shops, services, and eateries, anchored by four department stores: Macy's, Dillard's, Sears, and JC Penney. In addition, there are 15 shoe stores, a full array of apparel for the entire family (including maternity wear, petites, and large sizes), an extensive food court, and shops purveying toys, books, CDs and tapes, luggage, gifts, jewelry, home furnishings (The Bombay Company, among others), accessories, and so on. Fountains and trees enhance the Meadows' ultramodern, high-ceilinged interior, and a 1995 renovation added comfortable conversation/seating areas and made the mall lighter and brighter. It is divided into five courts, one centered on a turn-of-the-century carousel (a plus for kids). A natural history–themed court has a "desert fossil" floor, and an entertainment court is the setting for occasional live musical and dramatic performances. You can rent strollers at the Customer Service Center.

2 Factory Outlets

Las Vegas has two big factory outlets just a few miles past the southern end of the Strip. If you don't have a car, you can take a no. 301 CAT bus from anywhere on the Strip and change at Vacation Village to a no. 303.

Belz Factory Outlet World

7400 Las Vegas Blvd. S., at Warm Springs Rd. ☎ **702/896-5599.** Mon–Sat 10am–9pm, Sun 10am–6pm.

Belz houses 145 air-conditioned outlets, including a few dozen clothing stores and shoe stores. It offers an immense range of merchandise at savings up to 75% off retail prices. Among other emporia, you'll find Adolfo II, Casual Corner, Levi's, Nike, Dress Barn, Oshkosh B'Gosh, Leggs/Hanes/Bali, Esprit, Aileen, Bugle Boy, Carters, Reebok, Spiegel, Guess Classics, Oneida, Springmaid, We're Entertainment (Disney and Warner Bros.), Bose (electronics), Danskin, Van Heusen, Burlington, Royal Doulton, Lennox (china), Waterford (crystal), and Geoffrey Beene here. There is also a carousel.

Factory Stores of America

9155 Las Vegas Blvd., at Serene St. ☎ **702/897-9090.** Mon–Sat 10am–8pm, Sun 10am–6pm.

A 30-acre open-air mall with Spanish-style architecture, this is the only outlet center in the country with a casino bar/lounge on its premises. Its 41 stores include Corning/Revere, Izod, Mikasa, American Tourister, Van Heusen, B.U.M. Equipment, Spiegel, London Fog, VF (sportswear), Book Warehouse, Geoffrey Beene, and Adolfo II. Come here for clothing, housewares, shoes, china, and much, much more.

3 Hotel Shopping Arcades

Just about every Las Vegas hotel offers some shopping opportunities. The following have the most extensive arcades. *Note:* The Forum Shops at Caesars—as much a sightseeing attraction as a shopping arcade—are in the must-see category.

BALLY'S Bally's Avenue Shoppes number around 20 emporia offering pro team sports apparel, toys, clothing (men's, women's, and children's), logo items, gourmet chocolates, liquor, jewelry, nuts and dried fruit, flowers, handbags, and T-shirts. In addition, there are several gift shops, three restaurants, art galleries, and a pool-wear shop. There are blackjack tables and slot and video poker machines right in the mall, as well as a race and sports book. You can dispatch the kids to a video arcade here while you shop.

CAESARS PALACE Since 1978, Caesars has had an impressive arcade of shops called the Appian Way. Highlighted by an immense white Carrara-marble replica of Michelangelo's *David* standing more than 18 feet high, its shops include the aptly named Galerie Michelangelo (original and limited-edition artworks), jewelers (including branches of Ciro and Cartier), a logo merchandise shop, and several shops for upscale men's and women's clothing. All in all, a respectable grouping of hotel shops, and an expansion is in the works.

But in the hotel's tradition of constantly surpassing itself, in 1992 Caesars inaugurated the fabulous Forum Shops, an independently operated 250,000-square-foot Rodeo-Drive-meets-the-Roman-Empire affair complete with a 48-foot triumphal arch entranceway, a painted Mediterranean sky that changes as the day progresses from rosy-tinted dawn to twinkling evening stars, acres of marble, lofty scagliola Corinthian columns with gold capitals, and a welcoming goddess of fortune under a central dome. Its architecture and sculpture span a period from 300 B.C. to A.D. 1700. Storefront facades, some topped with statues of Roman senators, resemble a classical Italian streetscape, with archways, piazzas, ornate fountains, and a barrel-vaulted ceiling. The "center of town" is the magnificent domed Fountain of the Gods, where Jupiter rules from his mountaintop surrounded by Pegasus, Mars, Venus, Neptune, and Diana. And at the Festival Fountain, seemingly immovable "marble" animatronic statues of Bacchus (slightly in his cups), a lyre-playing Apollo, Plutus, and Venus come to life for a 7-minute revel with dancing waters and high-tech laser-light effects. The shows take place every hour on the hour. The whole thing is pretty incredible, but also very Vegas, particularly the Bacchus show, which is truly frightening and bizarre. Even if you don't like shopping, it's worth the stroll just to giggle.

More than 70 prestigious emporia here include Louis Vuitton, Plaza Escada, Bernini, Christian Dior, A/X Armani Exchange, bebe, Caché, Gucci, Ann Taylor, and Gianni Versace, along with many other clothing, shoe, and accessory shops. Other notables include: a Warner Brothers Studio Store (a sign at the exit reads thatius finitus folkus), The Disney Store, Kids Kastle (beautiful children's clothing and toys), Rose of Sharon (classy styles for large-size women), Sports Logo (buy a basketball signed by Michael Jordan for $695!), Field of Dreams (more autographed sports memorabilia), Museum Company (reproductions ranging from 16th-century hand-painted Turkish boxes to ancient Egyptian scarab necklaces), West of Santa Fe (Western wear and Native American jewelry and crafts), Antiquities (neon Shell gas signs, 1950s malt machines, Americana; sometimes "Elvis" is on hand), Endangered Species Store (ecology-themed merchandise), Brookstone (one-of-a-kind items from garden tools to sports paraphernalia), and Victoria's Secret. There's much more, including jewelry shops and art galleries.

A new 283,000-square-foot expansion, including 37 stores and two new restaurants, has just been completed. New residents include FAO Schwartz, Fendi, Polo, NikeTown, a Virgin Records megastore, and Wolfgang Puck's Asian Cafe. The centerpiece of the new area will be a Roman Great Hall of heroic proportions, featuring a dramatic high-tech interactive attraction called "Atlantis."

While you shop, send the kids downstairs for spine-tingling Motion-Simulator Cinema Rides in 3-D. Four 5-minute shows simulate a flight into outer space to destroy a runaway nuclear missile, a submarine race through the ancient ruins of Atlantis, a bicycle ride through a haunted graveyard, and a roller-coaster adventure. (Price is $6 for one film, $8 for a double feature. Children must be at least 42 inches high.)

Dining choices range from a pastrami on rye at the Stage Deli, to a thick, juicy steak at The Palm, to Wolfgang Puck's sublime Spago creations. Several Forum Shops restaurants are described in chapter 6.

The shops are open Sunday to Thursday from 10am to 11pm, Friday and Saturday 10am to midnight. An automated walkway transports people from the Strip to the shopping complex. Heralded by a marble temple housing four golden horses and a charioteer, it is flanked by flaming torchiers and fronted by a waterfall cascading over a bas-relief of the god Neptune—you can't miss it! Often a gladiator with sword and shield is there to greet you at the other end. Valet parking is available.

CIRCUS CIRCUS   About 15 shops between the casino and Grand Slam Canyon which offer a wide selection of gifts and sundries, logo items, toys and games, jewelry, liquor, resort apparel for the entire family, T-shirts, homemade fudge/candy/soft ice cream, and, fittingly, clown dolls and puppets. At Amazing Pictures you can have your photo taken as a pinup girl, muscle man, or whatever else your fantasy dictates. Adjacent to Grand Slam Canyon, there is a new shopping arcade themed along a European village, with cobblestone walkways and fake woods and so forth, decorated with replicas of vintage circus posters. It's much nicer than the tacky Circus Circus has had before. Among the stores are Marshall Russo, Headliners, The Sweet Tooth, and Carousel Classics.

EXCALIBUR   The shops of "The Realm," for the most part reflect the hotel's medieval theme. Dragon's Lair, for example, features items ranging from pewter swords and shields to full suits of armor, and Merlin's Mystic Shop carries crystals, luck charms, and gargoyles. Other shops carry more conventional wares—gifts, candy, jewelry, women's clothing, and Excalibur logo items. A child pleaser is Kids of the Kingdom, which displays licensed character merchandise from Disney, Looney Tunes, Garfield, and Snoopy. Wild Bill's carries Western wear and Native American jewelry and crafts. And at Fantasy Faire you can have your photo taken in Renaissance attire.

FLAMINGO HILTON   The Crystal Court shopping promenade here accommodates men's and women's clothing/accessories stores, gift shops, and a variety of other emporia selling jewelry, beachwear, Southwestern crafts, fresh-baked goods, logo items, children's gifts, toys, and games.

HARRAH'S   Harrah's is finishing up a massive new renovation which includes a new shopping center to be called Carnivale Court that will include party stores, Ghirardelli Chocolate, and a magic store. It will all be outdoors, and live entertainment will be strolling around, and playing on a bandshell.

LUXOR HOTEL/CASINO   Its new 20,000 square foot shopping arcade will be finished by 1998. Previously, it had The Source, on the lower level, where you'll find museum-quality Egyptian antiquities such as an alabaster portrait of Ptolemy V (205 B.C.) for $3,000 or a bronze Isis statue (664–25 B.C.) for $10,000. More affordable are beautiful Egyptian jewelry (both straight reproductions and Egypt-inspired designs), gift items (mother-of-pearl inlay boxes and tables, paintings, pottery, scarabs, and amulets), and books about ancient Egypt.

THE MGM GRAND   The hotel's Star Lane Shops include more than a dozen upscale emporia lining the corridors en route from the monorail entrance. The Knot Shop carries designer ties by Calvin Klein, Gianni Versace, and others. El Portal features luggage and handbags—Coach, Dior, Fendi, Polo Ralph Lauren, and other exclusive lines. Grand 50's carries *Route 66* jackets, Elvis T-shirts, photos of James Dean, and other mementos of the 1950s. MGM Grand Sports sells signed athletic uniforms, baseballs autographed by Michael Jordan, and the like; it is the scene of occasional appearances by sports stars such as Floyd Patterson and Stan Musial. You can choose an oyster and have its pearl set in jewelry at The Pearl Factory. Other Star Lane Shops specialize in movie memorabilia, Betty Boop merchandise, *EFX* wares, children's clothing, decorative magnets, MGM Grand logo items and Las Vegas souvenirs, seashells and coral, candy, and sunglasses. Refreshments are available at a Häagen-Dazs ice cream counter and Yummy's Coffees and Desserts. In other parts of the hotel, retail shops include a *Wizard of Oz* gift shop, Front Page (for newspapers, books, magazines, and sundries), a spa shop selling everything from beachwear to top-of-the-line European skin care products, a liquor store, a candy store, Kenneth J. Lane jewelry, and Marshall Rousso (men's and women's clothing). In addition, theme park emporia sell Hollywood memorabilia, cameras and photographic supplies, MGM Grand and theme park logo products, toys, fine china and crystal, animation cels, collectibles (limited-edition dolls, plates, figurines), Hollywood-themed clothing and accessories, and Western wear. At Arts and Crafts you can watch artisans working in leather, glass, wood, pottery, and other materials, and at Photoplay Gallery, you can have your picture taken as *Time* magazine's man or woman of the year.

MONTE CARLO An arcade of retail shops here includes Bon Vivant (resort wear for the whole family, dress wear for men), Crown Jewels (jewelry, leather bags, crystal, Fabergé eggs, gift items), a florist, logo shop, jeweler, food market, dessert store, and Lance Burton magic paraphernalia shop.

RIO The new 60,000-square-foot Masquerade Village is a nicely done addition to the Rio. It's done as a European village, and is two stories, featuring a wide variety of shops including the nation's largest Nicole Miller, Speedo, and the N'awlins store, which includes "authentic" voodoo items, Mardi Gras masks, and so forth. It's attached to a cafe that sells beignets (from Cafe Du Monde mix) and chicory coffee.

THE RIVIERA The Riviera has a fairly extensive shopping arcade comprising art galleries, jewelers, a creative photographer, and shops specializing in women's shoes and handbags, clothing for the entire family, furs, gifts, logo items, toys, phones and electronic gadgets, and chocolates.

SAM'S TOWN Though Sam's Town does not contain a notably significant shopping arcade, it does house the huge Western Emporium (almost department-store size) selling Western clothing for men and women, boots (an enormous selection), jeans, belts, silver and turquoise jewelry, Stetson hats, Native American crafts, gift items, and old-fashioned candy. You can have your picture taken here in period western costume. Open daily at 9am; closing hours vary.

STRATOSPHERE Shopping is no afterthought here. The internationally themed second floor Tower Shops promenade, which will soon house 40 stores, is entered off an escalator from the casino. Some shops are in "Paris," along the Rue Lafayette and Avenue de l'Opéra (there are replicas of the Eiffel Tower and Arc de Triomphe in this section). Others occupy Hong Kong and New York City streetscapes. Already-extant emporia include: The Money Company (money-motif items from T-shirts to golf balls), a T-shirt store, a magic shop, Key West (body lotions and more), Victoria's Secret, a magnet shop, Norma Kaplan (for glitzy/sexy women's footwear), an electronics boutique, a logo shop, and several gift shops. There are branches of Jitters (a coffee house) and Häagen-Dazs, and stores are supplemented by cart vendors.

TREASURE ISLAND Treasure Island's shopping promenade—doubling as a portrait gallery of famed buccaneers (Blackbeard, Jean Lafitte, Calico Jack, Barbarosa)—has wooden ship figureheads and battling pirates suspended from its ceiling. Emporia here include the Treasure Island Store (your basic hotel gift/sundry shop, also offering much pirate-themed merchandise, plus a section devoted to Calvin Klein clothing), Loot 'n' Booty, Candy Reef, Captain Kid's (children's clothing), and Damsels in Dis'Dress (women's sportswear and accessories). The Mutiny Bay Shop, in the video-game arcade, carries logo items and stuffed animals. In the casino are the Buccaneer Bay Shoppe (logo merchandise) and the Treasure Chest (a jewelry store; spend those

---

Impressions

As for Vegas—it couldn't be much weirder if this town were on the moon. The place just seems to pulse with whatever it is that makes the weirdness weird. The place feeds on it. Likes it. And the weirdest thing is—it always has.
　　　　　　　　　　　　　—Michael Ventura, *Las Vegas: The Odds on Anything*

winnings right on the spot). And the Crow's Nest, en route to the Mirage monorail, carries Cirque du Soleil logo items. Cirque du Soleil and Mystère logo wares are also sold in a shop near the ticket office.

4 Vintage Clothing

The Attic

1018 S. Main St. ☎ **702/388-4088.** Daily 9am–6pm. MC, V.

Sharing a large space with **Cafe Neon,** a coffeehouse that also serves Greek-influenced cafe food (so you can raise your blood sugar again after a long stretch of shopping), and a comedy club stage, and upstairs from an attempt at a weekly club (as of this writing, the Saturday night Underworld), The Attic has plenty of clothing choices on many racks. During a recent visit, a man came in asking for a poodle skirt for his 8-year-old. They had one.

Buffalo Exchange

4110 S. Maryland Parkway, at Flamingo, near Tower Records. ☎ **702/791-3960.** Mon–Sat 11am–8pm, Sun 12pm–6pm. MC, V.

This is actually part of a chain of such stores spread out across the western United States. If the chain part worries you, don't let it—this merchandise doesn't feel processed. Staffed by plenty of incredibly hip alt-culture kids (ask them for what's happening in town during your visit), it is stuffed with dresses, shirts, pants, and so forth. Like any vintage shop, the contents are hit and miss; you can easily go in one day and come out with 12 fabulous new outfits, but you can just as easily go in and come up dry. It is probably the most reliable of the local vintage shops.

The Haight

1647 E. Charleston. ☎ **702/387-7818.** Mon–Sat 11am–6pm, Sun 12pm–5pm. Cash and checks only.

Upstairs from an antique store, this is in a small old house, and so not only is the stock in various rooms, they've turned the retro-tiled bathroom into the dressing room. They have a large selection of used Levi's and otherwise specialize in '60s and '70s vintage clothing.

Our House

1639 E. Charleston. Sun–Fri 11am–6pm, Sat 10am–6pm.

A tiny store filled with the most happening in new and vintage clothing (think club kid wear) and some new jewelry designs. Not a huge selection, but very kinda now, kinda wow. No phone at this time (you can always check Information) but they are right next door to the Haight and the start of the Charleston antique row.

5 Reading Material: Used Books, Comics & a Notable Newsstand

USED BOOKS

Dead Poet Books

3858 W. Sahara (corner of Valley View, near Albertson's). ☎ **702/227-4070.** Mon–Sat 10am–6pm, Sun 12pm–5pm. AE, DISC, MC, V.

Eliot? Byron? Tennyson? None of the above. Actually, the dead poet in question was a man from whose estate the owners bought their start-up stock. He had such good taste in books, they "fell in love with him" and wanted to name the store in his memory. Just one problem—they never did get his name. So they just called him "the dead poet." He wasn't a poet, but surely anyone with such fine taste in books must have been one in his soul. His legacy continues is this book-lover's haven.

Parkland Books

3661 Maryland Pkwy. (corner of Twain, in the Maryland Square). ☎ **702/732-4474.** Mon–Sat 10am–6pm. DISC, MC, V.

Heavy on the hardbacks and the nonfiction, this nicely musty store offers used and out-of-print stock.

A LAS VEGAS SPECIALTY STORE

Gambler's Book Shop

630 S. 11th St., just off Charleston Blvd. ☎ **800/522-1777** or 702/382-7555. Mon–Sat 9am–5pm.

Here you can buy a book on any system ever devised to beat casino odds. Owner Edna Luckman carries more than 4,000 gambling-related titles, including many out-of-print books, computer software, and videotapes. She describes her store as a place where "gamblers, writers, researchers, statisticians, and computer specialists can meet and exchange information." On request, knowledgeable clerks provide on-the-spot expert advice on handicapping the ponies and other aspects of sports betting. The store's motto is "knowledge is protection."

COMIC BOOKS

Alternative Reality Comics

4800 S. Maryland Pkwy. ☎ **702/736-3673.** Mon–Sat. 11am–7pm, Sun 12pm–6pm.

The place in Vegas for all your comic book needs. They have a nearly comprehensive selection, with a heavy emphasis on the underground comics. But don't worry, the superheroes are here, too.

A NOTABLE NEWSSTAND

International Newsstand

3900 Paradise (in Citibank Plaza). ☎ **702/796-9901.** Daily 8:30am–9pm. AE, MC, V.

Homesick for local news? No matter where you are from, come here. It's crammed full of seemingly every city newspaper in the land, plus a large selection of foreign cities. They surely don't have everything, but it seems like they do. Okay, the actual count is every major U.S., city, plus 10 other countries. One impressed shopper said this would put many a formerly worthy newsstand in any cosmopolitan city to shame. There is also a wide array of magazines, both foreign and domestic, though they get less space than at other newsstands thanks to the newspapers.

6 Antiques

Antiques in Vegas? You mean really old slot machines, or the people playing the really old slot machines?

Actually, Vegas has quite a few antique stores—nearly two dozen, of consistent quality and price, nearly all located within a few blocks of each other. We have one friend, someone who takes interior design *very* seriously, who comes straight to Vegas for most of her best finds (you should see her antique chandelier collection!).

To get there, start in the middle of the 1600 block of E. Charleston and keep driving east. The little stores, nearly all in old houses dating from the '30s, line each side of the street. Or you can stop in at **Silver Horse Antiques** (1651 E. Charleston) and pick up a map to almost all the locations, with phone numbers and hours of operation.

Las Vegas After Dark 10

You will not lack for things to do at night in Vegas. It is a town that truly comes alive only at night. Don't believe us? Just look at the difference between the Strip during the day, when it's kind of dingy and nothing special, and at night when the lights hit and the place glows in all its glory. Night is when it's happening in this 24-hour town. In fact, most bars and clubs don't even get going until close to midnight. That's because it's only around then that all the many restaurant workers and people connected with the shows get off the clock and can go out and play themselves. It's extraordinary. Just sit down in a bar at 11pm; it's empty. You might well conclude it's dead. Return in 2 hours and find it completely full and jumping.

But you also won't lack for things to do before 11pm. There are shows all over town, ranging from traditional magic to cutting-edge acts like *Mystère*. The showgirls remain, topless and otherwise; Las Vegas revues are what happened to vaudeville, by the way, as chorus girls do their thing in between jugglers, comics, magicians, singers, and specialty acts of dubious category. Even the topless ones are tame; all that changes is the that already scantily clad showgirls are even more so.

Every hotel has at least one lounge, usually offering live music. The days of fabulous Vegas lounge entertainment, where sometimes the acts were of better quality than the headliners (and headliners like Sinatra would join the lounge acts onstage between their own sets), are gone. Most of what remains are homogenous and bland, and serve best as a brief respite or background noise. On the other hand, finding the most awful lounge act in town can be rewarding on its own. (To this end, seek out Cook E. Jarr and the Crumbs, a rapidly aging and tasteless crew universally revered as the worst lounge act in Vegas. They were last spotted at the Continental Hotel.)

Vegas still does attract the best in headliner entertainment in its showrooms and arenas. Bette Midler did an HBO special from the MGM Grand in early 1997, and U2 started its PopArt tour at UNLV's stadium. Liza Minnelli, Harry Belafonte, Penn and Teller, Melissa Manchester, Wayne Newton, Chaka Khan, Johnny Mathis, Barbara Mandrell, Englebert Humperdick, and Wynnona have all played Vegas recently. (And up until just a few years ago, the legendary Sinatra still did regular stints there.) It is still a badge of honor for comedians to play Vegas, and there is almost always someone of marquee value playing one showroom or the other.

Of course, if you prefer alternative or real rock music, your choices are more limited. More rock bands are coming through town, attracted to either the Hard Rock Hotel's venue or the Huntridge Theater, so that means you can actually see folks like Marilyn Manson and Beck in Vegas. But otherwise, the alternative club scene in town is severely limited. Check out the listings below for bars and coffeehouses, several of which offer live alternative or blues music.

If want to know what is playing there during your stay, consult local free alternative papers the *Scope* (biweekly, with great club and bar descriptions in their listings) and *City Life* (weekly, with no descriptions but comprehensive listings of what's playing where all over town). Both can be picked up at restaurants, bars, record and music stores, and hep retail stores. Or you can call *Scope* directly; act nice, and they might just give you a tip on the spot. If you are looking for good alt-culture tips, try asking the cool staff at the **Buffalo Exchange** vintage clothing store; they have their fingers right on the pulse of the underground (☎ 702/791-3960).

Admission to shows runs the gamut, from about $18.95 for *An Evening at La Cage* (a female impersonator show at the Riviera) to $80 and more for top headliners or *Siegfried and Roy*. Prices usually include two drinks or, in rare instances, dinner.

To find out who will be performing during your stay, and for up-to-date listings of shows (prices change, shows close), you can call the various hotels featuring headliner entertainment, using toll-free numbers. Or call the **Las Vegas Convention and Visitors Authority** (☎ 702/892-0711) and ask them to send you a free copy of *Showguide or What's On in Las Vegas* (one or both of which will probably be in your hotel room.)

Every hotel entertainment option is described below with information on ticket prices, what is included in the price (drinks, dinner, taxes, and/or gratuities), showroom policies (as to preassigned or maître d' seating and smoking), and how to make reservations. Whenever possible, reserve in advance, especially on weekends and holidays. If the showroom has maître d' seating (as opposed to assigned seats), you may want to tip him to upgrade your seat. A tip of $15 to $20 per couple will usually do the trick at a major show, less at a small showroom. An alternative to tipping the maître d' is to wait until the captain shows you to your seat. Perhaps it will be adequate, in which case you've saved some money. If not, you can offer the captain a tip for a better seat. If you do plan to tip, have the money ready; maître d's and captains tend to get annoyed if you fumble around for it. They have other people to seat. You can also tip with casino chips (from the hotel casino where the show is taking place only) in lieu of cash. Whatever you tip, the proper etiquette is to do it rather subtly—a kind of palm-to-palm action. There's really no reason for this, since everyone knows what's going on, but being blatant is in poor taste. Arrive early at maître d' shows to get the best choice of seats.

If you buy tickets for an assigned-seat show in person, you can look over a seating chart. Avoid sitting right up by the stage if possible, especially for big production shows. Dance numbers are better viewed from the middle of the theater. With headliners, you might like to sit up close.

Note: All of these caveats and instructions aside, most casino-hotel showrooms offer good visibility from just about every seat in the house.

In addition to the below listed, consider the Fremont Street Experience and Sunset Stampede at Sam's Town, both described in chapter 7.

1 What's Playing Where

It used to be that a show was an essential part of the Vegas experience. Back in those days, a show was pretty simple: a bunch of scantily clad (and we mean scantily—topless shows were part of the fun) showgirls paraded around while a comedian engaged in some raunchy patter. The showgirls are still here, and still scantily clad (though not as often topless; guess cable TV has taken some of that thrill away), but the productions around them have gotten impossibly elaborate. And they have to be; they have to compete with a free pirate battle stunt show held several times nightly right on the Strip. Not to mention a volcano, a Mardi Gras parade in the sky, lounge acts galore, and the occasional imploding building. All for free. The big resort hotels, in keeping with their general over-the top-tendencies, are pouring mountains of money into high-spectacle extravaganzas, luring big-name acts into decades-long residencies and surrounding them with special effects that would put some Hollywood movies to shame.

Unfortunately, along with big budgets come big ticket prices. Sure, you can still take the family to a show for under $100, but you're not going to see the same production values for the same $100 that might almost get you two tickets to EFX. Which is not to say you always get what you pay for: There are some reasonably priced shows that are considerably better values than their more expensive counterparts.

OUR FAVORITES   The "Best Show" is definitely *Mystère* at the Treasure Island. The best magic show, and one of the most reasonably priced productions (and thus overall best value for the money) is Lance Burton at Monte Carlo. Best classic Vegas topless revue is *Jubilee!* at Bally's. Best modern-day Vegas production is *EFX* at MGM Grand.

The following section will describe, by name, each of the major production shows currently playing in Las Vegas. But we begin by listing each major hotel and the production show(s) playing there in the event you want to catch a show in a particular location:

- Aladdin Hotel, *Country Tonite* (country music review)
- Bally's, ✪ *Jubilee!* (Las Vegas–style review)
- Debbie Reynolds Hotel, ✪ *Kenny Kerr Show* (female impersonators) and the ✪ *Debbie Reynolds Show* (Las Vegas–style review featuring Debbie)
- Excalibur, *An Evening in Vienna* (afternoon show featuring the Lippizaner Stallions, described in chapter 7) and *King Arthur's Tournament* (medieval-themed review)
- Flamingo Hilton, *Forever Plaid* (off-Broadway review featuring '60s music) and *The Great Radio City Spectacular* (Las Vegas–style review featuring the Radio City Music Hall Rockettes)
- Golden Nugget, ✪ *Country Fever* (country music review)
- Harrah's, *Spellbound* (magic review)
- Imperial Palace, *Legends in Concert* (musical impersonators)
- Jackie Gaughan's Plaza, *The Xtreme Scene* (sexy Las Vegas–style review)
- Las Vegas Hilton, *Starlight Express* (Andrew Lloyd Webber's Broadway show)
- MGM Grand, ✪ *EFX* (special-effects review featuring David Cassidy)
- The Mirage, ✪ *Siegfried and Roy* (magical extravaganza)
- Monte Carlo, ✪ *Lance Burton: Master Magician* (magic show and review)
- Rio Suite Hotel, *Danny Gans* (impressions)
- Riviera Hotel, *An Evening at La Cage* (female impersonators), *Crazy Girls* (sexy Las Vegas–style review), and *Splash* (aquatic review)

- Stardust, *Enter the Night* (Las Vegas–style review)
- Stratosphere Tower, *American Superstars* (an impression-filled production show), *Viva Las Vegas* (Las Vegas–style review)
- Treasure Island, ✪ Cirque du Soleil's *Mystère* (unique circus performance)
- Tropicana, *Folies Bergère* (Las Vegas–style review)

2 The Major Production Shows

This category covers production shows major and minor, including country music shows, magic shows, female impersonator shows, and racy revues like Teeze and Xposed.

American Superstars
Stratosphere, 2000 Las Vegas Blvd. S. ☎ **800/99-TOWER** or 702/380-7777.

One of the increasing number of celebrity impersonator shows (cheaper than getting the real headliners), "American Superstars" is one of the few where said impersonators actually sing live. Five performers do their thing; celebs impersonated vary depending on the evening. A typical Friday night featured Gloria Estefan, Charlie Daniels, Madonna, Michael Jackson, and Diana Ross and the Supremes. The performers won't be putting the originals out of work anytime soon, but they aren't bad. Actually, they are closer in voice than in looks to the celeb in question (half the black performers were played by white actors), which is an unusual switch for Vegas impersonators. The "Charlie Daniels" actually proved to be a fine fiddler in his own right and was the hands-down crowd favorite. The live band actually had a look-alike of their own: Kato Kaelin on drums (it's good that he's getting work). The youngish crowd (by Vegas standards) included a healthy smattering of children, and seemed to find no faults with the production. The action is also shown on two large, and completely unnecessary, video screens flanking the stage, so you don't have to miss a moment.

- **Showroom Policies:** Smoking not permitted; maître d' seating.
- **Price:** Admission $25.25 includes tax.
- **Show Times:** Fri–Wed at 8 and 10pm. Dark Thurs.
- **Reservations:** up to 3 days in advance.

✪ Cirque du Soleil's *Mystère*
Treasure Island, 3300 Las Vegas Blvd. S. ☎ **800/392-1999** or 702/894-7723.

The in-house ads for *Mystère* (say miss-*tair*) say "Words don't do it justice," and for once, that's not just hype. The show is so visual that trying to describe it is a losing proposition. And simply calling it a circus is like calling the Hope Diamond a gem, or the Taj Mahal a building. It's accurate, but something seems a little left out of the description.

Cirque de Soleil began in Montréal as a unique circus experience, not only shunning the traditional animal acts in favor of gorgeous feats of human strength and agility, but also adding elements of the surreal and the absurd. The result seems like a collaboration between Salvador Dali and Luis Buñel, with a few touches by Magritte and choreography by Twyla Tharp. Mirage Resorts has built them their own theater, an incredible space with an enormous dome and super hydraulics that allow for the Cirque performers to fly in space. Or so it seems.

While part of the fun of the early Cirque was seeing what amazing stuff they could do on a shoestring, seeing what they can do with virtually unlimited funds is spectacular. Unlike, arguably, other artistic ventures, Cirque took full advantage of their new largess, and their art only rose with their budget. The show features one

Impressions

I've built my own world here. Wayne's world.
> —Las Vegas superstar Wayne Newton talking about his
> 52-acre estate, Casa de Shenandoah, 5 miles out of town

simply unbelievable act after another (seemingly boneless contortionists and acrobats, breathtakingly beautiful aerial maneuvers), interspersed with Dada-ist, commedia dell'arte clowns, and everyone clad in costumes like nothing you've ever seen before. All this and a giant snail. The show is dreamlike, suspenseful, funny, erotic, mesmerizing, and just lovely. At times, you might even find yourself moved to tears. However, for some children, it might be a bit too sophisticated and arty. Even if you've seen Cirque before, it's worth coming to check out, thanks to the large production values. It's a world-class show, no matter where it's playing. That this is playing in Vegas is astonishing.

- **Showroom Policies:** Nonsmoking with preassigned seating.
- **Price:** $64.90 adults, $32.40 for children under 11 (drinks and tax extra).
- **Show Times:** Wed–Sun at 7:30 and 10:30pm. Dark Mon–Tues.
- **Reservations:** You can reserve by phone via credit card up to 7 days in advance (do reserve early since it often sells out).

✪ Country Fever
Golden Nugget, 129 E. Fremont St. ☎ **800/777-4658** or 702/386-8100.

A few years back, the Golden Nugget redecorated its showroom walls with a display of Western paraphernalia, neon cacti, steer heads, and cowboy boots. It's the setting for *Country Fever:* the best foot-stompin', hand-clappin' country music show in town, featuring a cast of tremendously talented singers and dancers, including bare-buttocks showgirls in fringed country thongs and cowboy boots (this *is* Las Vegas!). They're backed up by an outstanding nine-piece band called The Posse. The cast also includes a gospel choir and a first-rate stand-up comic, Kirby St. Romaine. Special kudos to the exuberant star of the show, T. J. Weaver. Since light fare is served, arrive at least an hour early, so you're through with it when the show begins.

- **Showroom Policies:** Nonsmoking with maître d' seating.
- **Price:** $25 (including a drink and a basket of taco chips with two dipping sauces and chicken tenders; gratuity extra).
- **Show Times:** Sat–Thurs at 7 and 9:45pm. Dark Fri.
- **Reservations:** You can reserve up to 4 days in advance.

Country Tonite
Aladdin Hotel, 3667 Las Vegas Blvd. S. ☎ **800/637-8133** or 702/736-0240.

The Aladdin presents *Country Tonite*, a lively revue with plenty of singin', fiddlin', guitar strummin', and foot-stompin' Western dances. Highlights include Karen Brownlee's rendition of the legendary Patsy Kline's "Sweet Dreams," a lasso- and gun-twirling exhibition, cloggers, a "Devil Went Down to Georgia" fiddling contest, and the antics of ventriloquist Sammy King and his Mexican parrot dummy. The show ends in a patriotic finale, with American flags flanking the stage and the cast performing "America the Beautiful," "All Gave Some, Some Gave All," "God Bless the USA," "Stand Up," and "We Shall Be Free."

- **Showroom Policies:** Nonsmoking with maître d' seating.
- **Price:** $21.95 adults, $15.35 for children under 11. With buffet adults pay $26.20, children $18.55.

- **Show Times:** Wed–Mon at 7:15 and 10pm. Dark Tues.
- **Reservations:** You can reserve up to 2 weeks in advance by phone.

Crazy Girls
Riviera Hotel, 2901 Las Vegas Blvd. S. ☎ **800/634-3420** or 702/734-9301.

Crazy Girls, presented in an intimate theater, is probably the raciest revue on the Strip. It features sexy showgirls with perfect bodies in erotic song and dance numbers enhanced by innovative lighting effects. Think of *Penthouse* poses come to life. Perhaps it's best summed up by one older man from Kentucky: "It's okay if you like boobs and butt. But most of the girls can't even dance."

- **Showroom Policies:** Nonsmoking with maître d' seating.
- **Price:** General admission $23.36, VIP admission $28.86 (includes two drinks; gratuity extra).
- **Show Times:** Tues–Sun at 8:30 and 10:30pm, with an extra midnight show Sat. Dark Mon.
- **Reservations:** Tickets can be purchased at the box office and over the phone, in advance if you wish.

✪ Danny Gans: The Man of Many Voices
Rio Suites, 3700 W. Flamingo Rd. ☎ **800/PLAY-RIO** or 702/252-7777.

Danny Gans has taken over the newly refurbished Copacobana Showroom for an indefinite run. If he's still on when you visit, don't miss him. Gans, who has starred on Broadway, is an impressionist extraordinaire. Natalie Cole, who heard him perform her father's famous song, "Unforgettable," exclaimed, "No one has ever done a better impression of my dad." His show is also unforgettable. In addition to startlingly realistic impressions of dozens of singers (everyone from Sinatra to Springsteen), he does movie scenes (such as Fonda and Hepburn in *On Golden Pond),* Bill Clinton, weird duets (Michael Bolton and Dr. Ruth, or Stevie Wonder singing to Shirley MacLaine "I Just Called to Say I Was You"), and, of course, a first-rate Elvis. A mind-boggling highlight is Gans's rendition of "The Twelve Days of Christmas" in 12 different voices, which necessitates rapidly switching back and forth from such diverse impressions as Paul Lynde, Clint Eastwood, Peter Falk, and Woody Allen, among others. This show gets a standing ovation every night.

- **Showroom Policies:** Nonsmoking with maître d' seating.
- **Price:** $44.95 (including two drinks, tax and gratuities).
- **Show Times:** Wed–Sun at 8pm. Dark Mon–Tues.
- **Reservations:** Tickets can be ordered up to 30 days in advance.

Debbie Reynolds Show
Debbie Reynolds Hotel, 305 Convention Center Dr. ☎ **800/633-1777** or 702/7-DEBBIE.

Note: This is a show that occurs only when Debbie Reynolds is in town, which is hard to predict with her increasingly busy movie schedule.

The very talented and boundlessly energetic Debbie Reynolds projects a warmth and relaxed stage presence seen only in the most seasoned of pros. And her beautiful 500-seat, state-of-the-art Star Theatre (son Todd Fisher designed it) is filled to bursting with devoted fans at every performance. Debbie, as cute and exuberant as ever, sings shows clips from her famous movies (like *Singin' in the Rain* and *The Tender Trap),* does impressions (her repertoire includes Katharine Hepburn, Bette Davis, Mae West, Zsa Zsa Gabor, Dolly Parton, Edith Bunker, and Barbra Streisand), cracks jokes, tells stories about her Hollywood heyday, and mingles with the audience. She is ably assisted by the Uptown Country Singers, who perform popular country music songs and sing and dance with Debbie. The show ends with a tribute to the big-band era. After each performance Debbie meets fans in the showroom to sign autographs and pose for pictures.

- **Showroom Policies:** Nonsmoking with maître d' seating.
- **Price:** $39.95 (includes tax, two drinks, and gratuity).
- **Show Times:** Mon–Fri at 7:30pm. Dark Sat–Sun.
- **Reservations:** You can reserve by phone up to 3 days in advance.

✪ EFX

MGM Grand, 3799 Las Vegas Blvd. S. ☎ **800/929-1111** or 702/891-7777.

Essentially the first major show of the post–Cirque de Soliel era, *EFX*'s $40 million makeover (thanks to new star David Cassidy) has used its money wisely, updating the classic Vegas revue into essentially a live action version of the modern over-the-top Strip hotels. It's not so much cheese anymore, as expensive and occasionally jaw-dropping cheese. Which is not to say it's bad—quite the opposite. The nominal story line, about a man who has lost his imagination, allows the very likable Cassidy, playing on his regular guy image, to assume the personas of King Arthur, P. T. Barnum, Houdini, and H. G. Wells, in order to deliver set pieces of better than usual dancing, magic, singing, acrobatics, and illusion. And, of course, special effects ("EFX" is the movie industry term for same). The sets are lavish beyond belief; the costumes and some of the acting show the Cirque influence (faintly Grand Guignol); and the choreography is considerably more imaginative and fresh than any other such show in town. The songs are somewhat bland, but sung almost totally live, and some prove surprisingly hummable. And the effects (flying saucers and cast members, fire-breathing dragons, 3-D time travel, lots of explosions) show where the money is. Cranks may occasionally spot wires, and sometimes said effects are a little painful on the eyes and ears (and they overdo it on the fog machine). The ticket price isn't cheap, so it might be worth taking the less-expensive seats in the mezzanine, as the view is just as good from there.

- **Showroom Policies:** Nonsmoking with preassigned seating.
- **Price:** $51.50–$72.
- **Show Times:** Tues–Sat at 7:30 and 10:30pm. Dark Sun–Mon.
- **Reservations:** You can reserve by phone any time in advance.

Enter the Night

The Stardust, 3000 Las Vegas Blvd. S. ☎ **800/824-6033** or 702/732-6111.

It's kind of cute how the Stardust has tried to stage a full-size topless revue on a small-to medium-size stage. Okay, maybe not *cute,* but the production does seem to be busting at its seams, and it never quite reconciles its aspirations with its reality. There is no plot or point to this; the theme is "enter the night" (of course) and about the passion and mystery that will then ensue, but the songs and actions are vague as to how this is supposed to come about. Instead, what you get is one of those "why is that girl parading around in her underwear?" sort of shows. It's a question that can be quite relevant, depending on your seats, since a circular catwalk extends into the audience; some seats are perched right on the rail edge of this, virtually squashing the occupant's face into a showgirl's midriff. In fact, some of those topless breasts could put out an eye. (Besides, it spoils the illusion when you are close enough to see all that pancake makeup.) Your seat placement is worth noting for this reason, if you don't want to be that up close and personal with a virtually naked total stranger. Others might pay extra.

Anyway, it's a revue, featuring songs about listening to your heart, dancing (the Space Age Viking dance number was a camp highlight), and one blonde (presumably Aki, "Showgirl for the 21st Century") in a flesh-colored G-string performing nearly nude *en pointe* ballet. All this is delivered with a Mickey Mouse Club enthusiasm, which is a bit disconcerting when half the performers are partially naked. There is also nearly naked ice skating, which was actually better than you might think; the skaters are very good and make use of the world's tiniest patch of ice in dramatic and resourceful ways. They were also a huge crowd pleaser, as was the delightful Argentinean gaucho act.

- **Showroom Policies:** Nonsmoking with preassigned seating.
- **Price:** Most seats $29.85, booths $35 to $55 (includes two drinks, tax and gratuity).
- **Show Times:** Tues, Wed, Thurs, Sat at 7:30 and 10:30pm; Sun–Mon at 8pm only. Dark Fri.
- **Reservations:** You can reserve up to a month in advance by phone.

An Evening at La Cage

Riviera Hotel and Casino, 2901 Las Vegas Blvd. S. ☎ **800/634-6753** or 702/734-9301.

No, not inspired by the French movie nor the recent American remake, nor even the Broadway musical. Actually, it's more the stage show from *Priscilla, Queen of the Desert.* Female impersonators dress up as various entertainers (with varying degrees of success) to lip sync to said performers greatest hits (with varying degrees of success). Celebs lampooned can include Cher, Bette Midler, Judy Garland, Whitney Houston, Dionne Warwick and, intriguingly, Michael Jackson. A Joan Rivers impersonator, looking not unlike the original but sounding (even with the aid of, oddly, a constant echo) not at all like her is the hostess, delivers scatological phrases and stale jokes. They do make the most of a tiny stage with some pretty stunning lighting, though the choreography is bland. Still, it's a crowd pleaser—one couple was back for their fourth (all comped) visit.

- **Showroom Policies:** Nonsmoking with maître d' seating.
- **Price:** $26.66–$32.16 (includes two drinks; gratuity extra).
- **Show Times:** Wed–Mon at 7:30 and 9:30pm, with an extra show at 11:15pm Wed. Dark Tues.
- **Reservations:** Tickets can be purchased at the box office only, in advance if you wish.

Folies Bergère

Tropicana, 3801 Las Vegas Blvd. S. ☎ **800/468-9494** or 702/739-2411.

The Trop's famous *Folies Bergère* is the longest-running production show in town and one of the few remaining dinner shows. It's the quintessential Las Vegas extravaganza with a French accent—an enchanting mix of innovative scenery, lively music, barebreasted showgirls in lavish feathered/rhinestoned/sequined costumes, and fast-paced choreography. Scene one is set in a turn-of-the-century Parisian music hall. Scene two salutes American music—gospel, blues, movie melodies, and the big-band and swing eras—culminating in a medley of oldies from the '50s through the '90s. A highlight is a kaleidoscope dance number (they do it with mirrors). Scene three once more celebrates the belle epoque, leading up to a colorful cancan finale. Acts are punctuated by acrobatic numbers and comedy routines.

Note: If you'd like to take a backstage tour of the Folies set, they are scheduled Sunday through Thursday at 12:30, 1:30, and 2:30pm. Tickets cost $2; call the above phone number for details.

- **Showroom Policies:** Nonsmoking with preassigned seating.
- **Price:** $45 for a table seat, $55 for a booth seat (includes coupon for buffet discount).

- **Show Times:** Fri–Wed at 8pm and 10:30pm. Dark Thurs.
- **Reservations:** You can charge tickets in advance via credit card.

Forever Plaid

Flamingo Hilton, 3555 Las Vegas Blvd. S. ☎ **702/733-3333**.

The Flamingo Hilton presents the off-Broadway hit *Forever Plaid* in its Bugsy's Celebrity Theatre. The plot line is bizarre, to say the least. The Plaids, an early 1960s harmony quartet on the order of The Four Freshmen, are killed on their way to their first big gig (at an Airport Hilton) when their car is broadsided by a busload of parochial-school girls en route to see the Beatles' U.S. television debut on *The Ed Sullivan Show*. After 30 years, they've mysteriously returned to Earth (it has to do with the power of harmony and expanding holes in the ozone layer) to finally perform the show they never got to do in life. This totally weird context is just an excuse for a zany musical stroll down memory lane consisting of 29 oldies—songs like "Rags to Riches," "Sixteen Tons," "Love is a Many-Splendored Thing," "Three Coins in the Fountain," and "No, Not Much." If you're sentimental about that era, you'll love it.

- **Showroom Policies:** Nonsmoking with maître d' seating.
- **Price:** $21.95 (includes tax).
- **Show Times:** Tues–Sun 7:30 and 10:30pm.
- **Reservations:** Tickets can be reserved a week in advance.

The Great Radio City Spectacular

Flamingo Hilton, 3555 Las Vegas Blvd. S. ☎ **702/733-3333**.

This is the wholesome showgirls show. If you aren't familiar with the venerable Rockettes tradition, the short black-and-white film on their history that opens the production will get you up to date. It also sets the stage for the big entrance by the ladies, arguably the world's best-known chorus line. There is a headliner who accompanies them—this star changes frequently. As of this writing, it was Paige O'Hara, the voice of Belle from Disney's *Beauty and the Beast*. Regardless of who it is, the star's musical numbers are interspersed with a variety of dance productions by the Rockettes that serve as a veritable history of dance, ranging from tap to '40s swing, waltzes, March of the Wooden Soldiers, and the like. Of course, the signature Rockettes' high kicking line is worked into at least half the numbers. That's their greatest hit—if O'Hara remains with the show, you can count on seeing her do hers, from the aforementioned *Beauty and the Beast*. The variety acts are standard Vegas: A juggler who keeps up a disturbing, David Helfgott–like banter under his breath and a magician who tries too hard. The stand-out here was the trained dogs act, which reduced even cynical viewers to goo. These are all pound-rescued mutts with plenty of star quality, and they work the crowd like pros.

- **Showroom Policies:** Nonsmoking with maître d' seating.
- **Price:** Dinner show based on main-course price ($53.95–$64.28 includes tax, and gratuity). Cocktail show $46.12 (includes two drinks, tax and gratuity).
- **Show Times:** Nightly dinner show at 7:45pm, cocktail show at 10:30pm.
- **Reservations:** You can reserve by phone 2 weeks in advance.

✪ Jubilee!

Bally's, 3645 Las Vegas Blvd. S. ☎ **800/237-7469** or 702/739-4567.

A classic Vegas spectacular, crammed with singing, dancing, magic, acrobats, elaborate costumes and sets, and of course, bare breasts. It's a basic review, with production numbers featuring homogenized versions of standards (Gershwin, Cole Porter,

12 Inaccuracies in the Movie *Showgirls*

By the showgirls in Jubilee!

1. Nomi Malone wouldn't be in a Las Vegas production because she can't sing (or act).

2. Showgirls do not live in trailers.

3. Showgirls aren't discovered in strip bars.

4. Showgirls do not pimp themselves at conventions or trade shows.

5. Hotel owners do not throw lavish cast parties.

6. A lead dancer does not become a celebrity.

7. No one learns a show in a day.

8. Pushing someone down the stairs doesn't get you a lead role, it gets you fired.

9. Ice is used backstage to treat injuries, not to erect nipples.

10. Leaving rehearsal to go to Spago to drink champagne is generally frowned upon.

11. Showgirls are not coke-sniffing, champagne-drinking lesbians.

12. Anyway, showgirls do not drink champagne backstage—we prefer Jack Daniels!

some Fred Astaire numbers) sometimes sung live, sometimes lip-synched, and always accompanied by lavishly costumed and frequently topless showgirls. Humorous set pieces about Samson and Delilah and the sinking of the *Titanic* (!) show off some pretty awesome sets, while the finale features aerodynamically impossible feathered and bejeweled costumes and headpieces designed by Bob Mackie. So what if the dancers are occasionally out of step and the action sometimes veers into the dubious (a Vegas-style revue about a disaster that took more than 1,000 lives?) or even the inexplicable (a finale praising beautiful and bare-breasted girls suddenly stops for three lines of "Somewhere Over the Rainbow")? With plenty of rhinestones and nipples on display, this is archetypal Vegas entertainment and the best of those presently offered.

- **Showroom Policies:** Nonsmoking with preassigned seating.
- **Price:** $49.50 (tax included, drinks extra).
- **Show Times:** Sun–Mon at 8pm, Tues–Thurs and Sat at 8 and 11pm. Dark Fri.
- **Reservations:** You can reserve up to 6 weeks in advance.

✪ Kenny Kerr Show

Debbie Reynolds Hotel, 305 Convention Center Dr. ☎ **800/633-1777** or 702/7-DEBBIE.

A sophisticated female-impersonator revue starring "hostess" Kenny Kerr, *Boylesque* has been playing somewhere in Las Vegas since 1970. This now eponymously titled version is his best show yet: He's looking great, his repartee is sparkling, and his vast array of costumes is simply stunning. An evening with Kenny is marvelously outrageous and over-the-top, with lots of double-entendre jokes and even a bit of beefcake. A talented cast, backed up by a dance troupe, does take-offs (mostly lip-synching, but Kenny really sings) on Marilyn Monroe, Dolly Parton, Janet Jackson, Diana Ross, Barbra Streisand, Liza Minnelli, and others—even Pocahontas. But most impressive is the lively improvisational patter of Kerr himself, who fields questions, some of them very personal, with humor and panache and creates an intimate rapport with his audience.

- **Showroom Policies:** Nonsmoking with maître d' seating.
- **Price:** $21.95 (includes tax).
- **Show Times:** Mon–Sat 10:30pm.
- **Reservations:** You can reserve by phone up to 3 days in advance.

King Arthur's Tournament
Excalibur, 3850 Las Vegas Blvd. S. ☎ **702/597-7600.**

If you've seen the Jim Carrey movie *The Cable Guy,* you probably laughed at the scene in which the two protagonists went to a medieval dinner and tournament. Perhaps you thought it was satire, created just for the movie. You would be wrong. It's actually part of a chain, and something very like it can be found right here in Vegas. For a price, you get a modest dinner, which you eat with your hands (in keeping with the theme), and watch a "tournament" of knights (jousting and whatnot) that is every bit as unrehearsed and spontaneous as a professional wrestling match. The story is about the battle between an evil black knight and a heroic white knight for a princess's hand in marriage. Each section of the arena is given a knight to cheer, and the audience is encouraged to hoot, holler, and pound on the tables, which kids love but many adults will find tiresome, particularly when they insist you shout "huzzah!" and other period slang. In addition to the knightly battles there are dances, equestrian acrobatics, tumblers, jugglers, and stunt riders. It's all incredibly camp, and only big Renaissance Faire buffs, kids, and Jim Carrey fans will really enjoy it. Dinner includes a pot of creamy chicken soup, Cornish game hen, stuffed baked potato, vegetable, biscuits, apple tart, and beverage.

- **Showroom Policies:** Nonsmoking with preassigned seating.
- **Price:** $29.95 (including dinner, beverage, tax, and gratuity).
- **Show Times:** "Knightly" at 6 and 8:30pm.
- **Reservations:** You can reserve up to 6 days in advance by phone.

✪ Lance Burton: Master Magician
Monte Carlo, 3770 Las Vegas Blvd. S. ☎ **800/311-8999** or 702/730-7000.

Magic acts are a dime a dozen in Vegas of late. Along with impersonator acts, they seem to have largely replaced the topless showgirls of yore. Most seem more than a little influenced by the immeasurable success of Siegfried and Roy. So when someone pops up who is original—not to mention charming and, yes, actually good at his job—it comes as a relief.

Monte Carlo dumped a lot of money into building the lush Victorian music hall–style Lance Burton Theater for the star, and it was worth it. Handsome and folksy (he hails from Lexington, Kentucky), Burton is talented and engaging, for the most part shunning the big-ticket special effects that seem to have swamped most other shows in town. Instead, he offers an extremely appealing production that starts small, with "close-up" magic. These rather lovely tricks, he tells us, are what won him a number of prestigious magic competitions. They are truly extraordinary (we swear that he tossed a bird up in the air, and the darn thing turned into confetti in front of our eyes. Really.) Burton doesn't have patter, per se, but his dry, laconic, low-key delivery is plenty amusing and in contrast to other performers in town who seem as if they have been spending way too much time at Starbucks. He does eventually move to bigger illusions, but his manner follows him—he knows the stuff is good, but he also knows the whole thing is a bit silly, so why not have fun with it? Accompanying him are some perky showgirls, who border on the wholesome, and talented comic juggler Michael Goudeau. The latter is a likable goofball who instantly wins you over

> ### 🎭 Family-Friendly Shows
>
> Appropriate shows for kids, all described in this chapter, include the following:
> - King Arthur's Tournament at Excalibur *(see p. 227)*
> - Siegfried and Roy at the Mirage *(see p. 229)*
> - Lance Burton at the Monte Carlo *(see p. 227)*
> - *Starlight Express* at the Hilton *(see p. 230)*
> - *EFX* at the MGM Grand *(see p. 223)*
> - Cirque du Soleil's *Mystère* at Treasure Island *(see p. 220)*
>
> As a general rule, early shows are less racy than late-night shows.

(or should) when he juggles three beanbag chairs. All this and extremely comfortable movie theater–style plush seats with cup holders. And for a most reasonable price.

- **Showroom Policies:** Nonsmoking with preassigned seating.
- **Price:** $34.95 (includes tax, drinks extra).
- **Show Times:** Tues–Sat at 7:30 and 10:30pm. Dark Sun–Mon.
- **Reservations:** Tickets can be purchased 60 days in advance.

Legends in Concert
Imperial Palace, 3535 Las Vegas Blvd. S. ☎ **702/794-3261**.

A crowd pleaser, which is probably why it's been running since May 1983. Arguably the best of the Vegas impersonator shows (though it's hard to quantify such things), "Legends" does feature performers live, rather than lip-synching. Acts vary from night to night (in a showroom that could use a face-lift) on a nice large stage with modern hydraulics but twinkle lighting that is stuck in a *Flip Wilson Show* time warp. The personal touches here include scantily clad (but well-choreographed) male and female dancers, and an utterly useless green laser. When we went, the performers included Neil Diamond (whose "America" was accompanied by red-, white-, and blue–clad showgirls covered in flags of all nations), an actual piano-playing Elton John, the Blues Brothers (a reasonable John Belushi, but a not even close Dan Ackroyd), and the inevitable Diana Ross, Four Tops, and the young thin Elvis (who performs hits from the fat old Elvis years). The latter, by the way, was preceded by a reverent multimedia presentation (the stage also has video screens that show not only the live action but clips by the real celebs). Best of all, Wayne Newton was there. Yes, the *real* one. During the Blues Brothers bit, the band showed a rare display of spontaneity. When one audience member called out a request for "country," they actually broke into the theme from *Rawhide*. Maybe it was a planned moment, but we were impressed that it didn't seem that way.

- **Showroom Policies:** Nonsmoking, with maître d' seating.
- **Price:** $29.50 (includes two drinks or one Polynesian cocktail such as a mai tai or zombie; tax and gratuity extra).
- **Show Times:** Mon–Sat at 7:30 and 10:30pm. Dark Sun.
- **Reservations:** You can make reservations by phone up to 2 weeks in advance.

Luxor Production Show
Luxor Las Vegas, 3900 Las Vegas Blvd. S. ☎ **702/262-4900.**

Luxor is building a giant showroom, to be completed sometime in 1997, for a production called "Imagine: A Theatrical Odyssey." It will be a modern Vegas show (think *EFX* and *Mystère*). Call for details.

✪ Siegfried & Roy

The Mirage, 3400 Las Vegas Blvd. S. ☎ **800/627-6667** or 702/792-7777.

A Vegas institution for more than 2 decades, illusionists Siegfried and Roy started as an opening act, became headliners at the Frontier, and finally were given their own $30 million show and $25 million theater in the Mirage. They (and their extensive exotic animal menagerie) have amply repaid this enormous investment by selling out every show since. No wonder the Mirage has them booked "until the end of time."

But while the spectacle is undeniable (and the money right on the stage), the result is overproduced. From the get go, there is so much light, sound, smoke, and fire; so many dancing girls, fire-breathing dragons, robots, and other often completely superfluous effects; not to mention an original (and forgettable) Michael Jackson song, that it overwhelms the point of the whole thing. Or maybe it's *become* the point of the whole thing. The magic, which was the Austrian duo's original act, after all, seems to have gotten lost. Sometimes literally. The tricks are at a minimum, allowing the flash pots, lasers, and whatnot to fill out the nearly 2-hour show. More often than not, when a trick is actually being performed, our attention was elsewhere, gawking at an effect, a showgirl, or something. Only the gasps from the audience members who actually happened to be looking in the right place let us know we missed something really neat.

Tellingly, the best part of the show is when all that stuff is switched off, and Siegfried and Roy take the stage to perform smaller magic and chat with the audience. The charm that helped get them so far shines through, and spontaneity is allowed to sneak in. The white tigers are certainly magnificent, but they don't do much other than get cuddled (charmingly) by Roy and badly lip-synch to pretaped roars. The duo is clearly doing something right, judging from the heartfelt standing ovations they receive night after night. But more than one couple was heard to say it was not the best show they had seen, and also to express a feeling that it was overpriced. At these ticket costs (essentially $90 *per person!*) almost anything is. Go if you can't live without seeing a true, modern Vegas legend, but one can find better entertainment values in town.

- **Showroom Policies:** Nonsmoking with preassigned seating.
- **Price:** $89.35 (includes 2 drinks, souvenir brochure, tax, and gratuity).
- **Show Times:** Performances are Fri–Tues at 7:30 and 11pm, except during occasional dark periods.
- **Reservations:** Tickets can be purchased 3 days in advance.

Spellbound

Harrah's, 3475 Las Vegas Blvd. S. ☎ **800/392-9002** or 702/369-5111.

Now, a warning. Be prepared: Out of nowhere, this magic show revue opens with a deafening explosion and blinding lights. Unfortunately, the magic that follows doesn't live up to this grandiose (and irritating) opening. The variety acts in between come as a relief, because frankly, the magic isn't very good. The ostensible headliner (at this writing, it was Jouquin Ayala) delivered high-drama, big-spectacle magic that was strangely disappointing. Further, unless you aren't watching all that closely, you could see the wires, so to speak. Perhaps his tendency to overdramatize every tiny feat he did was an attempt to distract you from the clumsy execution. But if the magic isn't on par with other such shows in Vegas, the dancing and choreography is among the best for the major shows. The routines are fun and infectious, precise but not formal. The dancers execute everything from terrific tap to a trash can and stick rhythm routine clearly influenced by *Stomp* (it was probably only a matter of time before Vegas jumped on that one). Another respite comes in the form of an amazing contortionist act and the "comedy juggler," who juggled two bowling balls and an M&M (peanut).

- **Showroom Policies:** Nonsmoking with preassigned seating.
- **Price:** $35.
- **Show Times:** Mon–Sat at 7:30 and 10pm. Dark Sun.
- **Reservations:** You can charge tickets up to 30 days in advance via credit card.

Splash

Riviera Hotel, 2901 Las Vegas Blvd. S. ☎ **800/634-6753** or 702/734-9301.

Many Vegas shows teeter on the edge of the inexplicable, but this one topples over into the truly bizarre. Set in a showroom badly in need of a facelift, it begins promisingly (from a camp perspective) as mermaids and synchronized swimmers cavort in a 20,000-gallon tank. Surrounding this are waterfalls and fountains, as dancers in highly silly, aquatic-themed costumes (shells and seaweed) prance and pose. The indication is that we are in for the sort of goofy stage spectacular that used to characterize Vegas. But after this, things go badly awry. The water theme all but vanishes, replaced by some unfortunate production numbers. In one, the lead singer and dancing girls come out in leather biker outfits (albeit ones that show off more skin than leather), riding motorcycles and sing a medley of songs, most of which have nothing to do with motorcycles. There is a series of celebrity impersonators—Michael Jackson, the artist formerly known as Prince, Madonna—lip-synching to several of said celebs greatest hits. The best moment is when the Madonna tribute turns into live-action highlights from the movie *Evita,* which raised certain questions in our minds: Is having girls dance in their underwear really a fitting tribute to Eva Peron? Why turn the fountains back on at this particular moment? A high point of sorts is hit with a likable bird act and an equally likable juggler, but the absolute nadir of any show in Vegas comes with the "comic antics" of some guy whose "talent" is truly mystifying: He prances, lip-synchs to lines from movies and waves props in the air. He was insulting, awful, and pointless. Meanwhile, there were glitches in the sound system, and the water spigots occasionally dripped on the performers. *Seating warnings:* Patrons in the front row get raincoats, while seats on the sides are so bad that fully three-quarters of the stage might be obscured.

- **Showroom Policies:** Nonsmoking with preassigned seating.
- **Price:** $45.58–$56.76, the latter for best seats in the house (includes tax; drinks and gratuity extra).
- **Show Times:** Nightly at 7:30 and 10:30pm (10:30pm show is topless).
- **Reservations:** You can reserve by phone up to a month in advance.

Starlight Express

Las Vegas Hilton, 3000 Paradise Rd. ☎ **800/222-5361** or 702/732-5755.

Starlight Express does seem perfectly appropriate for Vegas: It's both flashy and fast paced. In 1993, the Hilton transformed its famed showroom into a gorgeous 1,500-seat oval theater to house it. The plot involves a little boy's train set as the individual cars race for some championship title. The gimmick is that the trains are played by actors on roller skates. As opposed to evoking actual trains, the actors never seem like more than actors on roller skates, wearing (admittedly extremely heavy) costumes that

---

Impressions

If I stand still while I'm singing, I'm a dead man. I might as well go back to driving a truck.

—Legendary Las Vegas headliner Elvis Presley

look like they were assembled at a junkyard. The songs are forgettable, the main plot hard to follow, the love story inexplicable. On the other hand, the actors work very hard as they whiz about a set that goes into and through the audience; they hit impressive speeds, and some perform break-neck flips. It also seems to inspire repeat visits; a good portion of the audience cheers when key figures make their entrances. It also seems like a good show for kids, with clean content and a solid moral.

- **Showroom Policies:** Nonsmoking with preassigned seating.
- **Price:** $19.50–$45 (tax and drinks extra); $19.50 for children 4 to 12.
- **Show Times:** Tues, Thurs, Sat, Sun at 7:30 and 10:30pm; Mon and Wed at 7:30pm. Dark Fri.
- **Reservations:** You can reserve by phone up to 3 months in advance.

Viva Las Vegas

Stratosphere, 2000 Las Vegas Blvd. S. ☎ **800/99-TOWER** or 702/380-7777.

An everything-but-the-kitchen-sink Vegas variety show, good only if you really need an hour's respite in the afternoon from the slots. Which isn't a bad idea, since the preshow warm-up comic's "funny" gaming tips prove actually useful, though not actually all that funny. A lead singer and a small troupe of dancers perform numbers ranging from "Les Miz" to "Viva Las Vegas" (oh, was that a surprise?). A comedian delivered some very adult humor (fat jokes, gay jokes, breast jokes) given the time of day and the number of kids in the audience. The inevitable magician had some adequate close-up magic and an all too obvious mind-reading act. One bright point was when the white, female dancers donned Jackson Five outfits and lip-synched "ABC," fully aware of the giggles this sight engendered (unlike, unfortunately, the Elvis impersonator who closed the show).

Note: Discount coupons are often found in those free magazines in your hotel room. Sometimes the discount gets you in free, with just the price of a drink.

- **Showroom Policies:** Nonsmoking with maître d' seating.
- **Price:** $11.
- **Show Times:** Mon–Sat 2pm and 4pm. Dark Sun.
- **Reservations:** Not accepted.

The Xtreme Scene

Jackie Gaughan's Plaza, 1 Main St. ☎ **800/634-6575** or 702/386-2444.

An all-new revue that has replaced Xposed. A standard, racy production show that includes totally naked dancers (yep, topless and bottomless), singers, magicians, and comedians. Xposed featured a production number that had dancers clad in black cloaks suggesting figures of Death. Since Xtreme should be more extreme, one can only imagine what replaced that little number.

- **Showroom Policies:** Smoking permitted, maître d' seating.
- **Price:** $21.95 (includes one drink from the bar).
- **Show Times:** Sat–Thurs at 8 and 10pm. Dark Fri.
- **Reservations:** You can reserve up to a week in advance by phone.

3 Headliner Showrooms

Aladdin Theatre for the Performing Arts

Aladdin Hotel, 3667 Las Vegas Blvd. S. ☎ **800/637-8133** or 702/736-0419.

The 7,000-seat Theatre for the Performing Arts—a major Las Vegas entertainment venue—hosts headliner concerts has featured such acts as Kenny Rogers, Pearl Jam, the Allman Brothers, Yanni, Alan Jackson, the Scorpions, Sawyer Brown, Luther

Vandross, Tears for Fears, and Meatloaf. These alternate with Broadway shows (with touring-company casts) such as *Phantom of the Opera, Nutcracker on Ice, Dreamgirls,* and *Cats* and professional boxing and wrestling matches. There are several bars in the theater.

- **Showroom Policies:** Nonsmoking with preassigned seating.
- **Price:** $13–$100, depending on the event (tax included; drinks extra).
- **Show Times:** Vary with the performer or show.
- **Reservations:** Policy varies with the performer, theatrical production, or event. Most shows can be reserved via **Ticketmaster** (☎ **702/474-4000** or your local outlet) or the Aladdin Theatre box office as soon as they are announced.

Bally's Celebrity Room

Bally's, 3645 Las Vegas Blvd. S. ☎ **800/237-7469** or 702/739-4567.

Superstar headliners play the 1,400-seat Celebrity Room. Dean Martin inaugurated the facility. Today, frequent performers include Barbara Mandrell, Engelbert Humperdinck, Bernadette Peters, Liza Minnelli, Jeff Foxworthy, Hall and Oates, Steve Lawrence and Eydie Gorme, George Carlin, Andrew Dice Clay, Paul Anka, Anne Murray, Louie Anderson, and Penn and Teller.

- **Showroom Policies:** Nonsmoking and preassigned seating.
- **Price:** $25–$45, depending on the performer (tax included, drinks extra).
- **Show Times:** There are one or two shows a night at varying times (this also depends on the performer).
- **Reservations:** You can reserve up to 6 weeks in advance.

Caesars Circus Maximus Showroom

Caesars Palace, 3570 Las Vegas Blvd. S. ☎ **800/445-4544** or 702/731-7333.

From its opening in 1966, Caesars' 1,200-seat Circus Maximus Showroom has presented superstar entertainment—everyone from Judy Garland to Frank Sinatra. Many current headliners started out here as opening acts for established performers, among them Richard Pryor for singer Bobbie Gentry, Jay Leno for Tom Jones, and the Pointer Sisters for Paul Anka. The current lineup of luminaries includes Julio Iglesias, David Copperfield, Howie Mandel, Clint Black, Jerry Seinfeld, Natalie Cole, Diana Ross, Chicago, The Moody Blues, Wynonna, and Johnny Mathis. The luxurious showroom keeps to the Roman theme. Illuminated shields along the wall are replicas of those used by the legions of Caesar, and plush royal purple booths are patterned after Roman chariots.

- **Showroom Policies:** Nonsmoking with preassigned seating.
- **Price:** $45–$75, depending on the performer (including tax, drinks optional).
- **Show Times:** One or two shows nightly; times depend on performer.
- **Reservations:** You can reserve any time in advance (as soon as a show is confirmed) via credit card.

Desert Inn Crystal Room

3145 Las Vegas Blvd. S. ☎ **800/634-6906** or 702/733-4444.

The Desert Inn has a long history of superstar entertainment. Frank Sinatra's Las Vegas debut took place in the hotel's Painted Desert Room in 1951, and other early performers included Maurice Chevalier, Noël Coward, Buster Keaton, and Marlene Dietrich. Jimmy Durante once broke the piano board on a new spinet and yelled to the audience, "Mr. Hughes, it was broke when I got it!" And on one memorable night the entire Rat Pack (Dean Martin, Frank Sinatra, Joey Bishop, Sammy Davis Jr., and

Peter Lawford) invaded the stage when Eddie Fisher was performing! Today this historic showroom has been renamed the Crystal Room. Currently among its current major headliners are Smokey Robinson, The Temptations, The Golden Boys (Frankie Avalon, Fabian, and Bobby Rydell), Dennis Miller, Neil Sedaka, and Rita Rudner.

- **Showroom Policies:** Nonsmoking with maître d' seating.
- **Price:** $35–$50, depending on the performer (including two drinks; tax and gratuity extra).
- **Show Times:** Days vary; shows are usually at 9pm.
- **Reservations:** You can reserve up to 3 engagements in advance.

Hard Rock Hotel's The Joint

Hard Rock Hotel, 4455 Paradise Rd. ☎ **800/693-7625** or 702/693-5000.

When the Hard Rock Hotel opened in 1995, The Eagles were the first act to play its 1,400-seat state-of-the-art, live-concert venue, The Joint. Other performers during the hotel's opening festivities were Melissa Etheridge (with Al Green), B. B. King, Iggy Pop, Duran Duran, and Sheryl Crow. Since then the facility has presented Bob Dylan, Ziggy Marley, Marilyn Manson, Hootie and the Blowfish, the Black Crowes, Donna Summer, Stephen Stills, Jimmy Cliff, Tears for Fears, Johnny Cash, Lyle Lovett, and James Brown. It's rapidly becoming the place in town for rock acts to play.

- **Showroom Policies:** Smoking permitted; seating preassigned or general, depending on the performer.
- **Price:** $20 to $100, depending on the performer (drinks and tax extra).
- **Show Times:** 8:30pm (nights of performance vary).
- **Reservations:** You can reserve up to 30 days in advance.

Las Vegas Hilton: Fabulous Fridays

3000 Paradise Rd. ☎ **800/222-5361** or 702/732-5755.

Before it became the venue for Andrew Lloyd Webber's *Starlight Express,* the Hilton showroom presented superstar headliners for more than 2 decades. Barbra Streisand was the first in 1969, Gladys Knight the last in 1993, and in between Elvis played 837 sold-out shows over a 10-year period. On Fridays, when *Starlight Express* is dark, the Hilton has begun presenting headliners once again. Among those who've appeared so far are Creedence Clearwater, political comedian Bill Maher, Nancy Wilson (on a double bill with Ramsey Lewis), Lou Rawls, The Monkees, Johnny Cash and The June Carter Family, Al Jarreau, K. C. and The Sunshine Band, and Peaches and Herb.

- **Showroom Policies:** Nonsmoking with preassigned seating.
- **Price:** $29 to $59, depending on the performer (drinks and tax extra).
- **Show Times:** Usually 9pm.
- **Reservations:** You can reserve up to 60 days in advance.

MGM Grand Garden Events Arena

MGM Grand, 3799 Las Vegas Blvd. S. ☎ **800/929-1111** or 702/891-7777.

The 15,222-seat MGM Grand Garden Events Arena is a major venue for sporting events. It also hosts big-name concerts. Barbra Streisand returned to the stage here after an absence of 25 years on New Year's Eve 1993. Others who have played the Arena include Neil Diamond, Sting, Jimmy Buffett, Luther Vandross, Janet Jackson, The Rolling Stones, Bette Midler, Billy Joel, Elton John, and Whitney Houston. Grand Garden Events tickets are generally also available through **Ticketmaster** (☎ 702/474-4000).

Headliner Stadiums

Three arenas are worth a special mention since they often feature major entertainers. **Sam Boyd Stadium,** the outdoor stadium at the University of Nevada, Las Vegas (UNLV), has been host to such major acts as Paul McCartney, U2, the Eagles, and Metallica. **Thomas and Mack Center,** the university's indoor arena, has a more comprehensive concert schedule, including such names as Van Halen, Michael Bolton, and Celine Dion, as well as shows like *Disney on Ice* and Ringling Bros. Circus. Both are located on the **UNLV campus** at Boulder Highway and Russell Road (☎ 702/895-3900). Ticketmaster (☎ 702/474-4000) handles ticketing for both arenas. The **Huntridge** is a local theater venue where big alternative acts are likely to show up (Beck, Slash's Snakepit, Jim Rose Sideshow Circus, and so forth), though irregularly. It's located at 1208 E. Charleston Blvd. (☎ **702/477-0242**).

- **Showroom Policies:** Nonsmoking with preassigned seating.
- **Price:** Varies with event or performer.
- **Show Times:** Vary with event or performer.
- **Reservations:** Advance-reservations policy varies with event or performer.

MGM Grand Hollywood Theatre

MGM Grand, 3799 Las Vegas Blvd. S. ☎ **800/929-1111** or 702/891-7777.

The 650-seat Hollywood Theatre hosts headliners such as Wayne Newton, Tom Jones, the Righteous Brothers, Jeff Foxworthy, Dennis Miller, Rita Rudner, and Randy Travis. It has also featured occasional live telecasts of *The Tonight Show* with Jay Leno.

- **Showroom Policies:** Nonsmoking with preassigned seating.
- **Price:** Usually $44–$55, varies with performer (tax and drinks extra).
- **Show Times:** Vary with performer; there's usually a show at 9pm.
- **Reservations:** Tickets can be ordered anytime in advance as soon as they become available.

Orleans Showroom

Orleans Hotel, 4500 W. Tropicana. ☎ **800/ORLEANS.**

A pleasant, medium-sized showroom with theater seating and cup holders. Performers booked there so far have included Chuck Berry, the Pointer Sisters, the Everly Brothers, and the Oakridge Boys.

- **Showroom Policies:** Nonsmoking with preassigned seating.
- **Price:** Varies with performer.
- **Show Times:** Varies with performer.
- **Reservations:** Tickets can be ordered anytime in advance as soon as they become available.

Sahara Hotel Showroom

2535 Las Vegas Blvd. S. ☎ **702/737-2878.**

Since the Sahara was just completing a major renovation at press time, few details were available about its showroom. It will present headliner performers. Call for details or check local show listings when you're in town.

- **Showroom Policies:** Nonsmoking with preassigned seating.
- **Price:** Usually $22–$36, varies with performer (tax and drinks extra).

- **Show Times:** Vary with performer; there's usually a show at 9pm.
- **Reservations:** Tickets can be ordered anytime in advance as soon as they become available.

4 Comedy Clubs

Catch a Rising Star

MGM Grand, 3799 Las Vegas Blvd. S. ☎ **800/929-1111** or 702/891-7777.

Like The Improv, Catch a Rising Star presents nationally known talent from the comedy circuit. Three comedians perform each night.

- **Showroom Policies:** Nonsmoking with maître d' seating.
- **Price:** $12.50 (tax and drinks extra).
- **Show Times:** Nightly at 8 and 10:30pm.
- **Reservations:** You can charge tickets up to 30 days in advance via credit card.

Comedy Club

Riviera Hotel, 2901 Las Vegas Blvd. S. ☎ **800/634-6753** or 702/734-9301.

The Riviera's comedy club, on the second floor of the Mardi Gras Plaza, showcases four comedians nightly. Once a month, usually on the last weekend, the club hosts a late-night XXXTREME Comedy Showcase for shock and X-rated comedians. Other special events include the *All Gay Comedy Revue* and R-rated hypnotist Frank Santos.

- **Showroom Policies:** Nonsmoking with maître d' seating.
- **Price:** $18.96–$24.96 (includes two drinks and tax).
- **Show Times:** Nightly at 8 and 10pm, with an extra show Fri and Sat at 11:45pm.
- **Reservations:** Tickets can be purchased at the box office only, in advance if you wish.

Comedy Max

Maxim, 160 E. Flamingo Rd. ☎ **800/634-6987** or 702/731-4423.

The Maxim's very attractive nightclub features three comics nightly, and every seat is good.

- **Showroom Policies:** Nonsmoking, maître d' seating.
- **Price:** $16.25 (includes two drinks, tax, and gratuity). For $19.95 you can enjoy a buffet dinner as well.
- **Show Times:** Nightly at 7, 9, and 10:30pm.
- **Reservations:** You can reserve up to a week in advance by phone.

Comedy Stop

Tropicana, 3801 Las Vegas Blvd. S. ☎ **800/468-9494** or 702/739-2411.

Similar to clubs described above, the Comedy Stop here features three nationally known comedy headliners nightly.

- **Showroom Policies:** Smoking permitted with maître d' seating.
- **Price:** $14.30 (includes two drinks; tax and gratuity extra).
- **Show Times:** Nightly at 8 and 10:30pm.
- **Reservations:** You can charge tickets in advance via credit card.

The Improv

Harrah's, 3475 Las Vegas Blvd. S. ☎ **800/392-9002** or 702/369-5111.

This offshoot of Budd Friedman's famed comedy club (the first one opened in 1963 in New York City) presents about four comedians per show in a 400-seat showroom.

These are talented performers—the top comics on the circuit who you're likely to see on Leno and Letterman. You can be sure of an entertaining evening.

- **Showroom Policies:** Nonsmoking with preassigned seating.
- **Price:** $14.95 (tax and drinks extra).
- **Show Times:** Tues–Sun at 8 and 10:30pm. Dark Mon.
- **Reservations:** You can charge tickets up to 30 days in advance via credit card.

The Unknown Comic

Holiday Inn Boardwalk, 3750 Las Vegas Blvd. S. ☎ **702/735-2400.**

The Unknown Comic is Murray Langston, so called because he performs a large part of his act with a bag over his head. Come early to see preshow video clips of his numerous TV appearances on everything from *The Tonight Show* to *Oprah*. Langston is zany (some might say insane) and very manic, a king of one-liners such as, "What's the most successful pick-up line in the South?" "Nice tooth." He also does a bit of ventriloquism with a little bag face called Sad Sack for a dummy. It's weird, but fun.

- **Showroom Policies:** Smoking permitted; seating is first come, first served.
- **Price:** $5.95 (drinks and tax extra).
- **Show Times:** Tues–Sun at 9pm. Dark Mon.
- **Reservations:** You can make reservations by phone up to 7 days in advance.

5 Coffeehouses

Coffeehouses are both a day and nighttime activity; so far, not too many stay open past midnight. They can either be pretentious or the center of youth culture, depending on your demographic group. They can also be an oasis for those seeking alternative culture or just a respite from the usual Vegas hangouts. We've listed a range here, from ordinary rooms in strip malls to two very nice cafes. Many also offer live music and/or poetry readings; check the listings in *Scope* and *City Life* for details (or just call the place in question).

✪ Cafe Copioh

4550 S. Maryland Pkwy., near Harmon. ☎ **702/739-0305.**

A typical Gen X alt-rock coffeehouse with clientele to match. The low-tech decor includes mixed thrift store furniture and a collection of books to borrow. They have a large assortment of specialty coffee drinks, smoothies, and a few sandwich/bagel/pastry items if you get hungry. A crowded, bustling, smoky hang out at 11:30 on a Saturday night makes one wonder why it closes at midnight. The Goth crowd in Vegas makes this a vampire hangout on certain nights after 10pm (then they wander over to the Wet Stop bar just down the street)—catch them if you can. Open Monday to Friday from noon to midnight, Saturday and Sunday from 5am to midnight.

Cafe Espresso Roma

4440 W. Maryland Pkwy., near Harmon. ☎ **702/369-1540.**

Despite the vintage sofa look, the truth is told by the clean tile counter—this is an artificially manufactured attempt at the coffeehouse scene and, arguably, a successful one. Most of the patrons are University of Nevada students. They do have poetry and live music on certain nights, but they close too early. Open Monday to Friday from 7am to 10pm, Saturday from 8am to 9pm, Sunday from 8am to 10pm.

Cafe Neon

1018 So. Main, near Charleston. ☎ **702-388-4088.**

Located on the second floor of the Attic vintage clothing shop, this cafe provides you a place to sit and rest your shopped-till-you-dropped aching feet. Basic, mismatched coffeehouse furniture sits in a space carved out behind the clothes (some large triangle-shaped aquariums separate it from the racks). It even has a small stage where live comedy (presented by "Guppy Stop Theater") is performed. They have a small but adequate range of cold sandwiches and Greek-influenced salads and desserts. Open Monday to Friday from 10am to 6pm, Saturday and Sunday from 10am to 7pm (sometimes later).

Cyber City Cafe

3945 S. Maryland Pkwy., near Flamingo. ☎ **702-732-2001.**

Not just for tech-heads and geek girls. Actually, for a cyber cafe, this is a pretty friendly place, with plenty of chat space that has nothing to do with computers, a gay information center at the back, a large collage by a local artist, and a newsstand filled with a variety of alternative press and comics. And of course, there is a bank of computer terminals offering Internet access for a small fee. Go ahead, get wired and get on line. Open 24 hours.

✪ Enigma Cafe

918$^1/_2$ S. Fourth St., and Charleston. ☎ **702/386-0999.**

Though they have fine food here (see chapter 6 for a restaurant review), the menu is more than two-thirds beverages, a seemingly endless variety of coffee drinks, smoothies, and the like. You can sit in the garden patio or in the 1930s house-turned-art-gallery and listen to whatever music they are playing (classical in the morning, Liz Phair in the afternoon), or come back at night when it turns into a real candlelit scene, with poetry readings, "obscure and interesting movies" (shown by the owner of the antique camera store in the front), and live acoustic and folk music. This is a hangout for the neighborhood artists or anyone seeking an oasis of calm and culture in Vegas. It's very close to both downtown (in particular) and the Strip. Open Monday from 7am to 3pm, Tuesday to Friday from 7am to midnight, and Saturday and Sunday 9am to 12am.

✪ Jazzed Cafe & Vinoteca

2055 E. Tropicana, at Eastern. ☎ **702/798-5995.**

This genuine European-style (well, by way of California) cafe is owned and operated by the charming and friendly Kirk, a choreographer who lived in Italy for 10 years. It's tiny but intimate, featuring candlelight and cool jazz, with hot art on the walls. They serve multiple coffee drinks (be sure to try the terrific Illy, a renowned Italian brand) and average wine. There's a small but satisfying food menu featuring inexpensive ($4 to $6.50) authentic Italian specialties—simple pastas, focaccia bread, and so forth, all made by Kirk on the spot. It's a great respite from the maddening crowds (and a cheap place to eat well), though it fills up after the shows let out with the owner's show and dance pals. (By the way, this is just a quick drive up from the Strip.) A sign warns you *not* to order lemon peel with your espresso—if you do, be prepared to be sworn at (sweetly) in Italian. Open Tuesday to Sunday from 6pm to 3am. Credit cards accepted include American Express, Discover, MasterCard, and Visa.

Wayne Newton's Top-10 Favorite Lounge Songs

Wayne Newton is the consummate entertainer. He has performed more than 25,000 concerts in Las Vegas alone, and in front of more than 25 million people worldwide. Wayne has received more standing ovations than any other entertainer in history. Along with his singing credits, his acting credits are soaring—one of his more recent credits is Vegas Vacation. *Make sure you catch him playing at the MGM Grand. No trip to Vegas is complete without seeing the "King of Las Vegas" . . .* WAYNE NEWTON!

1. "You're Nobody, Til Somebody Loves You" (*You don't have a body unless somebody loves you!*)

2. "Up a Lazy River" (*or "Up Your Lazy River!"*)

3. "Don't Go Changin' (Just the Way You Are)" (*The clothes will last another week!*)

4. "Having My Baby" (*Oh God!!*)

5. "The Windmills of My Mind" (*A mind is a terrible thing to waste!*)

6. "The Wind Beneath My Wings" (*Soft and Dry usually helps!*)

7. "Copacabana"

8. "When the Saints Go Marching In"

9. "I Am, I Said" (*HUH?!*)

10. "The Theme from the Love Boat" (*or "Would A Dingy Do?"*)

6 Piano Bars

In addition to the establishments listed below, consider the ultraelegant **Palace Court Terrace Lounge,** adjoining the Palace Court restaurant at Caesars (see chapter 6). This romantic piano bar has a stained-glass skylight that retracts for a view of open starlit sky. Off the lounge is an intimate crystal-chandeliered, European-style casino for high-stakes players only. **Gatsby's** at the MGM Grand (see chapter 6) also has a sophisticated and stunning adjoining piano bar. And **Cafe Niccole** (see chapter 6) has a small, but agreeable genuine piano bar.

Alexis Park Resort: Pisces Bistro

375 E. Harmon Ave. ☎ **702/796-3300.** No cover or minimum.

The very upscale Alexis Park offers live entertainment in a beautiful room under a 30-foot domed ceiling; planters of greenery cascade from tiered balconies. When the weather permits, it's lovely to sit at umbrella tables on a terra-cotta patio overlooking the pool. Live music is featured Tuesday through Saturday nights from 8pm till about midnight; a versatile pianist and vocalist perform everything from show tunes to oldies to Top 40. Light fare is available.

The Carriage House: Kiefer's

105 E. Harmon Ave. ☎ **702/739-8000.** No cover or minimum.

This rooftop restaurant has a plushly furnished adjoining piano bar/lounge. Windowed walls offer great views of the Las Vegas neon skyline, making this a romantic setting for cocktails and hors d'oeuvres. There's piano music Thursday through Saturday from 7 to 11pm.

Club Monaco

1487 E. Flamingo Rd., between Maryland Pkwy. and Tamarus St. (on your right as you come from the Strip; look for the LA-Z-BOY Furniture Gallery). ☎ **702/737-6212.** No cover or minimum.

This low-key, sophisticated piano bar—its walls lined with oil paintings of icons such as Elvis, Bogart, James Dean, and Marilyn Monroe (not to mention Rodney Dangerfield, finally getting respect)—is a romantic setting for cocktails and classic piano-bar entertainment. There's a small dance floor. Friday and Saturday a talented vocalist is on hand as well. Club Monaco is far from a meat market, but it is a relaxed atmosphere in which to meet people. The crowd is over 30. A menu offers salads, burgers, steak sandwiches, pastas, and gourmet appetizers such as oysters Rockefeller and escargot-stuffed mushrooms. Open 24 hours.

Nicky Blair's

3925 Paradise Rd., between Flamingo and Twain. ☎ **702/792-9900.** No cover or minimum.

A Los Angeles legend, Nicky Blair closed the doors of his venerable L.A. establishment to open a new version here. Pity the Rat Pack is gone; this would be their hangout in the '90s. A U-shaped bar dominates an elegantly dark space, with hardwood floors and banquettes up against one wall. There are plenty of bartenders and waitresses on hand to serve the middle-aged, upscale (and largely local) clientele. The tables seem well spaced, so a romantic tête-à-tête should be possible. You can order the full menu from the restaurant. The piano goes from 7pm until close, which is midnight Monday through Thursday, 2am Friday and Saturday.

7 Gay Bars

Hip and happening Vegas locals know that some of the best scenes and dance action can actually be found in the city's gay bars. And no, they don't ask for sexuality ID at the door. All are welcome at any of the following establishments—as long as you don't have a problem with the people inside, they aren't going to have a problem with you. For women, this can be a fun way to dance and not get hassled by overeager lotharios. (Lesbians, by the way, are just as welcome at any of the gay bars.) If you want to know what's going on in gay Las Vegas during your visit, pick up a copy of *The Las Vegas Bugle,* a free, gay-oriented newspaper that is available at any of the places described below. Or call ☎ **702/369-6260.**

Angles/Lace

4633 Paradise Rd., at Naples St. ☎ **702/791-0100.** No cover or minimum.

This 24-hour gay bar (Lace is the lesbian bar attached to it), though among the most upscale in Las Vegas, is a casual neighborhood hangout compared to gay bars in other cities. The clientele is mostly local—about 85% men (including drag queens) in their mid-20s to early 30s. Wednesday nights there's a drag show in the front room, while the back room hosts Gothic Night. Weekends, male and female strippers perform from midnight till about 4 or 5am. There's a dance floor (the music's pretty loud), a small outdoor courtyard, and a game room with pool tables, darts, and pinball machines. Right next door, by the way, is the 24-hour **Mariposa Cafe,** which features cheap, tasty food.

The Buffalo

4640 Paradise Rd., at Naples. ☎ **702/733-8355.** No cover or minimum.

Close to both Angles and Gipsy, this is a leather/Levi's bar popular with motorcycle clubs. It features beer busts (all the beer you can drink for $5) Friday nights from 9pm to midnight. Open 24 hours.

The Eagle

3430 E. Tropicana Ave, at Pecos. ☎ **702/458-8662.** No cover.

Off the beaten track in just about every sense of the phrase, The Eagle is the place to go if well-lit bars make you nervous. Open 24 hours, it's dark, slightly seedy, and lacks even video poker machines (they might get in the way of your drink and/or ashtray). All in all, it's a refreshing change from the overprocessed slickness that is Las Vegas. The crowd, tending toward middle age, is mostly male and is of the Levi's/leather group. There is a small dance area (calling it a dance floor would be generous), a pool table, and a nice-sized bar. Drinks are inexpensive, and special events make them even more so. For instance, The Eagle is rapidly becoming famous for its twice-weekly underwear parties (if you check your pants, you receive draft beer and well drinks for free). That's right: free. The 20-minute drive from the strip makes it a questionable option, but if you've got a sense of adventure go see for yourself.

✪ Gipsy

4605 Paradise Rd., at Naples St. ☎ **702/731-1919.** Cover $4 (except Wed and Sun).

For years, Gipsy reigned supreme as the best gay dance place in the city, and for good reason: great location (Paradise Road near the Hard Rock), excellent layout (sunken dance floor and two bars), and very little competition. More recently some of its spotlight, along with a good portion of the clientele, has been stolen by fiercer competitors. This may be why Gipsy planned to close for a couple of months in 1997 for a top-to-bottom remodeling. Details on the plans were sketchy at press time, but may include an expanded dance floor, upgraded sound and lighting systems, a bigger bar, a VIP room, and fresh decor throughout. It may worth checking out on your next trip, especially if the redo turns out as nice as it sounds. Drink specials, beer and liquor busts, and a moderate cover charge on weekends along with special events, shows, male dancers, and theme nights have always made this place a good party bargain. In the past (call to see what they are doing now), Monday featured Latin female-impersonator shows, Tuesday was Variety Night (amateur strip shows and dance revues), and Thursday featured lip-synching contests for cash prizes. Open daily 10pm to 6am.

Good Times

1775 E. Tropicana, at Spencer (in the Liberace Plaza). ☎ **702/736-9494.** No cover.

This quiet, 24-hour neighborhood bar is located (for those of you with a taste for subtle irony) in the same complex as the Liberace Museum, a few miles due east of the MGM Grand. There is a small dance floor, but on a recent Friday night nobody was using it, the crowd preferring instead to take advantage of the cozy bar area. A small conversation pit is a perfect spot for intimate conversations. Of course, there are the omnipresent pool and video poker if you're not interested in witty repartee. We remember this place as being a lot more crowded than it was during our most recent visit (but perhaps we were there on an off night). It makes a nice after respite after the Liberace Museum (after which you may very well need to go next door for a stiff drink).

✪ Inferno

3340 S. Highland Ave, near Spring Mountain. ☎ **702/734-7336.** Web site: http://members.aol.com/inferno. Cover varies.

This new 24-hour dance club opened in late 1996 and quickly stole the crown from Gipsy as the gay hot spot in Vegas. It's conveniently located less than a mile off the strip near Treasure Island in an Industrial-type strip mall. The interior features exposed cinder-block walls and girders plus a few miles of chain link fencing to create an austere look, but that's balanced by a warm and friendly staff. A huge bar dominates the room, and there's a good-size dance floor and a first-rate lighting and sound system. When you add the pool tables, the inescapable video poker, and plenty of seating, you get a package that is accommodating and designed for fun. There always seems to be a crowd (about a 50/50 mix of locals and tourists), which tends to be younger and male (though not exclusively so). Be prepared for a line and a moderate cover on the weekends. Regular drink prices are average, but rotating specials and theme nights help give more bang for your buck.

8 Other Bars

In addition to the venues listed below, consider hanging out at **Country Star,** the **Hard Rock Cafe,** and **Planet Hollywood,** all described in chapter 6. You might also check out the incredible nighttime view at the bar atop the **Stratosphere Hotel**—nothing beats it. There's also the **Viva Las Vegas Lounge** at the Hard Rock Hotel, where eventually every rock-connected person in Vegas will eventually pass through.

Champagnes Cafe
3557 S. Maryland Pkwy. ☎ **702/737-1699.**

Wonder where old Vegas went? It ossified right here. Red- and gold-flocked wallpaper and other such trappings of "glamour" never die—in fact, with this ultralow key lighting, they will never even fade. A seedy old bar with seedy old scary men leering away. They even serve ice cream shakes spiked with booze—two indulgences wrapped into one frothy package. And quite a double addiction delight. Some might run screaming from the place, while others will think they've died and gone to heaven. Just remember—this is the kind of place director Quentin Tarantino or this year's alt-cult hit movie will make famous. It can't be long. And then it will be overrun with hipsters. Beat the rush, go there now, and brag that you knew about it back before it was so cool it became passé. Again.

Debbie Reynolds Hotel: Jazz & Jokes with Debbie Reynolds and Friends
305 Convention Center Dr. ☎ **702/737-0711.**

Every Friday and Saturday night from 10pm to 2am, this informal "show" takes place in the comfortable Celebrity Café. Basically, it's an intimate after-hours place where Strip entertainers, who are usually too keyed up to go home immediately after their shows, can hang out and unwind with Debbie. And being entertainers, they love to take the mike and belt out a few numbers. Among those who have already dropped by are Tony Bennett, blues singer Bobby Jones, Keely Smith, and comedian Steve Rossi. At its best, this is great impromptu entertainment with a chance to stargaze at close quarters. There is a $5 cover, plus a two-drink minimum.

The Dispensary
2451 E. Tropicana, at Eastern. ☎ **702/458-6343.**

Stuck in a '70s time warp (the waterwheel and the ferns are the tip-off, though the songs on the Muzak confirm it), this is a fine place for a nice, long, quiet drink. One that lasts decades, perhaps. It's very quiet, low key, and often on the empty side. Things pick up on weekends, but it still isn't the sort of place that attracts raucous drunks. (Of course, if it were on the Strip instead of tucked away, it probably would.) "We leave you alone if you don't want to be bothered," says the proprietor. (We still worry about what happens if you sit here long enough.) If you are a hepcat, but one on the mild side, you will love it.

✪ Double Down
4640 Paradise Rd., at Naples. ☎ **702/791-5775.**

"House rule: you puke, you clean." Okay, that about sums up the Double Down. Well, no, it doesn't really do the place justice. This is a big local hangout, with management quoting *Scope* magazine's description of its clientele: "Hipsters, blue collars, the well heeled lunatic fringe." Rumored to have been spotted there: director Tim Burton and Dr. Timothy Leary. Need to know more? Okay, trippy hallucinogenic graffiti covers the walls, the ceiling, the tables, and possibly you if you sit there long enough. Decor includes Abby Rents–type chairs and thrift store battered armchairs and sofa, a couple of pool tables, and a jukebox that holds everything from the Germs and Frank Zappa to Link Wray, Dick Dale, and the Rev. Horton Heat. On Wednesday nights they have a live blues band, while other nights might find local alternative, punk, or ska groups performing. No cover unless they have some out-of-town band that actually has a label deal.

Holy Cow
2432 Las Vegas Blvd. S., at Sahara Ave. ☎ **702/732-COWS.**

Okay, so maybe you go to serious bars for serious drinking, but anyplace with a giant bovine on the roof and an extensive cow theme on the inside can't be all bad. Cows are everywhere—cow paintings, cow-motif lighting fixtures, a "sidewalk of fame" of cow hoof prints outside, even slot machines called (irresistibly) "Moolah"—so if you are heifer-a-phobe, stay away. The microbrew pub upstairs offers a free tour, or you can taste its four hand-crafted microbrews: pale ale, wheat beer, brown ale, and a monthly changing brewmaster's special, which sometimes contains the word *blueberry* in it. Pub grub is also offered, which they assure us requires only one stomach to consume. Frankly, once you get past giggling at all the cow-related puns around (which can take awhile), you notice it's a bit busy on the eyes and aggressive with gambling devices. Indeed, this is more casino than bar.

✪ Main Street Station: Triple 7 Brew Pub
100 Main St. ☎ **702/382-1896.**

Yet another of the many things the new(ish) Main Street Station hotel has done right. Stepping into its microbrew pub feels like stepping out of Vegas. Well, maybe except for the dueling piano entertainment. Part modern warehouse look (exposed pipes, microbrew fixtures visible through exposed glass at back, very high ceiling), but with a hammered tin ceiling that continues the hotel's Victorian decor, this is a look more appropriate to North Beach in San Francisco. Dare we say it? The result produces an environment that is a bit on the yuppified side, but escapes being pretentious. And frankly, it's a much needed modern touch for the downtown area. They have their own brewmaster, a number of microbrews ready to try, and if you are feeling like a quick bite, there is also an oyster and sushi bar, plus fancy burgers and pizzas. It can get noisy during the aforementioned piano duel act, but otherwise casino noise stays out. And downtown being all too heavy on the old Las Vegas side (which is fine for a time but not *all* the time), this is good for a suitable breather.

✪ Peppermill's Fireside Lounge
2985 Las Vegas Blvd. S. ☎ **702/735-7635.**

Walk through the classic Peppermill's coffee shop (not a bad place to eat, by the way) on the Strip, and you land in its dark, plush, cozy lounge. A fabulously dated view of hip, it has low, circular banquette seats, fake floral foliage, low neon, and electric candles. But best of all is the water and fire pit as the centerpiece—a piece of kitsch thought long vanished from the earth, which attracts nostalgia buffs like moths to flames. It all adds up to a cozy, womblike place. Perfect for crashing down a bit after some time spent on the hectic Strip. The enormous, exotic froufrou tropical drinks (including the signature basketball-sized margaritas) will ensure that you sink into that level of comfortable stupor.

Pink E's
4170 S. Valley View. ☎ **702/252-4666.**

Sick of the attitude at Club Rio (and well you should be)? Escape directly across the street to Pink E's, where the theme is pink. You were expecting maybe seafoam? Anyway, at least one regular described this as "the only place to go if you are over 25 and have a brain." And like pink. Because everything here is: the many pool tables, the Ping-Pong tables, the booths, the lighting, the lava lamp on the bar, and even the people. In its own way, it's as gimmick-ridden as the Beach dance club, but surely no one would put out a pink pool table in all seriousness? Yeah, they're a ludicrous heresy, but don't you want to play on one? Anyway, Pink E's offers retro diner food and a DJ on weekends. The dress code basically translates to "no gangsta wannabe wear." Go, but wear all black just to be ornery.

Sand Dollar Blues Lounge
3355 Spring Mountain. ☎ **702/871-6651.**

The kind of funky, no decor (think posters and beer signs), atmosphere-intensive, slightly grimy, friendly bar you either wish your town had or wish it had something other than. Just up the road from Treasure Island, this is a great antidote to artificial Vegas. Attracting a solid mix of locals and tourists (employees claim the former includes everything from bikers to chamber of commerce members), the Sand Dollar features live blues (both electric and acoustic, with a little Cajun and Zydeco thrown in) every night. We wondered how Vegas had enough blues bands to fill out a whole weekly bill. The answer? All the musicians play in multiple bands in different configurations. The dance floor is tiny and often full. The minimal cover always goes to the band. Depending on your desires, it's either refreshingly not Las Vegas, or just the kind of place you came to Vegas to escape. Go before someone has the idea to build a theme hotel based on it.

The Sky Lounge (at the Polo Towers)
3745 Las Vegas Blvd. S. ☎ **702/261-1000.**

It may not quite be the view offered by the Stratosphere Hotel's bar, but it's pretty darn good and easier to get to. You see too much of the Holiday Inn Boardwalk directly across the street and not quite enough of the MGM Grand to the left, but otherwise there are no complaints. The decor is too modern (heavy on '80s black and purple), but overall the place is quiet (especially during the day) and civil. A jazz vocal/piano performs at night (when the views are naturally best). The atmosphere produced by all this is classic Vegas in the best sense (with only a slight touch of necessary kitsch). Worth a trip for an escape from the mob, though you won't be the only tourist fighting for window seats.

The Wet Stop
4440 S. Maryland Pkwy. ☎ **702/791-0977.**

This is a college bar (it's across the street from University of Nevada, Las Vegas), but the crowd changes radically depending on what live band is happening that night. (The acts are usually pretty good, too, both local groups and out-of-town bands.) Blues happens on Friday and Saturday, while Thursday offers the only live reggae in Vegas. The latter brings out the dreadlocks and the hippies. After Utopia closes early Sunday morning at 3am, they open up an after-hours club until 11am so that the club kids will have a place to hang. Other nights of the week alternative groups pop up. This also a hangout for the Gothic/vampire crowd; they drift over when Cafe Copiah closes, or when local group Blood Count is playing. The set this changing cast plays against is a basic, dark, friendly, busy bar with zero ambience—but who needs it? The crowd does it for you.

9 Dance Clubs

✪ The Beach

365 S. Convention Center Dr., at Paradise Rd. ☎ **702/731-9298.** $10 cover most nights (higher on some nights and for special events, lower and nonexistent on others).

If you are a fan of loud, crowded, 24-hour party bars filled with tons of good looking fun seekers, then bow in this direction, for you have found mecca. This huge, tropical-themed (hence the whole "Beach" thing) nightclub is right across the street from the Convention Center and is, according to just about anyone you ask, the "hottest" club in the city. It's a two-story affair with five separate bars downstairs and another three up. Just in case walking the 20 feet to the closest one is too much of an effort, they also have bikini-clad women serving beer out of steel tubs full of ice (they also roam the floor with shot belts). The drinks are on the pricey side ($3.75 for an 8-ounce domestic beer) but the unfailingly gorgeous, 4% body-fat bartenders (both men and women) are friendly and offer rotating drink specials that might keep you from busting your budget. Also downstairs is the large two-story dance floor, which dominates the center of the room and is built around a full-service bar at one end. The sound system is top-of-the-line, as is the lighting design (but the wash from the rest of the bar made it a little too bright on the floor to appreciate). Nobody really seemed to care though—there wasn't one square inch of space available on a recent Friday night. Upstairs, there are balconies overlooking the dance floor, pool tables, darts, foosball, pinball, and various other arcade games plus slot machines, video poker, and a sports book. Other neat touches include tarot card readings by the stairs and hot-pizza vendors. And let's not forget those Jell-O shot contests where club-goers try to eat shaky cubes of alcohol-spiked gelatin off each other's partially bared bodies. The crowd is aggressively young and pretty, more men than women (70/30 split), and about 60% tourist, which is probably why the place can get away with charging a $10 cover. Party people look no further. There's free valet parking, and, if you've driven here and become intoxicated, they'll drive you back home at no charge.

Cleopatra's Barge Nightclub

Caesars Palace, 3570 Las Vegas Blvd. S. ☎ **702/731-7110.** No cover; there's a 2-drink minimum Fri and Sat only.

Live bands play Top 40 dance tunes aboard Cleopatra's Barge, a replica of the majestic ships that sailed the Nile in ancient Egypt. This waterborne dance club is also afloat on "the Nile," complete with oars, ostrich-feather fans, statues of ancient pharaohs, and furled sails. You board via gangplanks, and hydraulic mechanisms rock the barge gently. There's seating on the main barge and on the dock. Nubian-inspired cocktail waitresses in diaphanous togas bring drinks. In the early days of this facility, Caesars found it necessary to construct a dockside fence to keep awestruck sightseers from falling into the river. It's open Tuesday to Sunday from 10pm to 4am.

Club Rio

Rio Suite Hotel, 3700 W. Flamingo Rd. ☎ **702/252-7777.** As advertised: $10 cover for men, local women free, out-of-state women $5—but frequently when we went by on a weekend night, the cover was $20 for everyone.

This is the hottest night spot in Vegas (along with Beach) as of this writing, but apparently made so by people who don't mind long lines, restrictive dress codes, attitudinal door people, hefty cover charges, and bland dance music. Waits can be interminable and admittance denied thanks to the wrong footwear or shirt. Once inside, you find a large, circular room, with the spacious dance floor taking up much of the space. Giant video screens line the upper parts of the walls, showing anything from shots of the action down below to catwalk footage. Comfy circular booths fill out the next couple of concentric circles; these seem mostly reserved, and when empty they leave the impression that the place isn't very full—so why the wait? The dress code (no sneakers, shirts must have a collar) is supposed to make the clientele look more sophisticated than grungy; the effect is the opposite, as most of the men end up in combinations of chinos and button-down shirts. Of course, it's so dark you can't tell if someone *is* wearing sneakers. Music on a recent visit included a Madonna medley and the perennial "Celebration," not the most au courant of tunes. The total effect is of a grown-up, not terribly drunken frat and sorority mixer.

✪ Drink

200 E. Harmon Ave., at Koval Lane ☎ **702/796-5519.** Cover $5–$10 ($15–$25 when major artists are performing); women are admitted free Tues nights. No minimum.

Where Gen X Vegas hangs out. Decor is hip, which in this case means an odd mix of industrial warehouse, peeling plaster, and brick country cottage exterior; somehow, it works. The rooms are all good looking (all are candle-lit, and at least one rope hammock swings in case you need to relax), though much of the detail is lost in the obligatory dark nightclub lighting. Soundproofing is impressive; you can literally pass from the hard rock room to the dance room with only a second's worth of the two overlapping into each other. (Of course, getting there can be a problem—the hallways from room to room are narrow and bottlenecks frequent. Be patient.) A recent saunter in the hard rock room heard a mix of retro and more current rock. (A song by The Cult segued into "Magic Carpet Ride," which went into "Spill the Wine," which went into some anonymous '90s faux metal/hard rock song.) The different sounds means different appeals for different rooms, thus something for everyone. So if you are traveling in a group, you don't need to have a consensus on music taste. Despite a young, fashion-conscious crowd, it's friendlier than you would imagine, with virtually no attitude, surprisingly enough. (If you go there after Club Rio, the difference in attitude is almost palpable.) Jay Leno, Matthew Perry, Dennis Rodman, and Charles Barkley have apparently been spotted there, but don't hold that against it. They serve food, too. Of the nightly dance clubs, this is the one to go to, unless a hip quotient frightens you. Open Monday to Thursday till 3am, Friday and Saturday till 5am. Closed Sunday. Self-parking is free, valet parking $3.

Monte Carlo Pub & Brewery

Monte Carlo Resort, 3770 Las Vegas Blvd. S. ☎ **702/730-7777.** No cover or minimum.

After 9pm nightly, this immense warehouselike pub and working microbrewery (see details in chapter 6) turns from a casual restaurant into a rollicking, high-energy dance club that is very popular with Gen-X-to-thirtysomething locals. Rock videos blare forth from a large screen and 40 TV monitors around the room, while, onstage, dueling pianos provide music and audience-participation entertainment. The Pub is cigar friendly and maintains a humidor. There's a full bar, and, of course, the house microbrews are featured; you can also order pizza. Open until 1am Sunday to Thursday, till 3am Friday and Saturday.

Sam's Town Western Dance Hall

Sam's Town, 5111 Boulder Hwy. ☎ 702/456-7777. No cover or minimum.

Attracting a large local crowd, Sam's Town houses a rustic dance hall, its weathered barnwood walls hung with steer horns, neon beer signs, wagon wheels, and other things Western. You can dance here to music provided by a DJ from 9pm to 3am. Come by from 7:30 to 9pm for free lessons in line dancing and West Coast swing. Sunday is karaoke night, with a DJ on hand from 9pm.

Utopia

3765 Las Vegas Blvd., S. (in the Epicenter). ☎ 702/593-5935. Cover varies.

According to *Scope* Magazine, Utopia is "less a discotheque and more a revolution"—which is an apt description, considering that in Las Vegas, underground once-a-week nightclubs usually disappear in a matter of weeks. (And for that matter, the underground itself is a shaky, hard-to-find thing.) Utopia is still going strong (as of this writing), despite the tragic death (in a car accident) of its founder, Aaron Britt. The music is progressive house, tribal, trance, techno, and rave. The atmosphere is industrial, foggy, and heavy with lasers and other dazzling visuals. A cool and outrageous crowd fills three rooms with fun, peace, and love, in a heart-pounding, techno way. It's for the tragically hip, but isn't it good to know they are out there in Vegas? Internationally known DJs spin and live rave acts play. It's open Saturday only, from 11pm to 3am (or so); 21 and over.

10 Strip Clubs

No, not entertainment establishments on Las Vegas Boulevard South. This would be the *other* kind of "strip." Yes, people come to town for the gambling and the wedding chapels, but the lure of Vegas doesn't stop there. Though prostitution is not legal within the city, the sex industry is an active, and obvious, force in town. Every other cab carries a placard for a strip club, and a walk down the Strip at night will have dozens of men thrusting flyers at you for clubs, escort services, phone sex lines, and more. And some of you are going to want to check it out.

And why not? An essential part of the Vegas allure is decadence, and naked flesh would certainly qualify, as does the thrill of trying something new and daring. Of course, by and large, the nicer bars *aren't* particularly daring, and if you go to more than one in an evening, the thrill wears off, and the breasts don't look quite so bare.

In the finest of Vegas traditions, the "something for everyone" mentality extends to the strip clubs. Here is a guide to the most prominent and heavily advertised; there are plenty more, of increasingly seediness, out there. You don't have to look too hard. The most crowded and zoolike times are after midnight, especially on Friday and Saturday nights. Should you want a "meaningful" experience, you might wish to avoid the rush and choose an off-hour for a visit.

Cheetah's

2112 Western Ave. ☎ 702-384-0074. MC, V (but cash preferred—they have an ATM machine). Cover $5. Topless.

This is the strip club used in the movie *Showgirls,* but thanks to the magic of Hollywood and later renovations by the club, only the main stage will look vaguely familiar to those few looking for Nomi Malone. There is also a smaller stage, plus three tiny "tip stages" so you can really get close to (and give much money to) the woman of your choice—and it gets them closer to the bar. Eight TVs line the walls; the club does a brisk business during major sporting events. The management believes, "If you treat people right they will keep coming back," so the atmosphere is friendlier than at other clubs. They "encourage couples—people who want to party come here. We get a 21 to 40 aged party kind of crowd," the manager told us. And indeed there is a sporty, frat bar feel to the place. (Though on a crowded Saturday night some unescorted women were turned away, despite policy.) Check out bikini-clad "beer babe" Kim at the beer bar—she's cute and friendly. $10 table dance, $20 couch dance. Open 24 hours.

Club Paradise

4416 Paradise Rd. ☎ **702-734-7990.** $10 cover, 2 drink minimum (drinks $4.50 and up). MC, V. Unescorted women allowed. Topless.

Possibly the nicest of the strip clubs (the outside looks a lot like the Golden Nugget), the interior and atmosphere are rather like that of a hot nightclub where most of the women happen to be topless. The glitzy stage looks like something from a miniature showroom: The lights flash and the dance music pounds, there are two big video screens (one featuring soft porn, the other showing sports!), the chairs are plush and comfortable, the place is relatively bright by strip club standards, and they offer champagne and cigars. Not too surprisingly, they get a very white collar crowd here. The result is not terribly sleazy, which may please some and turn off others. The girls ("actual centerfolds") are heavy (and we do mean heavy) on the silicone. They don't so much dance as pose and prance, after which they don skimpy evening dresses and come down to solicit lap dances, which eventually fills the place up with writhing girls in thongs. The club says it is "women friendly," and indeed there were a few couples, including one woman who was receiving a lap dance herself—and didn't seem too uncomfortable. Occasionally the action stops down for a minirevue, which ends up being more like seminaked cheerleading than a show. Lap dances $20. Open Monday to Sunday from 6pm to 6am.

Crazy Horse, Two

We've omitted the address of this place on purpose. Full of so much obnoxious jerk attitude, with overly aggressive girls soliciting lap dances, that even the other clubs in town sneer at them. There are plenty of strip bars—pass this one by.

Glitter Gulch

20 Fremont St. ☎ **702-385-4774.** No cover, 2-drink minimum (drinks $5.75). Topless.

Right there in the middle of the Fremont St. Experience, Glitter Gulch is either an eyesore or the last bastion of Old Las Vegas, depending on your point of view. The inside is modern enough: black light and bubble fountains, arranged around a runway strip. The shows are basic—the women take off sequined gowns to reveal G-strings. Customers sit in comfortable booths, and the dancers then come around and offer up close and personal table dances, often chatting merrily away while they expose themselves. The women are not too thin—fully fleshed, but not fat. As you enter, you are assigned your own (overly clothed) waitress who escorts you to your table. They also offer limo service to the hotels. There is even a line of souvenir clothing. Given such services and its convenient location, this is the perfect place for the merely curious—you can easily pop in, check things out, goggle and ogle, and then hit the

---

Two Strippers Give 9 Strip-Bar Etiquette Tips

Brittany and Kitty each have several years' experience working in strip bars, so they know what they're talking about. And they both really are sweet girls, honest.

1. Bathe.

2. Don't lie and say you never go into these places.

3. Don't take off your wedding ring—we can still see the mark it leaves.

4. Don't ask if we take credit cards. Bring cash!

5. Don't fall asleep—just because we are open 24 hours, we aren't a hotel.

6. Don't wear wool pants—they scratch.

7. Don't ask for our phone number.

8. Don't lick us. We're not Popsicles.

9. Don't forget: We *aren't* dumb strippers. We are a lot smarter than you think.

---

road, personal dignity intact. Table dances cost $20. Open Sunday to Thursday from noon to 4am, Friday to Saturday from noon to 6am.

Little Darlings

1514 Western Ave. ☎ **702/366-0145.** $10 cover plus $10 all you can drink (includes souvenir florescent mug). No unescorted women. Totally nude.

They call themselves the "Pornocopia of Sex," and given the number of services they offer, you can see why. In addition to a fully stocked adult store, they have private nude dances in booths (dancers must stay 6 inches from the customer at all times). This is one of the few clubs where the women are not allowed any physical contact with the customer. There are also rooms where you can watch a nude woman take a shower (in theory doing erotic things with soap), and "Fantasy Rooms" where a glass pane separates you from a woman performing still more erotic stunts. The women are all healthy and athletic, including some who do impressive work with the poles on stage (using their legs to climb all the way to the rafters). Despite all the nude offerings, the resultant atmosphere is not especially dirty, just rowdy. (Tellingly, they do promotions with a local radio station.) At least one late 20s customer felt it was all too much like high school and that the cover was prohibitively expensive. $15 totally nude private dance in booth. $15 "shower"; $15 table dance; $15 Fantasy room. Open Monday to Saturday from 11am to 6am, Sunday 2pm to 6am.

Olympic Gardens

1531 Las Vegas S. Blvd. ☎ **702/385-8987.** Cover $15 (includes 2 drinks). AE, DISC, MC, V (they have an ATM machine). Unescorted women allowed. Topless.

Possibly the largest of the strip clubs, this almost feels like a family operation, thanks to the middle-aged women handling the door. They also have a boutique selling lingerie and naughty outfits. (Since they get a lot of couples coming in, perhaps this is in case someone gets inspired and wants to try out what they learned here at home.) There are two rooms, one with large padded tables for the women to dance on, the other featuring a more classic strip runway. The girls all seemed really cute—perhaps the best looking of the major clubs. The crowd is a mix of 20s to 30s blue-collar guys and techno geeks. As the place fills up and the chairs are crammed in next to each other, it's hard to see how enjoyable, or intimate, a lap dance can be when the guy next to you is getting one as well. That didn't seem to stop all the guys there who all seemed appropriately blissed out. Table dances $20, more in VIP room. Open Monday to Sunday from 2pm to 6am.

Palomino

1848 Las Vegas Blvd., N. ☎ **702/642-2984.** Cover $10, plus 2-drink minimum (drinks $6). Totally nude.

Once the nicest strip club in town, it now edges into the seedy end of things. It's also a bit out of the way. On the other hand, it does offer total nudity in a classic red-walled setting. It's two levels, with the downstairs consisting of a large stage where featured dancers ("all have appeared in *Playboy* or *Penthouse* or some kind of publication") do themed dances with specific music, costumes, and props (one healthy surfer blonde gal used a big, white bed and satin nightie in her set), which can result in some incongruous sights, like an essentially interpretive dance with pauses for gynecological shots. Upstairs has two or three small stages with dancers doing their thing up close and personal. The girls here are more prone to cellulite. There is also a large room off to the side where they take you for lap dances, ensuring a small measure of privacy. Topless lap dance $20, totally nude $40. Open Monday to Sunday from 1:30pm to 4am.

11 Side Trips from Las Vegas

Anyone who has seen the cascades of neon and outsized hotels along the Strip would agree that the Las Vegas way is to do things on a grand scale. What most visitors to Las Vegas don't realize is that the sense of being somewhere extraordinary only shifts gears at the city limits; seeing the stark grandeur of the surrounding desert is an unforgettable experience in its own right. Also within easy reach are some of the country's most imposing artificial and natural wonders, such as the Hoover Dam and Red Rock Canyon; ghost towns, and other places where you can experience the flavor of the Old West; and innumerable opportunities for outdoor recreation, from whitewater rafting, to precipitous downhill skiing, to desert hiking—all in a landscape like none other.

The following excursions will take you from 20 to 60 miles out of town. Every one of them offers a memorable travel experience.

1 Goodsprings: A Ghost Town

35 miles SW of Las Vegas

The shadowy phenomenon of ghost towns—once-flourishing areas that were later deserted and abandoned—has always been an intriguing and romantic image. Many of these towns began with one lone traveler who serendipitously stumbled upon mineral-rich rocks while out on another pursuit—perhaps tracking game or strayed livestock. He would mark off his area, stuff his pockets and knapsacks with specimens, and rush off to register his claim. Soon adventurers, drifters, and raggedy prospectors would flock to the area, set up meager lodgings, break out picks and shovels, and get to work. If the yield was promising, word would spread quickly, and entrepreneurs would arrive with provisions. A main street would develop around a general-merchandise store, followed by other shops and the inevitable mining-camp saloons, gambling houses, and red-light district. Eventually a real town would emerge.

But then the mines would begin drying up. Little by little, businesses would fold, and the population would dwindle. Vandalism, wind, and fire would ravage the remaining structures, leaving only ghost-inhabited remnants of what had been. And so the town died. Nevada has at least 40 such towns, of which Goodsprings is the closest to Las Vegas.

Excursions from Las Vegas

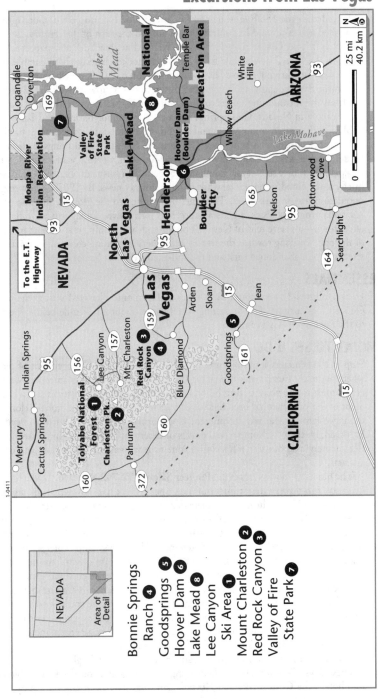

To the E.T. Highway

NEVADA

Area of Detail

Bonnie Springs Ranch ④
Goodsprings ⑤
Hoover Dam ⑥
Lake Mead ⑧
Lee Canyon ①
Mount Charleston ②
Red Rock Canyon ③
Ski Area ①
Valley of Fire State Park ⑦

Founded in the 1860s, and named for Joseph Good, a prospector, Goodsprings flourished as a silver and lead mining town around the turn of the century. During World War I, the Goodsprings Hotel was advertised in New York newspapers as "the finest in the West," and people from Las Vegas flocked here to shop, gamble, and see shows. The thriving metropolis had a population of 2,000, nine bars, several restaurants, a theater, churches, homes, and businesses. A narrow-gauge railroad carried ore from the surrounding mines to the Union Pacific tracks at nearby Jean. As the biggest town in Nevada, Goodsprings was a regular stop for Barnum and Bailey.

Shortly thereafter, mining days ended, and the town began its decline. It has had only one brief brush with fame since. On January 16, 1942, Goodsprings made headlines because it was the closest town to Potosi Mountain, where a plane lost in a storm crashed with movie star Carole Lombard on board. Her husband, Clark Gable, stayed briefly at the Goodsprings Hotel while awaiting further news. By 1967, Goodsprings's population had shrunk to 62. The hotel had burned to the ground, and one of its last remaining businesses, a general store, was torn down. Today it is an authentic ghost town—an eerie relic of Nevada's boom-and-bust mining era. All that remains of the once-thriving town is the rotting machinery of mining companies, discarded wrecks of old, abandoned cars, and the still-extant Pioneer Saloon.

ESSENTIALS

By car, follow I-15 south out of Las Vegas and turn onto Nev. 161 west at the Jean-Goodsprings turnoff. The first thing you'll pass—about a half mile before you get to the town itself—is a cemetery.

WHAT TO SEE & DO

Stop at the cemetery and poke around a bit. It's a down-at-the-heels sort of place where perpetual care has not been a big thing. A couple of markers are wood, weathered almost to the point of illegibility. Most of the standard headstones are in a segment of the yard that has been fenced off by a low rail. All of these stones belong to the Fayle family, who were prominent Goodsprings citizens in the town's heyday. Surprisingly, there are some recent graves of desert-rat bikers here. In the area near the cemetery, you can search for Native American arrowheads, spearheads, and other artifacts.

The heart of Goodsprings is the **Pioneer Saloon** (☎ 702/874-9362), which from its dusty, run-down exterior does not look operative. It has, however, been a going concern since 1913. The only complete decorative-metal building left standing anywhere in the United States, the saloon has pressed-tin walls (interior and exterior) and ceiling. If you're nostalgic about old-time Western saloons, you'll love the Pioneer. It's heated by a potbellied stove in winter and cooled by a swamp cooler in summer. Many of its fixtures and furnishings (even the curtains) are original to the saloon. Bartenders at the century-old cherry and mahogany bar regale customers with anecdotes about Goodsprings's past. A copy of the 1916 *Goodsprings Gazette* that carries an advertisement for the saloon is displayed on one wall; while you're looking at the walls, note the bullet holes, a legacy of a long-ago gunfight over a poker game. In addition to authentic ambience, the Pioneer offers such diverse entertainments as a pool table, dart board, jukebox, and poker machines. It's quite a thrill to play pool in a ghost town. The Pioneer is open daily from 10am to midnight.

These days, Goodsprings may be making something of a comeback. Two big casino hotels, the **Gold Strike** and **Nevada Landing,** have been erected nearby, and the population is now up to about 130.

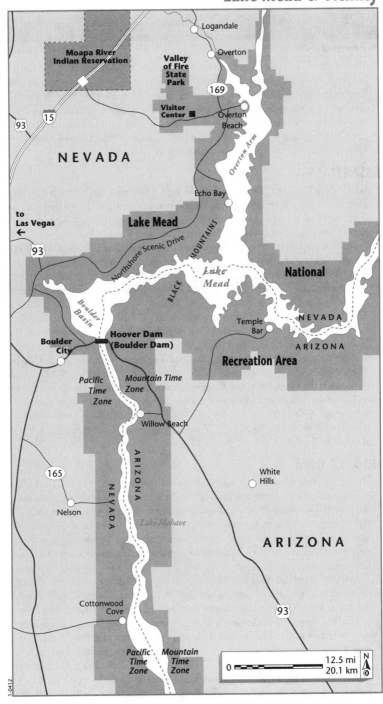

Lake Mead & Vicinity

Logandale

Overton

Moapa River
Indian Reservation

Valley
of Fire
State
Park

15

169

93

Visitor
Center

Overton
Beach

NEVADA

Overton Arm

Echo Bay

to
Las Vegas
←

93

Lake Mead

Northshore Scenic Drive

BLACK MOUNTAINS

*Lake
Mead*

National

NEVADA

Boulder
Basin

Temple
Bar

ARIZONA

Boulder
City

Hoover Dam
(Boulder Dam)

Recreation Area

*Pacific
Time
Zone*

*Mountain Time
Zone*

Willow Beach

White
Hills

165

ARIZONA

NEVADA

Nelson

Lake Mohave

ARIZONA

Cottonwood
Cove

93

*Pacific
Time
Zone*

*Mountain
Time
Zone*

N

0   12.5 mi
     20.1 km

1-0412

2 Hoover Dam & Lake Mead

30 miles SE of Las Vegas

This is one of the most popular excursions from Las Vegas, visited by 2,000 to 3,000 people daily. Wear comfortable shoes; the dam tour involves quite a bit of walking. The best plan would be to tour the dam in the morning, have lunch in Boulder City, take the Lake Mead dinner cruise, and stay a night or two at Lake Mead Lodge (details below), enjoying the area's scenic beauty and recreation facilities. Drive back to Las Vegas through the Valley of Fire, which is about 60 magnificently scenic miles from Lake Mead (purchase gas before your start!).

ESSENTIALS

GETTING THERE   By Car   Take U.S. 93 south from Las Vegas (it's a continuation of Fremont Street downtown). As you near the dam, you'll see a five-story parking structure tucked into the canyon wall on your left. Park here and take the elevators or stairs to the walkway leading to the new Visitor Center.

If you would rather go on an **organized tour, Gray Line** (☎ **702/384-1234**) offers several Hoover Dam packages, all of them including admission and a tour of the dam. When you're in Las Vegas, look for discount coupons in numerous free publications available at hotels. The 6¹/₂-hour **Hoover Dam Express** excursion, departing daily at 8am and noon, includes a stop at Cranberry World; price is $25.95 for adults, $23.50 for children 10 to 16 and seniors over 62, $21.50 for children under 10. The full-day **Deluxe Hoover Dam and City Highlights Tour,** departing daily at 10am, includes a stop at the Heritage Museum to view mining and ranching artifacts of frontier days, a buffet lunch at the Railroad Pass Casino, and a visit to Cranberry World; adults $31.95, children 10 to 16 and seniors $29.50, under 10 $27.50. Most elaborate is the **Grand Hoover Dam and Lake Mead Cruise Tour,** also departing daily at 10am, which includes a visit to Ethel M Chocolates and a 45-minute paddlewheeler cruise on Lake Mead with a light lunch; adults $39.95, children 10 to 16 and seniors $37.50, under 10 $34.95. You can inquire at your hotel sightseeing desk about other bus tours.

HOOVER DAM

Until Hoover Dam was built, much of the southwestern United States was plagued by two natural problems: parched, sandy terrain that lacked irrigation for most of the year and extensive flooding in spring and early summer when the mighty Colorado River, fed by melting snow from its source in the Rocky Mountains, overflowed its banks and destroyed crops, lives, and property. On the positive side, raging unchecked over eons, the river's turbulent, rushing waters carved the Grand Canyon.

In 1928, prodded by the seven states through which the river runs during the course of its 1,400-mile journey to the Gulf of California, Congress authorized construction of a dam at Boulder Canyon (later moved to Black Canyon) under the auspices of the Bureau of Reclamation, U.S. Department of the Interior, the agency that still operates it today. The Senate's declaration of intention was that "A mighty river, now a source of destruction, is to be curbed and put to work in the interests of society." Construction began in 1931. Because of its vast scope, and the unprecedented problems posed in its realization, the project generated significant advances in many areas of machinery production, engineering, and construction. An army of more than 5,200 laborers was assembled, and work proceeded 24 hours a day. Completed in 1936, 2 years ahead of schedule, the dam stopped the annual floods and conserved

---

Fast Facts: Hoover Dam

- The amount of concrete used in the construction of the dam could pave a standard highway from San Francisco to New York.
- The minimum wage paid on the project was $4 a day.
- Ninety-six men died while building, excavating, blasting, and scaling mountains during construction, and on-the-job injuries totaled about 1,500 a month.
- In summer, the canyon rocks are so hot you could literally fry an egg on them.
- Lake Mead contains enough water to cover the entire state of Pennsylvania to a 1-foot depth.
- The dam was originally called Boulder Dam because of its first-designated canyon site, then renamed Hoover Dam in 1930 to honor Herbert Hoover's years of work making the project a reality. Unofficially it was renamed Boulder Dam by FDR, who did not wish to honor Hoover; it finally regained the name Hoover Dam under Truman, who, in 1947, asked the 80th Congress to find out just what the "dam" name really was. Both names are still in popular usage.

---

water for irrigation, industrial, and domestic use. Equally important, it became one of the world's major electrical generating plants, providing low-cost, pollution-free hydroelectric power to a score of surrounding communities. Hoover Dam's $165 million cost has been repaid with interest by the sale of inexpensive power to a number of California cities and the states of Arizona and Nevada. The dam is a government project that paid for itself—a feat almost as awe-inspiring as its engineering.

The dam itself is a massive curved wall, 660 feet thick at the bottom and tapering to 45 feet where the road crosses it at the top. It towers 726.4 feet above bedrock (about the height of a 60-story skyscraper) and acts as a plug between the canyon walls to hold back up to 9.2 trillion gallons of water in Lake Mead—the reservoir created by its construction. Four concrete intake towers on the lake side drop the water down about 600 feet to drive turbines and create power, after which the water spills out into the river and continues south. All the architecture is on a grand scale, with beautiful art deco elements unusual in an engineering project. Note, for instance, the monumental 30-foot bronze sculpture, *Winged Figures of the Republic,* flanking a 142-foot flagpole at the Nevada entrance. According to its creator, Oskar Hansen, the sculpture symbolizes "the immutable calm of intellectual resolution, and the enormous power of trained physical strength, equally enthroned in placid triumph of scientific achievement."

The dam has become a major sightseeing attraction along with Lake Mead, America's largest artificial reservoir and a major Nevada recreation area.

Seven miles northwest of the dam on U.S. 93, you'll pass through **Boulder City,** which was built to house managerial and construction workers. Sweltering summer heat (many days it is 125°F) ruled out a campsite by the dam, whereas the higher elevation of Boulder City offered lower temperatures. The city emerged within a single year, turning a desert waste into a community of 6,000 with tree-shaded lawns, homes, churches, parks, restaurants, hotels, and schools. By 1934 it was Nevada's third-largest town. Today, it continues to thrive with a population of 13,500; you might plan on having lunch here at **Totos,** a reasonably priced Mexican restaurant at 806 Buchanan Blvd. (☎ 702/293-1744); it's in the Von's shopping center. About 300 yards past Boulder City, at the top of a slight incline, Lake Mead comes into view.

TOURING THE DAM

The **Hoover Dam Visitor Center,** a vast three-level circular concrete structure with a rooftop overlook, opened in 1995. You'll enter the Reception Lobby, where you can buy tickets, peruse informational exhibits, photographs, and memorabilia, and view three 12-minute video presentations in a rotating theater (respectively, about the importance of water to life, the events leading up to the construction of Hoover Dam, and the construction itself as well as the many benefits it confers). Additional exhibition galleries are in the works at this writing. Those on the Plaza Level will house interactive displays on the environment, habitation and development of the Southwest, the people who built the dam, and related topics. Yet another floor up, galleries on the Overlook Level demonstrate, via sculpted bronze panels, the benefits of Hoover Dam and Lake Mead to the states of Arizona, Nevada, and California. The Overlook Level additionally provides an unobstructed view of Lake Mead, the dam, the power plant, the Colorado River, and Black Canyon. You can visit an exhibit center across the street where a 10-minute presentation in a small theater focuses on a topographical map of the 1,400-mile Colorado River and the 14 dams and diversions along it. This building also houses a turbine and generator model and an information desk. A gift shop and food concession are under construction in the parking structure.

Thirty-minute tours of the dam depart from the Reception Lobby every few minutes daily, except Christmas. The Visitor Center opens at 8:30am, and the first tour departs soon after. The last tour leaves at 5:30pm, and the center closes at 6:30pm. Admission is $5 for adults, $2.50 for senior citizens and children 10 to 16, free for children under 10. More extensive, and expensive, hard-hat tours, offered every half hour between 9:30am and 4pm, can be arranged by calling in advance (☎ 702/294-3522).

The tour begins with a 520-foot elevator descent into the dam's interior, where an access tunnel leads to the Nevada wing of the power plant. The power plant consists of two similar wings, each 650 feet long, on either side of the river. From the visitor's balcony of the Nevada wing, you'll see eight huge hydroelectric generators (nine from the Arizona wing). These generators are driven by individual turbines located 40 feet below the floor. Water is delivered from the reservoir to the turbines (through canyon walls) via massive 30-foot-diameter pipes called penstocks. You'll learn about the manufacture of these generating units, each of which produces sufficient electrical energy to supply the domestic needs of a city of 95,000 people. Units lighted at the top are in operation. After visiting the generating room below, you'll go outside to see a tunnel through the 600-foot canyon wall that provides access to vehicles entering the power-plant area. However, heavy equipment is lowered by a cable way that has a capacity of 150 tons! Looking up, you can see the control room for the cable operation. During construction, entire railroad cars loaded with materials were lowered into the canyon via this cable way. The drumlike tanks on the deck above are electrical transformers.

With the aid of a diagram, your guide will explain construction procedures of the four tunnels that were drilled and blasted through solid rock and used to divert the river around the dam site. These diversion tunnels averaged 4,000 feet in length and

Impressions

Everybody knows Las Vegas is the best town by a dam site.
—Masthead slogan of the *Las Vegas Review Journal*

56 feet in diameter. When construction work advanced beyond the point where it was no longer necessary to divert water around the dam site, the tunnels were permanently sealed off. You'll also learn about the four intake towers that control the supply of water drawn from Lake Mead for the power plant turbines, and the spillways that, one on each side of the lake, control its maximum depth and ensure that no flood will ever overflow the dam. Finally, visitors stand in one of the diversion tunnels and view one of the largest steel water pipes ever made (its interior could accommodate two lanes of automobile traffic).

LAKE MEAD NATIONAL RECREATION AREA

Under the auspices of the National Park Service, the 1.5-million-acre Lake Mead National Recreation Area was created in 1936 around Lake Mead (the reservoir lake resulted from the construction of Hoover Dam) and later Lake Mohave to the south (formed with the construction of Davis Dam). Before the lakes emerged, this desert region was brutally hot, dry, and rugged—unfit for human habitation. Today it is one of the nation's most popular playgrounds, attracting about nine million visitors annually. The two lakes comprise 290.7 square miles. At an elevation of 1,221.4 feet, Lake Mead itself extends some 110 miles upstream toward the Grand Canyon. Its 550-mile shoreline, backed by spectacular cliff and canyon scenery, forms a perfect setting for a wide variety of water sports and desert hiking.

Visitor Information   The **Alan Bible Visitor Center,** 4 miles northeast of Boulder City on U.S. 93 at Nev. 166 (☎ **702/293-8990**), can provide information on all area activities and services. You can pick up trail maps and brochures here, view informative films, and find out about scenic drives, accommodations, ranger-guided hikes, naturalist programs and lectures, bird watching, canoeing, camping, lakeside RV parks, and picnic facilities. The center also sells books and videotapes about the area. It's open daily 8:30am to 4:30pm. For information on accommodations, boat rentals, and fishing also, call **Seven Crown Resorts** (☎ **800/752-9669**).

OUTDOOR ACTIVITIES

HIKING   The best season for hiking is November through March (too hot the rest of the year). Some ranger-guided hikes are offered via the Alan Bible Visitor Center, which also stocks detailed trail maps. Three trails, ranging in length from ³/₄ mile to 6 miles, originate at the visitor center. The 6-mile trail goes past remains of the railroad built for the dam project. Be sure to take all necessary desert-hiking precautions (see details in chapter 7).

CAMPING   Lake Mead's shoreline is dotted with campsites, all of them equipped with running water, picnic tables, and grills. Available on a first-come, first-served basis, they are administered by the **National Park Service** (☎ **702/293-8990**). There's a charge of $10 per night at each campsite.

BOATING & FISHING   A store at **Lake Mead Resort and Marina** under the auspices of Seven Crown Resorts (☎ **800/752-9669** or 702/293-3484), rents fishing boats, ski boats, personal watercraft, and patio boats. It also carries groceries, clothing, marine supplies, sporting goods, water-skiing gear, fishing equipment, and bait and tackle. You can get a fishing license here ($45.50 a year or $17.50 for three days; $9 a year for children 12 to 15, under 12 free). The staff is knowledgeable and can apprise you of good fishing spots. Largemouth bass, striped bass, channel catfish, crappie, and bluegill are found in Lake Mead, rainbow trout, largemouth bass, and striped bass in Lake Mohave. You can also arrange here to rent a fully equipped houseboat at **Echo Bay,** 40 miles north.

Other convenient Lake Mead marinas offering similar rentals and equipment are **Las Vegas Bay** (☎ 702/565-9111), which is even closer to Las Vegas, **Callville Bay** (☎ 702/565-8958), which is the least crowded of the five on the Nevada Shore.

SCUBA DIVING   October to April, there's good visibility, lessened in summer months when algae flourishes. A list of good dive locations, authorized instructors, and nearby dive shops is available at Alan Bible Visitor Center. There's an underwater designated diving area near Lake Mead Marina.

RAFTING   Rafting trips on the Colorado River are offered February 1 through November 30 by **Black Canyon,** 1297 Nevada Hwy. in Boulder City (☎ 800/696-7238 or 702/293-3776). Twelve-mile trips begin at the base of Hoover Dam. You'll see canyon waterfalls and wildlife (bighorn sheep, wild burros, chuckwalla lizards, mallards, grebe, and the occasional golden eagle) and stop at a quiet cove for a picnic lunch. There are stunning rock formations en route, and the area is rich in history—southern Paiute rock shelters and 1920s river-gauging stations and cable ways. Guides are quite knowledgeable about local lore. Prices (including lunch): $64.95 for adults, $35 for children ages 5 to 12, under 5 free. Bus transportation back to Las Vegas is available. Even if you don't go rafting, stop by Black Canyon, Inc.'s Boulder City headquarters to see exhibits about the area and a film on Hoover Dam. Their office also functions as an information center and tour operator for a wide array of area activities (Grand Canyon flights, jet-skiing, skydiving, and more).

CANOEING   The Alan Bible Visitor Center can provide a list of outfitters who rent canoes for trips on the Colorado River. There's one catch, however: A canoeing permit ($5 for one; $10 for 2 to 5 canoes) is required in advance from the Bureau of Reclamation. Call ☎ 702/293-8204 Monday through Thursday for information.

LAKE CRUISES   A delightful way to enjoy Lake Mead is on a cruise aboard the *Desert Princess* (☎ 702/293-6180), a Mississippi-style paddle wheeler. Cruises depart year-round from a terminal near Lake Mead Lodge (see below) and a dock right at Hoover Dam (inquire at the Visitor Center). It's a relaxing, scenic trip (enjoyed from an open promenade deck or one of two fully enclosed, climate-controlled decks) through Black Canyon and past colorful rock formations known as the "Arizona Paint Pots" en route to Hoover Dam, which is lit at night. Options include buffet breakfast cruises ($21 adults, $10 children under 12), narrated midday cruises ($16 adults, $6 children), cocktail/dinner cruises ($29 adults, $15 children), and sunset dinner/dance cruises with live music ($43 adults, children not allowed). Add $1 to all rates if you depart from Hoover Dam. Dinner is served in a pleasant, windowed, air-conditioned dining room. There's a full bar on board. Call for departure times.

WHERE TO STAY

Lake Mead Lodge

322 Lakeshore Rd., Boulder City, NV 89005. ☎ 800/752-9669 or 702/293-2074. 42 rms. A/C TV. Early Mar to late Nov $50–$65, the rest of the year $35–$50. Extra person $6. Children under 5 stay free in parents' room. DISC, MC. V.

If you aren't properly outfitted for camping at Lake Mead (see above), it's heavenly to spend a few nights relaxing at this tranquil lakeside resort, enjoying the area's numerous recreational activities. It's an easy drive from Hoover Dam. The rooms, housed in terra-cotta–roofed cream-brick buildings, are comfortable and attractive with wood-paneled ceilings and walls of white-painted brick or rough-hewn pine. All offer full baths and cable TVs. A lovely pool glitters in its lakeside setting, surrounded by mountains and beautifully landscaped grounds planted with pines, palm trees, and flowering oleander bushes. Weathered-wood roped dock posts add a nautical look to the resort. You might want to relax with a good book in one of the gazebos on the property. About a half mile down the road is the marina, where you can while away a few hours over cocktails on a lakeside patio. The marina is headquarters for boating, fishing, and water sports; it also houses a large shop (see details above under "Boating and Fishing"). And Boulder Beach, also an easy walk from the lodge, has waterfront picnic tables and barbecue grills.

Dining/Entertainment: There's a nautically themed restaurant called **Tale of the Whale** (☎ **702/293-3484**) at the marina, its rough-hewn pine interior embellished with harpoons, figureheads, ship lanterns, ropes, pulleys, and steering wheels. Open from 7am to 9pm Sunday to Thursday, till 10pm Friday and Saturday, it serves hearty breakfasts; sandwiches, salads, and burgers at lunch; and steak-and-seafood dinners, all at moderate prices. Sometimes there's live music Friday and Saturday nights.

3 Valley of Fire State Park

60 miles NE of Las Vegas

Most people visualize the desert as a vast expanse of undulating sands punctuated by the occasional cactus or palm-fringed oasis. The desert of America's Southwest bears little relation to this Lawrence of Arabia image. Stretching for hundreds of miles around Las Vegas in every direction is a seemingly lifeless tundra of vivid reddish earth, shaped by time, climate, and subterranean upheavals into majestic canyons, cliffs, and ridges.

The 36,000-acre Valley of Fire State Park, typifying the mountainous red Mojave Desert, derives its name from the brilliant sandstone formations that were created 150 million years ago by a great shifting of sand and continue to be shaped by the geologic processes of wind and water erosion.

Although it's hard to imagine in the sweltering Nevada heat, for billions of years these rocks were under hundreds of feet of ocean. This ocean floor began to rise some 200 million years ago, and the waters became more shallow. Eventually the sea made a complete retreat, leaving a muddy terrain traversed by ever-diminishing streams. A great sandy desert covered much of the southwestern part of the American continent until about 140 million years ago. Over eons, winds, massive fault action, and water erosion sculpted fantastic formations of sand and limestone. Oxidation of iron in the sands and mud—and the effect of groundwater leaching the oxidized iron—turned the rocks the many hues of red, pink, russet, lavender, and white that can be seen today. Logs of ancient forests washed down from faraway highlands and became petrified fossils, which can be seen along two interpretive trails.

Human beings occupied the region, a wetter and cooler one, as far back as 4,000 years ago. They didn't live in the Valley of Fire, but during the Gypsum period (2000 B.C. to 300 B.C.), men hunted bighorn sheep (a source of food, clothing, blankets, and hut coverings) here with a notched stick called an *atlatl* that is depicted in the park's petroglyphs. Women and children caught rabbits, tortoises, and other small game. In the next phase, from 300 B.C. to A.D. 700, the climate became warmer and dryer. Bows and arrows replaced the atlatl and the hunters and gatherers discovered farming. The Anasazi people began cultivating corn, squash, and beans, and communities began replacing small nomadic family groups. These ancient people wove watertight baskets, mats, hunting nets, and clothing. Around A.D. 300 they learned how to make sun-dried ceramic pottery. Other tribes, notably the Paiutes, migrated to the area. By A.D. 1150 they had become the dominant group. Unlike the Anasazis, they were still nomadic and used the Valley of Fire region seasonally. These were the inhabitants white settlers found when they entered the area in the early to mid-1800s. The newcomers diverted river and spring waters to irrigate their farmlands, destroying the nature-based Paiute way of life. About 300 descendants of those Paiute tribespeople still live on the Moapa Indian Reservation (about 20 miles northwest) that was established along the Muddy River in 1872.

ESSENTIALS

GETTING THERE   By Car   From Las Vegas take I-15 north to Exit 75 (Valley of Fire turnoff). However, the more scenic route is to take I-15 north, then travel Lake Mead Boulevard east to North Shore Road (Nev. 167), and proceed north to the Valley of Fire exit. The first route takes about an hour, the second 1½ hours.

Numerous **sightseeing tours** go to Valley of Fire. **Gray Line** (☎ **702/384-1234**), has a 7-hour tour from Las Vegas, including lunch, that costs $29.95 for adults, $24.50 for children 17 and under. Inquire at your hotel tour desk.

Valley of Fire can also be visited in conjunction with Lake Mead. **From Lake Mead Lodge,** take Nev. 166 (Lakeshore Scenic Drive) north, make a right turn on Nev. 167 (North Shore Scenic Drive), turn left on Nev. 169 (Moapa Valley Boulevard) west—a spectacularly scenic drive—and follow the signs. Valley of Fire is about 65 miles from Hoover Dam.

WHAT TO SEE & DO

There are no food concessions or gas stations in the park; however, you can obtain meals or gas on Nev. 167 or in nearby **Overton** (15 miles northwest on Nev. 169). Overton is a fertile valley town replete with trees, agricultural crops, horses, and herds of cattle—quite a change in scenery.

At the southern edge of town is the **Lost City Museum,** 721 S. Moapa Valley Blvd. (☎ **702/397-2193**), commemorating an ancient Anasazi village that was discovered in the region in 1924. Its population reached one of the highest levels of Native American culture in the United States. Artifacts dating back 12,000 years are on display, as are clay jars, dried corn and beans, arrowheads, seashell necklaces, and willow baskets of the ancient Pueblo culture that inhabited this region between A.D. 300 and 1150. Other exhibits document the Mormon farmers who settled the valley in the 1860s. A large collection of local rocks—petrified wood, fern fossils, iron pyrites, green copper, and red iron oxide—along with manganese blown bottles turned purple by the ultraviolet rays of the sun are also displayed here. The museum is surrounded by reconstructed wattle-and-daub pueblos. Admission $2, free for children under 18. The museum is open daily from 8:30am to 4:30pm. Closed Thanksgiving, Christmas, and New Year's Day.

Information headquarters for Valley of Fire is the **Visitor Center** on Nev. 169, 6 miles west of North Shore Road (☎ **702/397-2088**). It's open 7 days a week from 8:30am to 4:30pm. Exhibits on the premises explain the origin and geologic history of the park's colorful sandstone formations, describe the ancient peoples who carved their rock art on canyon walls, and identify the plants and wildlife you're likely to see. Postcards, books, slides, and films are on sale here, and you can pick up hiking maps and brochures. Rangers can answer your park-related questions.

There are hiking trails, shaded picnic sites, and two campgrounds in the park. Most sites are equipped with tables, grills, water, and rest rooms. An $11 per night camping fee is charged for use of the campground; if you're not camping, it costs $4 to enter the park.

Some of the notable formations in the park have been named for the shapes they vaguely resemble—a duck, an elephant, seven sisters, domes, beehives, and so on.

Mouse's Tank is a natural basin that collects rainwater, so named for a fugitive Paiute called Mouse who hid there in the late 1890s. And Native American petroglyphs etched into the rock walls and boulders—some dating from as early as 3,000 years ago—can be observed on self-guided trails. Petroglyphs at Atlatl Rock and Petroglyph Canyon are both easily accessible. Always awe-inspiring, the park is especially beautiful in early spring when the desert blooms with wildflowers—mallow, desert marigold, and indigo bush—in dramatic contrast to the predominant earth tones. Other desert life forms include bighorn sheep, ground squirrels, bats, kit foxes, jackrabbits, gila monsters, rattlesnakes, and lizards. And numerous birds—cactus and rock wrens, ravens, finches, and sage sparrows, as well as migrant species—are best observed in the early morning or late afternoon. In summer, when temperatures are usually over 100°F, you may have to settle for driving through the park in an air-conditioned car.

4 Mount Charleston & Lee Canyon Ski Area

Mount Charleston: 40 miles NW of Las Vegas; Lee Canyon: 47 miles NW of Las Vegas

In summertime, the mountains that encircle Toiyabe National Forest are as much as 30° to 40° cooler than the sweltering desert city. These mountains, once an island in an ancient sea, are today a cool oasis in the desert. The highest peak towers 11,918 feet above sea level. It's a beautiful drive. Nev. 157 winds up for about 21 miles through gorgeous canyon scenery, and, as you ascend, desert vegetation—cactus, yucca, creosote bush, and Joshua trees—gives way to stands of juniper, dense ponderosa forest, aspen firs, and bristlecone pine. The highway ends at the lovely **Mount Charleston Resort.** You can plan a day around lunch here, with activities like hiking, camping, bird watching, and horseback riding. In winter, there are sleigh rides, and you can ski at nearby **Lee Canyon.** In summer, there are hayrides, scenic chairlift rides in the ski area, barbecues, and a music festival.

It's a twilight-zone feeling to come from hot and air-conditioned Las Vegas to this sometimes snowy region where you can sit in front of a blazing fire sipping hot buttered rum. Both the Mount Charleston Resort and the Mount Charleston Hotel serve as information centers for area activities. In addition to the attractions listed below, see "Staying Active" in chapter 7.

ESSENTIALS

GETTING THERE   By Car   Take I-15 north and stay in the Reno Lane to U.S. 95 north. Make a left on Nev. 157.

During ski season you can catch a **bus** to the Lee Canyon Ski Area. Departure points vary each year. For details, call ☎ **702/878-5465.** There is no bus transportation to Mount Charleston.

WHAT TO SEE & DO

Under the auspices of the Mount Charleston Resort are the **Mt. Charleston Riding Stables** (☎ **800/955-1314** or 702/872-5408), offering marvelously scenic trail rides to the edge of the wilderness. These depart from stables on Kyle Canyon Road. Since the schedule varies, it's best to call in advance for details. Weather permitting, the stables also offer horse-drawn sleigh rides Thanksgiving Day through March ($8 for adults, $4 for children 10 and under) and hayrides Memorial Day through Labor Day ($5 for adults, $3 for children).

Forty pine-sheltered and secluded picnic groves are equipped with barbecue grills.

There are numerous **hiking trails,** ranging from short panoramic walks to waterfalls near the restaurant/lounge to more difficult hikes farther afield. A popular 5-mile trail beginning at Lee Canyon Highway takes you through a canyon of aspen and into forested areas of ponderosa, white fir, and bristlecone pine. There are picnic areas and campsites along some trails. For information on camping and hiking trails, contact the **U.S. Forest Service,** 2881 S. Valley View Blvd., Suite 16, Las Vegas, NV 89102 (☎ 702/873-8800). For camping information and reservations, you can also call **800/280-CAMP.** Both the Mount Charleston Resort and the Mount Charleston Hotel can provide trail maps.

The **Las Vegas Ski and Snowboard Resort,** at the end of Nev. 156 (☎ 702/385-2-SKI), has a base elevation of 8,510 feet which, along with an extensive snow-making system, provides an almost ideal climate and snow cover for skiing Thanksgiving Day through Easter Day. Facilities include a lodge, a complete ski school, an extensive ski-rental shop, a snowboard park, a coffee shop, and a lounge with blazing fireplace and sundeck. Three double chair lifts carry skiers over 40 acres of well-maintained slopes (in summer, you can ride them for scenic views Friday through Sunday). And summer weekends, the resort is the scene of a country/bluegrass and rock music festival.

WHERE TO STAY

The Mount Charleston Inn Hotel & Restaurant

2 Kyle Canyon Rd. (on Nev. 157). ☎ 702/872-5500. 60 rms. 3 suites. A/C TV TEL. Single or double Sun–Thurs $49–$69, Fri–Sat $59–$89; $109–155 suite. Extra person $5. Children under 12 stay free in parents' room. Inquire about ski packages. AE, CB, DC, DISC, MC, V.

Nestled in the mountains, this three-story property offers lodgings in a rustic log and stone building. Its lobby, with massive stone fireplaces, mounted deer heads, and a lofty beamed pine ceiling, resembles a ski lodge. The accommodations aren't fancy, but they're attractively decorated in earth tones and forest green; cathedral ceilings and balconies make third-floor rooms especially desirable. And nicest of all are the suites with convertible sofas in the living rooms, larger balconies, and wood-burning stone fireplaces. Facilities include a Jacuzzi and sauna in a windowed room, a small video-game arcade, and a gift shop. Room service is available from 8am to 9pm.

Dining/Entertainment: The hotel's hexagonal **Canyon Dining Room** has a lot of rustic charm, with two working fireplaces, windows all around overlooking beautiful mountain scenery, and heavy wrought-iron chandeliers suspended from a cathedral pine ceiling. At night it's romantically candlelit. All meals are available here including full and continental breakfasts. Lunch fare includes moderately priced burgers, sandwiches, fajitas, pizzas, and salads. And dinner entrees offer a choice of lighter fare (pizzas and pasta dishes) along with a steak-and-seafood menu. Like the restaurant, the simpatico Cliffhanger Lounge—scene of live music Friday through Sunday nights (Monday, football games are aired in-season)—has a full window wall and a working fireplace.

✪ Mount Charleston Resort

End of Nev. 157. ☎ 800/955-1314 or 702/872-5408. 24 cabins. Sun–Thurs Honeymoon Cabin (for one or two) $125, Family Cabin (for up to four) $155; Fri–Sat Honeymoon $180, Family $220. Extra person $10. AE, CB, DC, DISC, MC, V.

These charmingly rustic pine log cabins, built right into the mountainside to ensure stunning scenic views, are a delight. Beautifully decorated with southwestern and Native American artifacts (Paiute drums and decorative blankets, sheepskin rugs, steer horns), they have peaked ceilings beamed with rough-hewn logs, oak parquet floors, and lots of windows. Knotty-pine furnishings are complemented by oversized king beds and attractively upholstered armchairs and sofas, each room has a working gas fireplace and a whirlpool tub big enough for two, and in-room amenities include fan

A Close Encounter with Area 51

With the anniversary of the Roswell "incident" (where people persist in believing that aliens landed in New Mexico some 50 years ago), the recent mission to Mars, and, of course, the success of such movies as *Independence Day* and *Men in Black,* aliens are hotter than ever. For years, people have been spotting aliens—so they say—along a 98-mile stretch of Highway 98. Nearby is—so they say—the secret military air base known as "Area 51" where—so they say—experiments are done on captured aliens and their downed aircraft. The highway was even named the "Extraterrestrial Highway" in 1996. Why don't you go join the fun and decide for yourself: Aliens, weather balloons, jack rabbits, mass hallucination, or . . . something else? If you'd like to explore it, take I-15, to U.S. 93, to the ET Highway, returning via U.S. 6 and U.S. 95. You can do the trip in a day from Las Vegas. Even if you don't meet up with any aliens, you'll enjoy the stark desert scenery. Stop in the town of **Rachel,** where the oddly named Little A'Le'Inn is headquarters for UFO watchers; it offers information, dining, groceries, gas, and lodging. You might also want to detour 28 miles east at the junction of ET Highway and U.S. 6 to see the **Lunar Crater,** a volcanic field, 100 miles square, that was used in the late 1960s to train astronauts for the Apollo moon mission. On the return trip via U.S. 6 and 95, if you have an extra day or two, visit old mining and ghost towns like Tonapah, Goldfield, and Rhyolite. For more information call the Nevada Commission on Tourism (☎ **800/NEVADA-8**), and ask them to send you their "Pioneer Territory" brochure and a list of ET Highway services (gas stations, lodgings, chambers of commerce, restaurants, and more). On the Internet, check out **http://www.ufomind.com** and **http://www.ufo-hyway.com**.

chandeliers and coffeemakers (coffee, tea, and cocoa are provided). A big plus: each cabin has a furnished mountain-view terrace that would be a good place to enjoy the sunset and the warm chocolate-chip cookies that arrive to your door at about 7pm. This serene getaway is the perfect antidote to Las Vegas glitz and glitter, and, for couples, it would be hard to come by a more romantic setting.

WHERE TO DINE

Mount Charleston Resort

End of Nev. 157. ☎ **800/955-1314** or 702/872-5408. Reservations recommended. Breakfast main courses $4.50–$9.75, lunch main courses $3–$9.75, dinner main courses $13.50–$19.50. AE, CB, DC, DISC, MC, V. Sun–Thurs 8am–9pm, Fri–Sat until 10pm; the bar/lounge is open 24 hours. AMERICAN/CONTINENTAL.

This warmly inviting mountain chalet centers on a vast hooded fireplace stacked high with massive ponderosa pine and cedar logs. Wagon-wheel chandeliers are suspended from a lofty beamed ceiling, and large windows provide magnificent vistas. Mid-May to the end of October, you can sit at umbrella tables on a patio nestled in the wooded mountains, and you'd be hard pressed to find a more exquisitely peaceful setting. The lounge isn't fancy; it's a casual, kick-back kind of place. At night, however, it is romantically candlelit, and there's dancing to live music weekends and holidays. At lunch weekends and holidays, a Bavarian oompah-pah band called the Dummkopfs entertains.

The restaurant serves all meals, beginning with hearty country breakfasts (available through 5pm) such as eggs with wild-game sausages, hash browns, homemade biscuits, and gravy. Mexican breakfasts (eggs wrapped in tortillas with chili and cheddar) are another tempting option. At lunch there are sandwiches, salads, and full entrees ranging from Dijon-honey-glazed broiled salmon with rice pilaf and a vegetable to broiled pork chops served with applesauce, vegetable, and fries. Dinner entrees include wild-game specialties such as marinated elk steak topped with snow crabmeat, asparagus, and sauce béarnaise. Other choices include steaks, pasta dishes, and seafood. Everything is fresh and cooked on the premises, including homemade breads and desserts. At night the bar here is quite popular. Come by after dinner for a hot buttered rum or Mount Charleston coffee, a Jamaican blend spiked with brandy and Scotch liqueur, topped with homemade vanilla ice cream and a dollop of real whipped cream.

5 Red Rock Canyon

19 miles W of Las Vegas

Less than 20 miles from Las Vegas, Red Rock Canyon is worlds away experientially, a magnificent unspoiled vista that, in its timeless beauty, is the perfect balm for your casino-overloaded soul. You can simply drive the panoramic 13-mile **Scenic Drive** (open daily 7am till dusk) or explore in depth. There are many interesting sights and trail-heads along the drive itself. The wider **National Conservation Area** offers hiking trails and internationally acclaimed rock-climbing opportunities (especially notable is the 7,068-foot Mt. Wilson, the highest sandstone peak among the bluffs). There are picnic areas along the drive and also in nearby **Spring Mountain Ranch State Park,** 5 miles south. Since Bonnie Springs Ranch (see the next section) is just a few miles away, it makes a great base for exploring Red Rock Canyon.

ESSENTIALS

GETTING THERE   By Car   You simply drive west on Charleston Boulevard, which becomes Nev. 159. Look for the visitor center on your right.

You can also go on an **organized tour. Gray Line** (☎ 702/384-1234), among other companies, runs bus tours to Red Rock Canyon. Inquire at your hotel tour desk.

Finally, you can go **by bike.** Not very far out of town (at Rainbow Boulevard), Charleston Boulevard is flanked by a bike path that continues for about 11 miles to the visitor center/scenic drive. The path is hilly but not difficult if you're in reasonable shape. However, exploring Red Rock Canyon by bike should be attempted only by exceptionally fit and experienced bikers. For bike-rental information, see chapter 7.

Just off Nev. 159, you'll see the **Red Rock Canyon Visitor Center** (☎ 702/363-1921), where you can pick up information on trails and view history exhibits on the canyon. The center is open daily from 8:30am to 4:30pm. Red Rock Canyon can be combined with a visit to Bonnie Springs Ranch.

ABOUT RED ROCK CANYON

The geological history of these ancient stones goes back some 600 million years. Over eons, the forces of nature have formed Red Rock's sandstone monoliths into arches, natural bridges, and massive sculptures painted in a stunning palate of gray-white limestone and dolomite, black mineral deposits, and oxidized minerals in earth-toned sienna hues ranging from pink to crimson and burgundy. Orange and green lichens add further contrast, as do spring-fed areas of lush foliage. And formations like Calico Hill are brilliantly white where groundwaters have leached out oxidized iron. Cliffs cut by deep canyons tower 2,000 feet above the valley floor.

During most of its history, Red Rock Canyon was below a warm shallow sea. Massive fault action and volcanic eruptions caused this seabed to begin rising some 225 million years ago. As the waters receded, sea creatures died and the calcium in their bodies combined with sea minerals to form limestone cliffs studded with ancient fossils. Some 45 million years later, the region was buried beneath thousands of feet of windblown sand. The landscape was as arid as the Sahara. As time progressed, iron oxide and calcium carbonate infiltrated the sand, consolidating it into cross-bedded rock. Shallow streams began carving the Red Rock landscape, and logs that washed down from ancient highland forests fossilized, their molecules gradually replaced by quartz and other minerals. These petrified stone logs, which the Paiute Indians believed were weapons of the wolf god, Shinarav, can be viewed in the Chinle Formation at the base of the Red Rock Cliffs. About 100 million years ago, massive fault action began dramatically shifting the rock landscape here, forming spectacular limestone and sandstone cliffs and rugged canyons punctuated by waterfalls, shallow streams, and serene oasis pools. Especially notable is the Keystone Thrust Fault, dating back about 65 million years when two of the earth's crustal plates collided, forcing older limestone and dolomite plates from the ancient seas over younger red and white sandstones. Over the years, water and wind have been ever creative sculptors, continuing to redefine this strikingly beautiful landscape.

Red Rock's valley is home to more than 45 species of mammals, about 100 species of birds, 30 reptiles and amphibians, and an abundance of plant life. Ascending the slopes from the valley, you'll see cactus and creosote bushes, aromatic purple sage, yellow-flowering blackbrush, yucca and Joshua trees, and, at higher elevations, clusters of forest-green piñon, juniper, and ponderosa pines. In spring, the desert blooms with fiery red globe mallow, magenta monkeyflowers, pink-blossomed redbud trees, pristine white forget-me-nots, golden desert marigolds, and lavender phacelia. Among the animal denizens of the canyon are bighorn sheep, antelope ground squirrels, mule deer, kangaroo rats, lizards, California jackrabbits and desert cottontails, gray and kit foxes, tortoises, coyotes, bobcats, rattlesnakes, reclusive gila monsters, even mountain lions. Burros and wild horses are not indigenous but descended from animals that were set free by, or escaped from, miners in the 1800s. And commonly observed birds include eagles and hawks, roadrunners, turkey vultures, loggerhead shrike, cactus wrens, quail, mourning doves, broad-tailed hummingbirds, woodpeckers, horned larks, western bluebirds, American robins, northern mockingbirds, yellow warblers, and sage sparrows.

Archaeological studies of Red Rock have turned up pottery fragments, remains of limestone roasting pits, stone tools, pictographs (rock drawings), and petroglyphs (rock etchings), along with other ancient artifacts. They show that humans have been in this region since about 3000 B.C. (some experts say as early as 10,000 B.C.). You can still see remains of early inhabitants on hiking expeditions in the park. The Anasazi (also known as the "Basketmaker" people and "the Ancient Ones") lived here from the 1st century A.D. Originally hunter-gatherers, they learned to farm maize (corn), squash, and beans and began forming communities. From pit houses, they progressed to elaborate structures of up to 100 rooms and became known as the Pueblo Indians. They departed from the area (no one knows why) about A.D. 1150, and the Paiutes, who were still essentially hunter-gatherer nomads, became the dominant group. Until the mid-1800s, the Paiutes lived here in perfect harmony with nature—a harmony destroyed when white settlers arrived and began felling the pine forests for timber, introducing grazing livestock that destroyed food and medicinal plant sources, and decimating the Native American population with European diseases to which they had no immunity. By the 1880s, the Paiutes were forced onto reservations, their culture and way of life in shambles.

In the latter part of the 19th century, Red Rock was a mining site and later a sandstone quarry that provided materials for many buildings in Los Angeles, San Francisco, and early Las Vegas. By the end of World War II, as Las Vegas developed, many people became aware of the importance of preserving the canyon. In 1967 the secretary of the interior designated 62,000 acres as Red Rock Canyon Recreation Lands under the auspices of the Bureau of Land Management, and later legislation banned all development except hiking trails and limited recreational facilities. In 1990, Red Rock Canyon became a National Conservation Area, further elevating its protected status; its current acreage is 197,000.

Today Red Rock Canyon affords visitors the opportunity to experience nature's grandeur and serenity—to leave the stresses of daily life behind and get in touch with greater realities.

WHAT TO SEE & DO

First, you'll want to stop off at the visitor center. There you can view exhibits, enhanced by an audio tour, that tell the history of the canyon and depict its plant and animal life. You'll also see a fascinating video here about Nevada's thousands of wild horses and burros, protected by an act of Congress since 1971. At the center, you can obtain trail maps, brochures, permits for hiking and backpacking, and other information about the canyon. Call ahead to find out about ranger-guided tours as well as informative guided hikes offered by groups like the Sierra Club and the Audubon Society. Hiking trails range from a 0.7-mile loop stroll to a waterfall (its flow varying seasonally) at Lost Creek to much longer and more strenuous treks involving rock scrambling. A popular 2-mile round-trip hike leads to Pine Creek Canyon and the creekside ruins of a historic homesite surrounded by ponderosa pine trees. On trails along Calico Hills and the escarpment, look for "Indian marbles," a local name for small rounded sandstone rocks that have eroded off larger sandstone formations. And, if you're traveling with children, ask about the free *Junior Ranger Discovery Book* filled with fun family activities. Books and videotapes are on sale here, including a guidebook identifying more than 100 top-rated climbing sites. After you tour the canyon, drive over to Bonnie Springs Ranch (details in the next section) for lunch or dinner. See chapter 7 for further details on biking and climbing.

6 Bonnie Springs Ranch / Old Nevada

About 24 miles W of Las Vegas, 5 miles past Red Rock Canyon

Bonnie Springs Ranch / Old Nevada is a kind of Wild West theme park with accommodations and a charmingly rustic restaurant. If you're traveling with kids, a day or overnight trip to Bonnie Springs is recommended, but there's much for adults, too. It could even be a romantic getaway, offering horseback riding, gorgeous mountain vistas, proximity to Red Rock Canyon, and temperatures 5° to 10° cooler than on the Strip.

ESSENTIALS

GETTING THERE   If you are traveling **by car,** a trip to Bonnie Springs Ranch can be combined easily with a day trip to Red Rock Canyon; it is about 5 miles. But you can also stay overnight.

For those without transportation, there are **Desert Action Jeep Tour** to and from Las Vegas. Call ☎ 702/796-9355 for details.

For additional information, you can call **Bonnie Springs Ranch / Old Nevada** at ☎ **702/875-4191.**

WHAT TO SEE & DO AT BONNIE SPRINGS RANCH

Old Nevada attractions are detailed below. However, even if you just come out here for lunch, you can enjoy several things free of charge. A **small zoo** on the premises is home to dozens of animals—burros, mouflon sheep, buffalo, steer, raccoons, ferrets, ducks, red squirrels, coyotes, coatis, an Arctic fox (donated by singer Wayne Newton), bobcats, guinea pigs, and rabbits. There are always baby animals, and llamas, potbelly pigs, deer, and miniature goats roam free and can be petted and fed.

There's also an **aviary** housing peacocks (including a rare white peacock), Polish chickens, peachface and blackmask lovebirds, finches, parakeets, ravens, ducks, pheasants, and geese.

Riding stables offer guided trail rides into the mountain area on a continuous basis throughout the day (from 9am to 3:15pm spring through fall, until 5:45pm in summer). Children must be at least 6 years old to participate. Cost is $18 per hour.

And scenic 20-minute **stagecoach rides** offered weekends and holidays cost $5 for adults, $3 for children under 12.

WHAT TO SEE & DO IN OLD NEVADA

Old Nevada (☎ **702/875-4191**) is a microcosm of a mid-1800s western Nevada town, its main street lined with weathered-wood buildings fronted by covered verandas. It has a rustic turn-of-the-century **saloon** complete with red flocked wallpaper and wagon-wheel chandeliers overhead. Country music is played in the saloon during the day, except when **stage melodramas** take place (at frequent intervals between 11:30am and 5pm). In response to cue cards held up by the players, the audience boos and hisses the mustache-twirling villain, sobs in sympathy with the distressed heroine, laughs, cheers, and applauds. It's quite silly, but lots of fun; kids adore it. Drinks and snacks can be purchased at the bar.

Following each melodrama a **Western drama** is presented outside the saloon, involving a bank robbery, a shoot-out, and the trial of the bad guy. A judge, prosecuting attorney, and defense attorney are chosen from the audience, the remainder of whom act as jury. The action always culminates in a hanging. We're not talking Neil Simon or anything, but the dialogue is quite funny.

Throughout the area, cowboys continually interact with visiting kids. There are also ongoing **stunt shoot-outs** in this wild frontier town, and some rather unsavory characters languish in the town jail.

A **wax museum** displays tableaux with replicas of John C. Frémont and Kit Carson (who actually stopped at this site in the 1840s), an animated Abraham Lincoln reading the proclamation that made Nevada a state, early trailblazers and mountain men, Brigham Young, 19th-century Paiute chief Old Winnemucca, and early Nevada madam Julia Bulette, among others. A 9-minute film on Nevada history is shown in the wax museum throughout the day.

In the **Old Nevada Photograph Shoppe** you can have a tintype picture taken in 1890s Wild West costume with a 120-year-old camera. There are replicas of a turn-of-the-century church and stamp mill; the latter, which has original 1902 machinery, was used for crushing rocks to separate gold and silver from the earth. Movies (one about nearby Red Rock Canyon, one a silent film) are shown in the **Old Movie House** throughout the day from 10:30am to 5pm. You can test your skills in a **shooting gallery**, peek into an old-fashioned **dentist/barbershop** (and surprise a man in his bath), see a **Bootleg Hill still**, and tour the remains of the **old Comstock lode**

silver mine. The **Trading Post,** a museum and gift shop, displays a variety of 19th-century items (a switchboard, a craps table and slot machine, cash registers, radios, Victrolas, typewriters, a printing press, shotguns, and the remains of a New Mexico drugstore with many old-fashioned remedies). Other Old Nevada shops sell hand-blown glass, old-fashioned candy, Native American items (rugs, moccasins, silver and turquoise jewelry, baskets), and things Western. Eateries in Old Nevada are discussed below. There's plenty of parking; weekends and holidays, a free shuttle train takes visitors from the parking lot to the entrance.

Admission to Old Nevada is $6.50 for adults, $5.50 for seniors 62 and over, $4 for children ages 5 to 11, and free for children under 5. The park is open daily from 10:30am to 5pm November through April, and until 6pm the rest of the year.

WHERE TO STAY & DINE

Bonnie Springs Motel

1 Gunfighter Lane, Old Nevada, NV 89004 ☎ **702/875-4400.** 50 rms, including 13 suites and 5 fantasy rms. A/C TV TEL. Standard double $55–$65 Sun–Thurs, $65–$75 Fri–Sat; fantasy suite $110 Sun–Thurs, $125 Fri–Sat; family suite $85 Sun–Thurs, $95 Fri–Sat. An optional breakfast trail ride for motel guests is $20 per person; it departs at 9am every morning. Staying at the motel also entitles you to discounted tickets for Old Nevada. AE, MC, V.

The motel, housed in two-story weathered-wood buildings, is, like Old Nevada, evocative of a 19th-century Western town. Even standard rooms offer scenic mountain views and are delightfully decorated with pine-plank-motif carpets, floral-print calico drapes and bedspreads, and handcrafted pine furnishings. Some rooms are equipped with electric fireplaces, and all feature inviting individual touches—perhaps an antique oak mirror stand with a ceramic bowl and jug, Indian rugs, a Mexican serape artfully draped on a branch, lamps with ruffled calico shades, or Victorian-style lighting fixture/fans overhead. All rooms have full baths, in-room coffeemakers, and patios overlooking the mountains. There are beautiful family suites with fully equipped kitchens, bedrooms, living rooms (with convertible sofas), and dressing areas; these are equipped with two phones and two TVs. Fantasy rooms are romantic settings with sumptuous Jacuzzi tubs and mirrors over the bed. For instance, a Gay '90s room, decorated in mauve tones, is furnished with velvet-upholstered period chairs. It has a quaint bathtub on brass feet (in addition to an oversized faux-marble Jacuzzi), a lovely porcelain sink with hand-painted floral motifs, and a pink and black lace canopy over the bed. Other fantasy rooms are Chinese, Native American, Old West, and Spanish themed.

Dining: The **Bonnie Springs Ranch Restaurant** is cozily rustic, with rough-hewn pine walls, a beamed ceiling, and glossy cedar-slab tables. A wall of windows overlooks a serene pond with ducks and swans, and an aluminum-hooded wood-burning fireplace is ablaze in winter. Menus, printed on whiskey bottles, offer hearty breakfasts such as a chili-and-cheese omelet with ranch potatoes and homemade biscuits or thick slabs of Texas toast. Sandwiches, salads, burgers, and barbecued beef are featured at lunch, and dinner entrees include barbecued chicken and pork ribs, steaks, and seafood. Prices are moderate.

IN OLD NEVADA

The **Miner's Restaurant,** another rustic Western setting, is right in town and has unfinished pine-plank floors, a beamed ceiling, and ruffled curtains. Inexpensive snack fare (sandwiches, burgers, pizza, hot dogs) is served, along with fresh-baked desserts. There are tables out on the porch. In summer, you can also get beer and soft drinks in a similarly old-fashioned **Beer Parlor.**

Index

See also separate Accommodations, Dining, and Buffet indexes, below.

BUFFETS

This
Time
It's
Real.

STAR TREK
THE EXPERIENCE
LAS VEGAS HILTON

Beam aboard the most spectacular deep space adventure in the universe.

Introducing *STAR TREK: The Experience*™ at the Las Vegas Hilton. Engage your senses as you beam aboard the bridge of the U.S.S. Enterprise. Blast through distant galaxies at warp speed. Battle fearless Klingons. And when it's over, you can relax with alien creatures in Quark's Bar. Or shop and dine on the Deep Space Nine Promenade. So don't just watch a thrilling *Star Trek*® adventure. Be a part of one! *STAR TREK: The Experience*™ at the Las Vegas Hilton. There's nothing else like it in Las Vegas. Come to think of it, there's nothing else like it on Earth.

Wet'n Wild
on the
Las Vegas Strip

FOR RESERVATIONS CALL:

1-800-4-CHOICE

CHOICE HOTELS
INTERNATIONAL

Advance reservations are required. Discounts are based on availablility
at participating hotels and cannot be used in conjunction with other
discounts or promotions.

LIBERACE
MUSEUM
LAS VEGAS

Museum Hours: Open daily from 10 a.m. to 5 p.m.,
Sundays 1 p.m. to 5 p.m.
Donations: Proceeds benefit the Liberace Foundation for
the Performing and Creative Arts.
Closed: Thanksgiving, Christmas and New Year's Day.

800-322-8697
800-488-6283

Email: Room2@Las Vegas Weddings.com

**10%
OFF**

**10%
OFF**

Now you can save even more at any of more than 1,800
Days Inns throughout the United States and internationally.
Just present this coupon at check-in and Days Inn will take
10% off our regular room rate for your entire length of stay!
Advance reservations recommended, so call now!

1-800-DAYS INN

See details on back.

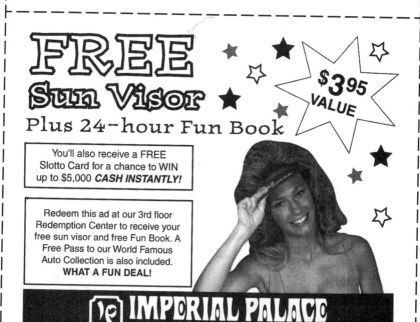

**FREE
Sun Visor** ★
Plus 24-hour Fun Book

$3 95 VALUE

You'll also receive a FREE
Slotto Card for a chance to WIN
up to $5,000 *CASH INSTANTLY!*

Redeem this ad at our 3rd floor
Redemption Center to receive your
free sun visor and free Fun Book. A
Free Pass to our World Famous
Auto Collection is also included.
WHAT A FUN DEAL!

IP IMPERIAL PALACE
HOTEL & CASINO • LAS VEGAS, NEVADA

Must be 21 or older. Management reserves the right to cancel or substitute offer. Expires 12/31/99

Follow the Sun

- Available at participating properties.
- This coupon cannot be combined with any other special discount offer.
- Limit one coupon per room, per stay.
- Not valid during blackout periods or special events.
- Void where prohibited.
- No reproductions accepted.
- Expires December 31, 1999.

1-800-DAYS INN

For Your Information:

Offer available at participating Hertz U.S. Corporate locations through 12/31/98. Leisure Weekly rentals require a 5 day minimum keep, including Saturday night. Minimum age is 25. Advanced reservations are required. Black out periods apply. This coupon has no cash value, must be surrendered at time of rental and may not be combined with any other discount, offer, coupon or promotion. Standard rental qualifications and return restrictions must be met. Car must be returned to renting location. Taxes and optional services, such as refueling, are extra and are not subject to discount.

Hertz rents Fords and other fine cars.

WHEREVER YOU TRAVEL, *H*ELP IS NEVER FAR AWAY.

From planning your trip to providing travel assistance along the way, American Express® Travel Service Offices are always there to help.

Las Vegas

American Express Travel Service
Caesar's Palace
3570 Las Vegas Blvd. South
Las Vegas
702/731-7705

Prestige Travel (R)
3870 East Flamingo Road
Suite A2
Las Vegas
702/731-2661

Mickey Cole Travel Service, Inc. (R)
Gold Coast Hotel & Casino
4000 W. Flamingo Road
Las Vegas
702/876-1410

Prestige Travel (R)
3504 Maryland Parkway
Las Vegas
702/794-2811

Travel

http://www.americanexpress.com/travel

**American Express Travel Service Offices
are located throughout Nevada.
For the office nearest you, call 1-800-AXP-3429.**